Public Health Research Methods for Partnerships and Practice

Melody S. Goodman and
Vetta Sanders Thompson

CRC Press
Taylor & Francis Group
Boca Raton London New York

CRC Press is an imprint of the
Taylor & Francis Group, an **informa** business

First published 2018
by Routledge
711 Third Avenue, New York, NY 10017
and
2 Park Square, Milton Park, Abingdon, Oxon, OX14 4RN

Routledge is an imprint of the Taylor & Francis Group, an informa business
© 2018 Taylor & Francis

The right of Melody S. Goodman and Vetta Sanders Thompson to be identified as the authors of the editorial material, and of the authors for their individual chapters, has been asserted in accordance with sections 77 and 78 of the Copyright, Designs and Patents Act 1988.

All rights reserved. No part of this book may be reprinted or reproduced or utilised in any form or by any electronic, mechanical, or other means, now known or hereafter invented, including photocopying and recording, or in any information storage or retrieval system, without permission in writing from the publishers.

Trademark Notice: Product or corporate names may be trademarks or registered trademarks, and are used only for identification and explanation without intent to infringe.

Library of Congress Cataloging-in-Publication Data

Names: Goodman, Melody S., editor. | Thompson, Vetta L. Sanders, editor.
Title: Public health research methods for partnerships and practice / edited by Melody S. Goodman and Vetta Sanders Thompson.
Description: Abingdon, Oxon ; New York, NY : Routledge, 2018. | Includes bibliographical references and index.
Identifiers: LCCN 2017019520| ISBN 9781498785068 (hardback) | ISBN 9781315155722 (ebook)
Subjects: | MESH: Research Design | Public Health Systems Research--methods | Qualitative Research | Community-Based Participatory Research
Classification: LCC RA440.85 | NLM WA 20.5 | DDC 362.1072--dc23
LC record available at https://lccn.loc.gov/2017019520

Visit the Taylor & Francis Web site at
http://www.taylorandfrancis.com

and the Routledge Web site at
http://www.routledgementalhealth.com

This book is dedicated to the CRFT Fellows past, present, and future. To those who look to build, develop, and nurture equitable community–academic partnerships to address health disparities.

Contents

Acknowledgments	x
Contributors	xi
Introduction	xiii

1 Community-based participatory research   1

VETTA SANDERS THOMPSON AND SULA HOOD

Introduction 1
Definitions of community 3
History of CBPR 4
CBPR implementation 6
Conclusions 15
Online resources 16
References 16
Activity 1: Group discussion 17
Activity 2: Group problem solving and planning 18

2 Health disparities—Understanding how social determinants fuel racial/ethnic health disparities   23

DARRELL HUDSON, WHITNEY SEWELL, AND TANYA FUNCHESS

Introduction 23
Prioritizing health 24
Defining health disparities 25
Racial/ethnic disparities in population health indicators 25
Social determinants of health—The roots of health inequities 29
Race/ethnicity, socioeconomic status, and health disparities 31
Stress and coping 33
Health behaviors, social context, and social norms 34
Towards achieving health equity 37

Contents v

Conclusions 42
References 42
Activity: The Last Straw! 47

3 Community health and community-based prevention 50

DEBORAH J. BOWEN AND CASSANDRA ENZLER

Introduction 50
Community analysis methods 52
How to use community analysis data 64
Engaging community members in the process 65
Identifying the health problems to target 66
Identifying the history of a community 66
Playing to a community's strengths 66
Avoiding difficult areas 67
Conclusions 67
References 68
Activity: Develop and evaluate a community health grant 69

4 Introduction to epidemiology 73

CASSANDRA ARROYO

Introduction 73
What is epidemiology? 74
Basic epidemiologic reasoning 76
Study design in epidemiology 77
Determining causality in observational studies 82
Basic epidemiologic measures 83
Conclusions 86
References 87
Activity 88

5 Cultural competency 91

VICTORIA WALKER AND VETTA SANDERS THOMPSON

Introduction 91
Race, ethnicity, and nationality 92
Culture in a broader context 92
An ever-changing culture 93
Diversity and culture 93
Cultural competence 94
Who should practice cultural competency? 96
The need for culturally competent research and practice 96

vi *Contents*

Health disparities 99
Social determinants of health and critical race theory 99
Conscious and unconscious bias 101
Consequences of culturally incompetent interventions 101
Implementing practice standards related to cultural competence 101
Conclusions 104
References 104
Activity 107

6 Health literacy 115

KIMBERLY A. KAPHINGST

Introduction 115
Definition of health literacy 116
Levels of health literacy in the United States 116
Effects of health literacy 116
Measurement of health literacy 119
Recommendations for materials development 121
Research example: Health literacy and genetics 122
Conclusions 123
References 124
Activity 128

7 Evidence-based public health 132

SANDRA C. HAYES

What is evidence-based public health? 132
Why is EBPH important? 133
Using data and information systems systematically 134
Making decisions using the best available data 134
Qualitative methods 138
Quantitative methods 138
Applying program-planning frameworks (that often have
  a foundation in behavioral science theory) 138
The logic model as a planning tool 139
Engaging the community in assessment and decision-making 139
Conducting sound evaluations to determine programmatic success 139
Disseminating what is learned to key stakeholders 143
Levels of evidence 143
Concerns 144
How does EBPH practice differ from evidence-based medical
  practice? 145
Future of EBPH 146

Contents vii

Conclusions 146
References 147
Activity 149

8 Program planning and evaluation 153

KRISTEN WAGNER, SHA-LAI WILLIAMS,
AND VETTA SANDERS THOMPSON

Introduction 153
Program planning processes 154
SMART goal development 158
Developing your evaluation plan 162
Selecting an evaluation method 164
Program design and evaluation considerations 166
Making sense of evaluation data 167
Writing evaluation reports 168
Conclusions 169
References 170
Activity 171

9 Research methods 174

BETTINA F. DRAKE, DANIELLE M. RANCILIO, AND JEWEL D. STAFFORD

Introduction 174
What is research? 175
The source of research questions 178
Independent and dependent variables 178
What is an association? 180
How data are gathered 181
Quantitative vs. qualitative 181
Data collection methods 181
Primary vs. secondary data 182
How to design a study 183
Conclusions 184
References 185
Summary activity 185

10 Quantitative research methods 188

MELODY S. GOODMAN AND LEI ZHANG

Introduction 188
Sampling methods 192
Data 195
Survey methods 197

viii   *Contents*

Questionnaire design 198
Analyzing survey data 202
Graphic methods 202
Hypothesis testing 208
Odds ratio 211
Conclusions 214
References 214
Activity 215

11   Roles, functions, and examples of qualitative research and methods for social science research

220

KEON L. GILBERT AND SUSAN MAYFIELD-JOHNSON

Introduction 220
What is qualitative research? 221
Qualitative data collection methods 222
Reporting qualitative findings 233
Conclusions 234
References 235

12   Research ethics

239

AIMEE JAMES AND ANKE WINTER

Introduction: What do we mean by research ethics? *239*
Historical milestones in research ethics 240
The three basic principles of the Belmont Report and their translation into research practice 243
Protection of vulnerable populations 246
Roles and responsibilities of the institutional review board 246
Responsible conduct of research and research misconduct 247
Ethical and not-so-ethical practice in research 250
Conclusions 253
References 253
Small group discussion questions 254

13   Health services and health policy research

258

KIMBERLY R. ENARD, TERRI LAWS, AND KEITH ELDER

Introduction 258
Social determinants of health 259
Role of health policy in influencing health 260
Health services research 267
Conclusions 273
References 273

Contents ix

Activity 276
Example: Opioid overdose deaths 277

14 Developing a grant proposal 280

JEWEL D. STAFFORD

Introduction 280
First things first: Why are you looking for a grant? 281
So you want to write a grant... 282
Finding the appropriate grant 285
Outline your plan of action 286
Grant proposal components 288
Conclusions 295
References 296
Activity 1: Analyze an abstract 296
Activity 2: Develop a grant pitch 297

15 Changing health outcomes through community-driven processes: Implications for practice and research 301

KEON L. GILBERT, STEPHANIE M. MCCLURE, AND MARY SHAW-RIDLEY

Introduction 301
Structuring community engagement processes 303
Building capacity for community change 305
Participation and membership in organizations 306
Building community and organizational capacity 308
Conclusions 310
References 311
Group discussion activity 313

Conclusion: CRFT program implementation and evaluation 316

MELODY S. GOODMAN AND VETTA SANDERS THOMPSON

Program implementation 316
Program evaluation 320
Evaluation metrics 322
Pilot projects and other program outcomes 322
Conclusions 325
References 325

Appendix: Self-assessment answer key 328
Index 333

Acknowledgments

This book would not have been possible without the dedicated faculty and staff of the Community Research Fellows Training (CRFT) program in St. Louis and Mississippi. Thank you for understanding the vision and helping to implement the program. Faculty members volunteered their time to the CRFT program for many aspects of the work, including developing lectures, handouts, and activities; facilitating sessions; and working collaboratively will fellows on pilot projects. We are immensely grateful to the Disparities Elimination Advisory Committee of the Program for the Elimination of Cancer Disparities for its initial acceptance and support of the CRFT vision and to Dr. Tanya Funchess for seeing the vision and bringing the CRFT program to Mississippi.

We would also like to thank the CRFT Fellows for their participation in the program and willingness to give quality feedback for program improvement. The content of the CRFT program has evolved over time, based on comprehensive program evaluation. We understand the burden on fellows to complete all of the necessary assessments and evaluations, and are exceedingly grateful for their commitment to the CRFT program and their participation in the comprehensive CRFT program evaluation.

Special thanks to the CRFT-St. Louis team. The team includes Goldie Komaie, who kept us on track, sent reminders to all the co-authors, collected all of the necessary documents from co-authors, developed additional homework assignments, formatted chapters and references, and handled the logistics necessary to bring this all together. Sarah Lyons developed pre- and posttest questions, formatted chapters and references, helped with the logistics, formatted homework assignments, and communicated with co-authors. Nicole Ackermann pulled samples and created figures for the Quantitative Research Methods chapter. Laurel Milam formatted chapters, developed self-assessment questions, and developed templates. Also, thanks to all of the Goodman Lab research assistants and practicum students who helped with the references.

Finally, we would like to thank the Siteman Cancer Center, Program for the Elimination of Cancer Disparities (National Cancer Institute grant U54 CA153460), Washington University Institute for Public Health and Institute for Clinical and Translational Sciences, The Staenberg Family Foundation, and The GrassRoots Community Foundation for their support of the CRFT-STL program, its fellows, and their community work.

Contributors

Cassandra Arroyo
Division of Public Health Sciences
Department of Surgery
Washington University School
 of Medicine
St. Louis, Missouri

Deborah J. Bowen
Department of Bioethics and
 Humanities
University of Washington
Seattle, Washington

Bettina F. Drake
Division of Public Health Sciences
Washington University School
 of Medicine
St. Louis, Missouri

Keith Elder
School of Public Health
Samford University
Birmingham, Alabama

Kimberly R. Enard
College for Public Health and Social
 Justice
Saint Louis University
St. Louis, Missouri

Cassandra Enzler
University of Washington
Seattle, Washington

Tanya Funchess
Office of Health Disparity
 Elimination
Mississippi State Department
 of Health
Jackson, Mississippi

Keon L. Gilbert
College for Public Health and Social
 Justice
Saint Louis University
St. Louis, Missouri

Melody S. Goodman
Department of Biostatistics
College of Global Public Health
New York University
New York, New York

Sandra C. Hayes
George A. and Ruth B. Owens Health
 and Wellness Center
Tougaloo College
Tougaloo, Mississippi

Sula Hood
Department of Social and Behavioral
 Sciences
Richard M. Fairbanks School of
 Public Health
Indiana University–Purdue University
Indianapolis, Indiana

xii *Contributors*

Darrell Hudson
George Warren Brown School
  of Social Work
Washington University
St. Louis, Missouri

Aimee James
Division of Public Health Sciences
Department of Surgery
Washington University School
  of Medicine
St. Louis, Missouri

Kimberly A. Kaphingst
Department of Communication
University of Utah
Salt Lake City, Utah

Terri Laws
University of Michigan-Dearborn
Dearborn, Michigan

Susan Mayfield-Johnson
Department of Public Health
University of Southern Mississippi
and
Center for Sustainable Health
  Outreach (CSHO) and the
  Community Health Advisor
  Network (CHAN)
University of Southern Mississippi
Hattiesburg, Mississippi

Stephanie M. McClure
Behavioral Science/Health Education
College for Public Health and Social
  Justice
Saint Louis University
St. Louis, Missouri

Danielle M. Rancilio
Washington University
St. Louis, Missouri

Vetta Sanders Thompson
George Warren Brown School
  of Social Work
Washington University
St. Louis, Missouri

Whitney Sewell
George Warren Brown School
  of Social Work
Washington University
St. Louis, Missouri

Mary Shaw-Ridley
Department of Health Promotion
  and Disease Prevention
Robert Stempel College of Public
  Health & Social Work
Florida International University
Miami, Florida

Jewel D. Stafford
George Warren Brown School
  of Social Work
Washington University
St. Louis, Missouri

Kristen Wagner
University of Missouri–St. Louis
St. Louis, Missouri

Victoria Walker
Mississippi State Department
  of Health
Jackson, Mississippi

Sha-Lai Williams
School of Social Work
University of Missouri–St. Louis
St. Louis, Missouri

Anke Winter
Division of Public Health Sciences
Department of Surgery
Washington University School
  of Medicine
St. Louis, Missouri

Lei Zhang
Office of Health Data and Research
Mississippi State Department
  of Health
Jackson, Mississippi

Introduction

*Melody S. Goodman and
Vetta Sanders Thompson*

Health disparities research has several phases: (1) the detect phase (do disparities exist?), (2) the understand phase (what causes disparities?), and (3) the solutions phase (development, implementation, and evaluation of potential solutions to address disparities).[1,2] Most of the current evidence base for racial disparities in health care is in the first two phases (detect and understand).[3] This book is intended to enhance the infrastructure for the development of solutions for health disparities by increasing the capacity of community health stakeholders to form equitable partnerships with academic researchers. These multistakeholder collaboratives are necessary to develop sustainable solutions for the complex interplay of the multiple risk factors that contribute to the persistent issue of health disparities.

Public Health Research Methods for Partnerships and Practice is designed to be a how-to reference for those who are interested in implementing a "solutions phase" program that involves community-academic partnerships to address health disparities. This book documents the training materials and curriculum implemented at multiple sites and by multiple partnerships to build the research acumen of community health stakeholders to equip them to participate in projects with the knowledge of standard research practices. The curriculum is based on a master of public health (MPH) degree, but the content is designed to be delivered to lay audiences with practical examples and activities. Content and materials are developed by leading community-engaged researchers across disciplines and are supplemented with fieldwork assignments designed to move learning from the classroom to the community. The training materials cover the entire research process, from developing a partnership and identifying a study question through data collection, analysis, and dissemination.

We have implemented the training model in multiple communities (i.e., Long Island, NY; St. Louis, MO; Jackson, MS; Hattiesburg, MS). In addition, we have continuously refined the program and training materials presented in the text on the basis of comprehensive (formative and summative), mixed-methods (quantitative and qualitative) program evaluation.[4-6] Using the feedback from the comprehensive program evaluations has allowed us to create an evidence-based curriculum, homework assignments, and activities that can be used by

xiv *Introduction*

other community-academic partnerships. The book is based on the successful implementation of the Community Research Fellows Training (CRFT) program in St. Louis (three cohorts to date) and the adaptation by the Mississippi State Department of Health, Office of Health Disparities Elimination in Jackson (two cohorts to date) and Hattiesburg (one cohort to date).

Similar to the course, this book covers a broad range of topics with just enough depth for clear understanding. Several books and numerous journal articles—many of them referenced in this work—are entirely devoted to each of the topics covered in this book. However, the topics are not covered in similar depth here because the purpose of this book is not to create research experts, but rather good consumers of research.

Structure of the book

Each chapter is based on a weekly session and is written by the CRFT faculty who facilitated the session.[4,6] This book includes 15 chapters, which cover community-based participatory research (CBPR), health disparities, community health and prevention, an introduction to epidemiology, cultural competency, health literacy, evidence-based public health, program planning and evaluation, research methods, quantitative research methods, qualitative research methods, research ethics, health services and health policy research, how to develop a research proposal, and how to engage in community organizing.

In this book, we define *communities* as self-identified affinity groups. Community is an important concept in partnerships and may be designated by geography (e.g., neighborhood, block, city, town, county) but can also be designated by other sociodemographic characteristics (e.g., gender, age, race, ethnicity, sexual orientation) or some combination of geographic and sociodemographic characteristics (e.g., black males in New York City, LGBTQ youth in St. Louis). We also include community health stakeholders (e.g., community health centers, hospitals, social services, social workers, nurses) as potential members of community-academic partnerships.

Each of the topical chapters starts with a set of learning objectives and a brief self-assessment consisting of a few open-ended questions. These questions are designed to encourage the readers' thinking about the topic and the consideration of what they already know in the area. Chapters include a small group activity (where appropriate) and provide additional references beyond those covered in the chapter. Group activities are designed for experiential learning, moving concepts beyond the classroom to real-world examples (e.g., brainstorming for a grant proposal, gathering data for a debate on school nutrition offerings). Each chapter concludes with a self-assessment consisting of multiple choice questions adapted from the pre-/posttest used for the in-person training sessions. The final chapter is on program implementation and evaluation. On the book website, we provide templates for session evaluations, baseline and final assessments, the CRFT application for participation, application review criteria, participant agreement, ground rules, sample

Introduction xv

agenda, sign-in sheet, faculty evaluation, mid-training evaluation, request for proposals, proposal review template, sample certificate of completion, follow-up interview questions and consent form, and homework assignments.

A research methods curriculum for community members: The origins

To increase organizational capacity and enhance the infrastructure for CBPR, community members themselves initiated the idea to receive training on public health research methods. The request came during community organization and coalition-building work to address minority health issues in Suffolk County, NY. The Center for Public Health and Health Policy Research at Stony Brook University School of Medicine hosted several planning meetings during the development of the Suffolk County Minority Health Action Coalition. The meetings consisted of three mini-summits on minority health— half-day workshops with a broad array of community health stakeholders— and two annual Suffolk County Minority Health Summits.[7]

The purpose of the mini-summits on minority health was to identify areas of concern (first mini-summit), to develop attainable goals (first and second mini-summits), to determine recommended strategies for reaching goals (first and second mini-summits), and to form a minority health community coalition (third mini-summit). Each mini-summit had a theme: (1) race, class, and public health; (2) community-based participatory research; and (3) coalition building. At the third mini-summit on minority health, the Suffolk County Minority Health Action Coalition was officially formed with four working committees: (1) coalition structure, (2) data collection, (3) cultural competency, and (4) insurance. Although the intended outcome of the mini-summits on minority health was to form working committees, sometimes the unanticipated outcomes offer the most impact.[7]

The topic of the second mini-summit on minority health was CBPR, as a recommended strategy for developing and implementing solutions to address health disparities in the county. The mini-summits had the same structure. Each started with a short presentation on the designated topic. Participants were then divided into small groups for facilitated, semistructured roundtable discussions. These discussions were shared with the larger group as part of a facilitated group discussion.[7]

In the larger group discussion during the second mini-summit, a participant raised a good point. Although CBPR seemed to have great potential for addressing community health concerns, how could community members and community health workers participate in research as equal partners if the community members did not have adequate knowledge of research methods? This point started a lively discussion about some of the pitfalls of previous community-academic partnerships in the region. Mini-summit participants discussed frustrations about past work with researchers who told them their ideas were not research questions or that research did not work in the ways

xvi *Introduction*

that the community members articulated. The previous experiences of poor collaboration made the effort to build new partnerships a challenging task.

Community health stakeholders bring a wealth of important information, resources, and skills to community-academic partnerships. In evidence-based and data-driven fields, community health stakeholders need the skills to be good consumers of research. In order to build equitable partnerships, community partners do not need to be research experts but need to have basic research literacy (basic knowledge of research methods, study design, and research terminology).[5] The community's request for research training just made sense so that they would have the knowledge necessary to be partners in the research process. Academic institutions are designed to train; this important resource and the existing infrastructure allow institutions to give the resource of training to the community before they take the resource of information. This act of goodwill has been well received by community stakeholders in various settings in which it has been offered.

The community-driven idea to train community members and increase community research literacy to enhance the infrastructure for CBPR was developed into a training program based on the core competencies embedded in the MPH degree at the university. Simultaneously, in 2007, the National Institutes of Health (NIH) was interested in funding new community-academic research partnerships through the Partners in Research mechanism, the purpose of which was "to support studies of innovative programs designed to improve public understanding of health care research and promote collaboration between scientists and community organizations."[8] Furthermore, the aim of the studies was to "help in the development of strategies to increase the public awareness and trust in both the role of NIH and the importance of new directions of research for advancing the public health."[8] The funding mechanism required an academic institution and a community-based organization to jointly propose a project.

The Center for Public Health and Health Policy Research at Stony Brook University developed a collaboration with Literacy Suffolk and wrote a proposal to develop the Community Alliance for Research Empowering Social Change (CARES). The CARES program included training for community fellows and funding for small pilot CBPR projects. Literacy Suffolk focused on countywide change by improving individual adult literacy skills and had recently expanded into health literacy; research literacy was a natural extension of their work. An ideal partner in this initiative, Literacy Suffolk was affiliated with Suffolk County, NY Public Libraries; library branches became the training sites. Each partner library designated a CARES librarian who was knowledgeable about the program and who could help fellows use the library to conduct health research.[9]

Unlike most trainings for community members that are purposefully short (usually limited to a few hours), training for the CARES fellows was designed like a semester-long course with weekly 3-hour sessions for 15 weeks. The full commitment also included two additional weeks, with orientation the week before the training and the certificate ceremony the week after the training

(17 weeks total).[9,10] Each session was a condensed version of an MPH course and was facilitated by an expert in the field (e.g., research methods, research ethics, quantitative methods, qualitative methods, health literacy, cultural competency, community health, epidemiology, and grant writing). The survey course was designed to cover a broad range of topics with enough depth for clear understanding. After completing the training program, which included a certification to conduct research with human subjects, fellows were eligible to apply for CBPR pilot grant funding in collaboration with an academic researcher.

Adapted from the CARES fellows training program, the CRFT program was developed for the St. Louis region with the support of a community advisory board (CAB) and funding from the Program to Eliminate Cancer Disparities (PECaD) at the Alvin J. Siteman Cancer Center (SCC) and the National Cancer Institute. The CRFT CAB consisted of a diverse group of community stakeholders who collaborated with the CRFT project team to implement three successful cohorts (in years 2013, 2014, and 2015), training more than 100 community health stakeholders in the St. Louis greater metropolitan area.[6]

Unlike CARES, the CRFT training took place on a university campus—specifically, Washington University School of Medicine (WUSM). We believe that this change in location was key in fellows feeling connected to the university, becoming familiar with the campus, and having a willingness to collaborate in other community-academic initiatives. Most CRFT alumni were involved in the community before participating in the program, but subsequent to completing the program, several joined community-academic partnerships (e.g., PECaD colorectal community partnership, CRFT CAB), worked on research projects in collaboration with academic institutions (e.g., Washington University in St. Louis, University of Missouri-St. Louis, Saint Louis University), and participated in grant reviews (e.g., Missouri Foundation for Health, WUSM Institute for Clinical and Translational Sciences, Washington University Institute for Public Health).[6] Homework assignments were also a new addition to the CRFT program. They were designed to be easy to complete, and they placed course material in a community context.

The importance of community-academic partnerships

The public health problems faced by communities today are extremely complex and often involve an amalgam of biological, social, environmental, and economic factors. One of the most challenging public health issues today is the persistence of racial/ethnic and socioeconomic disparities in health. Although academic researchers and others are still working to understand all of the multifactorial causes of health disparities, it is clear that research conducted in an academic vacuum is not the way to develop sustainable solutions to address known causes. The development, implementation, and evaluation of potential solutions to address these problems will require multiple stakeholders working together and blending their knowledge, skills, and resources.

xviii *Introduction*

The kinds of robust collaborations among stakeholders that are needed to diminish health disparities are often threatened by historical mistrust and bad personal experiences that make community stakeholders wary of collaborating with researchers at academic institutions. Much of the mistrust is owed to the record of how participants in the Tuskegee Syphilis Experiment—all African American men—were treated. The breaches in ethical research conduct were many. The researchers did not fully disclose the details of the research study to the participants, they did not offer a widely used and accepted treatment for syphilis once it became available, and the study continued well beyond its initially projected timeline of six months. The study lasted 40 years.[11] The history and notable ethical lapses of this study are discussed in detail in Chapter 12.

Although the Tuskegee Syphilis Experiment may be the most well-known instance of such egregious research misconduct, racial and ethnic minority groups besides African Americans (e.g., Hispanics, Native Americans) have also been subjected to research misconduct. Additionally, the mistrust that communities of color often have for institutions extends beyond health-related institutions; it also encompasses those that are designed to "serve" (e.g., police, criminal justice, social services). Thus, the issue of institutional mistrust is culturally embedded and may pose a substantial barrier to collaboration, so community members frequently do not benefit from the knowledge of academic researchers.

Despite researchers' knowledge of the role of place—or where people live, work, pray, and play—in determining social networks, social resources, and access to health-promoting resources,[12–15] successful community-based implementation of evidence-based programs, interventions, and policies is difficult to achieve in real-world settings.[16–18] Several academic institutions and researchers have been working to bridge this gap through community-academic partnerships.

Most community-academic partnerships have a goal of creating equitable, mutually beneficial partnerships to address a health concern. However, many community organizations ideal for these sorts of partnerships lack the organizational capacity and research literacy necessary to participate fully in community-engaged and community-based research. Similarly, many academic institutions lack the infrastructure for the development of equitable participatory partnerships between faculty and community members. Nonetheless, community-academic partnerships have demonstrated potential for the development and implementation of interventions to address health disparities through multi-sectoral collaboration.[19–23] An intricate balance exists between research and practice, which makes community-academic partnerships with high levels of community engagement essential for the development and implementation of solutions in community-based settings. However, partnerships often face many challenges in development, progression, and sustainability due to lack of equity, an imbalance of power, limited funding, lack of transparency, differing agendas of stakeholders, and minimal benefit to community stakeholders.[24,25] The guiding purpose of the CRFT program has been to address such complications in community-academic partnerships. The knowledge base and the lessons learned during this program and its predecessor, the CARES

Introduction xix

program, are infused in the chapters to follow so that stakeholders in various communities might work together as true partners toward solutions to health disparities that are pertinent to their contexts.

Resources section with links

The companion website for this book provides resources for program implementation (e.g., CRFT application, homework, sample certificate of completion) and evaluation (e.g., baseline assessment, session evaluation template, faculty evaluation, interview guide) in the form of editable templates that can be adapted for use by others. Each of these resources are described in greater detail in the conclusion which describes program implementation and evaluation in detail. Available online only at https://www.routledge.com/978498785068

Homework

Available online only at https://www.routledge.com/978498785068

References

1. Thomas SB, Quinn SC, Butler J, Fryer CS, Garza MA. Toward a fourth generation of disparities research to achieve health equity. *Annu Rev Public Health.* 2011;32(c):399–416. doi:10.1146/annurev-publhealth-031210-101136.
2. Kilbourne AM, Switzer G, Hyman K, Crowley-Matoka M, Fine MJ. Advancing health disparities research within the health care system: A conceptual framework. *Am J Public Health.* 2006;96(12):2113–2121. doi:10.2105/AJPH.2005.077628.
3. Goodman MS, Gilbert KL, Hudson D, Milam L, Colditz GA. Descriptive analysis of the 2014 race-based healthcare disparities measurement literature. *J Racial Ethn Heal Disparities.* August 2016. http://www.ncbi.nlm.nih.gov/pubmed/27571958.
4. D'Agostino McGowan L, Stafford JD, Thompson VL et al. Quantitative Evaluation of the Community Research Fellows Training program. *Front Public Heal.* 2015; 3(July):179. doi:10.3389/fpubh.2015.00179.
5. Komaie G, Ekenga CC, Thompson VLS, Goodman MS. Increasing Community research capacity to address health disparities: A qualitative program evaluation of the Community Research Fellows Training Program. *J Empir Res Hum Res Ethics.* 2017;12(1):55–66. doi:10.1111/j.1749-6632.2009.05089.x.
6. Coats J V., Stafford JD, Sanders Thompson V, Johnson Javois B, Goodman MS. Increasing research literacy: The Community Research Fellows Training Program. *J Empir Res Hum Res Ethics.* 2015;10(1):3–12. doi:10.1177/1556264614561959.
7. Goodman MS, Stafford JD, Suffolk County Minority Health Action Coalition. Mini-Summit Health Proceedings. In: *Center for Public Health & Health Policy Research.* Stony Brook, NY: Community Engaged Scholarship for Health; 2011. doi:Product ID#FDKMG47P.
8. National Institutes of Health. The NIH Public Trust Initiative Launches the "Partners in Research" Program; 2007. https://www.nih.gov/news-events/news -releases/nih-public-trust-initiative-launches-partners-research-program. Accessed January 12, 2017.
9. Goodman MS, Dias JJ, Stafford JD. Increasing research literacy in minority communities: CARES fellows training program. *J Empir Res Hum Res Ethics.* 2010;5(4):33–41. doi:10.1525/jer.2010.5.4.33.

xx   *Introduction*

10. Goodman MS, Si X, Stafford JD, Obasohan A, Mchunguzi C. Quantitative assessment of participant knowledge and evaluation of participant satisfaction in the CARES training program. *Prog Community Heal Partnerships Res Educ Action.* 2012;6(3):359–366. doi:10.1353/cpr.2012.0051.
11. Centers for Disease Control and Prevention. Tuskegee Study—Timeline. https://www.cdc.gov/tuskegee/timeline.htm. Accessed February 2, 2017.
12. González G, Wilson-Frederick Wilson SM, Thorpe RJ. Examining place as a social determinant of health: Association between diabetes and US geographic region among non-Hispanic Whites and a diverse group of Hispanic/Latino men. *Fam Community Health.* 2015;38(4):319–331. doi:10.1097/FCH.0000000000000081.
13. Laveist T, Pollack K, Thorpe R, Fesahazion R, Gaskin D. Place, not race: Disparities dissipate in southwest Baltimore when blacks and whites live under similar conditions. *Heal Aff.* 2011;30(10):1880–1887. doi:10.1377/hlthaff.2011.0640.
14. Boardman JD, Saint Onge JM, Rogers RG, Denney JT. Race differentials in obesity: The impact of place. *J Health Soc Behav.* 2005;46(3):229–243. doi:10.1177/002214650504600302.
15. Chang VW. Racial residential segregation and weight status among US adults. *Soc Sci Med.* 2006;63(5):1289–1303. doi:10.1016/j.socscimed.2006.03.049.
16. Glasgow RE, Askew S, Purcell P et al. Use of RE-AIM to address health inequities: Application in a low-income community health center based weight loss and hypertension self-management program. *Transl Behav Med.* 2013;3(2):200–210. doi:10.1007/s13142-013-0201-8.
17. Brown CH, Kellam SG, Kaupert S et al. Partnerships for the design, conduct, and analysis of effectiveness, and implementation research: Experiences of the prevention science and methodology group. *Adm Policy Ment Heal.* 2012;39(4):301–316. doi:10.1007/s10488-011-0387-3.
18. Highfield L, Hartman MA, Bartholomew LK, Balihe P, Ausborn VM. Evaluation of the effectiveness and implementation of an adapted evidence-based mammography intervention. *BioMed Research International.* 2015;2015:Article ID 240240. doi:10.1155/2015/240240.
19. Thompson VLS, Drake B, James AS et al. A community coalition to address cancer disparities: Transitions, successes and challenges. *J Cancer Educ.* 2014;30(4):616–622. doi:10.1007/s13187-014-0746-3.
20. Nguyen G, Hsu L, Kue KN, Nguyen T, Yuen EJ. Partnering to collect health services and public health data in hard-to-reach communities: A community-based participatory research approach for collecting community health data. *Prog Community Heal Partnerships Res Educ Action.* 2010;4(2):115–119.
21. Gwede CK, Castro E, Brandon TH et al. Developing strategies for reducing cancer disparities via cross-institutional collaboration outreach efforts for the partnership between the Ponce School of Medicine and the Moffitt Cancer Center. *Health Promot Pract.* 2012;13(6):807–815. doi:10.1177/1524839911404227.
22. Israel BA, Lichtenstein R, Lantz P et al. The Detroit Community-Academic Urban Research Center: Development, implementation, and evaluation. *J Public Heal Manag Pract.* 2001;7(5):1–19.
23. Israel BA, Coombe CM, Cheezum RR et al. Community-based participatory research: A capacity-building approach for policy advocacy aimed at eliminating health disparities. *Am J Public Health.* 2010;100(11):2094–2102.
24. Adams A, Miller-Korth N, Brown D. Learning to work together: Developing academic and community research partnerships. *WMJ.* 2004;103(2):15–19.
25. Ross LF, Loup A, Nelson RM et al. The challenges of collaboration for academic and community partners in a research partnership: Points to consider. *J Empir Res Hum Res Ethics.* 2010;5(1):19–31. doi:10.1525/jer.2010.5.1.19.

1 Community-based participatory research

Vetta Sanders Thompson and Sula Hood

LEARNING OBJECTIVES

- Describe history and principles of Community-Based Participatory Research (CBPR) project.
- Critically evaluate participants' positions within their communities and their potential roles within CBPR projects.
- Describe methods to ensure that CBPR research benefits all partners.
- Share lessons learned from CBPR.

SELF-ASSESSMENT—WHAT DO YOU KNOW?

1. What is community engagement?
2. What two research trends contributed to the development of CBPR?
3. What are the principles of CBPR?
4. What are the benefits of CBPR?
5. In a CBPR project, who determines the health problem to be studied or analyzed?
6. What are the key components of a partnership plan?

Introduction

A core value of the public participation process is that those who are affected by a decision have a right to be involved in the decision-making process.[1] Public participation allows an organization to consult with important stakeholders—such as interested or affected people, organizations, and government entities—before making a decision; it requires, at minimum, two-way communication, collaborative problem solving, and attempts to obtain better

2 Public health research methods for partnerships and practice

and more acceptable decisions.[1] Community engagement is a component of public participation and is believed to achieve its aims by bringing together community stakeholders to reach mutually agreed-upon goals or to resolve mutually agreed-upon concerns.[2]

Community engagement can be conducted through partnerships, collaborations, and coalitions that help to mobilize resources to influence systems and that help to improve equity in the relationships among those engaged.[3] The results of community engagement serve as catalysts for changing policies, programs, and practices.[3] To be effective, the resulting interactions and collaborations rely on the establishment of trust—building and enhancing community relationships, resources, and capacity.[2,3] Fundamental to community engagement is a requirement of respect for the community and the incorporation of community attitudes, beliefs, and insights regarding needs and problems when developing programs, interventions, and research.[3,4] Ideally, community engagement strategies are implemented in ways that assure that the communities and members most likely to be affected by decisions about programs, services, and resources have involvement and voice from the point of activity initiation to the completion of relevant projects and services.[5] These principles apply to the research enterprise, as well as other civic or social change and engagement endeavors.[2]

It is increasingly acknowledged that although research can and should benefit communities, many examples exist of the failure to do so, in addition to instances of harm.[6] Examples of harm have included exposure of marginalized communities to greater likelihood of poor health outcomes and the potential for stigma and discrimination in the case of small, identifiable groups of people negatively perceived in society.[6] Theoretically, engagement strategies that allow communities to be fully engaged in the process of mobilization and organization for change can address these issues.[6] In addition, community engagement strategies increase the likelihood that programs and policies designed to improve well-being are accepted by those they are designed to serve and that they are also successful.[7–9]

Community-based participatory research (CBPR) is one of several community engagement models. According to Wallerstein and Duran, CBPR "bridges the gap between science and practice through community engagement and social action."[10] With a goal of societal transformation,[11] CBPR involves community partners in all aspects of the research process, with all partners contributing expertise and sharing decision-making.[11,12] By promoting equitable power and strong collaborative partnerships, CBPR offers a positive alternative to traditional "top-down research,"[13] and, although very prominent in public health research, it is increasingly applied across disciplines as diverse as nursing, sociology, social work, psychology, and others.[14]

This chapter provides a brief history of CBPR and, then, describes key concepts and principles of the model. The steps required to initiate and sustain CPBR are discussed, and an example of a successful CBPR partnership

Community-based participatory research   3

is presented. The chapter ends with a discussion of strategies to improve partnership functioning and sustainability.

Definitions of community

What does community mean to you?

Before discussing implementation of CBPR, it is important to understand the complexity of defining *community*. It is common to define community on the basis of geographic characteristics, using a synonym of community in the term *neighborhood*. Administrative boundaries (e.g., census tracks, blocks) and areas between natural or man-made barriers are often used to define the relevant location.[6] However, some people within a geographic area do not have the same sense of group belonging, which has implications for participation, defining issues, and setting the goals and objectives of interventions, research, and activities designed to promote change.

Community may also be socially or psychologically defined on the basis of group identity, affiliation, or membership.[15] Groups may be based on shared characteristics such as race, ethnicity, religion, nationality, sexual orientation, profession, or other characteristics. Examples of communities defined in this way are the Latino/a community, the Muslim community, the lesbian/gay/bisexual/transgender/queer community, or the business community. In the examples provided, community is dynamic, and multiple identities and interests may be present and relevant for participants.[16] All of these issues can affect the development of successful collaborations and implementation of the CBPR process. One key to the success of CBPR is the presence of shared identity among participants in the process.[16]

What is a good community/neighborhood? What is a bad community/neighborhood?

In CBPR partnerships, people affiliated with or self-identified as a geographically close entity (neighborhood), special interest, or social or political group act to address issues affecting the well-being of the community—for example, the South Side of Chicago, prostate cancer survivors, or the progressive wing of the Democratic party. Members of a community may view their group and its boundaries differently from those who are outsiders of the group.[16] The differences in perceptions regarding who or what is community may lead to differences in what are seen as strengths, weaknesses, and resources, as well as whether the community is viewed as "good" or "bad." Therefore, it is important that all members of partnerships, particularly researchers, spend some time considering what community means to them, as well as time exploring their definitions of constructs such as the idea of good and bad communities. The self-awareness gained through reflection and

4 *Public health research methods for partnerships and practice*

dialogue with partners and collaborators about appropriate definitions of community and geographic boundaries is a first step in the CBPR process and will assist in honest discussions of issues, goals, and objectives.

Trust is an important aspect of CBPR that cannot be overemphasized. Building the trust necessary for a successful partnership requires that researchers, stakeholders, and community members share information on how they see the potential, the ability to change, and the strengths and problems of the defined community. Additionally, when possible, researchers should get to know the communities they are working with, beyond the surface level (or understandings conveyed through data). This process involves them spending time in the communities being studied and interacting with community members, experiences that are often facilitated by key community stakeholders. As "outsiders," researchers must seek to overcome their own biases and assumptions about communities by intimately learning about the communities that they are working with, including norms and formal and informal structures. In CBPR, it is imperative that research partners be sensitive to community norms, as these factors will likely influence intervention preferences, adoption or uptake, and sustainability.

History of CBPR

A negative history of academic–community research relations, particularly in communities of color, has resulted in a strong mistrust toward colleges and universities that is based on unethical research practices.[17,18] The Tuskegee Syphillis Experiment serves as one example of unethical research practice. (See Chapter 12 for a detailed discussion.) However, other research and intervention examples have fueled mistrust as well, with research and outside interference in Native American communities' affairs serving as an example.[17,18] During the 1970s, researchers began to express concerns about the ways that they conducted research, as well as the accuracy and usefulness of the data collected, and interventions developed to address social issues. Most efforts to provide a history of CBPR refer to two distinct historical traditions that have informed the development of the research strategy known as CBPR: Northern (also referred to as *traditional action research*) and Southern (also referred to as *radical action research*).[19,20]

It is from Kurt Lewin that CBPR draws its emphasis on the active involvement of "those who are most affected."[13] Lewin, a social psychologist, is typically identified as the first to use the term *action research*.[20] This Northern, or traditional, approach to participatory research began in the 1940s, with Lewin advocating for the use of scientific data by community leaders. He hoped that university researchers and their institutions would facilitate action research and emphasized that the relationship among researchers, those who participate in studies, and a variety of stakeholder groups was an important factor in how useful the research could be in promoting social change.[20]

As an important aspect of CBPR, co-learning is understood as the process of two or more parties learning together to solve a problem and learning from each other.[12] CBPR's emphasis on co-learning is drawn from Brazilian adult educator and social activist Paulo Freire in his work on critical thinking, which encourages oppressed people to closely examine their circumstances and to understand the nature and causes of their oppression and activities, and the strategies of their oppressors.[13,19] The Southern, or radical, form of action research is associated with philosophies and scholarship that emerged in underdeveloped or developing nations (e.g., Brazil, Colombia, India).[20] Scammell suggests that the most important characteristic of this tradition is a focus on political and socioeconomic inequities.[20] Proponents of the Southern tradition believe that social science researchers have an important role to play in reducing the disparities and inequities observed among members of poor and underserved communities.[20] This aspect of CBPR may provide the greatest opportunity for change as communities and institutions of all sorts collaborate to address social problems.

Marullo and Edwards suggest that engaged scholarship requires a transformation of colleges and universities into institutions that enter into "collaborative arrangements with community partners to address pressing social, political, economic, and moral ills."[21] CBPR is one part of the efforts to create this transformation and seeks to overcome historic tensions between researchers and community members to address disparities and injustice.[3,20] Scammel highlights the role of the environmental justice movement in the form of CBPR that emerged in the United States and further notes the role of the 1999 Institute of Medicine (IOM) report *Toward Environmental Justice: Research, Education, and Health Policy Needs*.[20] In the IOM report, participatory research was discussed as a method for addressing health disparities and environmental injustice. This report was important because it offered an alternative to traditional epidemiological methods. A CBPR approach not only encourages community participation in research, but also encourages community participation in determining how data are used to inform the policies that may contribute to injustices.

Despite interest in this methodology, its adoption and implementation has been variable. A systematic review of CBPR clinical trials involving racial and ethnic minorities showed that most CBPR studies reported community involvement in identifying study questions, recruitment efforts, development and delivery of the intervention, and data collection methods.[22] However, very few studies involved the community in the interpretation of research findings or in efforts to disseminate findings.[22] The development of the relationships, trust, and rapport required for CBPR can be inhibited by imbalances in power and knowledge that may exist among researchers, treatment providers, and the community members and organizations engaged in research efforts.[23]

6 *Public health research methods for partnerships and practice*

CBPR implementation

CBPR stands in contrast to standard "top down" research practices in which researchers and providers decide the issues, goals, strategies, and methods employed in the research and intervention studies.[12] In summary, the most cited CBPR principles stress collaboration, community involvement, shared decision-making, building on community strengths and assets, a balance between the desire to increase knowledge and the desire to act to improve social conditions, co-learning, and capacity building in the community.

BOX 1.1   NINE KEY PRINCIPLES OF COMMUNITY-BASED PARTICIPATORY RESEARCH

- Community is defined using identity.
- The collaboration identifies and builds on strengths and resources within the community.
- The process is structured to facilitate collaborative, equitable involvement of all partners in all phases of the research.
- Knowledge, activities, and interventions are structured to assure mutual benefit for all partners.
- The established processes promote co-learning and empowerment, and attend to social inequities.
- A cyclical and iterative process is involved.
- Health promotion is addressed from both positive and ecological perspectives.
- Knowledge, findings, and outcomes are shared with all partners.
- The collaboration involves long-term commitment by all partners.

(Adapted from Israel BA et al., Annu Rev Public Health, *19, 173–202, 1998.)*

Benefits of CBPR

The literature notes numerous benefits of CBPR.[8,11,14,19] First, this approach promotes the development of trust and rapport between community members and researchers, making it more likely that community partners will share their concerns with the researchers, and the approach increases the likelihood that community needs can be addressed.[8,11,19] In addition, community participation, particularly feedback on findings, will likely increase the accuracy of the data collected and how those data are interpreted. CBPR approaches allow the researchers to gain an insider's perspective, in which community partners can offer valuable information related to the phenomenon being studied and can offer culturally relevant and potentially effective solutions. When CBPR strategies are used, findings and resulting interventions from the collaborative work may have increased acceptance, adoption, and sustainability within the community, given the community's awareness that their input and perspectives influenced the efforts.[8,11,14] Finally, it is suggested that CBPR empowers and changes people's perceptions of themselves and what they can accomplish.[19]

BOX 1.2   BENEFITS OF COMMUNITY-BASED PARTICIPATORY RESEARCH

Institutional Partner
- Learns more about local resources and services.
- Obtains improved ecological validity of research.
- Gains understanding of how interventions in other communities may or may not apply to local circumstances.
- Gains additional knowledge and perspective on the community's history and culture.
- Sees evidence of how community experiences can improve the research process.

Community Partner
- Gains understanding of how certain decisions about research design could impact the credibility of the results.
- Sees evidence of how their experiences can improve the research process.
- Obtains data that validate their concerns to the "outside world."
- Provides "proof" that policy makers, the media, and other high-level decision makers require before they believe that the issue deserves their attention.
- Sees resulting benefits in the community.

Developing the partnership

When thinking about conducting CBPR, it is important to realize that rather than doing research *on* or *in* the community, by engaging in partnerships, CBPR researchers conduct research *with* the community, as equal partners.[12] As equal contributors to the research, community partners are valued and recognized for the unique strengths, assets, resources, and experiential knowledge that they bring to the table.[13] Additionally, CBPR promotes mutually beneficial relationships between academic and community partners so that both parties gain.[14] Closely related to the idea of mutual benefit, CBPR

8 *Public health research methods for partnerships and practice*

embraces co-learning through partnerships, which consist of reciprocal knowledge translation and transmission, such that all involved parties gain insight and skills from one another.[10] For example, research partners gain invaluable insight and information about community structure or norms that they otherwise would not have been privy to, which increases their understanding of community needs. Similarly, by working with researchers, community partners gain knowledge pertaining to community-based research, ranging from project conceptualization and implementation to data interpretation and evaluation.

A key characteristic of CBPR is that the focus of the issue under study is community driven, meaning that a CBPR project always begins with a topic of concern that has been voiced by members of the community.[13] Cornwall and Jewkes note that participatory research not only requires acknowledgment of the importance of community knowledge and perspectives, but also prioritizes these as the basis for research.[24] Moreover, community partners are involved in every aspect of the research process, from start to finish, including research design, intervention development, evaluation of interventions, interpretation, and dissemination of findings. Community members of a CBPR team should contribute to the dissemination of research findings, including making presentations and coauthoring scholarly works with researchers and other academic partners.[14] By involving community partners in every aspect of the research process, CBPR is a systematic effort to integrate community voice, needs, and knowledge into research.[10] As noted by Minkler, "CBPR breaks down the barriers between the researcher and the researched."[13]

Community partners may consist of community members, community organization leaders, and other community-based stakeholders. Much of the CBPR work has been conducted with low-income communities and other disadvantaged populations, with researchers seeking to provide a platform for the needs, concerns, and suggestions of "those who are most affected" by inequalities and disparities to be heard.[14] Examinations of CBPR efforts suggest that institutional and faculty commitment to engagement principles, flexible and inclusive governance structures, and strategies to educate community members must be developed to assure that the barriers to CBPR frequently identified in the literature do not inhibit success.[23]

Researchers and community organizations and members have a number of motivations for participating in research and research partnerships. Some motivations are not compatible with the principles observed in CBPR, particularly those that involve opportunism and self-interest. For researchers primarily interested in obtaining grant funding to support an academic position, the need to demonstrate a community partnership to meet funder requirements, and community partnership as a vehicle to recruit individuals from underserved communities as research participants, CBPR partnership participation is inappropriate. If community members are looking for credibility that they believe comes from working with an academic institution for grant funding to support or sustain community programs, or a job, CBPR partnership participation is inappropriate.

As outlined in the CBPR principles, CBPR partnerships involve a cyclical and iterative process that requires a long-term commitment to producing community change.[12] In addition, all partners must examine their capacity to commit the resources, time, and effort required for a specific CBPR partnership. For example, if an organization is only interested in services or community interventions, then participating in research may not be feasible or appropriate. This is because community service projects have different timelines and overall goals and objectives compared to research interventions. Although an organization or agency might participate effectively in a service project with an evaluation component, a CBPR research project might be frustrating because of difficulty agreeing on research goals and objectives.

Another significant characteristic of CBPR is equity. The need for equity is not unique to research relationships; equity is important in any partnership or relationship. To achieve equity, there must be good communication, which requires a common vocabulary. For community members and researchers to communicate well and for partnerships to progress, each participant must gain access to the knowledge and skills of the other. This is why co-learning is so important.[10] In order to facilitate equity in the partnership, members must have a process for the following:

- Addressing power imbalances between community members and academics.
- Acknowledging and valuing the expertise and skills of community organizations.
- Developing strategies for building a common language among partners.
- Examining and resolving differences and conflicts that develop within and between partner organizations because of differences in funding, resources, and constituencies.
- Handling issues of ownership of data, resources, and control of funding.
- Dealing with research fatigue amongst certain communities. Researchers should consider how many research or intervention requests are made to a single community and the burden that participation produces.

The CBPR process: Making it work

As the development of the partnership begins, it is important to remember that the values, perspectives, contributions, and confidentiality of everyone in the community must be respected. It is important for partners to decide how respect and confidentiality will be assured. Partnership information is of importance, as are community input and feedback in addition to data obtained as part of the research process. Questions to be answered include the

10 *Public health research methods for partnerships and practice*

following: who owns the data, who will be responsible for shared data, where and how will the data be stored, who will have access to the data, and what level of identification will be maintained when data are stored. The group must determine whether participating partners are required to undergo training on protecting human subjects and the level training (if any).

A complete CBPR partnership plan outlines a governance structure that explains partnership oversight; how members are added to the partnership; who leads the partnership meetings; the frequency of these meetings; the research, intervention, and activity implementation responsibilities of partnerships; the structure for obtaining group and community feedback; information sharing and dissemination of data; a process for managing communication between meetings; and a mechanism for systematic partnership review and evaluation. Governance structures take many forms and are decided on the basis of the partners' specific purpose, goals, and outcomes of the partnership. While the specific governance structures of CBPR partnerships may vary, what is consistent across partnerships is that governance is developed with input and agreement from all members.

The governance document must also specify how the community will be involved in the development of research plans and activities from the beginning of the partnership. Community partners should have real influence on the direction of activities and research. In this instance, plans for co-learning can be strategic.[10] Opportunities for co-learning can be structured into activities that support the research—such as interviewing, data entry, and interpretation—so that community members gain practical knowledge of the process, as well as skills that may benefit their organizations.

The partnership document should also indicate what the structure for decision-making will look like, who participates in the decision-making (e.g., every meeting attendee, one participant per organization, all partnership members, or designated partnership members), and which issues require partnership awareness, input, and approval. CBPR principles suggest that community input be obtained on the partnership purpose, outcomes of interest, major activities, results, and recommendations based on data obtained.[14] The partnership assists in shaping the process for obtaining both community input and the dissemination of these results. Finally, rules must be developed for access and use of the data compiled, within and outside of the partnership.

The remainder of the partnership plan requires information on all partners, the overall purpose of the partnership, partnership outcomes (expected results), the resources needed to support the partnership, and the major activities to be completed to achieve the outcomes. This section of the partnership plan contains information that is transferred to a memorandum of understanding (MOU), which is used to document partner commitments and obligations. This document and associated MOUs should be periodically reviewed at intervals agreed upon by the partners.

The information on partners should include their mission, location, longevity in the community, demographics of those they serve, expertise, the

Community-based participatory research   11

BOX 1.3   MEMORANDUM OF UNDERSTANDING OUTLINE

Partners (List those organizations, agencies, and individuals who have agreed to participate.):

CBPR Principles Guiding the Processes of the Partnership (Select the CBPR principles that the group believes are most important to the initiation and maintenance of the partnership. State how these principles are to be applied to the operations and activities of the partnership. Keep in mind your past collaborations, research experiences, reasons for participating, needs, and concerns.)

Goals (What does the partnership hope to accomplish? Attempt to use goals that are specific, measurable, achievable, realistic, and timely.):
1.
2.
3.

Activities (What will the group do to accomplish the goals of the collaboration?):
1.
2.
3.

Responsibilities (Specify what the partner organization, agency, or individual is expected to do for each goal and each activity related to that goal. Include any resources that the partner will provide, resources that the partner can expect to receive, or both.)

Organization A agrees to do the following:

Organization B agrees to do the following:

Signature_____   Date_____
Signature_____   Date_____

---

services or activities they provide, resources and skills relevant to the partnership, potential barriers to participation, and the organization's partnership representative. Every partnership will add and subtract information categories from this list, depending on partnership purpose and the stage of partnership development.

12   *Public health research methods for partnerships and practice*

Planning for sustainability begins with the initiation of the partnership. Careful assessment of the physical, economic, and social assets of the community permits partners to anticipate the need to seek additional funding, partners from sectors not initially included, and availability of volunteers and in-kind resources in order to facilitate continued activity and pursuit of new goals and directions. Areas sometimes overlooked, but important, are financial strength, longevity, quality, and reputation strength of partners. The analysis of assets should consider the extent to which assets and resources can or will be directed to support the partnership.

The overall purpose and desired outcomes of the partnership are developed on the basis of partnership dialogue, community input, and data on community concerns. Partnership members must agree not only on the data required, but also on dialogue processes and strategies; who facilitates discussions; and whether the process includes literature and archival research, qualitative (e.g., facilitated workshops, focus groups, key informant and individual interviews, photovoice) or quantitative (e.g., Delphi method, surveys or questionnaires, etc.) methods of obtaining data on community-identified concerns, or a combination of these approaches. The data are summarized and shared in the format most appropriate for the partnership. (See Chapter 10 for a discussion of quantitative methods and Chapter 11 for a discussion of qualitative methods.)

Outcomes are determined on the basis of partnership purpose and the data reviewed. The standard criteria for outcomes are that they be specific, measurable, achievable, realistic, and timely (discussed further in Chapter 8). The use of specific and measurable goals facilitates review and evaluation of partnership activity and is important to understanding partnership progress and the need for changes in activities.[25] As the partnership meets goals, expands, or shifts interests and community needs, partnership purpose and outcomes can be reviewed and revised. Optimally, a schedule and plan for reviews are discussed and developed during the planning process.

The selected outcomes drive decisions on the major activities of the partnership (i.e., what is done to achieve the partnership outcomes). The discussion of outcomes should include consideration for how the selected outcomes and activities will serve the community.[12] Outcomes and associated activities can be structured for community benefit by sustaining useful projects, developing community capacity (e.g., jobs, training), or generating long-term benefits such as improved health. The resources required to complete each activity should be determined during the planning process as well. The ability to obtain needed resources can help to determine whether an outcome is realistic. As activities are decided and refined, the following are also determined: the responsibilities of each partner; the timeline; and resources provided, received, and shared by partners and partner contacts. Partnerships often develop logic models (described in detail in Chapter 8) during this part of the process to assist in developing and documenting their objectives, inputs (resources), activities, outcomes, and timeline. Again, as the partnership changes, expands, or contracts, activities will shift, as will other elements of the logic model.

CBPR example

To address the excess cancer burden among minority and medically underserved populations, the Program for the Elimination of Cancer Disparities (PECaD) was developed by the Alvin J. Siteman Cancer Center (SCC) of Washington University School of Medicine (WUSM) located in St. Louis, Missouri.[26] This partnership was developed in 2003 as an attempt to create a national model for eliminating cancer disparities and, from its inception, has applied the principles of CBPR to its programmatic approaches in community outreach and engagement, research, and training. In 2005, PECaD became one of the centers of the Community Networks Program (CNP), which was an initiative of the Center to Reduce Cancer Health Disparities. PECaD programs and activities focus on breast, lung, prostate, and colorectal cancers, using culturally competent methods developed with input from community representatives to increase reach among African Americans and low-income individuals. A more complete overview of the history of the partnership is available for review.[26]

The Disparities Elimination Advisory Committee (DEAC) is a community advisory group for PECaD and was established in 2003 at its inception. DEAC is made up of cancer survivors and advocates, representatives from health care and social service organizations, academic researchers, clinicians, and PECaD program staff. Members of DEAC are selected through a nomination process that includes review of résumés and nomination statements for evidence of community participation and consideration of the organizations and diverse populations represented. The group provides guidance and direction for PECaD programs; development, implementation, and evaluation of cancer control and prevention activities; recommendations for additional collaborations; and sharing of information on programs and resources.

Initially, the committee was led by academic researchers who were interested in CBPR as a method of achieving program goals. However, the group eventually acknowledged that this structure was not consistent with its CBPR philosophy. In 2010, DEAC began electing a community co-chairperson to serve with the academic researcher co-chairperson. The co-chairpersons plan the agenda for quarterly DEAC meetings; they also colead the DEAC meeting and monthly meetings of the PECaD internal leadership team. The leadership team is composed of the DEAC co-chairpersons, the researchers leading the research projects, individuals leading the training and community outreach activities, and the project coordinator. When the community co-chairperson was incorporated into DEAC governance, this individual also became a member of the internal leadership team, which introduced community input into the leadership team. The leadership team works in conjunction with DEAC and is responsible for guiding the implementation of PECaD

14 *Public health research methods for partnerships and practice*

programs and translating ongoing discussion within DEAC into relevant programmatic plans. The shifts in governance structure illustrate the need for partnerships to engage in an iterative process of review and evaluation, with flexibility to change and grow.

The CBPR process began with several activities that permitted identification of concerns about community cancer disparity that were within PECaD's capacity to respond. Community input resulted in a focus on sustained community outreach; educational programs to raise awareness about the benefits of screening, including a lay speaker's corps; state policy advocacy through SCC's government relations representative, as well as community service by PECaD leaders and staff; a research mentorship program to train and support junior faculty, postdoctoral fellows, graduate students, and undergraduates to conduct research projects examining cancer disparities; pilot research efforts, and SCC's minority recruitment in clinical trials monitoring.

One of the first research-related activities was based on a community request that WUSM researchers engage in a process to improve the conduct, relevance, and impact of research on local health concerns. This led to the assembly of a project team that conducted interviews with community leaders and key minority physicians and that also conducted focus groups.[27] The results and recommendations of the work group helped to focus the work of PECaD. The study revealed community support for the idea of research but noted as major barriers to participation the mistrust of researchers, the failure of the researchers to provide research descriptions that were easy to understand, and the lack of dissemination or poor dissemination of research results back to the community. The minority physicians who were interviewed also supported these issues and raised additional concerns. The results contributed to PECaD's early and ongoing focus on researcher training. The lessons continue to guide research efforts to seek community input, guidance, and support for all community-based cancer research.

The first programmatic effort was oversight of the development of partnerships regarding four diseases (i.e., breast, colon, lung, and prostate). Each of the four partnerships, with community input, identified its own priorities, including delays in accessing treatment after an abnormal mammogram, the difficulties navigating the system to get colon cancer screening for uninsured patients, spreading the message about prostate cancer screening, and supporting smoke-free environments. The partnerships have changed over a decade, and flexible governance and membership structures have been assets in managing change.[26] The lung partnership dissolved after achieving its original goal of supporting smoke-free legislation in the region.[26] The colorectal cancer community partnership, originally one of the smallest and least active partnerships, was revived and is now one of the most active groups. The breast cancer partnership has raised issues of accountability[28] and continually pushes for more frequent data sharing. The prostate partnership has challenged the PECaD leadership to be more active in assisting the community to understand shifting screening guidelines.[26] Review and evaluation[29] and a commitment to community input into all phases of the research and intervention process[12,13] have encouraged community members to challenge researchers and partnerships to dissolve, grow, and change to meet shifting community concerns and needs.

Conclusions

Examinations of CBPR efforts suggest that university and faculty commitment to engagement principles, development of flexible and inclusive governance structures, and strategies to educate community members are needed to assure that the barriers to CBPR frequently identified in the literature do not inhibit success.[23] There is no predetermined way for partnerships to function, as each community partnership is composed of different stakeholders. Partnership members set the levels of interaction and input with which they are comfortable. However, there will be variation in community organizations' expectations and desired input that can lead to frustration. It is important to have processes in place to address tensions as they arise. Partnership sustainability is more likely when participants are responsive to their unique social environments, develop programs consistent with available resources, and address community-defined social and health concerns.

Partnerships should be planned with periodic review and assessments to ensure that appropriate and meaningful activities continue.[28] Those activities that allow partners and researchers to respond to changing community needs, organizational interests, policies, and funding environments should be retained, with the option to add new activities to be responsive to current community circumstances and to delete activities that do not serve community needs.[28] An aspect of these periodic reviews is systematic evaluation, which has the potential to strengthen adherence to CBPR principles. Adherence to CBPR principles is important to assure that researchers and partners maintain the trust and respect required to continuously identify research priorities and gaps in needed services and interventions. Fidelity to the CBPR principles is also necessary to continually work to collaborate in ways that address disparities and community needs.

In addition, over time, the nature of partnership relationships and interactions should show growth. For example, joint applications for funding and joint publications should increase if there is true equity in the partnership and community involvement in all phases of the work.[10,12] Finally, community attitudes about the research, willingness to participate, and the ability to use partnership data for problem solving should be examined within mature partnerships, as these are signs of trust and empowerment that should be facilitated by CBPR.

When done with strong, collaborative partnerships, CBPR has significant potential for capacity building and sustainability, increasing the ability to make a large-scale impact on the issue(s) being addressed. Trust and respect are key elements of CBPR and are the foundation of successful partnerships.

16 Public health research methods for partnerships and practice

Collaboratively developed plans for governance and processes for operation that include co-learning facilitate identification of issues, planning and implementation of interventions, as well as dissemination of outcomes. Often forgotten, but important, strategies for obtaining feedback on interactions, level of participation, and satisfaction with the experience all allow partnerships to mature—expanding and contracting as needed.

Online resources

International Association for Public Participation. IAP2 Core Values: http://www .iap2.org/

Community-Campus Partnerships for Health: Promoting Health Equity and Social Justice: https://ccph.memberclicks.net/cbprcurriculum

Community Tool Box. Section 2. Community-Based Participatory Research: http:// ctb.ku.edu/en/table-of-contents/evaluate/evaluation/intervention-research/main

References

1. IAP2 core values. International Association for Public Participation Web site. http://www.iap2.org/?page=A4. Accessed June 12, 2016.
2. Zakus JDL, Lysack CL. Revisiting community participation. *Health Policy Plan.* 1998;13(1):1–12.
3. Jones L, Wells K. Strategies for academic and clinician engagement in community-participatory partnered research. *JAMA.* 2007;297(4):407–410.
4. Sapienza JN, Corbie-Smith G, Keim S, Fleishman, AR. Community engagement in epidemiological research. *Ambul Pediatr.* 2007;7(3):247–252.
5. Minkler M, Blackwell AG, Thompson M, Tamir H. Community-based participatory research: Implications for public health funding. *Am J Public Health.* 2003; 93(8):1210–1213.
6. Tindana PO, Singh JA, Tracy CS et al. Grand challenges in global health: Community engagement in research in developing countries. *PLoS Med.* 2007;4(9):e273.
7. D'Alonzo KT. Getting started in CBPR: Lessons in building community partnerships for new researchers. *Nurs Inq.* 2010;17(4):282–288. doi:10.1111/j.1440-1800 .2010.00510.x.
8. Israel BA, Eng E, Schulz AJ, Parker EA. *Methods in Community-Based Participatory Research for Health.* San Francisco, CA: John Wiley & Sons; 2005.
9. Viswanathan M, Ammerman A, Eng, E et al. Community-based participatory research: Assessing the evidence. In: *AHRQ Evidence Report Summaries.* Rockville, MD: Agency for Healthcare Research and Quality; 2005:99. http://www.ncbi.nlm .nih.gov/books/NBK11852/?report=reader. Accessed June 12, 2016.
10. Wallerstein N, Duran B. Community-based participatory research contributions to intervention research: the intersection of science and practice to improve health equity. *Am J Public Health.* 2010;100(suppl 1):S40–S46.
11. Minkler M. *Community Organizing and Community Building for Health.* New Brunswick, NJ: Rutgers University Press; 2003.
12. Israel BA, Shulz A, Parker EA, Becker AB. Review of community-based research: Assessing partnership approaches to improve public health. *Annu Rev Publ Health.* 1998;19:173–202.
13. Minkler M. Ethical challengers for the "outside" researcher in community-based participatory research. *Health Educ Behav.* 2004;31(6):684–697.

Community-based participatory research   17

14. Israel BA, Eng E, Shulz A, Parker E. *Methods for Community-Based Participatory Research for Health*. 2nd ed. Somerset, NJ: John Wiley & Sons; 2012.
15. Campbell C, Jovchelovitch S. Health, community and development: Towards a social psychology of participation. *J Community Appl Soc*. 2000;10(4):255–270.
16. MacQueen KM, McLellan E, Metzger DS et al. What is community? An evidence-based definition for participatory public health. *Am J Public Health*. 2001;91(12): 1929–1938.
17. Hurt T. Connecting with African American families: Challenges and possibilities. *The Family Psychologist*. 2009;25(1):11–13.
18. Murray VM, Kotchick BA, Wallace S et al. Race, culture, and ethnicity: Implications for a community intervention. *J Child Fam Stud*. 2004;13(1):81–99.
19. Minkler M, Wallerstein N, eds. *Community-Based Participatory Research for Health*. San Francisco, CA: Jossey-Bass; 2002.
20. Scammell MK. Roots of community research: Primer on the legacy of participatory research partnerships. *Race, Poverty and the Environment*. http://www.reimaginerpe.org/node/158. Accessed June 11, 2016.
21. Marullo S, Edwards B. From charity to justice: The potential of university-community collaboration for social change. *Am Behav Sci*. 2000;43(5):895–912.
22. De las Nueces D, Hacker K, DiGirolamo A, Hicks LS. A systematic review of community-based participatory research to enhance clinical trials in racial and ethnic minority groups. *Health Serv Res*. 2012;47:1363–1386. doi:10.1111/j.1475 -6773.2012.01386.x.
23. Weerts DJ, Sandmann LR. Building a two-way street: Challenges and opportunities for community engagement at research universities. *Rev High Educ*. 2008;32: 73–106.
24. Cornwall A, Jewkes R. What is participatory research? *Soc Sci Med*. 1995;41(12): 1667–1676.
25. Arroyo-Johnson C, Allen ML, Colditz GA et al. A tale of two Community Networks Program Centers: Operationalizing and assessing CBPR principles and evaluating partnership outcomes. *Prog Community Health Partnersh*. 2015;9(suppl):61–69. doi:10.1353/cpr.2015.0026.
26. Thompson Sanders VL, Drake B, James A et al. A community coalition to address cancer disparities: Transitions, successes and challenges. *J Cancer Educ*. 2015;30(4): 616–622. doi:10.1007/s13187-014-0746-3.
27. Scharff DP, Matthews KJ, Jackson P, Hoffsuemmer J, Martin E, Edwards D. More than Tuskegee: Understanding mistrust about research participation. *J Health Care Poor Underserved*. 2010;21(3):879–897. doi:10.1353/hpu.0.0323.
28. Cargo M, Mercer SL. The value and challenges of participatory research: Strengthening its practice. *Annu Rev Public Health*. 2008;29:325–350. doi:10.1146/annurev .publhealth.29.091307.083824.
29. Scarinci I, Johnson R, Hardy C, Marron J, Partridge E. Planning and implementation of a participatory evaluation strategy: A viable approach in the evaluation of community-based participatory programs addressing cancer disparities. *Eval Program Plann*. 2009;32:221–228. doi:10.1016/j.evalprogplan.2009.01.001.

Activity 1: Group discussion

This exercise is designed to stimulate awareness and thinking about attitudes, behaviors, and actions that can interfere with the process of developing a CBPR partnership that has equity and full community participation as core values. Participants should complete Step A on their own. The facilitator

18 *Public health research methods for partnerships and practice*

should assign the students to break into pairs, for discussion, after the completion of Step A.

This activity requires 20 to 30 minutes.

A. Think about your collaborations and participation on teams, in partnerships, or in coalitions, specifically:
   i. Your reasons for participating.
   ii. The assumptions that you made about your partners.
   iii. Your thoughts on how you and the other members would work together.
   iv. Your assumptions about what would be accomplished.
B. Exchange stories with your partner about your collaborative/team/partnership assumptions, expectations, and experiences.
C. Discuss the assumptions that you made that proved false. Looking back, how aware were you of your assumptions? What triggered your awareness of discrepancies in expectations and assumptions?
D. Discuss any efforts that you made to address discrepancies in expectations, attitudes, or beliefs that might affect the partnership or collaboration?

Activity 2: Group problem solving and planning

This activity is designed to facilitate consideration of the issues and associated activities and tasks required for the development of CBPR partnerships. Activity groups should consist of 4 or 5 participants. Assign each group a health focus (e.g., smoking, obesity, physical activity, diet, cancer screening). The activity requires 90 minutes to complete.

Part 1

Your group is engaged in the planning of the first full meeting of your CBPR partnership. Reflecting on your assigned health focus, share information and knowledge relevant to the issue. Consider the questions listed on the activity form in Table 1.1. Complete the lists, and compile any information requested. Identify sources of quantitative data. What strategies might you use to solicit ideas and opinions from members of the community not participating in planning meetings? Allow 45 to 60 minutes to complete.

Part 2

Agenda setting and development are important to meeting success. The effectiveness of meetings can affect perceptions of partnership communication and interactions. Participants engaged in this activity will gain an understanding of the complexities of the process of developing an agenda, as well as the

Community-based participatory research 19

Table 1.1 Group activity 2: Part 1

Question	Response
Who should be involved in the partnership?	
Who will be affected by the research?	
Who are the key stakeholders (who can help)?	
What CBPR principles are key to partnership members?	
What are the community's issues of concern?	
What are the needs of the community?	
What factors contribute to the issue or concern?	
What activities or strategies can be used to prioritize these issues for action?	
What data should be gathered and shared so that all participants begin with similar information?	
What community strengths might the partnership draw on?	
What barriers and issues might adversely affect the work of the partnership?	
What resources will be needed to overcome these barriers?	
What are the goals of the partnership? (Responses should be specific, measurable, achievable, realistic, and timely.)	
What skills will be important to the partnership?	
Which agencies, organizations, or individuals possess the needed skills and expertise?	

importance of advance planning. Once you have completed the form from Part 1, use the lists and information compiled to develop the agenda for the first partnership meeting. Be prepared to present and discuss your agenda and its rationale. What power dynamics would you want to consider in a discussion of the type required by agenda items? Allow 30 minutes to complete.

Tips for developing an effective agenda include the following:

1. Obtain and use input from the entire group.
2. Provide the meeting purpose and goal.
3. Indicate who will serve as the meeting chair(s).
4. Provide the meeting time frame, and stick to it.
5. Describe each item on the agenda clearly, as well as the time allotted for the item.
6. Indicate who will facilitate each discussion.
7. Indicate whether the item is listed to allow information sharing, obtain input, or decision-making.
8. Prioritize the items that require input from all partners.
9. Provide information on participant preparation if required.

All meeting agendas should be distributed with enough time for participant preparation.

20   Public health research methods for partnerships and practice

---

BOX 1.4   AGENDA TEMPLATE

Date: _____
Time: _____
Location: _____

Meeting Purpose *(type of meeting)*:   Please read:

Chairperson(s):   Please bring:

Agenda Items

	Topic	**Presenter**	**Time Allotted**

I.

II.

III.

IV.

V.

VI.

VII.

SELF-ASSESSMENT—WHAT DID YOU LEARN?

1. In a community-based participatory research (CBPR) project, who determines the health problem to be studied or analyzed?
   a. University researchers
   b. Community members
   c. Government policy makers
   d. University researchers and community members together

2. What is community engagement?
   a. A process of inclusive participation that supports mutual respect of values, strategies, and actions
   b. A method of teaching that combines classroom instruction with meaningful community service

c. The use or involvement of volunteer labor, especially in community services

d. The full participation of all people in community life

3. What is the unit of focus for a CBPR project?
   a. The individual
   b. The family
   c. The community
   d. The state

4. CBPR requires a change in _____.
   a. Approach
   b. Funding received
   c. Problem studied
   d. Population studied

5. Which of the following is a principle of CBPR?
   a. Data collection must be conducted by people who do not live in the community to be studied.
   b. Collaborative partnership must occur in all phases of the research.
   c. Researchers from the university must decide the methods of evaluation used in the research project.
   d. None of the above

6. What factors prevent effective CBPR collaborations?
   a. Governance structures that are not inclusive
   b. Imbalances in power and knowledge between researchers and community members
   c. Inflexible governance structures
   d. All of the above

7. What document's components include information on all partners along with the overall purpose and desired outcomes of a CBPR project?
   a. Memorandum of understanding
   b. Partnership contract
   c. Letter of intent
   d. Cooperation agreement

8. Who has sole control over funding in a CBPR project?
   a. Researchers
   b. Community members

22   *Public health research methods for partnerships and practice*

    c. Government officials
    d. Researchers and community members together

9. In a CBPR setting, researchers should begin their discussion with community members by _____.
    a. Offering blanket solutions
    b. Offering money for community problems
    c. Asking what is needed in the community
    d. Describing institutional problems

10. Community members who are part of a CBPR project should expect to play a role in _____.
    a. Developing the research question
    b. Collecting and interpreting data
    c. Disseminating project findings
    d. All of the above

2 Health disparities—Understanding how social determinants fuel racial/ethnic health disparities

Darrell Hudson, Whitney Sewell, and Tanya Funchess

LEARNING OBJECTIVES

- Define health disparities.
- Identify major health disparities, including those related to gender, race/ethnicity, geographic location, and socioeconomic status.
- Understand and provide examples of the causes of health disparities with respect to prevention, incidence, and mortality.
- Define social determinants of health.
- Describe public health strategies and interventions for reducing health disparities.

SELF-ASSESSMENT—WHAT DO YOU KNOW?

1. What are racial/ethnic health disparities?
2. What causes racial/ethnic disparities in health? Are these disparities due to biological differences?
3. What are some prominent examples of health disparities?
4. What are social determinants of health?
5. How do social determinants affect racial/ethnic health disparities?
6. What is meant by the terms *upstream* and *downstream* in relation to health disparities?
7. What are some approaches to achieving health equity?

Introduction

Health disparities are differences in health outcomes, such as life expectancy and morbidity, among different groups. Whereas the overall definition of *health disparities* is quite simple, the factors that explain the existence of health disparities are complex and multifaceted. The in-depth analysis of all the different determinants of health and health disparities as well as the strategies

24   *Public health research methods for partnerships and practice*

needed to address disparities is beyond the scope of this chapter. Rather, the goals of this chapter are to provide a definition of health disparities, focusing on racial/ethnic disparities in health; to provide a number of prominent examples of health disparities found when examining population health indicators; to explain via the lens of the social determinants of health why health disparities exist; and to explain how this lens is critical in addressing disparities in health. We conclude by describing efforts at the national and local levels, particularly the importance of partnerships developed across multiple sectors to address racial/ethnic health disparities.

Prioritizing health

Before our conversation about health disparities or social determinants of health, it is important to discuss the concept of health. A popular definition of *health* that almost any person who has been exposed to public health literature can nearly recite from memory is the World Health Organization (WHO) definition—"health is a state of complete physical, mental, and social well-being and not merely the absence of disease or infirmity."[1] This is such a widely used definition because it acknowledges the comprehensive nature of health and that health encompasses general well-being, not just whether a person is sick. Despite this comprehensive definition of health, there is often a mismatch between what individuals consider to be health and what public health practitioners or medical professionals consider to be health. For public health practitioners and medical professionals, health often requires individuals to make lifestyle choices, like maintaining a balanced diet or getting regular physical activity. However, this priority may not be in alignment with the priorities that individuals have, particularly those who disproportionately bear the burden of health disparities.

Often, social determinants of health such as employment, financial capabilities, school quality, and the safety and well-being of family members and friends take priority over maintaining normative blood pressure levels or getting regular health screenings. Medical professionals often remark that individual patients are deeply concerned about their jobs, family responsibilities, and the health and well-being of their loved ones.[2,3] These are the things people truly care about, sometimes even above their own personal health.

These competing demands at the individual level help to explain how individuals might not seek regular medical treatment or obtain preventive screenings for diseases such as cancer, cardiovascular disease, and diabetes. However, it is not just individual choice that explains health disparities, and many of the social and economic determinants that affect health are beyond individual control. Individuals may perceive that the costs associated with maintaining a healthy lifestyle, such as the cost of fresh produce, learning how to prepare a healthy, balanced meal, or growing accustomed to the tastes or portion size of a new dish, outweigh the benefits associated with changing a health behavior.[4] Additionally, the stress of being marginalized because of

Health disparities 25

race/ethnicity, gender, or sexual orientation can also preclude one's concerns about personal health.[5-7] In addition, often, *socioeconomic status* (SES) plays a key role in determining whether individuals choose to seek medical care, as poorer people often perceive the costs associated with health care to be more stressful than knowing their actual disease status.[8-10]

Although health might not be the first thing on the minds of individuals in their respective communities, good health is absolutely essential to an individual's ability to perform well in school or at work and to function in other roles as caregivers, spouses, parents, and the like. At the population level, good health is associated with improved educational attainment and work productivity.[11] Again, as with the WHO definition of health, any definition of health must stretch beyond diseases or conditions. Rather, individuals' overall well-being, including their social, economic, and emotional well-being, is critical to their ability to be healthy, productive citizens.

Defining health disparities

A prominent goal of Healthy People 2020 is to eliminate health disparities and to achieve health equity.[12] Many definitions of health disparities exist. The definition of *health disparities* offered by the National Institutes of Health (NIH) is the following: "differences in the incidence, prevalence, mortality, and burden of diseases and other adverse health conditions that exist among specific population groups in the United States."[13] Paula Braveman describes health disparities as "potentially avoidable differences in health between groups of people who are more or less advantaged socially."[14] Furthermore, Braveman describes health disparities as differences in health that are not fueled by immutable gulfs in health status (e.g., "bad genes") between racial/ethnic groups that are unlikely to close no matter what interventions, programs, and policies are developed.[14] Rather, Braveman argues that health disparities are systematic and avoidable. To summarize, health disparities can be described as differences in health across different population groups (e.g., racial/ethnic groups) that are systematic and plausibly avoidable, that are influenced by policies, and that place disadvantaged groups at further disadvantage with respect to their health.

Racial/ethnic disparities in population health indicators

In the examination of various health outcomes, racial/ethnic disparities are evident, particularly in population health indicators. Population health indicators provide valuable insight into the incidence, prevalence, and trends of health and help direct the preventive measures needed to address disparities in health. Top health indicators in the United States include life expectancy, infant mortality, and overall morbidity. Health risk factors, such as obesity, smoking, diabetes, heart disease, HIV/STDs, and hypertension influence life expectancy and mortality and are often the target of health prevention and intervention efforts. Life expectancy and mortality provide information about the overall health status of a population.

Life expectancy at birth measures the average number of years a cohort of infants would live if the group experienced the present age-specific mortality rate. An increase in years of life expectancy is indicative of a healthy population, and a decrease of years reflects a need to implement stronger health prevention and treatment efforts. According to data from the Centers for Disease Control and Prevention (CDC), as of 2014, the life expectancy at birth of the total population in the United States was 78.8 years.[15] The life expectancy was 76.4 years for males and 81.2 years for females. Since 2004, the life expectancy at birth has increased 1.4 years for males and 1.1 years for females; however, there still remains a substantial 4.8-year disparity between males and females. Since 2004, the gap in life expectancy between the white and black populations has narrowed to 3.6 years; in 2014, life expectancy for white persons was 78.8 years, 75.2 years for black persons, and 81.8 years for Hispanic persons.[16] As the statistics reflect, life expectancy rates vary across groups, including race/ethnicity and gender (Figure 2.1). Critical to our understanding of these disparities is an awareness of the social determinants of health and well-being (e.g., SES, urban/rural residence, education) that influence the prevalence of health risks in a specific population.

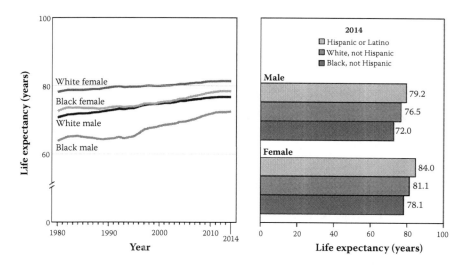

Figure 2.1 Life expectancy by race/ethnicity and gender. Life expectancy data by Hispanic origin were available starting in 2006 and were corrected to address racial and ethinic misclassification. (From the Centers for Disease Control and Prevention/National Center for Health Statistics, *Health, United States, With Special Feature on Racial and Ethnic Health Disparities.* Hyattsville, MD: National Center for Health Statistics; 2016, https://www.cdc.gov/nchs/data/hus/hus15.pdf, accessed July 29, 2016, 2015, Figure 18. Data from the National Vital Statistics System.)

Infant mortality, another population health indicator, reveals a twofold racial difference in infant mortality between blacks and whites.[16] The infant mortality rate decreased significantly between 1999 and 2013, when the United States had a 14% decrease overall, a 13% decrease in neonatal mortality rates, and a 17% decrease in postneonatal mortality rates (i.e., for infants aged 28 days to 11 months).[16] Despite a slight decrease in rates between 1999 and 2013, infant mortality rates remain the highest among infants born to black women (11.11 per 1000 live births).[16] Since 1999, the disparity in infant mortality rates between black infants (the group with the highest rate) and Asian or Pacific Islander infants (the group with the lowest rate) has narrowed from 9.41 in 1999 to 7.21 in 2013.[16] These trends in infant mortality reflect public health efforts to improve maternal health and access to quality health care, including modern medical technology.

Additionally, due to advancements in medical technology and large-scale public health efforts, such as reducing the overall rate of smoking and improving sanitation and occupational safety, the average life expectancy in the United States has increased dramatically. An examination of the leading causes of death in the United States reveals how important health behaviors and overall lifestyle are to health (Figure 2.2). According to the CDC, most of the top 10 leading causes of death are preventable chronic diseases and accounted for 74% of the 2.6 million deaths in 2014.[16] These 10 causes of death were heart disease, cancer, chronic

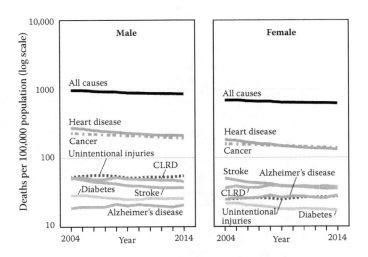

Figure 2.2 Selected causes of death by gender. CLRD indicates chronic lower respiratory diseases. A change in the coding rules for nephritis syndrome and nephrosis caused an increase in the number of deaths attributed to diabetes beginning with 2011 data. Thus, the trend for diabetes death rates should be interpreted with caution. (From the Centers for Control and Prevention/National Center for Health Statistics. *Health, United States, 2015*, Figure 2 and Table 17. Data from the National Vital Statistics System.)

lower respiratory diseases, unintentional injuries, stroke, Alzheimer's disease, diabetes, influenza and pneumonia, nephritis, and suicide. Comparatively, the leading causes of death in the United States in the 1900s (e.g., pneumonia, diarrhea, tuberculosis) are substantially different from leading causes of death in 2014 (e.g., heart disease, cancer, diabetes). Rates of death related to infectious disease have drastically declined in the United States, and most of the current leading causes of death, including heart disease, stroke, and diabetes, are now related to health behaviors.[16] Health risk factors such as obesity, smoking, diabetes, heart disease, HIV/STDs, and hypertension influence life expectancy and mortality and are often the target of health prevention and intervention efforts. In order to close racial/ethnic disparities in overall life expectancy, intervention efforts regarding health behaviors such as poor diet, lack of exercise, and smoking are necessary to address the risk factors for leading causes of morbidity and mortality.

One of the four goals of Healthy People 2020 is to "attain high-quality, longer lives free of preventable disease, disability, injury, and premature death."[12] Hypertension is a risk factor for heart disease, as well as several other health conditions (i.e., stroke, kidney failure). Black men and women are at an increased risk of having hypertension compared to other racial groups. Despite public health efforts to increase awareness, education, and access to quality care, these racial disparities persist. They remained constant between 1999 and 2014 (Figure 2.3).[16] Another common risk factor associated with heart disease, diabetes, morbidity, mortality, and other health conditions is obesity.[16] Females are at greater risk (8.9%) of having high-risk (grade 3) obesity than males (4.9%).[16] From 1999 to 2014, the prevalence of obesity among those aged 2 to 19 remained stable.[16] In 2014, Hispanic children had the highest percentage of obesity (21.9%), and Asian/Pacific Islander children had the lowest percentage (8.6%).[16] The prevalence of obesity among black children and adolescents was 19.5%, followed by 14.7% among white children and adolescents.[16]

Each year in the United States, one in five deaths is due to smoking tobacco products. Smokers are at an increased risk of numerous health issues, including cancer, heart disease, diabetes, stroke, arthritis, and stillbirth.[16] In 2014, across racial groups, men were more likely to be current smokers than women.[16] The percentage of current smokers among men was 19%. African American men comprised the highest proportion of smokers (22%) compared with white (20%), Asian (14%), and Hispanic (13.8%) men.[16] Among women, over the period 1999 to 2014, white women had the highest percentage of current smokers (18.3%) compared with any other racial group, followed by black women (13.7%), Hispanic women (7.4%), and Asian women (5.1%).

Despite overall preventive efforts and improvements in many of the factors linked to major causes of morbidity and mortality in the United States, the differences in risk factors reviewed in this section indicate disparities by race/ethnicity and gender among key health indicators. Race/ethnicity and gender are not the sole sites of health disparities; however, they are often proxies for a number of social determinants such as SES, residential setting (urban/rural), access to quality health care, education, religion, and others. Prevention

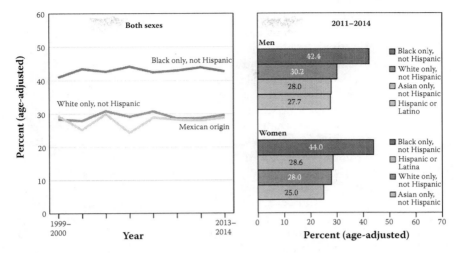

Figure 2.3 Hypertension by race/ethnicity and gender. Estimates are age adjusted. Hypertension is defined as having measured high blood pressure (systolic pressure of at least 140 mm HG or diastolic pressure of at least 90 mm Hg) and/or a respondent report of taking antihypertensive medication. (From the Centers for Control and Prevention/National Center for Health Statistics. *Health, United States, With Special Feature on Racial and Ethnic Health Disparities.* Hyattsville, MD: National Center for Health Statistics; 2016, https://www.cdc.gov/nchs/data/hus/hus15.pdf, accessed July 29, 2016, 2015, Figure 23. Data from the National Health and Nutrition Examination Survey.)

efforts to reduce the disparities that exist among these health indicators must take into account the multidimensional nature of health and wellness.

The evidence presented previously in this chapter suggests that health behaviors such as obtaining preventive screenings for cancer, abstaining from smoking, eating a balanced diet, and getting physical activity are prominent factors in the prevention of many top killers in the United States. Regardless of the health condition one explores, health behaviors and lifestyle factors often play a large role in the distribution of morbidity and adverse health. Additionally, these factors are inextricably linked to social determinants of health, factors that go beyond an individual's lifestyle choices. Indeed, the CDC's white paper on social determinants of health states that these determinants of health are "not controllable by the individual but affect the individual's environment."[17]

Social determinants of health—The roots of health inequities

Social determinants of health, although largely out of the control of individuals, affect health through a number of different pathways and mechanisms. These effects are manifest in many day-to-day ways and are easily observed in

30 *Public health research methods for partnerships and practice*

different neighborhoods and communities across the country. Healthy People 2020 defines *social determinants of health* as the conditions in the environment in which people are born, live, learn, work, play, and age that affect a wide range of health outcomes and risks that are shaped by social, political, and economic forces.[12] WHO argues that social determinants include individuals' social and environmental context—where they are born, where they live, and where they work.[12] According to WHO, these contexts are strongly influenced by the distribution of resources, particularly money and power, at the societal level all the way down to the individual nested within a particular community. Again, those who have the least amount of power, wealth, and other resources are at a further disadvantage with regard to their health.[14] WHO, through its Committee on the Social Determinants of Health, has concluded that the social determinants of health are the leading causes of inequalities in health.[18]

No matter what the precise definition may be, social determinants of health, including race/ethnicity, SES, and place-based resources such as schools, access to quality food outlets, and safe spaces to recreate are critical to all aspects of health. In a 2014 policy brief published in *Health Affairs* on social determinants of health, the authors concluded that there are five major categories of health determinants: genetics, behavior, social circumstances, environmental and physical influences, and medical care.[18] They emphasized the importance of examining multiple determinants of health and the interactions between those determinants, as well as the need to examine the multiple levels—ranging from the intrapersonal level to the society level—that influence health.

Another way to think about social determinants of health is to consider them as "fundamental causes."[19] Link and Phelan[19] describe fundamental causes of health as resources that can be used to avoid risks, minimize causes, affect multiple health outcomes over time, and continue to affect different health outcomes when risk profiles change. If interventions focus on risk factors for specific diseases and conditions without addressing the fundamental causes of health, diseases and conditions eventually shift to the most vulnerable populations—populations without many socioeconomic resources or power. Syme argues that people in the most vulnerable groups will eventually replace those who are considered most at risk, regardless of the actual risk factors for a disease or condition.[20]

Examples of social determinants of health include race/ethnicity, SES, gender, immigration status, and sexual orientation. These are important factors to consider because they can increase risk of marginalization. Social determinants are closely intertwined and together affect health through multiple pathways. After this section, we use the lens of social determinants of health to explain how race/ethnicity is associated with health, not only because racial/ethnic minorities receive different treatment within health care settings, but also because of how race/ethnicity is intertwined with SES, neighborhood context, and social disadvantage.

Race/ethnicity, socioeconomic status, and health disparities

Although health behaviors are critical to health and the persistence of racial/ethnic health disparities, there are many factors beyond individual health behavior that fuel disparities in health. Individuals are embedded in families, neighborhoods, communities, states, countries, and society. Susser asserts that "states of health do not exist in a vacuum apart from people. People form societies and any study of the attributes of people is also a study of the manifestations of the form, the structure, and the processes of social forces."[21] Understanding how humans organize themselves, particularly around a social hierarchy, is important in our understanding of racial/ethnic and socioeconomic health disparities. Indeed, the association between stress derived from low social status and poorer health has been thoroughly documented in the literature.[22–26]

Race and racism clearly illustrate the effects of social stratification on health disparities in the United States. Gee and Ford[6] define *structural racism* as "the macro-level systems, social forces, institutions, ideologies, and processes that interact with one another to generate and reinforce inequities among racial and ethnic groups." They further argue that structural racism "emphasizes the most influential socioecologic levels at which racism may affect racial and ethnic health inequities."[6] One prevalent example of structural racism in the United States that is pertinent to African American men involves the prison-industrial complex and racial sentencing disparities within the criminal justice system.[6,27] Race/ethnicity is inextricably linked to SES in the United States,[28] and another prominent example of racism on the structural level is racial residential segregation throughout the United States, which plays a major role in the resources individuals have access to and serves to perpetuate health disparities.[29,30] Williams and Collins assert that "residential segregation shapes socioeconomic mobility and socioeconomic conditions across multiple levels including individual, household neighborhood and community."[30] Several researchers have described racial residential segregation as the "structural lynchpin" of racial relations in the United States,[31–33] and rates of racial residential segregation remain stubbornly high.

Racial residential segregation is largely responsible for many blacks residing in neighborhoods of poorer quality that have reduced access to equitable services and institutions, ranging from full-service grocery stores to quality public schools and libraries.[30,32,34] Importantly, researchers have noted neighborhood effects on health, independent of individual SES markers. High levels of racial residential segregation in the United States constrain the health-promoting resources available in neighborhoods that are predominantly composed of racial/ethnic groups. Not only are there fewer outlets for healthy, affordable food, there is a preponderance of fast food restaurants as well as stores that largely sell calorie-dense products of low nutritional value. Poorer neighborhoods are often characterized by high levels of poverty and community violence, which weaken the levels of neighborhood trust and organization. Negative neighborhood attributes such as excessive noise,

32 Public health research methods for partnerships and practice

inadequate lighting, and heavy traffic were associated with the loss of physical functioning in later life. These factors contribute to the stress that individuals in poorer communities feel on a day-to-day basis and increase their risk of poor health outcomes.[35]

As discussed previously in this chapter, racial/ethnic health disparities are not naturally occurring, immutable differences in health. These are differences that are fueled by policies and practices. Racial residential segregation is not only fueled by discrimination among individual real estate agents, homeowners, and buyers, but also by historical practices and policies. For instance, one of the most significant investments in social policies in the United States were found in the government policies of the New Deal* era, initially adopted shortly before World War II.[36–38] These policies of the New Deal era included the Servicemen's Readjustment Act of 1944, most commonly known as the GI Bill, which provided free postsecondary education for veterans of the armed forces. Black veterans were systematically denied equal access to the GI Bill.[38] For instance, Katznelson illustrates how blacks in the southern states were allowed to use their GI Bill education benefits only to attend a vocational school rather than a 4-year college.

Another policy of the New Deal era was low-interest home loans. Prior to the New Deal era, homebuyers would have to save a much larger proportion of the total home cost. Low-interest, federally backed housing loans instituted during the New Deal era allowed a much larger proportion of Americans to buy homes since it reduced the down payment to about 20% of the final price.[36] However, people of color were systematically denied these low-interest home loans because of redlining practices† used by mortgage companies. Banks "redlined" neighborhoods that were predominantly minority, refusing to lend to home buyers in these neighborhoods. Furthermore, Federal Housing Authority (FHA) loans were used widely in the suburbs of major American cities, leading to the depopulation of many central cities—stripping the central cities of employment opportunities and investments in new residential and commercial developments, along with straining the capacity of city services. The vestiges of these historical policies and practices are manifest in the racial/ethnic composition of neighborhoods today along with the resources embedded in these neighborhoods.

Additionally, there are tremendous racial/ethnic gaps in wealth, and these wealth differences are partially rooted in residential segregation. Home equity comprises a large proportion of the wealth that Americans hold.[37,39]

---

* Coined by President Franklin D. Roosevelt, the New Deal refers to a set of policies initially adopted by the US government between 1933 and 1938. During the administrations of Franklin Roosevelt and Harry Truman, progressive policies such as Social Security, protective labor laws, and the GI Bill were adopted.[38]

† Redlining is described as the practice in which banks would not administer loans to certain residential areas in cities, often populated by blacks.[36] Banks color coded maps of entire cities, and red was the color assigned to the areas in which banks would not offer home loans.[32,36]

Residential segregation has yielded wide differences in home value according to the racial composition of neighborhoods and communities. Homes located in predominantly white neighborhoods are, on average, worth substantially more than homes in predominately African American neighborhoods.[37,39,40] So, differences in home values also undergird the staggering underlying differences in the structure of wealth between African Americans and whites that may never close so long as racial residential segregation levels persist. Of course, in addition to wealth, racial segregation affects a broad range of health-promoting resources, including education quality, neighborhood safety, employment opportunities, social capital, and neighborhood services.

The exclusion of blacks from the government policies of the New Deal era has led to immense wealth disparities and has helped to fuel the deep-seated levels of racial residential segregation described previously. However, the examination of such radical, large-scale policies offers clear examples of how to improve the overall health and well-being of an entire population. Additionally, these policies provide important evidence that social, economic, and health disparities have, indeed, been fueled by policies and practices.

Stress and coping

Stress, particularly chronic stress, has been implicated as a key factor in the production of racial/ethnic health disparities.[41,42] Our bodies are hardwired to handle stress, allowing us to adapt to changes in the environment and avoid threats.[43] Yet, our bodies are not sensitive enough to discern physical threats to our lives from social stressors, like financial distress or a fear of public speaking. This means that exposure to social stressors elicits the same stress response as actual threats to our lives, and the chronic activation of this stress process can cause dysregulation over time.[43,44]

A number of theoretical frameworks and models have been developed to illustrate how stress "gets under the skin" and has both short-term and long-term effects on health. For instance, Krieger describes how psychosocial stressors "embody" themselves over time—a process in which the society is biologically incorporated into individuals' bodies.[45] McEwen describes allostatic load as the "wear and tear" on the body that occurs and is exacerbated with greater exposure to chronic stress.[46] Another theoretical framework described in the health disparities literature is weathering.[42] Developed by Geronimus, weathering is the notion that people under chronic stress experience accumulated disadvantage over the life course in addition to accelerated aging.[42,47] For instance, Geronimus has found that the weathering process could potentially explain black-white differences in birth outcomes. Although women may be the same chronological age, weathering could lead to black women being an older maternal age.

The different theoretical concepts discussed above have been developed to delineate the pathways between experience of social stress and the development of poor health. Researchers interested in addressing racial/ethnic

34 *Public health research methods for partnerships and practice*

health disparities are often deeply interested in understanding how stress gets under the skin to negatively affect health. Common stressors examined in the health disparities literature include SES-related stressors such as socioeconomic deprivation or exposure to poverty as well as the experience of racial discrimination.[48-51] Racial discrimination, for instance, is considered to be a unique, socially patterned stressor thought to play an important role in the health of African Americans and other racial/ethnic minority groups in the United States.[51,52] Kessler and colleagues argue that the experience of racial discrimination is highly stressful, ranking in significance with other major stressful life events such as job loss, divorce, and the death of a loved one.[52] Stress produces negative emotions and psychological distress that can have negative impacts on health, and some researchers hypothesize that stress may lead to fundamental changes in physiological systems.[42,53,54]

People of color often face multiple stressors at the same time, ranging from socioeconomic deprivation to perceptions of racial discrimination. In addition to understanding the biological underpinnings of the relationship between stress and health, it is also important to note how stress and coping operate to affect health. In the transactional model of stress and coping, stressful experiences are defined as "person–environment transactions," in which the impact of an external stressor is mediated by a person's appraisal of the stressor and the psychological, social, and cultural resources at the person's disposal.[55] The social context in which people are embedded is incredibly important to the stress and coping process. Not only can social contexts produce stressful experiences, but they can also inform the resources that individuals have to cope with and dictate what socially acceptable coping behaviors are within different contexts. The next section describes the importance of health behaviors, social context, and social norms in the production of racial/ethnic health disparities.

Health behaviors, social context, and social norms

As noted previously, place has a profound effect on health disparities between racial/ethnic groups in the United States, and place is fueled by racist policies and practices. Social context not only shapes the social norms and health behaviors of individuals from an early stage in life, but context also influences the stressors and coping resources. As mentioned previously, the effects of chronic stress exposure accumulated over the life course are posited to cascade into dysregulation on the cellular level. Examples of these include shortened telomere length, increased levels of inflammatory markers, and decreases in immune system functioning.[42,53,56,57] For instance, it is hypothesized that chronic stress negatively affects telomeres, which affect how cells age, as they cap and protect the ends of our chromosomes.[56,57] Additionally, stress has a negative effect on immune system functioning, which may cause chronically stressed individuals to be more susceptible to infections and disease.[43,56] Evidence from the field of psychoneuroimmunology indicates that dysregulation due to chronic stress leads to inflammation, which can increase susceptibility to conditions such as atherosclerosis, the narrowing and hardening of arteries and a key factor in the development of cardiovascular disease.[58]

In addition to the competing demands that individuals face in their day-to-day lives, people are also embedded within social networks and may adhere to social norms that do not promote the lifestyle changes that public health and health care professionals would like.[59–61] For instance, many people connect through food, so there are important social and cultural considerations that must be made in the development of programs and policies geared toward improvement of dietary practices. Asking individuals to change their health behavior is often asking them to make substantial changes to their participation in their social networks as well. Additionally, social norms may influence the likelihood of people to abstain from eating foods that public health professionals might consider unhealthy.[60,61] If an individual is part of a family that holds regular dinners and delicious, calorie-dense foods are part of the menu, it may be difficult to ask someone to refrain from indulging in the food that one's family has prepared. This is not only because individuals are being asked to deny themselves foods that they have grown to love, but also because refraining from the foods may be interpreted as a negative or offensive behavior on the part of the family members who have prepared the food.

Predominantly African American neighborhoods often have a preponderance of fast food restaurants and liquor stores as well as the proliferation of tobacco and alcohol advertisements and the absence of full-service grocery stores.[34,62] These environmental factors could promote the adoption of unhealthy behaviors due to the close proximity of large numbers of outlets that serve high-fat, calorie-dense foods as well as provide increased access to alcohol and illicit drug use. Using data drawn from the Baltimore Epidemiologic Catchment Area study, Mezuk and colleagues[63] found that poor health behaviors provide an effective means of coping with the stress of social disadvantage and mitigating the negative effects of stress on depression. Specifically, as stress exposure increased, African Americans who engaged in more poor health behaviors had lower risk of depression. This finding indicates that coping with poor health behaviors could provide temporary psychological relief from exposure to chronic stress and social disadvantage. However, in the long term, adoption of poor health behaviors could come at an increased risk of physical health problems.

There is no doubt that health is strongly influenced by individual choices—diet, exercise, buckling safety belts, and obtaining preventive health screenings. However, the social determinants of health, such as where people live and the resources embedded in their neighborhoods, are beyond the control of individuals. Considering social determinants of health allows one to envision a way to facilitate health at the individual level by removing barriers to positive health behaviors. This perspective also encourages researchers, practitioners, and policy makers to consider influences of health at multiple levels, including the individual, family, community, organizational, and policy levels.

Thinking about health as multilayered can help produce solutions at a broader level and encourage thinking about health from a population perspective.

Social determinants of health are especially challenging to address because they affect multiple disease outcomes over time and are deeply intertwined with each other. Social determinants drive racial/ethnic disparities in health because they determine resources, including but not limited to access to healthy food outlets and health care, which help to protect health.[19] Simply put, people with greater resources may be more likely to maintain better health behaviors. Simultaneously, greater amounts of resources such as higher levels of income, education, and social capital, can be used to avoid proximal and distal causes of disease and premature death.

Although the term *social determinants of health* is well-defined and widely used, there have been limited efforts to truly address the social determinants that drive health. Researchers have attempted to identify the "upstream" determinants of health, shifting the focus from individual choices and lifestyle factors and looking at the underlying social conditions and structural factors that have created health disparities.[64] A constant tension exists in public health between "upstream" and "downstream" approaches to understanding health disparities. Instructors often use the "babies in the river" example to explain upstream approaches to understanding health disparities.

Imagine that you are on the shore of a river and you find that there are drowning babies in the river. You decide to jump in to save the babies, but no faster can you pull them out before more are bobbing in the water. Downstream, there is an immediate need—to save babies from drowning. Yet upstream, one has to wonder how the babies are getting into the water in the first place and what can be done to prevent this from occurring.

As ridiculous as an example the analogy of the babies in the river may be, there are parallels in the health care and public health infrastructure in the United States and how efforts and resources are allocated to address health. In the immediate sense, lives must be saved. People enter emergency rooms with acute health threats that need to be fixed immediately, and the United States health care system is strongly oriented to and adept at saving the lives of individuals who have found themselves treading water downstream. The upstream solutions to disparities, such as changes to the built environment or policies to promote racial equity in socioeconomic resources, are expensive and often difficult to achieve because of the political climate.

For instance, people of color disproportionately bear the burden of disease and premature mortality, as evident from countless data sources.[65-67] However, the data do not tell the story of how people end up as numbers in a figure. The lives that people who are socially disadvantaged live are stressful, and some people endure exposure to stress and the effects of poor contextual environments for their entire lifetimes. The upstream forces—ranging from school districts' funding by communities with widely varying tax bases to immense wealth disparities between racial/ethnic groups—are seemingly impossible to alter. Similarly, pronounced gaps exist in education quality across race and ethnicity in the United States. Relative to other wealthy countries, there is a pronounced lack of investment in social services in the United States. These factors are certainly beyond any one individual's control. Yet, these upstream determinants fuel health disparities and pose significant challenges in the quest to achieve health equity. Both upstream and downstream solutions are necessary to reduce disparities in health.[45] Although increasing access to health-promoting resources, such as fresh produce and safe places to recreate, is absolutely essential, individuals must still make healthy choices and adopt healthy lifestyles. Considering the social determinants lens allows one to contextualize the factors that fuel disparities in health.

Whereas the precise mechanisms that link social stress or low SES to discrete health outcomes have not been fully elucidated, there is no question that structural racism affects health disparities. However, the political will to address these factors is often low, and it is not clear what the right way to elicit change will be. Political ideology plays a large role in how social determinants of health are framed and what efforts are developed to address disparities in health.

From a research perspective, there are many papers that have documented the associations between social determinants such as racial residential segregation and economic deprivation with poor health and the presence of racial/ethnic health disparities.[30,68] Similarly, within the practice realm, efforts to address health disparities are often limited in both scope (e.g., focusing on one particular health behavior or health outcome) and scale (e.g., mostly focusing on the intra- and interindividual level). Furthermore, many of the existing health behavior interventions do not take into account social context, such as built environment and access to resources. Authors often conclude that interventions do not work because of inadequate participation rather than admitting that perhaps the theories guiding their work are not appropriate or that the context in which individuals reside can trump change intervention efforts regarding individual health behavior.

Towards achieving health equity

If the goal of the nation is to eliminate health disparities, then health equity must be pursued. *Health equity* is defined as obtaining the highest level of health for all people.[14] The concept of health equity implies that everyone should be able to obtain the highest level of health possible and should not be disadvantaged because of their social position or other socially determined circumstances. Whitehead et al. state that "health equity involves creating opportunities and removing barriers to achieving the fullest health potential for all people."[69] Health equity, according to the United States Department of Health and Human Services (HHS), is attainment of the highest level of health for all people. Due to the existence of inequalities, not all Americans can achieve optimal health.[14] Therefore, a growing body of research has made a persuasive argument that health is a human right, and everyone should have the right to obtain the highest level of health in their society. Accepting the

38 *Public health research methods for partnerships and practice*

concept that health is a human rights issue requires looking at health equity through a social justice lens.

Addressing health disparities is not just a public health issue; reaching the lofty goal of health equity requires multisector and multilevel solutions. Consequently, researchers have implored the field of public health to consider health in all policies, ranging from zoning and housing to education and workforce development in order to effectively address social determinants of health.[5,66] Although overwhelming at times, there are ways that partnerships can effectively craft solutions to racial health disparities. Due to the various factors that may impede individuals from reaching their optimal level of health, collaborating with nontraditional partners outside of the health care arena is imperative. Health starts before entering the health care system—in our homes, schools, work places, neighborhoods, and communities. Therefore, multiple partners are needed to address health disparities and to reduce inequalities on the quest to achieve health equity. This section will provide an example of the various types of partnerships or initiatives developed to address health disparities.

An example of a multisector solution is the establishment of medical-legal partnerships that have the opportunity to move beyond services to individuals by detecting patterns of systemic need that can be addressed through institutional policy changes or changes in public policy.[70] Medical-legal partnerships are partnerships established between health care and civic legal aid entities to better care for vulnerable populations.[71,72] These partnerships are solidified through a MOU used to form the foundation of the partnership and to detail the expectations for both health and legal partners. There are two guiding principles for medical-legal partnerships as described by the National Center for Medical-Legal Partnership: (1) both partners use trainings, screening, and legal care to improve patient and population health and (2) legal care is integrated into the delivery of care with engaged health, and legal partners at the frontline and administrative levels.[71] Medical-legal partnerships differ from referrals to legal services because the lawyers are present on site in the health care settings and are a part of the clinical team. Several examples exist of how medical-legal partnerships can address the social determinants of health: addressing concerns for public benefit (e.g., appeal denials of food stamps, health insurance, cash benefits, and disability benefits); improving substandard housing conditions; preventing evictions; protecting against utility shutoff; securing specialized education services; preventing and remedying employment discrimination; resolving veteran discharge status; clearing criminal/credit histories; assisting with asylum applications; securing restraining orders for domestic violence; and securing adoption, custody, and guardianship for children.[72] Additionally, the National Center for Medical-Legal Partnership hosts the Social Determinants of Health Academy, a virtual training to assist health care centers and primary care providers in the development and implementation of sustainable solutions to social determinants of health.

Health disparities 39

It is important to note that those who bear the disproportionate burden of health disparities are the ones who are hardest to reach in health interventions and programs.[73-75] Many contextual factors exist, such as the built environment and SES, that interfere with people's ability to fully participate in the initiatives that public health and medical professionals design.[2,10] Engaging different sectors such as social work and education may lead to the development of more effective solutions to disparities. Developing spaces for place-based initiatives that allow colocation of comprehensive services may be an effective strategy in reaching underserved and socially disadvantaged communities.[76] Examples of this include colocating health services in schools along with the presence of social service workers or incorporating health into settings such as community centers. In addition, to address the economic barriers to health screenings, clinicians and health agencies may provide free screenings at community health fairs, schools, and work sites. Additionally, workplace incentives and competitions increase healthy behaviors, help to change social norms within environments, and provide access to exercise facilities and walking trails that may not be available in the communities where workers live.[69]

At the local level, organizations like PolicyLink, headquartered in Oakland, California, have led the way in health equity and have developed multisector strategies to improve the economic, social, and health status of various neighborhoods. PolicyLink provides a set of equity tools on its Web site, www .policylink.org, including an equitable development tool kit that centers on the development of communities of opportunity that will lead to equitable outcomes. PolicyLink also has a number of opportunities to highlight the innovative work that is being done in different communities across the country through its Equity Summits and regular webinars.

It is critical to consider the factors that allow people to thrive in the face of adversity. Despite the facts and figures about racial/ethnic disparities in health, some individuals are able to survive and thrive. Social connectedness is considered a major factor in the risk and resilience of individuals and communities.[77,78] It is important to develop a clear understanding of assets that are embedded in neighborhoods that might be considered socially or economically disadvantaged throughout the country. For instance, the social networks and the social support that people are able to offer each other is critical to buffer against stress and to offer an avenue to pool resources.[79-81] Government social services may not meet the needs of disadvantaged communities, and informal networks are often the lifelines that individuals rely upon within their networks. Fostering the organic social networks that exist within communities represents a way to strengthen the levels of trust, feelings of safety, collective efficacy, and norms of reciprocity within neighborhoods.[77,81-83] Furthermore, providing linkages between communities and other sectors such as business and policy can empower communities to advocate for the resources that communities need for individuals to thrive.[77,83-85]

Various organizations are deeply committed to health equity and are helping to lead the way. For instance, the Robert Wood Johnson Foundation is

40 *Public health research methods for partnerships and practice*

devoted to establishing a "culture of health." This culture of health is characterized by good health and well-being across sociodemographic factors like race/ethnicity and place.[86] To achieve this culture of health, the foundation has developed an action plan in which health equity is at the center. The plan calls for including opportunities for individuals and families to make health choices and for forging multisector collaborations with government, business, individuals, and organizations working together to build healthy communities. To this end, the foundation uses the Culture of Health Prize to highlight and elevate the work that different communities across the United States are doing to achieve health equity.

Efforts toward health equity are also being guided by the development and implementation of policies and initiatives at different levels. For instance, at the federal level, Healthy People 2020 aims to inform and improve health policies and practices on the national, state, and local levels, as well as increase public, individual, and community awareness of the prevention of chronic disease, morbidity, disability, and premature death.[12] Access to health care through affordable health insurance coverage is a health policy approach that has linked individuals to quality prevention and treatment services. The Affordable Care Act (ACA) is a health policy that has increased access to health care for individuals who may be low income, uninsured, or undocumented.[87,88] In addition to helping to expand the health care coverage for Americans, the ACA has also helped expand nonprofit health organizations' community benefit programs. The ACA now requires health care organizations to provide community needs assessments and health improvement plans, guiding these organizations to invest in the communities they serve beyond providing charity care. It is in the nation's best interest to have a healthy population, and investments in communities across multiple sectors and expansions beyond the provision of health care represent yet other ways to effectively address health disparities.

Critically, the provision of evidenced-based care is important to efforts to reduce health disparities. Access to quality care and its delivery by health professionals are critical to the prevention and detection of disease. Providers and their staff can adopt up-to-date evidence-based clinical practice guidelines for promoting healthy behaviors.[89] Activity and diet recommendations are important; however, clinicians should be aware of the economic barriers many individuals face in health care and should provide education and referrals for prescription-subsidizing programs, Medicaid-covered treatment options, or Medicare-covered treatment options for their patients.[76]

Examples of public policies that have been implemented at local and state levels include the taxation of tobacco and high-energy, low-nutrient foods (e.g., soft drinks), in addition to mandated food labeling, in order to reduce the consumption of unhealthy products.[90] Similarly, tobacco use policies have regulated access to tobacco products, banned tobacco advertisement and sponsorships, and regulated exposure to environmental tobacco smoke (e.g., in the workplace and in restaurants, public transportation, and public spaces).[89] Urban planning initiatives, such as the installation of walking and cycling paths as well as appropriate lighting, have been developed to improve built environments and increase physical activity in communities.[89] Other examples of local and state policies are zoning laws that regulate the location of fast food establishments and the provision of healthy foods in public school cafeterias.[3]

Although the efforts reviewed here are not exhaustive, they provide insight into the multilevel public health approach to reducing health disparities and increasing health and wellness. Designing prevention and intervention programs should consider several factors that are specific to the health issues, target population, and target behavior, in addition to the social, political, and environmental context. It is also critical to consider the assets that individuals and communities possess. Gaining more information about the protective factors that individuals possess will be critical to designing interventions at multiple levels. The insights from individuals who have the resilience to thrive in challenging social environments can provide ways to foster those assets and learn lessons that can inspire innovative solutions. The deliberate consideration of these factors leads to culturally tailored health programs, which research has identified as the most effective approach for health promotion.[91,92]

Relatedly, it is also necessary to incorporate the lens of the social determinants of health into the development of science policy, particularly national research funding priorities. As mentioned previously, the priorities of individuals and communities are oftentimes misaligned with the priorities of public health or medical professionals. Similarly, the funding priorities of agencies like the NIH can be misaligned with the needs of communities.[20] For instance, it is often the case that the priorities of the community of concern center on social determinants of health such as economic opportunities, school quality, and safety rather than a specific disease or condition. Therefore, in the development of programs geared toward addressing health disparities, it is often the case that the intervention efforts do not meet the needs that community members have identified. Yet, we know that racial/ethnic disparities are not immutable, unmodifiable biological differences in health.

Whereas everyone who is exposed to adversity does not have a poor outcome—health or otherwise—broader efforts are necessary to address the structural inequalities that have produced health disparities. Rose[93] states that the most likely solutions to population health problems are universal risks. Using the lens of the social determinants of health allows practitioners to consider how an individual or population is embedded within a social context. Consideration of social networks, social support, social norms, stress and coping, and structural forces are key to addressing racial/ethnic health disparities. The development of both upstream and downstream solutions is also critical to addressing health disparities. Also, because racial/ethnic health disparities are fueled by social determinants of health, we can examine the policies and practices that can effectively and broadly address health disparities.

Conclusions

In a 2010 paper, Tom Frieden, former director of the CDC, wrote that the social determinants of health constitute the most important factor in the production of deleterious health conditions that disproportionately affect marginalized members of society.[94] In this chapter, we have defined health disparities, provided some prominent examples of racial/ethnic health disparities in the United States, examined the role of social determinants of health in the production of racial/ethnic health disparities, and highlighted different pathways to health equity in the United States. We have sought to make clear that it is imperative to address the sociostructural factors that undergird racial/ethnic health disparities.

References

1. World Health Organization. Preamble to the Constitution of the World Health Organization as adopted by the International Health Conference. http://www.who.int/governance/eb/who_constitution_en.pdf. Accessed January 23, 2017.
2. Fiscella K, Franks P, Doescher MP, Saver BG. Disparities in health care by race, ethnicity, and language among the insured: Findings from a national sample. *Med Care*. 2002;40(1):52–59.
3. Fiscella K, Williams DR. Health disparities based on socioeconomic inequities: Implications for urban health care. *Acad Med*. 2004;79(12):1139–1147.
4. Ajzen I. Theory of planned behavior. In: Van Lange P, Kruglanski AW, Higgins ET, eds. *Handbook of Theories of Social Psychology*. Vol 1. London, UK: Sage Publications; 2011;438–459.
5. Braveman P, Egerter S, Williams DR. The social determinants of health: Coming of age. *Annu Rev Public Health*. 2011;32:381–398. doi:10.1146/annurev-publhealth-031210-101218.
6. Gee GC, Ford CL. Structural racism and health inequities. *Du Bois Review: Social Science Research on Race*. 2011;8(1):115–132. doi:10.1017/S1742058X11000130.
7. Meyer IH, Schwartz S, Frost DM. Social patterning of stress and coping: Does disadvantaged social statuses confer more stress and fewer coping resources? *Soc Sci Med*. 2008;67(3):368–379.
8. Hudson DL, Eaton J, Lewis P, Grant P, Sewell W, Gilbert K. "Racism?!?... Just Look at Our Neighborhoods": Views on racial discrimination and coping among African American men in Saint Louis. *J Mens Stud*. 2016;24(2):130–150. doi:10.1177/1060826516641103.
9. Hudson DL, Eaton J, Banks A, Sewell W, Neighbors H. "Down in the sewers": Perceptions of depression and depression care among African American men. *Am J Mens Health*. June 2016. doi:10.1177/1557988316654864.
10. Phillips KA, Mayer ML, Aday LA. Barriers to care among racial/ethnic groups under managed care. *Health Aff*. 2000;19(4):65–75. doi:10.1377/hlthaff.19.4.65.
11. Wilkinson R, Pickett K. *The Spirit Level: Why Greater Equality Makes Societies Stronger*. New York, NY: Bloomsbury; 2011.
12. Office of Disease Prevention and Health Promotion. Disparities. https://www.healthypeople.gov/2020/about/foundation-health-measures/Disparities. Published 2010. Accessed January 23, 2017.
13. US Department of Health and Human Services. HHS action plan to reduce racial and ethnic health disparities. https://minorityhealth.hhs.gov/npa/files/Plans/HHS/HHS_Plan_complete.pdf. Accessed February 18, 2017.

Health disparities 43

14. Braveman P. Health disparities and health equity: Concepts and measurement. *Annu Rev Public Health*. 2006;27:167–194.
15. Xu J, Murphy SL, Kochanek K, Bastian BA. Deaths: Final data for 2013. *Natl Vital Stat Rep*. 2016;64(2):1–119. http://www.cdc.gov/nchs/data/nvsr/nvsr64/nvsr64 _02.pdf. Accessed July 29, 2016.
16. *Health, United States, 2015: With Special Feature on Racial and Ethnic Health Disparities*. Hyattsville, MD: National Center for Health Statistics; 2016. https:// www.cdc.gov/nchs/data/hus/hus15.pdf. Accessed July 29, 2016.
17. Centers for Disease Control and Prevention. *Establishing a Holistic Framework to Reduce Inequities in HIV, Viral Hepatitis, STDs, and Tuberculosis in the United States*. Atlanta, GA: Centers for Disease Control and Prevention; 2010. https:// stacks.cdc.gov/view/cdc/11585. Accessed July 29, 2016.
18. McGovern L, Miller G, Hughes-Cromwick P. Health policy brief: The relative contribution of multiple determinants to health outcomes. *Health Affairs*, August 21, 2014. http://www.healthaffairs.org/healthpolicybriefs/brief.php?brief_id=123. Accessed January 31, 2017.
19. Link BG, Phelan J. Social conditions as fundamental causes of disease. *J Health Soc Behav*. 1995;35:80. doi:10.2307/2626958.
20. Syme SL. Reducing racial and social-class inequalities in health: The need for a new approach. *Health Aff*. 2008;27(2):456–459. doi:10.1377/hlthaff.27.2.456.
21. Susser M. *Causal Thinking in the Health Sciences: Concepts and Strategies of Epidemiology*. New York, NY: Oxford University Press; 1973.
22. Marmot MG, Stansfeld S, Patel C et al. Health inequalities among British civil servants: The Whitehall II study. *Lancet*. 1991;337(8754):1387–1393.
23. Adler NE, Boyce T, Chesney MA et al. Socioeconmic status and health: The challenge of the gradient. *Am Psychol*. 1994;49(1):15–24.
24. Adler N, Singh-Manoux A, Schwartz J, Stewart J, Matthews K, Marmot MG. Social status and health: A comparison of British civil servants in Whitehall-II with European- and African-Americans in CARDIA. *Soc Sci Med*. 2008;66(5):1034–1045. doi:10.1016/j.socscimed.2007.11.031.
25. Link BG, Phelan JC. McKeown and the idea that social conditions are fundamental causes of disease. *Am J Public Health*. 2002;92(5):730–732.
26. Cohen S, Janicki-Deverts D, Chen E, Matthews KA. Childhood socioeconomic status and adult health. *Ann N Y Acad Sci*. 2010;1186:37–55. doi:10.1111/j.1749 -6632.2009.05334.x.
27. Western B, Wildeman C. The black family and mass incarceration. *Ann Am Acad Pol Soc Sci*. 2009;621(1):221–242. doi:10.1177/0002716208324850.
28. Braveman PA, Cubbin C, Egerter S et al. Socioeconomic status in health research: One size does not fit all. *JAMA*. 2005;294(22):2879–2888. doi:10.1001 /jama.294.22.2879.
29. Diez Roux AV, Stein Merkin S, Arnett D et al. Neighborhood of residence and incidence of coronary heart disease. *N Engl J Med*. 2001;345:99–106.
30. Williams D, Collins C. Racial residential segregation: A fundamental cause of racial disparities in health. *Public Health Rep*. 2001;116(5):404–416. https://www.ncbi .nlm.nih.gov/pmc/articles/PMC1497358/pdf/12042604.pdf. Accessed January 31, 2017.
31. Bobo L. Keeping the linchpin in place: Testing the multiple sources of opposition to residential integregation. *Revue Internationale de Psychologie Sociale*. 1989;2:306–323.
32. Massey D, Denton N. *American Apartheid, Segregation and the Making of the Underclass*. Cambridge, MA: Harvard University Press; 1993.
33. Frey WH, Farley R. Latino, Asian, and Black segregation in U.S. metropolitan areas: Are multiethnic metros different? *Demography*. 1996;33(1):35–50.

44 *Public health research methods for partnerships and practice*

34. LaVeist T, Pollack K, Thorpe R, Fesahazion R, Gaskin D. Place, not race: Disparities dissipate in Southwest Baltimore when blacks and whites live under similar conditions. *Health Aff.* 2011;30(10):1880–1887. doi:10.1377/hlthaff.2011.0640.
35. Balfour JL, Kaplan GA. Neighborhood environment and loss of physical function in older adults: Evidence from the Alameda County study. *Am J Epidemiol.* 2002;155(6):507–515.
36. Conley D. *Being Black, Living in the Red.* Oakland, CA: University of California Press; 1999.
37. Shapiro TM. *The Hidden Cost of Being African American: How Wealth Perpetuates Inequality.* New York, NY: Oxford University Press; 2004.
38. Katznelson I. *When Affirmative Action Was White: An Untold Story of Racial Inequality in Twentieth Century America.* New York, NY: W.W. Norton and Co.; 2005.
39. Oliver ML. Sub-prime as a black catastrophe. *Am Prospect.* 2008;19(10). http://www.prospect.org/cs/articles?article=sub_prime_as_a_black_catastrophe. Accessed January 23, 2017.
40. Charles CZ. The dynamics of racial residential segregation. *Annu Rev Sociol.* 2003;29:167–207.
41. Meyer IH, Schwartz S, Frost DM. Social patterning of stress and coping: Does disadvantaged social statuses confer more stress and fewer coping resources? *Soc Sci Med.* 2008;67(3):368–379. doi:10.1016/j.socscimed.2008.03.012.
42. Geronimus AT, Hicken M, Keene D, Bound J. "Weathering" and age patterns of allostatic load scores among blacks and whites in the United States. *Am J Public Health.* 2006;96(5):826–833.
43. McEwen BS, Gianaros PJ. Central role of the brain in stress and adaptation: Links to socioeconomic status, health, and disease. *Ann N Y Acad Sci.* 2010;1186:190–222. doi:10.1111/j.1749-6632.2009.05331.x.
44. McEwen BS. Early life influences on life-long patterns of behavior and health. *Ment Retard Dev Disabil Res Rev.* 2003;9(3):149–154.
45. Krieger N. Theories for social epidemiology in the 21st century: An ecosocial perspective. *Int J Epidemiol.* 2001;30:668–677.
46. McEwen BS. Interacting mediators of allostasis and allostatic load: Towards an understanding of resilience in aging. *Metabolism.* 2003;52(10 Suppl 2):10–16.
47. Geronimus AT. Black/White differences in the relationship of maternal age to birthweight: A population-based test of the weathering hypothesis. *Soc Sci Med.* 1996;42(4):589–597.
48. Do DP, Frank R, Finch BK. Does SES explain more of the black/white health gap than we thought? Revisiting our approach toward understanding racial disparities in health. *Soc Sci Med.* 2012;74(9):1385–1393.
49. Seeman T, Merkin SS, Crimmins E, Koretz B, Charette S, Karlamangla A. Education, income and ethnic differences in cumulative biological risk profiles in a national sample of US adults: NHANES III (1988–1994). *Soc Sci Med.* 2008;66(1):72–87. http://www.sciencedirect.com/science/article/B6VBF-4R00FTG-2/2/74b4b9f774904cc90a8197b7b7bb57e2.
50. Shavers VL, Fagan P, Jones D et al. The state of research on racial/ethnic discrimination in the receipt of health care. *Am J Public Health.* 2012;102(5):953–966. doi:10.2105/AJPH.2012.300773.
51. Williams DR, Neighbors HW, Jackson JS. Racial/ethnic discrimination and health: Findings from community studies. *Am J Public Health.* 2003;93(2):200–208.
52. Kessler R, Mickelson K, Williams D. The prevalence, distribution, and mental health correlates of perceived discrimination in the United States. *J Health Soc Behav.* 1999;40:208–230.

Health disparities 45

53. Cohen S, Wills TA. Stress, social support, and the buffering hypothesis. *Psychol Bull.* 1985;98(2):310–357.
54. Massey DS. Segregation and stratification: A biosocial perspective. *Du Bois Rev Soc Sci Res Race.* 2004;1(1):7–25. http://journals.cambridge.org/action/display Abstract?fromPage=online&aid=209703&fulltextType=RA&fileId=S1742058X0 4040032RD 2004. Accessed January 23, 2017.
55. Glanz K, Schwartz MD. Stress, coping and health behavior. In: Glanz K, Rimer BK, Viswanath K, eds. *Health Behavior and Health Education: Theory, Research, and Practice.* San Francisco, CA: Jossey-Bass; 2008:211–230.
56. Kemeny ME, Schedlowski M. Understanding the interaction between psychosocial stress and immune-related diseases: A stepwise progression. *Brain Behav Immun.* 2007;21(8):1009–1018. http://www.sciencedirect.com/science/article/B6WC1 -4PPWMC0-1/2/80a35ee11f6585bd476c6875a2bdb499. Accessed January 23, 2017.
57. Buwalda B, Blom WAM, Koolhaas JM, van Dijk G. Behavioral and physiological responses to stress are affected by high-fat feeding in male rats. *Physiol Behav.* 2001;73(3):371–377. http://www.sciencedirect.com/science/article/B6T0P -43CBCN7-J/2/8636780a6c327d5ce043b7aee788defa. Accessed January 23, 2017.
58. McEwen BS. Protection and damage from acute and chronic stress: Allostasis and allostatic overload and relevance to the pathophysiology of psychiatric disorders. *Ann N Y Acad Sci.* 2004;1032:1–7.
59. Link BG, Phelan J. Social conditions as fundamental causes of disease. *J Health Soc Behav.* 1995;35:80. doi:10.2307/2626958.
60. Bandura A. Social cognitive theory: An agentic perspective. *Annu Rev Psychol.* 2001;52(1):1–26. doi:10.1146/annurev.psych.52.1.1.
61. Bandura A. Health promotion by social cognitive means. *Heal Educ Behav.* 2004;31(2):143–164. http://heb.sagepub.com/content/31/2/143.abstract. Accessed February 19, 2017.
62. Jackson JS, Knight KM, Rafferty JA. Race and unhealthy behaviors: Chronic stress, the HPA axis, and physical and mental health disparities over the life course. *Am J Public Health.* 2010;100(5):933–939. doi:10.2105 /AJPH.2008.143446.
63. Mezuk B, Rafferty JA, Kershaw KN et al. Reconsidering the role of social disadvantage in physical and mental health: Stressful life events, health behaviors, race, and depression. *Am J Epidemiol.* 2011;172(11)1238–1249. doi:10.1093/aje /kwq283.
64. Krieger N. Proximal, distal, and the politics of causation: What's level got to do with it? *Am J Public Health.* 2008;98(2):221–230. doi:10.2105/AJPH.2007.111278.
65. Geronimus AT, Bound J, Waidmann TA, Hillemeier MM, Burns PB. Excess mortality among blacks and whites in the United States. *N Engl J Med.* 1996;335(21):1552–1558.
66. Braveman P, Barclay C. Health disparities beginning in childhood: A lifecourse perspective. *Pediatrics.* 2009;124(suppl 3):S163–S175. doi:10.1542/peds .2009-1100D.
67. Adler NE, Stewart J. Health disparities across the lifespan: Meaning, methods, and mechanisms. *Ann N Y Acad Sci.* 2010;1186:5–23. doi:10.1111/j.1749-6632 .2009.05337.x.
68. Williams DR, Collins C. US socioeconomic and racial differences in health: Patterns and explanations. *Annu Rev Sociol.* 1995;21(1):349–386. doi:10.1146 /annurev.so.21.080195.002025.
69. Whitehead M, Burström B, Diderichsen F. Social policies and the pathways to inequalities in health: A comparative analysis of lone mothers in Britain and Sweden. *Soc Sci Med.* 2000;50(2):255–270.

46 *Public health research methods for partnerships and practice*

70. Sandel M, Hansen M, Kahn R et al. Medical-legal partnerships: Transforming primary care by addressing the legal needs of vulnerable populations. *Health Aff.* 2010;29(9):1697–1705.
71. National Center for Medical-Legal Partnership. Building resources to support civil legal aid access in HRSA-funded health centers. http://medical-legalpartnership .org/building-resources. Accessed January 23, 2017.
72. George Washington University School of Public Health and Health Services. The medical-legal partnership toolkit phase II. Building infrastructure. http://kresge .org/sites/default/files/Uploaded%20Docs/Medical-Legal-Partnership-toolkit-phase -2.pdf Accessed January 23, 2017.
73. Williams DR, Jackson PB. Social sources of racial disparities in health. *Health Aff.* 2005;24(2):325–334. doi:10.1377/hlthaff.24.2.325.
74. US Department of Health and Human Services. *Mental Health: Culture, Race, and Ethnicity: A Supplement to Mental Health: A Report of the Surgeon General.* Rockville, MD: Substance Abuse and Mental Health Services Administration; 2001.
75. Yerger VB, Przewozrik J, Malone RE. Racialized geography, corporate activity, and health disparities: Tobacco industry targeting of inner cities. *J Heal Care Poor Underserved.* 2007;18(4):10–38.
76. Gottlieb L, Sandel M, Adler NE. Collecting and applying data on social determinants of health in health care settings. *JAMA Intern Med.* 2013;173(11):1017–1020. http://dx.doi.org/10.1001/jamainternmed.2013.560.
77. Szreter S, Woolcock M. Health by association? Social capital, social theory, and the political economy of public health. *Int J Epidemiol.* 2004;33(4):650–667.
78. Krause N. Exploring the stress-buffering effects of church-based and secular social support on self-rated health in late life. *J Gerontol B Psychol Sci Soc Sci.* 2006;61(1):S35–S43.
79. Thoits PA. Stress, coping, and social support processes: Where are we? What next? *J Health Soc Behav.* 1995:53–79.
80. Newman K. *No Shame in My Game: The Working Poor in the Inner City.* New York, NY: Knopf/Russell Sage Foundation; 1999.
81. Link BG, Phelan JC, Miech R, Westin EL. The resources that matter: Fundamental social causes of health disparities and the challenge of intelligence. *J Health Soc Behav.* 2008;49(1):72–91. http://www.ncbi.nlm.nih.gov/pubmed/18418986.
82. House JS. Understanding social factors and inequalities in health: 20th century progress and 21st century prospects. *J Health Soc Behav.* 2002;43(2):125–142.
83. Israel BA, Checkoway B, Schulz A, Zimmerman M. Health education and community empowerment: Conceptualizing and measuring perceptions of individual, organizational, and community control. *Health Educ Q.* 1994;21(2):149–170.
84. Israel BA, Schulz AJ, Estrada-Martinez L et al. Engaging urban residents in assessing neighborhood environments and their implications for health. *J Urban Health.* 2006;83(3):523–539.
85. Cattell V. Poor people, poor places, and poor health: The mediating role of social networks and social capital. *Soc Sci Med.* 2001;52(10):1501–1516.
86. Culture of Health. Robert Wood Johnson Foundation Web site. http://www.rwjf .org/en/culture-of-health.html. Accessed January 23, 2017.
87. Sommers SR, Norton MI. Lay theories about white racists: What constitutes racism (and what doesn't). *Gr Process Intergr Relations.* 2006;9(1):117–138.
88. Koh HK, Sebelius KG. Promoting prevention through the Affordable Care Act. *N Engl J Med.* 2010;363(14):1296–1299. doi:10.1056/NEJMp1008560.
89. Halpin HA, Morales-Suarez-Varela MM, Martin-Moreno JM. Chronic disease prevention and the new public health. *Public Health Rev.* 2010;32(1):120–154.

Health disparities 47

90. Jacobson M, Brownell KD. Small taxes on soft drinks and snack foods to promote health. *Am J Public Health*. 2000;90(6):854–857. doi:10.2105/AJPH.90.6.854.
91. Kreuter MW, Sugg-Skinner C, Holt CL et al. Cultural tailoring for mammography and fruit and vegetable intake among low-income African-American women in urban public health centers. *Prev Med*. 2005;41(1):53–62. doi:10.1016/j.ypmed.2004.10.013.
92. Sanders Thompson VL. Cultural context and modification of behavior change theory. *Heal Educ Behav*. 2009;36(5 suppl):156S–160S. doi:10.1177/1090198109340511.
93. Rose G. Sick individuals and sick populations. *Int J Epidemiol*. 2001;30(3):427–432. doi:10.1093/ije/30.3.427.
94. Frieden TR. A framework for public health action: The health impact pyramid. *Am J Public Health*. 2010;100(4):590–595. doi:10.2105/AJPH.2009.185652.
95. Reeve K, Rossiter K, Risdon C. The last straw! A board game on the social determinants of health. *Med Educ*. 2008;42(11):1125–1126. doi:10.1111/j.1365-2923.2008.03215.x.

Activity: The Last Straw![95]

The Last Straw is a board game that provides an innovative, fun way to discuss social determinants of health. The goals of this game are to provide players with an understanding of social determinants of health and how social determinants affect health over the life course. In addition to the game apparatus, the developers have created a guide to aid in the facilitation of the game and have included detailed game scenarios and discussion questions.

SELF-ASSESSMENT—WHAT DID YOU LEARN?

1. "A state of complete physical, mental, social and spiritual well-being" defines which of the following terms?
   a. Optimism
   b. Health
   c. Happiness
   d. Wellness

2. Differences in the incidence, prevalence, mortality, and burden of diseases that exist among specific population groups are known as _____.
   a. Health disparities
   b. Burden differences
   c. Social disparities
   d. Epidemiological differences

3. The forces that shape the social determinants of health are
   _____.
   a. Politics
   b. Economics
   c. Social policies
   d. All of the above

4. Economic, social, cultural, and physical conditions that contribute to or detract from the health of individuals and communities are known as _____.
   a. The social determinants of health
   b. Healthy People 2020
   c. Public health
   d. Health disparities

5. The precise mechanisms that link social stress to discrete health outcomes have been fully elucidated.
   a. TRUE
   b. FALSE

6. Examples of the embodiment of chronic stress include
   _____.
   a. Shortened telomere length
   b. Increased levels of inflammatory markers
   c. Decreases in immune system functioning
   d. All of the above

7. Health disparities are differences in health that are _____.
   a. Systematic but never avoidable
   b. Systematic and plausibly avoidable
   c. Random but never avoidable
   d. Random and plausibly avoidable

8. Upstream determinants of health are _____.
   a. Environmental toxins such as secondhand smoke
   b. Easy solutions to health disparities
   c. Difficult-to-achieve solutions such as changing policies or built environment
   d. Undercurrents that cause infants to experience premature death

Health disparities 49

9. Approaches to achieving health equity include _____.
   a. Empowering communities to advocate for solutions
   b. Development of federal, state, and local policies
   c. Colocation of social and health services
   d. All of the above

10. A social determinants of health lens allows researchers to envision a way to facilitate interventions that remove barriers to positive health behaviors.
   a. TRUE
   b. FALSE

3 Community health and community-based prevention

Deborah J. Bowen and Cassandra Enzler

LEARNING OBJECTIVES

- Define public health.
- Define community health.
- Identify contributing factors that impact the health of a community.
- Describe community health activities.
- Discuss methods for community-based prevention.
- Assess the need for a program.

SELF-ASSESSMENT—WHAT DO YOU KNOW?

1. What are the core functions of public health?
2. What are some examples of community health activities?
3. What factors contribute to the health of a community?

Introduction

Public health matters

This volume is meant to articulate to readers how to use the tools of public health to improve the health outcomes of people all over the world. *Public health* can be thought of as a mission to protect and improve the health and well-being of all people as measured by increasing the number of healthy years that people live and by eliminating health disparities. This often means preventing disease and controlling its impact. We often speak of a population as all people living within a defined geographic area or boundary. However, not all people are healthy or unhealthy at the same level. This is why we look for disparities or differences in health among subgroups of people. These subgroups are often called communities.

Definition of community

Communities can be categorized by a variety of factors; often, definitions differ among scholars and public health experts. Among the vast number of studies that use community engagement, some may classify communities as populations that share social or cultural ties.[1] Examples of social and cultural ties can include community engagement activities such as book clubs, exercise groups, cooking classes, or regions where ethnic populations may congregate (such as the high proportion of Pakistani residents on Staten Island or the large Japanese and Korean communities in California).[2,3] Wells et al. defined *community* as "social groups with a collective identity or shared attitudes and experiences, whether social, cultural, political, occupational, or based on affiliation through geography, institutions, or communication channels."[4] However, in another definition, MacQueen et al.[5] classify community as "a group of people with diverse characteristics who are linked by social ties, share common perspectives, and engage in joint action in geographical locations or settings." As a combination of these definitions, the general term for community can be described as a population in which the individuals share some factor.

Within public health, community health is a topic that has received much focus in terms of interventions or studies. McKenzie and colleagues[6] defined *community health* as "the health status of a defined group of people and the actions and conditions, both private and public (governmental), to promote, protect, and preserve their health." Often, the first step is to try to understand where a community begins. In other words, a community analysis tells the public health expert where to begin with change, the pros and cons of different methods for community intervention, and the strengths and challenges of a specific community, in order to work toward a common goal of health. With these and other studies, one can consider using many methods to assess the starting place of communities. Each method is used to seek understanding of the health of communities, and each method has its strengths, limitations, and ideal conditions for use.

Purpose of the chapter

In this chapter are descriptions of many of the common community analysis methods used to better understand and support communities as they engage in change to improve health. These methods will be described in detail, to help users to understand which methods are most appropriate to analyze community health among varying communities. These methods range from using data that already exist to gathering new data to inform the user of something that is necessary and useful in efforts to improve health in a community. We will first discuss several common types of community analysis, from simple methods to more difficult and time-consuming methods that provide specific types of information. We will provide examples of how such methods can be

52   *Public health research methods for partnerships and practice*

used to inform community activities. We will close with thoughts about how to look for resources to conduct community analysis.

Community analysis methods

Table 3.1 lists several key methods for gaining an understanding of communities. Often these methods are used in combination and potentially are used over time to track progress. They provide a baseline, or preliminary, snapshot.

Key informant interviews

Key informant interviews are performed by interviewing individuals within a community who have a comprehensive knowledge of the interactions and factors that comprise this population. Interviewers must have knowledge of how to perform successful interviews, and they must be able to contact these individuals within a community. Some examples of key informants include town officials, pastors for congregational meetings, presidents at local universities or colleges, or persons in positions that interact with many members of their community. Especially in smaller communities, this method of community analysis is efficient, as key informants should have a good understanding of the surrounding population and its interactions. Upon completion of these key informant interviews, public health officials can qualitatively code the interviews. This entails several public health officials transcribing the interviews and then looking for main themes as provided by the interviewees' answers. This method of community analysis will allow for public health officials to determine the perceptions, beliefs, strengths, and needs of the community efficiently by interviewing one person instead of multiple sources. Public health officials can gain valuable information from this method of analysis, but they should be cautioned that in larger communities, key informants may not have comprehensive knowledge of the entire population. This method might work best in smaller communities where key informants can gain a comprehensive understanding of the surrounding population. An example of a study using key informant interviews is a study performed by Sherrieb et al.[7] in 2012 that used school principals as key informants to assess perceptions of community resilience according to varying degrees of school poverty.

General public interviews

General public interviews are performed by interviewing several members of the community. Interviewers must have knowledge of how to perform successful interviews, and they must be able to recruit several willing participants from the community. This method of analysis is efficient in both small and large communities, as long as an adequate number of diverse individuals are recruited for participation. This number will vary in accordance with the design and nature of the study. After interviewing members of the community, public

Type of method	What is learned from the method?	Specialized knowledge/statistics	Analysis	Gain/no gain	General conditions for use
Key informant interview	Both personal and public perception of the community and its needs and participant's beliefs, desires, etc.	• Must have someone trained to conduct interview • Must know how to code qualitative data • Must be able to contact qualified interviewees	Qualitatively code the interview and look for main themes among the interviews	Gain: Quick way to gain perspective of community through the eyes of community expert No gain: Interviewer bias, may not address full perception of larger communities	May be better used in smaller communities with champions of information within the population
General public interview	Personal perceptions of the community and its needs, their beliefs, desires, etc.	• Must have someone trained to conduct interview • Must know how to code qualitative data • Must be able to collect interviews from a range of individuals	Qualitatively code the interview and look for main themes among the interviews	Gain: Personal accounts of the community No gain: May not gain a comprehensive view of community if limited participation. May not address all of community's beliefs, problems, or needs	May be used in both small and large communities, useful when the population is extremely diverse. Especially useful for gaining perspective of marginalized communities

(Continued)

Table 3.1 (Continued) Methods of community analysis: knowledge of the methods and how to perform them[a]

Type of method	What is learned from the method?	Specialized knowledge/statistics	Analysis	Gain/no gain	General conditions for use
Group interview	Community perceptions, dynamic of community, needs on population basis	• Must have someone trained to conduct interview • Must be able to facilitate	Qualitatively code the interview and look for main themes among the interviews	Gain: Assess group interaction, perform qualitative research more efficiently No gain: Data may be difficult to analyze. Perceptions may differ about community	Useful in both small and large communities. Convenient when focus groups are already formed within the community. Useful if interested in a particular topic
Observation	Community interaction, view events/social sites that may not be captured in an interview	• Cannot participate in community, solely observe • Must be objective about observations	Qualitatively assess the observations by comparing with other observers	Gain: Facilitate further questions; knowledge of environment not gained by asking questions No gain: Discrepancies among what is observed	Useful in both small and large communities. Useful if interested in the interactions of diverse populations. Not to be used for in-depth analysis

(Continued)

Table 3.1 (Continued) Methods of community analysis: knowledge of the methods and how to perform them[a]

Type of method	What is learned from the method?	Specialized knowledge/statistics	Analysis	Gain/no gain	General conditions for use
Community/large meeting	Opinions from community, knowledge, disagreements, and discussions	• Cannot actively participate	Qualitatively code the dialogue among the participants and look for similar themes	Gain: Discussions and reactions in community setting. Directly hear about community needs No gain: Different perspectives and views. May not address everyone's needs	Useful in both small and large communities. Ideal for communities already gathering for meetings. Useful for focused topics. May be difficult to organize independently
Interpretation of records, transcripts	Community standing/ perception, behaviors, needs, demographics	• Must have access to documentation • Must have some statistical knowledge since it will be community data	Analyze documents qualitatively by looking for themes or quantitatively by using statistical software such as STATA or ATLAS	Gain: May prompt qualitative studies. Representative of community No gain: Does not provide perception or in-depth knowledge of community needs/ issues	Useful in both small and large communities. Not to be used for extremely in-depth analysis. Useful for collecting general information without recruiting individuals for interviews

(Continued)

Table 3.1 (Continued)   Methods of community analysis: knowledge of the methods and how to perform them[a]

Type of method	What is learned from the method?	Specialized knowledge/statistics	Analysis	Gain/no gain	General conditions for use
SWOT analysis	Strengths, weaknesses, opportunities, and threats	• Develop in group setting for best results • Must be able to facilitate • Must understand SWOT analysis	Qualitatively assess the strengths, weaknesses, opportunities and threats of a community by implementing a SWOT matrix or Force Field analysis	Gain: Identify strengths of community and opportunities as well as weaknesses and threats No gain: Does not prioritize factors. Does not figure out solutions for problems. Does not verify statements	Useful in both small and large communities. Ideally used within group settings to assess, primarily, perceived strengths, weaknesses, opportunities, and threats
PEST analysis	Political, economic, social, and technological factors	• Develop in group setting for best results • Must be able to facilitate • Must understand PEST analysis	Qualitatively assess the political, economic, social, and technological factors of a community by implementing a PEST matrix	Gain: Identify external influences and attempt to predict future. Identify forces and factors of community No gain: No prioritization; analysis of external factors can be complex	Used in both small and large communities. Ideally used within group settings to assess, primarily, perceived thoughts about the political, economic, social, and technological environment

(Continued)

Table 3.1 (*Continued*) Methods of community analysis: knowledge of the methods and how to perform them[a]

Type of method	What is learned from the method?	Specialized knowledge/statistics	Analysis	Gain/no gain	General conditions for use
Photovoice	Community point of view and explanations	• Must have people willing to take photos and share stories • Must have camera	Analyze qualitatively by looking for common themes among the pictures and stories shared by various participants	Gain: Perspective, especially from marginalized communities No gain: Individualized, may not encompass thoughts of community	Useful in smaller communities, especially among marginalized populations. Useful if equipment is available and the surrounding environment is a good depiction of the community
Analysis of existing datasets	Demographics and health problems at national, state, and other geographic level	• Must have access to datasets • Must be able to interpret datasets and ensure they encompass relevant information	Qualitatively or quantitatively analyze through the use of tools such as STATA or ATLAS	Gain: General view of community, health problems, sociodemographic factors No gain: Perspectives, pockets of health problems or community needs	Useful in both small and large communities. Not to be used for in-depth analysis. Useful if studies have already been performed on the community and the data are available

(Continued)

Table 3.1 (Continued) Methods of community analysis: knowledge of the methods and how to perform them[a]

Type of method	What is learned from the method?	Specialized knowledge/statistics	Analysis	Gain/no gain	General conditions for use
Survey	Sociodemographic factors, health, generalizable picture of community	• Must have access to community and ability to provide surveys • Must create surveys in a manner that is easily interpretable	Analyze qualitatively by coding answers or quantitatively by using statistical software such as STATA or ATLAS	Gain: General health or needs of community, sociodemographic factors No gain: No in-depth perspective of community, cannot analyze beyond surface-level answers	Useful in both small and large communities. Not to be used for in-depth analysis. Efficient way to gather surface-level information from a large number of individuals

Abbreviations: PEST, political, economic, social technological; SWOT, strengths, weaknesses, opportunities, threats.

[a] Along with the examples listed in the table, other resources, such as the following, provide additional details: Bensley RJ, Brookins-Fisher J. Community Health Education Methods: A Practical Guide. Sudbury, MA: Jones and Bartlett; 2003.

Community health and community-based prevention 59

health officials can transcribe the interviews and, then, qualitatively assess the transcripts by looking for main themes discussed among the participants. This method of community analysis will allow public health officials to determine a comprehensive view of the community as it pertains to its strengths, weaknesses, and needs. Public health officials can gain a comprehensive view from multiple sources, but should be warned that without sufficiently diverse sources, public health officials may not gain a comprehensive perception of the community. Various sources are needed in order to ensure that interview bias does not exist. An example of a study that uses public interviews was conducted in 2015 by Bell et al.[8] who approached smokers in public settings and analyzed several ethnographic factors regarding these participants.

Group interviews

Group interviews are performed by gathering several members of the community and interviewing them collectively. Public health officials must have knowledge of how to facilitate group interviews, and they must construct the interview in a manner that allows participants to share a comprehensive view of the community. This method of analysis is efficient in both small and large communities as long as a diverse group of people is recruited to participate in interview sessions. Upon the completion of group interviews, public health officials can qualitatively assess the data by transcribing the interviews and looking for main themes among the varying responses. This method of community analysis will allow for public health officials to efficiently gain a comprehensive view of the community, as several members can relate their perceptions during a single session. However, interview bias can arise from this method because group collaboration can lead to participants skewing their responses on the basis of the group's attitudes, beliefs, or opinions or the participants' perceptions of such. Interviewee perceptions about the community may also differ widely, which will lead to difficulty during analysis. Also, if interviewers do not facilitate the group interview well, a comprehensive view of the community may not be apparent. An example of a study using group interviews was conducted in 2014 by Robertson et al.[9] to assess parents' perspectives of helmet use in childhood. The methods in this study were representative of how to conduct group interviews, and the study also shows how a public health matter can be assessed through the use of this strategy. Another example of a study using group interviews is a 2002 study in which the researchers used this method to further understand children's perceptions of health-related issues.[10] As these examples show, group interviews can be conducted among a variety of participants. This strategy is important in gaining qualitative perspectives on important issues.

Observation

Observation is performed by simply assessing the surrounding community without intervening in the interactions of the population. Public health officials must know how to observe the community without interfering or becoming noticeable by the population. Public health officials must also be objective about the observations they make within the community. After observing the community, public health officials qualitatively assess their perceptions by comparing their views with other public health officials. This allows for analysis of common themes within the community. This method of community analysis will also allow public health officials to gain a more objective view of the community as well as generate further questions for discussion. This method is typically more effective in smaller communities because larger communities will require more time and more public health officials for observation; larger communities will also have many different interactions that may be difficult to capture through observation. Public health officials must be unbiased in their perceptions. An example of observation and how different situations call for different measures is cancer screening. Mammography screening occurs every 2 years for women between the ages of 50 and 74, mostly among females, and is noninvasive.[11] However, colonoscopy observation is much different. This procedure typically occurs every 10 years for people between the ages of 50 and 74 and is invasive.[12] Although these examples are medically related, it is important to be aware that observation will differ among various settings and differing populations. This method of analysis will not allow public health officials to gain a community perception of the environment or allow for deeper analysis from individuals within the community. An example of a study that used observation within a community was performed by Masson et al.[13] in 2016 to assess food storage behavior and its impact on health.

Community meetings

Community meetings are performed by hosting a public meeting in an accessible location and asking questions of the attendees while acting as an observer at these gatherings. Public health officials must act as passive listeners and not engage within the interactions but rather listen to what is being discussed. After attending community or large meetings, public health officials can transcribe the meeting and qualitatively assess the main themes that were discussed among the participants. Community meetings are effective in both large and small communities, but public health officials may need to attend more of these events as the population of the community increases. This is also an efficient way to gain differing perceptions of the community in a single event rather than recruiting various individuals for interviews. This type of community analysis method may also lead public health officials to generate further questions for discussion. However, public health officials must be cautious in using this method of analysis as well. Community/large meetings may be focused on certain topics, which may restrict public health officials from gaining a comprehensive view of the community. These events may also be dominated in conversation by certain individuals, which may lead

Community health and community-based prevention   61

to bias during analysis if a comprehensive view from various sources is not gathered. In addition, it is most likely that public health officials will not be able to discuss topics on a deeper level unless future interviews are scheduled. An example of a study that used community/large meetings for community analysis was conducted by Williamson[14] in 2013 to determine differing perceptions among participants and the larger population.

Interpretation of records and transcripts

Interpretation of records and transcripts involves public health officials accessing certain documents to better assess the community. Public health officials must have access to these documents and collect enough of these to gain a comprehensive understanding of the community. These records and transcripts may have both qualitative and quantitative data, so public health officials may need skill sets for the assessment of both of these types of data. For qualitative data, public health officials can look for main themes among the records and transcripts that provide perceptions of the community. For quantitative data, public health officials can use software such as STATA® or SPSS®, two statistical software packages that can be used to look for associations among the data collected. Public health officials often partner with academic researchers or others who have access and skill with these software packages to analyze survey data. The interpretation of records and transcripts is effective for both small and large communities as long as enough of the documents are collected for a comprehensive assessment. These documents will allow public health officials to gain an understanding of different community factors such as demographics, perceptions, strengths, and needs. Assessment of these documents may allow public health officials to generate qualitative questions for future research. However, this method of analysis will not allow public health officials to gain perceptions from individuals within the communities. This method is a surface-level assessment and does not provide for an in-depth review of the community. An example of a study using past records, observations, and transcripts was performed in 2016 by Evenson et al.[15] who cumulatively assessed multiple parks on the basis of transcripts, observations, and records from past research. A 2016 study by Casey et al.[16] is another example of how research has been conducted using records; the authors assessed how electronic health records have been used for population health research. (See Chapter 10 for a discussion of quantitative methods and Chapter 11 for a discussion of qualitative methods.)

SWOT analysis

To assess communities using the *strengths, weaknesses, opportunities, and threats* (SWOT) analysis tool, public health officials must have some knowledge of SWOT analysis and must be able to recruit individuals or groups within the community to answer questions about their perceptions of the

62   *Public health research methods for partnerships and practice*

strengths, weaknesses, opportunities, and threats within the surrounding population. This method of analysis is qualitative and can be interpreted by creating a SWOT matrix. This will allow public health officials to draw out main themes on each of the factors. This method of community analysis is effective in both large and small communities but may require more sources of information, depending on the size of the population. This analysis will allow public health officials to gain a rather comprehensive view of the community, as the factors in SWOT can depict many perceptions of the community. However, this method of analysis does not prioritize perceptions of the community, nor does it verify the statements made by individuals. Also, whereas it does highlight many aspects of the community, this method of analysis does not support methods for solving solutions. An example of SWOT analysis was depicted in a 2015 study conducted by Romero-Gutierrez et al.[17] to analyze students' perceptions of their current educational program. Another example of a SWOT analysis was performed by the Meeker-McLeod-Sibley community health board in 2008 to assess their community leadership team.[18] These examples represent how a SWOT analysis can be conducted.

PEST analysis

Public health officials can use *political, economic, social, and technological* (PEST) analysis to assess the environment of a community. Public health officials must have some knowledge of PEST analysis and must be able to recruit individuals or access documentation from various sources within the community in order to gain comprehensive knowledge of the population and its interactions. This method of analysis can be both qualitative and quantitative, so public health officials must have some understanding of both of these types of assessments. For qualitative data, public health officials can develop a PEST matrix and look for common themes of PEST factors as portrayed from the various sources of information. For quantitative data, public health officials can use statistical software such as STATA® or SPSS®, two of many software packages for analysis of numeric data, which can draw associations among collected data. This method of analysis is effective in both small and large communities, but more sources of information may be needed as the size of the population increases. PEST analysis will allow for public health officials to gain a comprehensive understanding of many internal and external factors that affect a community. However, similar to SWOT analysis, this method of analysis does not allow public health officials to prioritize factors. Public health officials may also find it difficult to analyze external factors and their association with the community as compared to internal factors within the community. An example of PEST analysis was used in a study performed by Igliński et al.[19] in 2016. This study was not related to community health but, instead, was a study of the aspects affecting renewable energy production.

Community health and community-based prevention 63

Photovoice

Photovoice methods allow public health officials to observe the ways that individuals perceive their community through both pictures capturing their point of view and stories that accompany their observations. Public health officials must have access to equipment that allows for individuals to both take pictures and relay their experiences with the observations they capture. Public health officials must also be able to recruit individuals from varying backgrounds, as bias can occur with limited observations. This method of analysis is qualitative, and public health officials can assess a community by looking for similar themes among the multiple photovoice images collected from different individuals. This method is more effective in smaller communities because larger communities will require more resources to complete a comprehensive view. Photovoice will allow public health officials to gain a deeper understanding of how individuals perceive the community, especially among marginalized populations. However, this method may also give results that are too individualized and that do not encompass a comprehensive perception of the community. In a photovoice study in 2016, Davtyan et al.[20] depicted a marginalized population experiencing stigma in daily life. Another example of a photovoice study captured the perception of homeless women in Auckland, New Zealand, and the barriers and facilitators that existed in their daily lives.[21]

Analysis of existing datasets

Analysis of existing datasets involves public health officials using data collected from past studies to gain a better understanding of the community. Public health officials must have access to existing datasets as well as have some background knowledge of how to perform both qualitative and quantitative analysis. For qualitative assessment, public health officials can use the datasets to look for main themes that portray the community or community issues analyzed. For quantitative data, public health officials can use the statistical software packages previously mentioned, which can be used to look for comparisons among the data. This method of analysis is effective in both small and large communities as long as the datasets are representative of the community being analyzed. By analyzing existing datasets, public health officials can gain an understanding of the community in a more efficient and less costly manner than collecting original data, as the data have already been collected. A variety of factors, such as economic issues or sociodemographic variables, can be analyzed through existing datasets. The information from existing datasets may also allow public health officials to formulate hypotheses for future studies. However, this method of analysis limits public health officials from performing more in-depth analysis. Datasets typically do not address perceptions of individuals within the community, and this method of analysis may not be effective if the collected data are not representative. An

64   *Public health research methods for partnerships and practice*

assessment of varying perspectives of end-of-life care provides an example of public health officials using a past dataset to understand community health attitudes.[22]

Surveys

Surveys involve public health officials formulating questions for communities to complete in order to gain a better understanding of concerns, needs, health issues, and other matters. Public health officials must be able to formulate surveys and have access to distribute these to the community. Surveys can be qualitative or quantitative, so public health officials must have some understanding of both forms of analysis. For qualitative information, public health officials can look for similar themes among the multiple survey responses. For quantitative information, public health officials can use software such as STATA® or SPSS® to look for associations among the survey responses. This method of analysis is effective in both small and large communities as long as enough responses are generated. Surveys allow public health officials to gain an understanding of the community in an efficient and less costly manner than conducting in-depth interviews. Surveys can also reach a large portion of the community and can thus allow for a comprehensive perception. Surveys can be tailored to assess many factors of a community, including needs, strengths, sociodemographic variables, and other topics. However, surveys can also be very limited. Surveys do not allow for explanation by both public health officials and participants, which may result in bias during analysis. Surveys can also restrict understanding of the community if there are not enough people who complete this method of analysis. Public health officials also cannot gain in-depth analysis of the community beyond the responses obtained by the survey. An example of a study using community surveys was conducted by Kessler et al.[23] in 2013 in which the authors assessed the prevalence of binge-eating disorders by administering population surveys. Surveys are a simple way to gather information from many people in a timely fashion and, thus, are ideal for many research projects as demonstrated by Dr. Julie Ponto.[24]

How to use community analysis data

The next step after conducting the community analysis is to use the information to guide the choice and implementation of intervention strategies. Many aspects need to be taken into consideration regarding how to use community analysis to choose community intervention strategies and to guide their implementation. Here, we will discuss methods for using community analysis to guide intervention choice. We will use an existing intervention as an example of how community analysis can and did aid in the design of a project to change community health outcomes and behaviors.

Salihu et al.[25] created an intervention program to address existing health disparities in a low-income, mostly African American community in

Tampa, FL. The objective of this pilot study was to assess the effectiveness of a novel community-based intervention program, which was called a *fortified dietary intervention* (FDI). The program was redesigned through structural modification of an existing, purely diet-based program by adding physical and mental health components.

The study methodology was similar to that used in a previous study.[25,26] Trained and certified community educators delivered a series of interactive lessons to low-income women in community settings. The lessons were adapted from the evidence-based Expanded Food and Nutrition Education Program (EFNEP) curriculum and addressed basic nutrition, food budgeting, and food preparation.[27] In graduated classroom instruction that included food demonstrations, worksheets, and interactive class discussions, participants learned about healthy eating and cooking at lower costs, saving money at the grocery store, and keeping food safe. Study participants monitored their daily goal attainment and returned the goal sheets the following week. At least 10 minutes of a personalized physical activity of participants' choosing took place at each FDI session, under the supervision of a certified trainer. In addition, participants in the program were encouraged to get at least 30 minutes of moderate physical activity or exercise each day and to adopt an active lifestyle. To address stress and mental health, women received education about the harmful effects of stress, the impact that stress has on overall well-being (i.e., mind, body, soul), and methods to cope with stressors. Participants engaged in stress-reducing activities as they explored their stressors and discussed ways to build a support system and how to identify support within the community. Finally, the mental health section included sessions on healthy sleep that addressed typical problems that contribute to sleep disturbances, practical solutions to these issues, and practical presleep relaxation methods that they could integrate as part of a daily routine that they practiced at home.

Engaging community members in the process

Good research involves connecting with community members on a variety of factors that include culture, ethnicity, and age. In a study that focused on improving nutrition among low-income African American women, Salihu et al.[25] implemented CBPR methods to assess the barriers and facilitators of good health for this group of women. An initial engagement period, in which project directors seek opinions and ideas about the intervention from community participants, can help provide direction on design and interpretation of the study and its data. Throughout the project, directors can also continue this seeking, including during the reviewing of results. One reason to conduct early interviews or group sessions of participants is to learn how to design the multiple components of the intervention so that it will be acceptable to potential participants. A community advisory board (CAB) might be part of such a project and usually is made up of members and leaders from the community

66   *Public health research methods for partnerships and practice*

who are interested in improving the health and resources of their community and who want to spend time and resources in doing the improvements. Bringing in these members from the start and continuing their involvement will help program designers understand what is happening at the community level and will potentially improve the choices made during the design process.

Identifying the health problems to target

Often survey data and data on health outcomes can help to identify the direction of efforts for interventions. For example, analysis of data from the Behavioral Risk Factor Surveillance System (BRFSS) for Tampa, Florida, and comparisons to other similarly sized cities might help to identify the need for such an intervention targeting eating and activity. Analysis of survey data for the specific community and presenting findings to the CAB might be a way to engage participants in the problem. Analyzing data that the community members want to increase their understanding of issues and concerns would demonstrate a shared commitment to the identification of problems that can be improved by community and project directors together.

In our example, the analysis of survey data for the community of Tampa might have provided information on the baseline preprogram levels of unhealthy eating and physical activity. It also might have given program officials the idea that in order to target eating and activity, one must help people reduce their stress levels and become more able to focus on health-promoting behaviors. Discussion with individuals or groups could inform the specific content of the sessions designed to help people change diet, activity, or stress. These bits of knowledge could come from a careful community analysis using some of the methods proposed in this paper.

Identifying the history of a community

Many communities have had some experience with programs and research in the past, and many of them have had negative experiences as well as positive ones. A better understanding of the community's experiences could help the program designers avoid the mistakes that led to negative experiences in the past. There may be more recent and immediate examples of harm due to projects or research, and these must be addressed before beginning. Success stories could exist that will shape the reactions of community members to a new project, and these must be considered as well.

Playing to a community's strengths

Communities enter projects with strengths, previous experiences, and connections that shape the choices that community members make and the events that people react to. Knowing about these experiences and strengths could help guide the program director's choice of intervention strategies. An example might be the existence of a successful lead exposure program that had been previously implemented in city public housing with positive results. This lead exposure prevention program—including both the people and the procedures—could be used to guide a program to prevent exposure to a different chemical or irritant. Understanding where a community has had success with health promotion programs in the past might provide direction for future activities.

Avoiding difficult areas

Similarly, negative experiences could affect future direction for health promotions. For example, if a community is known to have high distrust of police and law enforcement, then simply increasing police presence to help people feel safe as they exercise is not likely to work. Rather, introduction of a neighborhood watch group might be more effective. Another example of a negative experience is the set of recent events to identify and clean the water supply for Flint, Michigan;[28,29] it will have lasting effects on the residents' ability to trust government officials and public health programs in the future. Knowing about these difficult areas and understanding what the community has experienced could make the difference between success and failure of a health promotion opportunity, no matter how well meaning.

Conclusions

As Kofi Annan, former Secretary-General of the United Nations, has said, "Knowledge is power."[30] We have discussed that there are many ways to obtain information about communities. This information can be helpful, and even critical, to the success of the program under consideration. Learning about a community—its healthy and not so healthy behaviors, its strengths and weaknesses, and its history—is an important first step in designing programs to improve health. Many ways exist to learn about a community, and, generally, program officials do not have the resources or time to do all of them. There are always choices to be made in the design of a community intervention. These choices can and will be based on resources, time, previous expertise, and interest. Methods can also be combined in a variety of ways, and with the assessment of the players and setting involved, the appropriate methods to be used can be decided. However, the methods also can be based on where the community is starting and what they have experienced to date, both positively and negatively. Knowing the health outcome levels and the community's experiences with them might help to make more appropriate choices for improvement.

Many times, these types of data already exist and can be obtained from local, regional, or national health department officials. Where specialized skills are required to obtain such data, there are often people who have those

68 *Public health research methods for partnerships and practice*

skills who might help. Collaborating with local or regional health department officials to obtain relevant data is one strategy used by some to conduct community analysis. Another strategy is to collect data separate from what is already known, using the existing data as a guide. Multiple strategies exist for conducting community analysis, and many of these were highlighted in this chapter.

References

1. Ahmed SM, Palermo AS. Community engagement in research: Frameworks for education and peer review. *Am J Public Health.* 2010;100(8):1380–1387.
2. Fessenden F, Roberts S. Then as now—New York's shifting ethnic mosaic. *New York Times.* January 21, 2011. http://www.nytimes.com/interactive/2011/01/23/nyregion/20110123-nyc-ethnic-neighborhoods-map.html?_r=0. Accessed July 12, 2016.
3. Kim V. "Comfort women" and a lesson in how history is shaped in California textbooks. *Los Angeles Times.* February 7, 2016. http://www.latimes.com/local/education/la-me-comfort-women-curriculum-20160207-story.html. Accessed July 12, 2016.
4. Wells K, Miranda J, Bruce ML, Alegria M, Wallerstein N. Bridging community intervention and mental health services research. *Am J Psychiatry.* 2004;161(6): 955–963.
5. MacQueen KM, McLellan E, Metzger DS et al. What is community? An evidence-based definition for participatory public health. *Am J Public Health.* 2001;91(12): 1929–1938.
6. McKenzie JF, Pinger RR, Kotecki JE. *An Introduction to Community Health.* Boston, MA: Jones and Bartlett; 2005.
7. Sherrieb K, Louis CA, Pfefferbaum RL, Pfefferbaum JB, Diab E, Norris FH. Assessing community resilience on the US coast using school principals as key informants. *Int J Disaster Risk Reduc.* 2012;2:6–15.
8. Bell K, Dennis S, Robinson J, Moore R. Does the hand that controls the cigarette packet rule the smoker? Findings from ethnographic interviews with smokers in Canada, Australia, the United Kingdom and the USA. *Soc Sci Med.* 2015;142:136–144.
9. Robertson DW, Lang BD, Schaefer JM. Parental attitudes and behaviors concerning helmet use in childhood activities: Rural focus group interviews. *Accid Anal Prev.* 2014;70:314–319.
10. Heary CM, Hennessy E. The use of focus group interviews in pediatric health care research. *Pediatr Psychol.* 2002;27(1), 47–57. doi:10.1093/jpepsy/27.1.47.
11. What is breast cancer screening? Centers for Disease Control and Prevention Web site. https://www.cdc.gov/cancer/breast/basic_info/screening.htm. Published April 19, 2016. Accessed January 30, 2017.
12. Colorectal cancer screening guidelines. Centers for Disease Control and Prevention Web site. https://www.cdc.gov/cancer/colorectal/basic_info/screening/guidelines.htm. Published February 26, 2014. Accessed January 30, 2017.
13. Masson M, Delarue J, Blumenthal D. An observational study of refrigerator food storage by consumers in controlled conditions. *Food Qual Prefer.* 2017;56:294–300.
14. Williamson, AR. Public meetings as sources of citizen input: Comparing attendees with citizens at large. *Soc Sci J.* 2014;51(2):191–200.
15. Evenson KR, Jones SA, Holliday KM, Cohen DA, McKenzie TL. Park characteristics, use, and physical activity: A review of studies using SOPARC (System for Observing Play and Recreation in Communities). *Prev Med.* 2016;86:153–166.

Community health and community-based prevention 69

16. Casey JA, Schwartz BS, Stewart WF, Adler NE. Using electronic health records for population health research: A review of methods and applications. *Annu Rev Public Heal.* 2016;37(1):61–81. doi:10.1146/annurev-publhealth-032315-021353.
17. Romero-Gutierrez M, Jimenez-Liso MR, Martinez-Chico M. SWOT analysis to evaluate the programme of a joint online/onsite master's degree in environmental education through the students' perceptions. *Eval Program Plann.* 2016;54:41–49.
18. Meeker-McLeod-Sibley Community Health Board. *Community Leadership Team SWOT Analysis.* McLeod, MN: Minnesota Health Department; 2008.
19. Igliński B, Iglińska A, Cichosz M, Kujawski W, Buczkowski R. Renewable energy production in the Łódzkie Voivodeship. The PEST analysis of the RES in the voivodeship and in Poland. *Renew Sustain Energy Rev.* 2016;58:737–750.
20. Davtyan M, Farmer S, Brown B, Sami M, Frederick T. Women of color reflect on HIV-related stigma through photovoice. *J Assoc Nurses AIDS Care.* 2016; 27(4):404–418.
21. Bukowski K, Buetow S. Making the invisible visible: A photovoice exploration of homeless women's health and lives in central Auckland. *Soc Sci Med.* 2011;72(5):739–746. doi:10.1016/j.socscimed.2010.11.029.
22. Kendall M, Carduff E, Lloyd A et al. Different experiences and goals in different advanced diseases: Comparing serial interviews with patients with cancer, organ failure, or frailty and their family and professional careers. *J Pain Symptom Manage.* 2015;50(2):216–224.
23. Kessler RC, Berglund PA, Chiu WT et al. The prevalence and correlates of binge eating disorder in the World Health Organization world mental health surveys. *Biol Psychiatry.* 2013;73(9):904–914.
24. Ponto J. Understanding and evaluating survey research. *J Adv Pract Oncol.* 2015;6(2):168–171.
25. Salihu HM, Adegoke KK, Das R et al. Community-based fortified dietary intervention improved health outcomes among low-income African-American women. *Nutr Res.* 2016;36(8):771–779. doi:10.1016/j.nutres.2016.04.006.
26. Cullen KW, Lara Smalling A, Thompson D, Watson KB, Reed D, Konzelmann K. Creating healthful home food environments: Results of a study with participants in the expanded food and nutrition education program. *J Nutr Educ Behav.* 2009;41(6):380–388.
27. Expanded Food and Nutrition Education Program. National Institute of Food and Agriculture Web site. https://nifa.usda.gov/program/expanded-food-and-nutrition -education-program-efnep. Updated 2015. Accessed July 12, 2016.
28. Hanna-Attisha M, LaChance J, Sadler RC, Schnepp AC. Elevated blood lead levels in children associated with the flint drinking water crisis: A spatial analysis of risk and public health response. *Am J Public Health.* 2016;106(2):283–290. doi:10.2105/AJPH.2015.303003.
29. Rosner D. Flint, Michigan: A century of environmental injustice. *Am J Public Health.* 2016;106(2):200–201. doi:10.2105/AJPH.2015.303011.
30. Annan K. "Knowledge means power"—And those who provide honest information are best allies of UN, says Kofi Annan in BBC World Service Lecture. United Nations Web site. http://www.un.org/press/en/2002/SGSM8552.doc.htm. Published December 10, 2002. Accessed January 30, 2017.

Activity: Develop and evaluate a community health grant

Part 1: Develop a community health grant

This activity is designed to encourage thinking about the community resources that can be drawn upon to facilitate the reduction in a public health problem

70   *Public health research methods for partnerships and practice*

and the drafting of a community health intervention proposal. This activity requires 45 to 60 minutes to complete. The class will divide into groups of 8 to 10 participants and consider the following:

For this activity, imagine that you are a part of your governor's council on public health priorities for your state. It has come to the governor's attention that there is a possible grant for $10 million dollars to focus on a specific health problem in one or more states in the United States. You need to identify a public health problem that is pertinent to your state and establish an overview of a plan to spend the grant money as well as demonstrate that you have adequate knowledge of your community to implement a solution to the problem. Construct and present a short elevator pitch (3–5 minutes) that addresses the following:

A. *Introduction:* Identify a public health problem in your community.
B. *Background:* Describe the public health problem and the risk factors that you want to focus on. What data might you use to present to the reviewers?
C. *Impact on the community:* Describe the stories of the community targets and which community members are most impacted by the problem. What is important to convince a tough review group that your ideas are the best? Think about how you can synthesize anecdotes with data.
D. *Outcome:* Detail what your project will do with the funds. List three activities, three resources, and one service that you can implement with the grant funding. Describe two short-term goals (what knowledge, skills, and attitude changes will your intervention achieve?) and a long-term goal (what is the ultimate impact?).

Part 2: Evaluate a community health grant

This exercise is designed to facilitate consideration of the components that make a convincing research proposal. This activity requires 15 minutes to complete.

A. Keeping the request for proposals from Part 1 in mind, develop a list of standards to be used when evaluating the proposals. What data do you want to see? How will you decide which is the worthiest cause?
B. Swap your community health grant from Part 1 with another group's, or critically evaluate your own. Evaluate their proposal against your evaluation criteria. What standards does it meet? Where can it be improved? What percentage of the $10 million dollars, if any, would you award to this project?

Community health and community-based prevention 71

SELF-ASSESSMENT—WHAT DID YOU LEARN?

1. What is community health?
   a. The health status of an individual and the actions the government must take to improve the individual's health
   b. The study and improvement of the health characteristics of geographic areas of people
   c. The study and improvement of the health characteristics of individuals
   d. The health outcomes of a group of individuals

2. Which of the following is NOT a community health activity?
   a. Lobbying
   b. Community gardens
   c. Health promotion
   d. Program planning and evaluation

3. Which of the following is NOT a core function of public health?
   a. Research for solutions to health problems
   b. Increase revenue for the institution
   c. Assure the provision of health care when it is otherwise unavailable
   d. Inform and education people about health issues

4. Fluoridation of water would be an example of _____.
   a. A primary prevention strategy
   b. A secondary prevention strategy
   c. A tertiary prevention strategy
   d. None of the above

5. The three environments that affect community health are _____.
   a. Physical, social, and organizational
   b. Physical, mental, and emotional
   c. Social, spiritual, and organizational
   d. Social, educational, and location

6. Which of the following is NOT a physical factor that contributes to the health of the community?
   a. Geography
   b. Community size
   c. Religion
   d. Industrial development

7. What is the process of collecting information to develop an understanding of an issue, resources, or constraints of a population as related to the development of a health promotion program?
   a. Needs assessment
   b. Summative evaluation
   c. Social plan
   d. Community appraisal

8. Which is NOT a tool of community health practice?
   a. Epidemiology
   b. Community organizing
   c. Health education
   d. Pharmaceutical interventions

9. What causes public health problems?
   a. Behaviors
   b. Physical environment
   c Social environment
   d. All of the above

10. Public health _____ health status to identify and solve community health problems.
   a. Monitors
   b. Ignores
   c. Enforces
   d. Creates

4 Introduction to epidemiology

Cassandra Arroyo

LEARNING OBJECTIVES

- Define epidemiology.
- Identify major contributions of epidemiology.
- Identify frameworks for understanding disease processes.
- Compare and contrast observational studies versus clinical trials.
- Describe different types of study designs.

SELF-ASSESSMENT—WHAT DO YOU KNOW?

1. What is epidemiology?
2. Name a contribution of epidemiology.
3. Identify a difference between observational studies and clinical trials.

Introduction

Epidemiologists are often called "disease detectives" because many focus on finding evidence of the who, what, when, where, and why for diseases and health outcomes in populations. However, most people have never heard of an epidemiologist or epidemiology. Have you ever seen a special health report on the local news where the reporters mention something like "Losing X% of your body weight can lower your risk of developing type 2 diabetes by Y%"? There's epidemiology behind that statement. When you go to the doctor's office and are asked whether you smoke, drink, or have unprotected sex, epidemiology is behind those questions. Epidemiology and its benefits are everywhere in our communities and across the globe.

74 *Public health research methods for partnerships and practice*

What is epidemiology?

Many definitions of epidemiology have evolved over time. The root of the term *epidemiology* suggests that it is a combination of the following Greek words: (1) *epi*, meaning "on or upon;" (2) *demos*, meaning "the common people;" and (3) *logy*, meaning "study." How does that come together to define epidemiology? Simply, it means the study of that which falls upon the common people. However, with the evolution of the definition, the focus has shifted from early emphasis on the study of infectious disease to a more inclusive definition that reflects the broad spectrum of health outcomes (including disease). For the purpose of this chapter, we define *epidemiology* as the study of the frequency, distribution, and determinants of health outcomes (including disease) in human populations and the application of this study to control health problems. That is a lot of terminology. So let's develop this definition in more detail based on the terms used.

Population

In medicine, the individual is the focus. However, in public health, the population is the focus. Populations are the primary focus when epidemiologists are studying health outcomes. They are more concerned about how disease occurs in a population as opposed to in individuals. When speaking of a *population*, we are referring to a group of people with common characteristics. These characteristics can include, but are not limited to, gender, age, race, geographic location, or specific health care services used. Black males who live in East St. Louis, IL, are members of a population that is defined by race, gender, and geographic location. Not only is the definition of the population critical, but the size of the population is just as critical in epidemiology. Counting the presence or occurrence of the health outcome is best used in relation to the size of the population in order to determine the true disease frequency. In most cases, the size of the population is determined by a complete count of the population. A complete count is considered to be a census of the population. How we get the complete count data varies. One common source is the census conducted every 10 years by the federal government as an attempt to count every person in the United States. Another source could be medical records from a federally qualified health center (FQHC), from which researchers might obtain a count of people who use a specific center.

Frequency

In epidemiology, obtaining the *frequency* of a health outcome or disease simply means quantifying how much or how often disease occurs in a population. Epidemiologists use counting as a major tool in determining the frequency of disease in the population. There are three critical steps that have to take place in order to do the counting. First, the definition of disease has to be developed.

Introduction to epidemiology 75

Without a clear definition of the disease in question, it would be impossible to accurately determine who in the population should be counted as having disease. The definitions for diseases can be developed from different methods. Some of these methods include physical exams, lab examinations of body tissue or fluid, results from diagnostic tests, and even symptoms of disease. As an example, a case definition for metabolic syndrome would require the presence of at least three of five metabolic conditions defined by the National Heart, Lung, and Blood Institute of the National Institutes of Health. These conditions are, then, defined by physical and laboratory tests that are used to assess large waistline, high triglyceride level, low HDL cholesterol, high blood pressure, and high fasting blood sugar.[1]

The second step in counting disease in a population is putting a mechanism in place for actually counting cases of disease within the specific population of interest. A number of mechanisms can be used; cancer registries, death certificates, medical records, and national surveys are some examples. For instance, the National Health and Nutrition Examination Survey (NHANES), which began in the early 1960s, is a unique federally funded program of studies that combines interviews with physical examinations. The program was designed to assess both the health and nutritional status of adults and children in the United States.[2] The data are used to determine prevalence of major diseases and risk factors for health outcomes. In the case of using NHANES, the counts and population size are weighted to estimate the prevalence of health outcomes such as anemia, cardiovascular disease, obesity, physical fitness, and diabetes in the US population.

Distribution

In the most general sense, *distribution* is defined as the "position, arrangement, or frequency of occurrence over an area or throughout a space or unit of time."[3] With respect to public health outcomes, the distribution of disease consists of analyzing the disease patterns in relation to who gets disease (person), where disease happens (place), and how it changes over time (time). These patterns serve as the basis by which epidemiologists understand the health of a specific population; develop hypotheses about the factors contributing to disease; and inform the planning, implementation, and evaluation of public health initiatives and programs designed to prevent and control adverse health outcomes.

Determinants

Knowing the person, time, and place of health outcomes is important; however, that knowledge is not fully adequate for preventing and controlling disease in a population. In order to prevent and control disease, factors contributing to change in disease status must be identified. These factors are called determinants and can be causal or preventive. Although many determinants exist, they primarily fall into three categories: individual, environmental, or social. Individual determinants include age, gender, genetics, behaviors, preexisting conditions, and physical activity. A child who plays video games is more likely to be overweight or obese because of the time spent doing a sedentary activity.[4–10]

Environmental and social determinants cover a broad spectrum of factors by which external context changes an individual's health status. Examples of environmental determinants include, but are certainly not limited to, outdoor air pollution, particulate matter in ambient air, and temperature. Social determinants are focused on societal factors. Concentration of poverty, racial residential segregation patterns, and crime rates are just a few examples of societal factors. Social determinants also include features of the built environment like presence of sidewalks, access to safe playgrounds, number of fast food restaurants, and presence/absence of stores that sell fresh fruits and vegetables. Epidemiologists study the pathways and mechanisms by which the determinants of health affect health status.

Basic epidemiologic reasoning

At the core of epidemiology are two relatively basic assumptions. First, disease is not randomly distributed in a population. This lays the foundation for the determinants of health as measurable factors that influence the pattern of disease and the underlying causes of disease. The second assumption is that disease causation is multifactorial. Essentially, there are multiple determinants (i.e., social, individual) interacting to create an environment in which disease occurs. This can be seen in a simple epidemiology triangle using infectious disease as the example (Figure 4.1).

Now, let's consider the West Nile virus outbreak with respect to the epidemiology triangle. The agent is the causal factor—the actual virus. In other

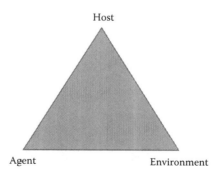

Figure 4.1 Epidemiology triangle for infectious disease. (From Stallybrass, CO, *The Principles of Epidemiology and the Process of Infection*, G Routledge and Son Ltd, London, England, 1931.)

Introduction to epidemiology 77

words, the agent is necessary for disease to occur. The virus alone is not blood-, water-, food-, or airborne, but vector-borne. This means that in order for a person to get West Nile virus, the virus requires a third party, or vector, to be transmitted. In the case of West Nile virus, the vector is known to be mosquitos. The human who catches the disease is the host. Developing disease once infected can be influenced by genetics, deficiencies in the immune system, and more. Environment, as discussed previously in this chapter, is external to the body. High temperatures and standing water create an ideal environment within which mosquitos can multiply. The mosquito is also an environment factor.

The representation of the epidemiologic triangle in Figure 4.1 assumes that the agent, host, and environment are all of equal importance for contracting disease. Although this model does work for most infectious diseases, it is insufficient for chronic diseases like cardiovascular disease, diabetes, and cancer. Chronic diseases are multifactorial in nature.

After much progress in the field of epidemiology since its early days, we can identify two distinct and necessary classes of epidemiology: descriptive and analytic.

Descriptive epidemiology

Descriptive epidemiology places emphasis on the distribution of disease in a population. Specifically, studying the patterns of disease within and across populations involves determining the person, place, and time characteristics. In descriptive epidemiology, an epidemiologist may want to know how avian influenza spreads across continents. One would be looking specifically at the geographic distribution. Epidemiologists use descriptive epidemiology to develop hypotheses that can be tested about the determinants of disease.

Analytic epidemiology

A more in-depth approach than descriptive epidemiology, *analytic epidemiology* focuses on the determinants of disease. Recall that determinants are the factors that influence prevention, occurrence, control, and outcome of disease. Epidemiologists utilize analytic epidemiology to study associations between determinants and the health outcome of interest. In these studies, questions such as "What are the factors that lead to obesity?" would require examining the association among multiple factors and obesity.

Study design in epidemiology

Several types of study designs are used in epidemiology. Before moving forward with descriptions of each study design, one must consider the basic premise for study design in epidemiology. Most studies are conducted in order to determine the relationship between a determinant and a health outcome.

78   *Public health research methods for partnerships and practice*

The study's design begins with the question "Is determinant A related to health outcome Y?" Specifically, the choice of study design highly depends on the research question. In that regard, epidemiologic study designs can be categorized into two major types of studies: experimental and observational.

Experimental study design

As a broad category, the underlying design of an *experimental study* involves assigning individuals to two or more groups. Each group receives a different exposure, drug, intervention, or public health program. The groups are then followed to track the health outcome. The groups are compared to see whether there are differences in the relationship between the determinant and health outcome. Although this is the underlying design, the *randomized controlled trial* (RCT) is a specific type of experimental study design used in public health and is the gold standard design for clinical research.

Randomized controlled trials

For illustrative purposes, RCTs are explained here with some form of treatment as the determinant of interest. Regarded as the gold standard of study designs, the RCT requires two necessary conditions to be considered an experiment. First, the investigator has to be able to manipulate, or control, the treatment. The second is that participants in the study must be randomly assigned to treatment conditions. It is important to note here that there is a difference between random assignment and random selection. *Random assignment* means that all participants have an equal chance of being assigned to any treatment condition. Random assignment happens after participants are selected for the study. Random assignment is used to make sure the treatment groups are comparable. In contrast, *random selection* is a procedure, based on probability, for selecting participants to make sure they are representative of the target population. Random assignment does not require random selection.

Recall that the population of interest must be defined for the purposes of epidemiologic studies. Once the population is defined, study participants are selected from the population based on predetermined eligibility criteria. Eligibility criteria may include, but are not limited to, age, gender, or presence of other health conditions. Eligible participants are then given the choice to participate in the study, typically by way of informed consent. People who choose to participate in the RCT are then randomly assigned to a treatment group, such as an intervention group or control group. A *control group* does not receive the intervention being studied; in most studies, they receive usual care for the condition being examined. These groups are then followed to determine which participants develop the health condition and which do not.

Introduction to epidemiology 79

Strengths of experimental study design

There are several strengths of experimental study design. As the gold standard, experimental studies provide the strongest and most direct evidence of cause-and-effect relationships between the determinant and health outcome.[11] This is a direct result of randomization to treatment group. Additionally, selection and confounding bias are eliminated through the randomization of the study population to treatment conditions. Recall that random assignment of participants ensures that the treatment groups are sufficiently equivalent such that they can be compared based on the treatment group. Finally, the intervention, or treatment/exposure, is controlled. This is particularly critical for attributing between-group differences to the treatment.

Limitations of experimental study design

One of the major limitations of experimental study design concerns sample size. Experimental studies can require large sample sizes in order to determine statistically significant differences between treatment groups. Because of the large sample size and depending on the health outcome, experimental studies can be very time consuming and expensive. Experimental studies may also have limited generalizability to other populations. This is a result of the population definition, eligibility/exclusion criteria, and control of the treatment. Controlling the treatment in a real-world setting is virtually impossible because the researcher no longer has control over the research setting. For example, Dietary Approaches to Stop Hypertension (DASH) was a randomized, controlled-feeding trial of two diets compared to a control diet similar to a typical American diet at the time of the study.[12] The study provided participants with all of their food over 11 weeks. In a real-world setting, income and access to fresh produce could affect whether someone can follow the DASH diet. Last, certain exposures present practical and ethical concerns. For instance, cigarette smoking is a known carcinogenic exposure; thus, it is unethical to expose study participants to cigarette smoke.

Observational study design

In an observational study, researchers observe participants and measure variables of interest without assigning treatment to subjects. Simply stated, the observational study design does not randomly assign participants to an exposure. Here, the investigator passively observes the natural progression of health outcomes in a population. In epidemiology, quasi-experimental, cohort, case-control, and cross-sectional study designs are the most commonly used observational study designs. Descriptions, strengths, and limitations are provided here.

80   *Public health research methods for partnerships and practice*

Quasi-experimental study design

The primary difference between experimental studies and quasi-experimental studies is random assignment. Where random assignment to a treatment condition group is a necessary condition in experimental study design, it is not a requirement for quasi-experimental studies. All other steps in conducting a quasi-experimental study are the same as the steps of an experimental study.

As with experimental study design, a strength of quasi-experimental study design is the intervention, or exposure, being controlled. Quasi-experimental studies can be used to evaluate quality improvement, public health interventions, or health policies for effectiveness. Unlike the experimental study design, quasi-experimental studies may have better external validity. This means that the results from the study can usually be generalized to other populations.[13] While external validity may be improved, the internal validity of a quasi-experimental study may be lacking in comparison to experimental studies. Internal validity refers to how reliable or accurate the study results are.[13] The lower internal validity is due to absence of random assignment of study participants in quasi-experimental studies. Recall that random assignment is used to make the treatment or intervention groups comparable. Ideally, random assignment removes the influence of factors that may cloud the true treatment or intervention effect.

Cohort study design

In a cohort study, eligibility is primarily based on the absence of the health condition of interest. Once eligibility has been determined and participation is chosen by eligible participants, the investigator collects baseline information to classify participants as *exposed* or *not exposed* to the determinant of interest. From *baseline*, or the start point of the study, participants are followed over time to see whether they develop the health condition. Typically, health status and other determinants of interest are assessed at predetermined intervals. For example, the Nurses' Health Study is a cohort study of health outcomes among nurses that began in the 1970s.[14] Follow-up with the participating nurses is done every 2 years. This means that participants have received questionnaires to complete every 2 years since they enrolled in the study.

A major strength of the cohort design is the ability to calculate incidence rates and relative risk. *Incidence* refers to new cases of the health outcome since baseline. *Relative risk* is used to compare the risk of developing the health outcome among participants who were exposed and participants who were not exposed. Cohort studies also allow for the study of multiple diseases over time. In addition, this study design is suitable for the study of rare exposures. In cohort studies, the exposure, by design, clearly occurred before the health outcome of interest.

The exposure of interest cannot be controlled in cohort studies, whereas it can in experimental studies. Cohort studies are also time consuming and

Introduction to epidemiology 81

expensive. Since the investigator is observing disease progression in a natural setting, cohort studies are not efficient for studying rare diseases. Finally, participants may drop out of the study over time. This is commonly referred to as *loss to follow-up*. Loss to follow-up can lead to bias in the results, especially if the loss to follow-up is due to the development of the disease.

Case-control study design

Eligibility in a case-control study is based on the presence of disease. Study participants are selected because they have the disease or health outcome of interest, and a suitable control group composed of participants who do not have the disease of interest is defined for comparison. Once the cases and controls have been selected, participants are then asked about their exposure history.

Case-control studies are suitable, often ideal, for the study of rare diseases since, by design, participants already have disease; researchers do not have to wait to determine whether disease will develop over time. Furthermore, case-control studies are suitable for the study of diseases with long latency periods. In contrast to cohort studies, case-control studies allow the investigator to study multiple exposures or determinants for a single disease. A major strength of the case-control design is that it is less expensive and less time consuming than other types of studies.

Although they have considerable strengths, case-control studies also have important limitations. Unlike cohort studies, case-control studies are inefficient for studying diseases with rare exposures. Also, it is more difficult to establish whether the exposure came before the disease since the investigator is relying on past exposure. In case-control studies, the investigator cannot calculate incidence, as disease is present at the start of the study. This also means the investigator cannot calculate the relative risk. In case-control studies, certain types of bias are more likely to occur. For example, recall bias is very likely since the investigator relies on the participant's exposure history. Finally, selecting a comparable control population is very challenging.

Cross-sectional study design

Unlike any of the previous study designs, the defining characteristic of cross-sectional studies is the assessment of exposure and outcome at the same time. It is considered to be a snapshot of population health at a specific point in time. For example, the National Health Interview Survey (NHIS) is conducted every year via an interview that asks questions about disease status and exposure status.

The cross-sectional study allows for characterizing the prevalence, or presence, of multiple exposures and health conditions in a population. Cross-sectional studies are far less time consuming than other study designs; thus, they can be conducted relatively quickly. Also, cross-sectional studies are ideal

82 *Public health research methods for partnerships and practice*

for generating hypotheses to test using other study designs. This study design is the most commonly used study design in public health practice because it is quick and less expensive than other study designs. A major, and most important, limitation of the cross-sectional study is that an investigator cannot determine the temporal sequence between exposure and disease. There is also no random assignment in cross-sectional studies.

Range of study validity

In this section describing study designs in epidemiology, they were described in order of validity of the scientific evidence. Experimental studies are, as previously stated, considered to be of highest validity of all study designs, whereas cross-sectional studies have low validity for studying the relationship between the exposure and health condition.[13]

Determining causality in observational studies

In 1965, Sir A. B. Hill[15] suggested several guidelines for determining the causal relationship between a determinant and a health outcome. These guidelines are not intended to be a fixed checklist for causality but more of a guide to determining whether causality is possible. Some of the critical Hill criteria are described here.

Strength of association

The stronger the association between the exposure and disease, the more likely it is that the exposure is causal in relation to the disease. When the association is strong, it is less likely to be attributable to bias than in the case of a weak association.[15] However, a weak association does not mean that the relationship between exposure and disease cannot be causal. Nonetheless, it does make it harder to rule out bias and confounding as reasons for the association between exposure and disease. A hypothetical example of a strong association would be that smokers are nine times more likely to develop lung cancer than nonsmokers.

Temporality

Temporality, or time sequence, requires that the exposure must occur prior to the development of disease. The exposure must be present for a time period that is consistent with the proposed biological mechanism driving the relationship between the exposure and disease.[15] This particular guideline is harder to prove in some study designs, such as a cross-sectional study design. For example, a cohort study of smokers and nonsmokers starts with these two groups when they are free of the disease of interest and follows them to determine the occurrence of lung cancer subsequently.

Introduction to epidemiology   83

Biological gradient

The *biological gradient* is often referred to as a *dose-response relationship*. This means that the strength of association between exposure and disease increases with intensity or duration of the exposure as predicted.[15] For example, lung cancer mortality increases with the number of cigarettes smoked. Some outcomes actually require a threshold to be met before incident disease is observed. Polycystic ovary syndrome, as an example, requires that a woman's serum anti-Müllerian hormone (AMH) be at least 35 pmol/L before being defined as incident disease.[16]

Consistency upon repeatability

Studies are often repeated using different populations and research methods to determine whether the relationship between exposure and disease are consistent. However, the absence or lack of consistency does not rule out a causal relationship. This inconsistency may be the result of studies using different exposure level definitions. In keeping with the lung cancer example, at least 36 cohort studies have shown smoking to be associated with lung cancer.

Biological plausibility

Plausibility means that there are known or claimed biological, or social, mechanisms that explain the relationship between exposure and disease. For example, cigarettes are known to contain carcinogenic substances.[15] Carcinogens, by definition, are known, potentially cancer-causing agents. It is important to point out that there are epidemiologic studies that have demonstrated and identified cause-effect relationships between exposure and disease prior to the discovery of the biological or social mechanisms. For example, in the 1848 cholera outbreak in England and Wales, it was demonstrated that the water from a specific pump was the source of disease and that cholera was not airborne.[17]

Basic epidemiologic measures

Up to this point, associations between exposure and disease have been discussed but not defined in detail. Fractions are important for studying associations; thus, division is often used in epidemiology as a technique for calculating associations. Fractions have both a numerator and a denominator. One of the most difficult tasks in epidemiology is determining the correct and most appropriate denominator to use. In this section, the basic epidemiologic measures are described to provide further understanding of how epidemiologists determine the association between an exposure and a disease.

As mentioned previously in this chapter, counts are a major part of epidemiology. In epidemiology, the count is a simple addition of all the cases (e.g.,

84   *Public health research methods for partnerships and practice*

550 cases of chlamydia on a private university campus). A proportion is a count divided by a meaningful denominator (e.g., 550 cases/24,000 [private university population] or 2.29%).

Rates in epidemiology

Rates are a special type of proportion used in epidemiology. As a requirement, some unit of time is always incorporated into a rate. Additionally, everyone in the denominator must be at risk for being in the numerator. This means that if a person is to be counted as a disease case in the numerator, that person has to be at risk for developing disease during that time period. It is important to note here that whereas all rates are proportions, not all proportions are rates. Time is the necessary factor for rates, not proportions. Several common types of rates in epidemiology are summarized below.

Crude rates

- Estimate actual disease frequency in a population.
- Can be used to provide data for the allocation of health resources and public health programming.
- Can be misleading if compared over time or across populations, as they do not take into account distribution of age or other factors.

Adjusted (or standardized) rates

- Are computed to remove effect of age or other factors from the crude rates.
- Allow for meaningful comparison across populations when age distributions are different for populations being compared.

Prevalence

- Indicates the number of existing cases of disease in a population at a given time.
- Is calculated using the following equation: (# existing cases)/(total population at a point in time).

Incidence rate (IR)

- Is used to describe the number of new cases of disease that develop in a population during a defined time period.
- Is a rate because
    - It incorporates a unit of time.
    - All persons in the denominator are at risk of being in the numerator (i.e., at risk of developing disease during the specified time period).

Introduction to epidemiology 85

- It is calculated using the following equation: (# new cases)/(total *person-time* of observation). A *person-time* is the time that an individual is at risk of disease during the study period.

Relative risk (RR)

- Is the ratio of two incidence rates.
- Provides risk of one group developing disease compared to another.
  - Example: Men are 1.5 times more likely to develop cardiovascular disease than women.
- Is also called *rate ratio* or *risk ratio*.
- Is a number ranging from 0 to infinity.
  - The number 1 indicates that there is no association between exposure and disease.
  - Relative risk that is greater than 0 and less than 1 (0 < RR < 1) indicates that incidence in those who are unexposed is higher than incidence in those who are exposed; i.e., the exposure is beneficial.
  - Relative risk that is greater than 1 (RR > 1) indicates that incidence among those exposed is greater than incidence among those who are unexposed; exposure is detrimental.

Odds ratio (OR)

- Is the ratio of two relative odds.
- Provides odds of disease occurring in one exposure group compared to another.
  - Example: The odds of having cardiovascular disease is 1.5 times higher among men compared to women.
- Is a number ranging from 0 to infinity.
  - The number 1 indicates exposure not associated with odds of disease.
  - An OR that is greater than 0 and less than 1 (0 < OR < 1) indicates that exposure is associated with lower odds of disease.
  - An OR that is greater than 1 (OR > 1) indicates that exposure is associated with higher odds of disease.
- Case-control and cross-sectional studies use ORs to approximate the RR.

Basic setup for epidemiologic studies

The most basic form of organizing the data from an epidemiologic study is a 2×2 table. There are 2 rows and 2 columns. The 2×2 table categorizes study participants by exposure status and disease status. Exposure is set up as the rows and disease status as the columns. The 2×2 table (Figure 4.2) is used to calculate a number of basic epidemiologic measures.

86   *Public health research methods for partnerships and practice*

Disease

Exposure	Yes	No
Yes	A	B
No	C	D

Figure 4.2 2×2 table for basic epidemiologic study.

Relative risk

- Incidence among exposed (IR_E) = a/(a + b)
- Incidence among unexposed (IR_U) = c/(c + d)
- Relative risk = IR_E/IR_U = [a/(a + b)]/[c/(c + d)]

Odds ratio

- Odds of disease given exposure $(O_{D|E})$ = a/c
- Odds of no disease given exposure $(O_{D-|E})$ = b/d
- Odds ratio = $O_{D|E}/O_{D-|E}$ = (a/c)/(b/d) = (a × d)/(b × c)

Conclusions

Epidemiology is the study of disease frequency, distribution, and determinants in populations and the control of disease through application of such study. Disease determinants are factors that impact disease distribution and are critical for understanding how to control and prevent disease. Three major categories of determinants are individual, environmental, and social. Environmental and social determinants of disease describe the context within which an individual lives. In epidemiology, it is assumed that disease is not randomly distributed in the population of interest and that disease causation is multifactorial. There are multiple ways to study the multifactorial nature of disease: RCTs, quasi-experimental studies, cohort studies, case-control studies, and cross-sectional studies. RCTs, quasi-experimental studies, and cohort studies establish the presence of determinants of health prior to developing disease, whereas the temporal nature of exposure and disease are less clear in case-control and cross-sectional studies. As suggested by Sir A. B. Hill,[15]

Introduction to epidemiology 87

guidelines for evaluating causality in observational studies include strength of association, time sequence, dose-response relationship, consistency upon repetition, and biological plausibility. Basic epidemiologic measures include counts, proportions, rates, prevalence, incidence, RR, and ORs. These measures are used to quantify and test associations between determinants and disease. Finally, epidemiologic measures comprise the scientific evidence for public health policy and program planning, implementation, and evaluation.

References

1. What is metabolic syndrome? National Heart, Lung, and Blood Institute Web site. https://www.nhlbi.nih.gov/health/health-topics/topics/ms#. Updated June 22, 2016. Accessed February 3, 2017.
2. National Health and Nutrition Examination Survey, 2013–2014 overview. National Center for Health Statistics Web site. https://wwwn.cdc.gov/nchs/nhanes /ContinuousNhanes/Overview.aspx?BeginYear=2013. Accessed February 23, 2017.
3. Distribution. Merriam-Webster Web site. https://www.merriam-webster.com /dictionary/distribution. Accessed February 5, 2017.
4. Whitt-Glover MC, Taylor WC, Floyd MF, Yore MM, Yancey AK, Matthews CE. Disparities in physical activity and sedentary behaviors among US children and adolescents: Prevalence, correlates, and intervention implications. *J Public Health Policy*. 2009;30(suppl 1):S309–S334. doi:10.1057/jphp.2008.46.
5. Nesbit KC, Kolobe TA, Arnold SH, Sisson SB, Anderson MP. Proximal and distal environmental correlates of adolescent obesity. *J Phys Act Heal*. 2014;11(6):1179–1186. doi:10.1123/jpah.2012-0245.
6. Liu J, Bennett KJ, Harun N, Probst JC. Urban-rural differences in overweight status and physical inactivity among US children aged 10–17 years. *J Rural Heal*. 2008;24(4):407–415. doi:10.1111/j.1748-0361.2008.00188.x.
7. Staiano AE, Harrington DM, Broyles ST, Gupta AK, Katzmarzyk PT. Television, adiposity, and cardiometabolic risk in children and adolescents. *Am J Prev Med*. 2013;44(1):40–47. doi:10.1016/j.amepre.2012.09.049.
8. Merchant AT, Dehghan M, Behnke-Cook D, Anand SS. Diet, physical activity, and adiposity in children in poor and rich neighbourhoods: A cross-sectional comparison. *Nutr J*. 2007;6:1. doi:10.1186/1475-2891-6-1.
9. Nelson MC, Gordon-Larsen P, Adair LS, Popkin BM. Adolescent physical activity and sedentary behavior: Patterning and long-term maintenance. *Am J Prev Med*. 2005;28(3):259–266. doi:10.1016/j.amepre.2004.12.006.
10. Carroll-Scott A, Gilstad-Hayden K, Rosenthal L et al. Disentangling neighborhood contextual associations with child body mass index, diet, and physical activity: The role of built, socioeconomic, and social environments. *Soc Sci Med*. 2013;95:106–114. doi:10.1016/j.socscimed.2013.04.003.
11. Guyatt G, Sackett D, Sinclair J et al. Users' guides to the medical literature. IX. A method for grading health care recommendations. *JAMA*. 1995;274(22):1800–1804. http://dx.doi.org/10.1001/jama.1995.03530220066035.
12. Sacks FM, Obarzanek E, Windhauser MM et al. Rationale and design of the Dietary Approaches to Stop Hypertension trial (DASH). A multicenter controlled-feeding study of dietary patterns to lower blood pressure. *Ann Epidemiol*. 1995;5(2):108–118. doi:10.1016/1047-2797(94)00055-X.
13. Godwin M, Ruhland L, Casson I et al. Pragmatic controlled clinical trials in primary care: The struggle between external and internal validity. *BMC Med Res Methodol*. 2003;3(1):28. doi:10.1186/1471-2288-3-28.

88 *Public health research methods for partnerships and practice*

14. Stampfer MJ, Willett WC, Colditz GA, Rosner B, Speizer FE, Hennekens CH. A prospective study of postmenopausal estrogen therapy and coronary heart disease. *N Engl J Med.* 1985;313(17):1044–1049. doi:10.1056/NEJM198510243131703.
15. Hill A. The environment and disease: Association or causation? *Proc R Soc Med.* 1965;58(8):295–300.
16. Dewailly D, Gronier H, Poncelet E et al. Diagnosis of polycystic ovary syndrome (PCOS): Revisiting the threshold values of follicle count on ultrasound and of the serum AMH level for the definition of polycystic ovaries. *Hum Reprod.* 2011;26(11):3123–3129. doi:10.1093/humrep/der297.
17. Parkes E. Mode of Communication of Cholera. By John Snow, MD: Second Edition - London, 1855, p 162. *Int J Epidemiol.* 2013;42(6):1543–1552. doi:10.1093/ije/dyt193.

Activity

At a block party, 100 community members are in attendance. Some people get sick after eating certain foods; numbers are provided in Table 4.1.

Which food (chicken, burgers, potato salad, or ice cream) is most likely to be the cause of sickness?

Table 4.1 Number of people who ate a certain food compared to the number of sick people

Food eaten (Number of people)	Number of sick people
Chicken (35)	10
Burger (20)	5
Potato salad (40)	23
Ice cream (60)	15

SELF-ASSESSMENT—WHAT DID YOU LEARN?

1. One of the fundamental premises underlying the study of epidemiology is that _____.
   a. Disease, illness, and ill health are randomly distributed in a population
   b. Disease, illness, and ill health are not randomly distributed in a population
   c. Disease, illness, and ill health are only randomly distributed in large populations
   d. Disease, illness, and ill health are very rarely distributed in large populations

Introduction to epidemiology   89

2. A framework for understanding disease processes should include _____.
   a.   Individual determinants only
   b.   Individual, environmental, and social determinants
   c.   Environmental and social determinants only
   d.   Social determinants only

3. Epidemiology is the study of the _____.
   a.   Occurrence of epidemics
   b.   Distribution and determinants of disease frequency on the population level
   c.   Determinants of an individual's likelihood to get a disease
   d.   Individual's future health

4. Epidemiologists are interested in learning about _____.
   a.   The causes of diseases and how to cure or control them
   b.   The frequency and geographic distribution of diseases
   c.   The causal relationships between diseases
   d.   All of the above

5. _____ are the causes and other factors that influence the occurrence of health-related events.
   a.   Grounds
   b.   Sources
   c.   Determinants
   d.   Contributing factors

6. Clinical trials differ from observational studies because _____.
   a.   Clinical trials only occur in hospitals
   b.   Clinical trials feature an intervention
   c.   Observational studies do not require informed consent
   d.   Observational studies occur only in the community

7. Prevalence refers to _____.
   a.   The number of existing cases of a disease or health condition in a population at some designated time
   b.   The occurrence of new disease within a defined period in a population
   c.   A summary rate based on the actual number of events in a population over a given time period
   d.   A measure that refers to the mortality rate associated with a specific cause of death

90   *Public health research methods for partnerships and practice*

8. Which is a major contribution of epidemiology?
   a. Surgeon General's warnings on cigarette cartons
   b. Development of vaccine for smallpox
   c. Discovery of cholera as a waterborne disease
   d. All of the above

9. When determining causation, the idea that an effect has to occur after the cause is known as _____.
   a. Consistency
   b. Plausibility
   c. Temporality
   d. Specificity

10. Incidence rates are calculated to estimate the presence of existing disease in a population.
    a. True
    b. False

11. An odds ratio can be used to estimate relative risk in a case-control study.
    a. True
    b. False

5 Cultural competency

Victoria Walker and
Vetta Sanders Thompson

LEARNING OBJECTIVES

- Define cultural competency.
- Describe the need for culturally competent research and practice, based on a historical perspective.
- Identify contributing risk factors for health disparities.
- Identify skills associated with cultural competent practices.

SELF-ASSESSMENT—WHAT DO YOU KNOW?

1. What is culture?
2. Why is it important for health care professionals to be culturally competent?
3. What are the components of cultural competence?
4. On what levels (e.g., individual, organizational, etc.) can there be cultural competency?

Introduction

Culture is heavily entwined in the human experience, and its complexity can make it difficult to grasp. Encounters with different cultural groups can create a shocking reality that life is not the same for all, and there is great variation in how people think, believe, behave, and interact. *Culture* can be defined as the thoughts, actions, beliefs, and values of a group. Culture also provides a frame and lens in which the world is viewed and how thoughts, actions, beliefs, and values outside of the group are interpreted and understood.[1] Culture does not stand outside the influences of political, economic, religious, biological, and psychological factors.[2] Instead, these factors contribute to the development of the beliefs and values that are embodied by thoughts and actions observed in the group.[2]

92 *Public health research methods for partnerships and practice*

Race, ethnicity, and nationality

Culture is often referenced by race or ethnicity and nationality. As a starting point, it can demonstrate the definitional aspects of culture and provide insight on the variability of culture. For example, the ethnic category of Hispanic/ Latino includes individuals whose origins are countries in South America and North America. The ethnic category does not provide context on which country (i.e., Bolivia, Puerto Rico, Mexico, Colombia, Peru, Ecuador, etc.) an individual claims as his or her homeland or origin. Inasmuch as *Hispanic/ Latino* provides a cultural reference, a person's nationality provides a cultural reference that alludes to variations that may differ from the larger cultural group. Examples of variation can include local dialects, customs, traditional clothing, music, food, practices, and much more. The level of variation can go further to include differences by geographical areas and residential context (urban cities and rural towns) within countries. This can also hold true for other race/ethnicity and nationality categories such as Asian, African, European, and American. From this example, it can be gleaned that culture is more complex than belonging to a race or ethnic group. The thoughts, actions, beliefs, and values of a racial or ethnicity group are fluid and susceptible to differences by other factors (e.g., national origin, income, residential context).

As important as it is to recognize cultural differences, it is equally important to recognize with what group(s) the individual self-identifies and that most individuals self-identify into multiple groups, creating intersectionality. To expound, intersectionality is at play when a black woman participates in feminist and racial justice efforts. Identifying as a woman, she sees the value of advancing women in society; identifying as black, she sees the importance of bringing an end to racism and racially discriminatory practices. Furthermore, it demonstrates that culture is both collective and individual, and it is more fluid than rigid. A person may belong to a cultural group, yet he or she may have attitudes and behaviors that are contrary to the more collective group. In a way, this makes it difficult to label, or stereotype, a person as having certain characteristics by belonging to a cultural group.

Culture in a broader context

The term *group* in the definition of culture is broader than race and ethnicity. Group can be more loosely defined as community, profession, organization, or association. Even in these terms, it is evident that there are differences in thoughts, actions, beliefs, and values among different cultural groups. These differences allow for a more complex view of an individual's culture beyond race or ethnicity and its variations. As a reference, the health care setting— particularly the professions of nursing and medicine (physicians)—has a culture that governs behaviors among colleagues and patients.[3] In these professional roles, race and ethnicity are not forgotten or neglected; they still impact the attitudes and behaviors of the physicians and nurses. Consider the

Cultural competency 93

situation of a Vietnamese primary care physician. The physician is trained to diagnose, treat, and provide medical counseling to all persons. However, if the physician were to treat a Vietnamese patient, a level of comfort and familiarity may be established between the two because of a shared cultural experience that may not be readily available with other non-Vietnamese patients. Ideally, the quality of care that the Vietnamese physician provides would not vary from patient to patient, but the effect of race and ethnicity on physician-patient interaction cannot be ignored and has the potential to impact patient outcomes.

An ever-changing culture

In this context, people are multicultural layers of lived experiences.[1] Each cultural lens helps people to decode and understand the world.[1] A more critical analysis indicates that culture does not exist within a vacuum and is not static, but dynamic in nature.[2] As stated previously, culture can be affected by many influential factors—political, religious, economic, etc.[2] These influential factors can affect the collective cultural group and individual culture for even more variation. The evidence of cultural shifts can be seen throughout the history of the world. In the history of the United States, political factors introduced a culture of freedom, equality, and fair representation that allowed 13 colonies to unify and break away from Great Britain. Almost 100 years after that conflict, religious and economic factors influenced a cultural shift that resulted in the Civil War, which still impacts US culture.

Cultural shifts can have historical significance in the collective or individual culture and lead to the development of new values and beliefs. As technological advancements have led to near-instantaneous global reach and access to information, considerably more influential factors exist to shift cultural groups' thoughts, actions, beliefs, and values. Whether these cultural shifts happen fast or slowly, resistance can occur from the collective or individual culture that desires to remain static. In this regard, the diverging of the culture can bring about cross-cultural conflicts that make evident the fragility of cultural bonds even within a cultural group.

Diversity and culture

So how does diversity relate to culture? *Diversity* is sometimes used politely to discuss cultural differences, racism, and oppressions that racial/ethnic minority groups experience.[4] At its core, the term *diversity* encompasses all the ways that differences may occur among people. Categorically, these differences can be seen by gender identity, sexual orientation, race/ethnicity, religion, SES, political ideology, and more. Diversity and culture are sides of the same coin. Culture provides a context in which a group has a shared life experience; in contrast, diversity points out the polarity of the shared life experiences among groups of people.

94 *Public health research methods for partnerships and practice*

Discussions on diversity focus often on the "respect, dignity, and inclusion for all people."[4] Approaches on how to reach this goal may vary and include building cross-cultural bridges; educating on the legal and federal laws for inclusion; pitching economic and business practices in the global economy and workforce; and calling out prejudices, racism, sexism, and all other "isms" as they are seen.[4] Each of these approaches addresses micro- and macro-level systems of power and domination that can repress and oppress minority groups so that they are not fully being included and allowed to participate in society.[4] Embracing diversity requires systems and infrastructures that are easily accessed and utilized by all people. Although no "one size fits all" solution exists, many guiding principles and standards exist that have been developed over the years for greater inclusion and cultural competence by individuals and within organizations.

Cultural competence

Over time, organizations with policy and regulatory authority have moved to define what is meant by cultural competence. These efforts are aimed at providing health care providers, as well as researchers, with clearer guidance on those activities that will promote health equity and reduce health disparities.[5] Cultural competence definitions acknowledge the need to accommodate the changing US demographic.[5] In the national standards of the Culturally and Linguistically Appropriate Services in Health and Health Care (known as CLAS), from the HHS Office of Minority Health (OMH), *cultural competence* is defined as "care and services that are respectful of and responsive to the cultural and linguistic needs of all individuals."[5,6]

In accordance with the CLAS definition, health care interventions, services, research explanations, and protocols should be delivered in the individual's preferred language and should take into account cultural preferences. In addition to being responsive to demographic shifts, it is believed that provision of sensitive health care services and CBPR are required to reduce gaps in health care outcomes among racial/ethnic minorities, individuals of low income and education, those with limited English proficiency and low health literacy, as well as other marginalized populations.

In 1997, the OMH undertook the development of national standards to provide organizations and providers with guidance on the implementation of culturally and linguistically appropriate services, and in December of 2000, CLAS standards were entered into the Federal Register.[5] The original CLAS standards were organized by themes: culturally competent care, language access services, and organizational supports for cultural competence. CLAS included three types of standards. The standards in the first category were mandates, which were required of all recipients of federal funds and were composed of four standards for language access services.[5] Although a great deal of attention focused on addressing the needs of speakers of limited English, these standards covered sensory-related communication needs also, including those of individuals who are deaf, hard of hearing, and blind, as

Cultural competency 95

well as those with limited health literacy.[7] The standards in the second category were guidelines, which consisted of nine provision and training standards for cultural competence services that OMH recommended that federal, state, and national accrediting bodies adopt. Finally, the standards included a recommendation for public reporting on the progress of CLAS implementation; public reporting was considered voluntary.[5]

Ongoing research spurred continued interest in cultural competence. In 2001, the Institute of Medicine (IOM) identified social and cultural influences as important to health outcomes and provided strong recommendations that research in these areas be advanced.[8,9] In *Crossing the Quality Chasm: A New Health System for the 21st Century*, the IOM suggested the need for studies of health behaviors and other social variables in the context of culture in order to understand why groups adopt or do not adopt health recommendations.[8] In *Unequal Treatment: Confronting Racial and Ethnic Disparities in Health Care*, the IOM examined the role that provider bias, lack of cultural competence, and communication barriers might play in health disparities, again suggesting the need for additional research.[9] Research and resulting reports contributed to policy efforts to speed progress toward equity and cultural competence in health and health care.

In 2003, The Joint Commission conducted an analysis of its standards for cultural and linguistic appropriateness in comparison to the CLAS standards.[10] The study's findings showed significant overlap in standards, although The Joint Commission standards were less prescriptive than the CLAS standards. The Joint Commission continued its reviews and analyses of practices and standards, resulting in new guidelines in 2009 and a document published in 2010 to assist hospitals and health care organizations with implementation.

The Joint Commission, which accredits and certifies health care organizations and programs in the United States, has noted that addressing patients' cultural and linguistic needs plays a role in the successful delivery of health care services.[10] According to The Joint Commission, cultural competence is "the ability of health care providers and health care organizations to understand and respond effectively to the cultural and language needs brought by the patient to the health care encounter."[10] In order to meet the definition of cultural competence, organizations and those they employ are expected to "value diversity, assess themselves, manage the dynamics of difference, acquire and institutionalize cultural knowledges, and adapt to diversity and cultural contexts of patients and the communities served."[10]

Other organizations have provided definitions that contribute to the understanding and implementation of cultural competence. For example, the National Alliance for Hispanic Health defines cultural proficiency as the ability of health care organizations to "do more than provide unbiased care as they value the positive role culture can play in a person's health and well-being."[11] The discussions by CLAS and The Joint Commission on cultural competence remind all involved in health care services and research that much of the cultural competence guidance provided has a foundation in federal law

96 *Public health research methods for partnerships and practice*

and regulation, including Title VI of the Civil Rights Act of 1964, Section 504 of the Rehabilitation Act of 1973, the Americans with Disabilities Act (ADA), Title XVIII of the Social Security Act, the Hill-Burton Act, and the Age Discrimination Act of 1975.[5,10]

Who should practice cultural competency?

It is important for those interested in public health and health-related research to understand that cultural competence applies to individuals (e.g., researchers, practitioners, educators) and organizations. Federal guidance is clear that all organizations receiving federal funds should adhere to the standards for culturally and linguistically appropriate services.[5] Health care organizations seeking accreditation from The Joint Commission are similarly held to the standards promulgated.[10] The Joint Commission and CLAS standards apply to organizations; however, each set of standards holds the organization accountable for assuring that all employees also meet standards of cultural competence at every point of the health care contact. Professionals working in the fields of health and public health should examine their codes of ethics and professional practice standards for requirements related to culturally competent practice, such as those published for nursing, psychology, and social work.[12–15] The researchers who are most likely to encounter requirements to engage in culturally competent research are those likely to be engaged in CBPR or community action research, both of which embrace the principles espoused in the definitions of cultural competence previously mentioned.[16,17] However, researchers who are not engaged in CBPR, but whose research focuses on minority and other vulnerable populations with cultures different from that of the researcher, may encounter requirements from their institutional review board (IRB), funding sources, or other entities responsible for research.

The need for culturally competent research and practice

One of the seminal works that pushed the cultural competence curriculum into medical school was *The Spirit Catches You and You Fall Down: A Hmong Child, Her American Doctors and the Collision of Two Cultures* by Anne Fadiman.[18] The book uses an anthropologic lens to give an account of how the Western biomedical view of health and sickness is not universal among cultural groups.[18] Although cultural competence curricula have become prominent in medical schools, the best methods to teach and to evaluate their impact on health outcomes are continuing to be developed.[19,20] Training on cultural competency still leaves a gap in personal responsibility and accountability at an organizational level.[21] The issues of engaging cultural groups and providing culturally appropriate care are not left solely to the practice of medicine, but also extend to research and public health practices.

The history of research misconduct in ethnic minority communities has fueled a level of mistrust that some argue inhibits participation in research.[22] The most prominent example of this misconduct is known as the Tuskegee Syphilis Study (explained in detail in Chapter 12).[22,23] More recently, public awareness of the case of Henrietta Lacks has renewed concerns about the ethics of health researchers working in diverse communities.[24] These cases are important, and scholars increasingly site the failure to recruit diverse research participants as an issue of concern.[23]

Equity is a key feature of efforts to reduce health disparities and improve health outcomes.[5,25,26] An equity focus suggests assurance of appropriate services, service delivery strategies, and the resources required for health without respect to race, education, health literacy, age, sexual orientation, ethnicity, religion, physical or mental disability, language, sex, gender identity, income, or class.[5,25,26] In addition, reviews suggest that research on culture and social determinants assists in understanding when, why, and how evidence-based interventions should be culturally adapted to increase health equity.[26–28] Thus, cultural competence is a key component of organizational efforts to improve the public's health.[27,28]

Growing recognition of the role of cultural and linguistic appropriateness in quality care stimulated the review, update, and revision of the original CLAS standards. The enhanced CLAS standards are broader and are intended to apply to every point of contact in health-promoting systems, including mental and social well-being, and they encompass services to individuals and group consumers of health care services.[5] The standards were designed to be consistent with and to support other national health policies, including the ACA, beginning with the principal standard that calls for "effective, equitable, understandable, and respectful quality care and services that are responsive to diverse cultural health beliefs and practices, preferred languages, health literacy, and other communication needs."[5]

BOX 5.1

How easy or difficult is it for you to talk about cultural difference or interact with people from other cultural backgrounds?

With calls for research on culture and social determinants, it became important that researchers, as well as practitioners, be culturally aware and competent. Researchers had to learn to work effectively in culturally diverse settings so that trust and partnerships could be developed and maintained.[16,17] In 2000, the Council of Psychological Associations for the Advancement of Ethnic Minority Interests issued guidelines for culturally competent psychological research.[15] In addition, CBPR principles provided guidelines for this

98 *Public health research methods for partnerships and practice*

work.[16,17] These and other guidelines required core considerations and activities that are described subsequent to this point in the chapter.

Culturally competent research requires that communities and participants be met with openness and acceptance, regardless of their cultural background.[5,15–17] The development of trusting relationships is particularly important if the research is to be long-term and is on sensitive topics.[16,17] To assure that all individuals have access to high-quality services and treatments, it is important that researchers obtain honest, high-quality evaluation and research data. Culturally appropriate evaluation and research assess the appropriateness of the methods and practices being utilized, not just the outcomes.[15] To accomplish this aim, researchers assure that interventions are designed using the best existing evidence and services to achieve the intended outcomes in a culturally appropriate manner. Asking the right question in research is very important, perhaps more important than the methods for finding an answer to the question. In addition, it is important to include members or appropriate community representatives in the development of design, methodology, and information dissemination. The community participates to assist, reflect on, and critique how research questions and the research design are constructed.[15–17]

It is critical that researchers ask whether they have the necessary cultural competence to do the work.[15] Appropriate experience includes examination of minority group experience, including any history of prejudice and discrimination. Researchers are responsible for assuring that appropriate theories, valid assessment tools, and internally and externally valid research methodologies are used. The questions that should be addressed include whether the reliability and/or validity of the measures selected have been established for the population or populations involved in the research; whether the language usage level is appropriate for the population; whether the length of the measure is appropriate; and whether the informed consents, research protocols, and research task instructions and descriptions are conveyed fully in language understandable to the participant.[15] A part of culturally competent research is understanding the heterogeneity of diverse groups and limitations to studies when samples are limited or restricted in some way. The enhanced CLAS standards established data collection categories, standards, and processes to assist in obtaining high-quality evaluation and research data.[5]

Efforts to deliver high-quality services require standards for cultural adaptation of evidence-based treatments and services. Castro et al.[29] identify steps to guide decisions to culturally adapt evidence-based interventions. The time and effort required to complete a cultural adaptation must be justified. Reasons for adaptation include failure of an intervention to sufficiently engage members of diverse populations and/or the presence of unique risk factors or symptoms. Once cultural adaptations have been justified, changes can be made in program content and delivery.[29] Early discussions of cultural adaptation emphasized "surface" and "deep structures" of modification.[30] Surface structure modifications involve inclusion of visual elements (photos,

Cultural competency 99

symbols), recruitment, and outreach strategies. Resnicow et al.[30] also refer to the "deep structure" of cultural adaptation that incorporates a group's cultural values, beliefs, and behaviors, which are recognized, reinforced, and built upon to provide context and meaning to important components of the intervention. The second form of cultural adaptation frameworks focuses on defining the steps of the intervention adaptation process.[29,31] Barrera et al.[31] reviewed the literature to identify five stages of cultural adaptation. These steps are information gathering, preliminary design, preliminary testing, refinement, and final trial. Barrera and colleagues suggest that interventions involving the inclusion of cultural elements in an adaptation are more effective than control or usual care conditions.

Health disparities

The 1985 publication of the *Secretary's Task Force Report on Black and Minority Health*, also known as the *Heckler Report*, was the first time in HHS history that health disparities of ethnic and racial minorities were documented.[32] Since this milestone, an extensive amount of research and resources have gone towards identifying the causes of health disparities. Historically, health disparities have been defined by the differences in morbidity, mortality, incidence, and prevalence of diseases among cultural groups.[33] Braveman et al.[33] introduced a more comprehensive definition of health disparities as "health differences that adversely affect socially disadvantaged groups" and that are systematic, plausibly avoidable health differences according to race/ethnicity, skin color, religion, or nationality; socioeconomic resources or position (reflected by, e.g., income, wealth, education, or occupation); gender, sexual orientation, gender identity; age, geography, disability, illness, political or other affiliation; or other characteristics associated with discrimination or marginalization.

This definition makes two poignant points: (1) health disparities can happen among an array of cultural groups, and (2) the presence of these systematic social disadvantages is causing unfair and unjust differences in health outcomes. Braveman et al.[33] argue that health disparities cannot be defined without addressing the "unfavorable social, economic, or political conditions" that are commonly known as the *social determinants of health*.

Social determinants of health and critical race theory

According to the WHO, the social determinants of health are "the conditions, in which people are born, grow, work, live, and age, and the wider set of forces and systems shaping the conditions of daily life."[34] (See Chapter 2 for an in-depth discussion of the social determinants of health.) If health disparities are defined by adverse social determinants of health, how do these determinants of health have an impact on cultural groups through the policies, systems, and infrastructures in society? Additionally, how do organizations

100 *Public health research methods for partnerships and practice*

and institutions address these social disadvantages through a culturally competent framework?

Critical race theory (CRT) provides a context to understand how these social disadvantages occur for racial and ethnic groups through the different systems and institutions of society (i.e., politics, criminal justice, economics, physical elements, and environment).[35,36]

As explained by Ford and Airhihenbuwa,[35] CRT can be adapted to a public health framework to explain health disparities and health equity and to better understand how race, racism, and racialization affect health. At its core, CRT draws on the foundation of critical consciousness to understand how concepts of bias and relationships function in the institutions of society and how they disproportionally affect racial and ethnic groups.[35] CRT also considers the historical context of these institutions' relationships with racial and ethnic groups and the pervasive structures of racism in policies and practices that have had the unintentional consequences of being exclusive.[36] Although intended to better understand the oppression that racial and ethnic groups experience, CRT's level of analysis can also extend to how other marginalized groups—involving gender identity, sexual orientation, socioeconomic status, religious views, and other indicators of marginalization—are able to access and utilize the health care system.

Many differing opinions exist on whether health is a human right. Good health is necessary for education attainment, job performance, political activities, civic engagement, and a quality of life for fully participating in society. In this regard, health can be considered a social justice issue in which poor health, due to systemic social disadvantages, hinders certain groups of people from being fully participating citizens and limits their potential and involvement in society.[34] Limited access to health care can have detrimental effects on health and lead to excessive and early deaths.

Access to health care includes insurance status, proximity to hospitals and clinics, linguistics services, appointment scheduling, and feasibility to adhere to medical counseling and appointments. In communities where there are no grocery stores or markets to obtain fresh fruits and vegetables or safe walkable spaces for exercise, it can be difficult to manage chronic diseases such as diabetes, hypertension, and heart disease. In additional, a hospital or a clinic that does not have a certified medical interpreter or translated materials is unable to provide adequate and effective care to persons who have limited English proficiency; thus, the health of such persons can continue to decline. A hospital or clinic located in an affluent area that does not have a nearby public transportation stop may not see some of its poorest and sickest community members. All of these contributing factors can lead to health disparities that require culturally relevant and competent solutions to provide high-quality care. Health care and health interventions are not entities that exist in a "if it is built they will come" silo. Even if strategies and practices are implemented, biased behavior may keep participants and patients from feeling welcomed or from receiving the best care.

Conscious and unconscious bias

We often think of discrimination as being blatant and conscious, but most is subtle and unconscious.[37] Because our biased behavior usually involves things like favoring or doing more for those like us, we do not see ourselves as racist, discriminating, or stereotyping, and it is unlikely that health care providers are saying, "I dislike African Americans and Latinos, and I am going to give them inferior care." Yet bias persists in our society and continues to operate in subtle ways. In health care, self-reported bias or discrimination is a good predictor of physicians' reactions to the patient encounter, but is not a good measure of the patient's reactions.[38] Often, implicit bias and the automatic reactions and responses that operate outside of consciousness or awareness are better predictors of the patient experience. Implicit biases are stereotypes invoked and expressed outside of the awareness/control of the actor.[37] Implicit biases seem to influence decisions and responses to and impressions of members of oppressed and marginalized communities when situations are subjective and there are no definite and specific protocols and requirements.[38] This suggests the need to assure that all staff are aware of research protocols that are designed to protect participants in marginalized communities from stereotypical attitudes or responses.

Consequences of culturally incompetent interventions

Sociocultural differences between patients and physicians influence communication and clinical decision making, and evidence exists that patient-physician communication is linked to patient satisfaction, adherence, and overall quality of care.[39] Data also indicate that ethnic-discordant health care relationships affect ratings of the quality of care, with ethnic minorities generally perceiving the health care system more negatively than whites.[40] Unexplored or misunderstood sociocultural differences between patients and physicians can lead to patient dissatisfaction, poor adherence to treatment, and poor health outcomes.[39,40] Current research suggests the need to pay greater attention to biases in the health care system.[40]

Implementing practice standards related to cultural competence

The CLAS standards

The CLAS standards (Figure 5.1) begin with the principal standard as described previously. To achieve the principal standard, standards 2 through 15 must be implemented, evaluated, reviewed, and revised as goals are met. Standards 2 through 15 are organized into three themes: (1) governance, leadership, and workforce—providing guidance on developing leadership capacity in promoting and sustaining CLAS; (2) communication and language assistance; and (3) engagement, continuous improvement, and accountability.[5,41]

102 *Public health research methods for partnerships and practice*

> **Principal standard**
>
> Standard 1
>
> Effective, equitable, understandable, respectful quality care and services responsive to diverse cultural beliefs and practices, preferred languages, literacy and communication needs

> **Governance, leadership, and workforce**
>
> Standards 2–4
>
> Guidance on leadership support and training to promote and sustain CLAS, as well as workforce diversity

> **Communication and language assistance**
>
> Standards 5–8
>
> Recommendations for addressing language and other communication barriers to adequately meet the needs of individuals with limited English proficiency and other communication needs

> **Engagement, continuous improvement, and accountability**
>
> Standards 9–15
>
> Addresses implementation and maintenance of culturally and linguistically appropriate policies and services regardless of one's role within an organization or practice

Figure 5.1 Enhanced National Culturally and Linguistically Appropriate Services (CLAS) Standards organized by category of activity. (From U.S. Department of Health and Human Services, Office of Minority Health. The national CLAS standards. https://minorityhealth.hhs.gov/omh/browse .aspx?lvl=2&lvlid=53.)

The first theme is focused on organizational governance, leadership, and workforce as they relate to culturally and linguistically appropriate standards.[5] Three standards (2–4) recognize the role that organizational policy, practices, and allocation of resources play in promoting CLAS standard and health equity in addition to the importance of recruiting and promoting a workforce that is diverse.[5] The CLAS standards ask that organizations review their workforce for diversity at all occupational levels and positions, including governance and leadership. In addition, education and training on CLAS is important for all executives, professionals, and staff of an organization.

The second theme addresses the most recognizable component of the CLAS standards—communication and language assistance.[5] These standards hold organizations and their employees responsible for meeting the communication needs of individuals with limited English proficiency and/or other communication needs, including informing them of their rights to communication assistance and assuring the competence of those providing assistance.[5] Finally, organizations are expected to provide easy-to-understand health information and assist with comprehension of and adherence to instructions and requirements for patients' health care and plans for their care. Adherence to these standards help organizations comply with Title VI of the Civil Rights Act and the ADA.[5]

BOX 5.2

Discuss how your organization might change its physical environment to be more inviting to partnership members from diverse backgrounds.
Discuss the social factors that might affect communication among partnership members, community members, groups, or among a combination of these.

The third theme acknowledges the role of social determinants of health in the production of health disparities[25] and the intersections among health disparity categories and social determinants. Engagement, continuous improvement, and accountability standards 12 through 14 provide guidelines for community engagement and include recommendations on conducting community assessments.[5,26] Assessments should determine the needs of the populations in the agency service area, identify community assets and the services available and not available to populations, determine the services to provide and how to implement them based on the results of the community assessment, and ensure that organizations obtain demographic, cultural, linguistic, and epidemiologic data regularly to better understand the populations in their service areas.

CLAS sets an expectation that those concerned with public health will partner with the community to establish appropriate and effective programs and services, a standard that is consistent with CBPR principles.[16,17] There is also recognition of the need for processes that facilitate the resolution of conflicts and grievances that may arise as organizations and communities interact around improved public health.[5]

To assist in effective implementation of the Enhanced CLAS standards, the OHM has produced *National Standards for CLAS in Health and Health Care: A Blueprint for Advancing and Sustaining CLAS Policy and Practice Standard.*[5] This resource makes it clear that implementation efforts are a continuous process of implementation, evaluation, and refinement of improved service delivery and intervention.[5] Communities' needs and community engagement efforts will vary. Engagement activities may include building coalitions with community partners to increase reach and impact in identifying and creating solutions; participation on joint steering committees and coalitions; offering education and training opportunities; convening town hall meetings and community forums; applying community-based participatory strategies when evaluating needs; and developing services, research, and other activities to improve community health.[16,17] The enhanced CLAS standards acknowledge

104 *Public health research methods for partnerships and practice*

the role of social determinants in creating inequity in health, and they push organizations to examine hiring and contracting practices and ways that these can be made more equitable; the enhanced standards also explore ways to hire community members to participate in health promotion and in the health care delivery system.[5] Training and hiring community health workers, advisors, and/or promoters are examples of these efforts.

Cultural Humility

As demographic changes and cultural shifts happen,[2] organizations need to be able to adapt to new dynamics in their service area. It is impossible for organizations to become competent with respect to all of the various cultural groups they serve. A viewpoint of cultural humility is needed for this ongoing process.[36] Cultural humility uses a process of self-reflection, self-critique, and learning to understand the relationship between the individual and the power structure.[36] Cultural humility embodies the cyclic process of assessment, knowledge gain, and skill development to address cultural differences.[1] Self-reflection can help researchers or providers to learn of their own personal biases and prejudices, to have cultural confidence in being ignorant, and to have a willingness to be uncomfortable in complex cultural scenarios.[42]

Conclusions

Culture plays an important role in how individuals seek health care, access the health care system, and make health decisions. Cultural competence is an organizational and individual responsibility to ensure a high quality of care, better health outcomes, and improved health care service, public health practices, and research protocols. The enhanced CLAS standards and The Joint Commission have given guidance for organizations to strategically become more culturally competent through implementation, evaluation, review, and revision. Cultural competence is also important to eliminating health disparities and reducing disadvantages to many marginalized cultural groups. Culture's dynamic and variant nature requires the health care and public health sectors to be available to adapt and be sensitive to the nuances of cultural groups.

References

1. The Cross Cultural Health Care Program. *Closing the Gap: Cultural Competence in Health and Human Services.* Seattle, WA: The Cross Cultural Health Care Program; 2014.
2. Kleinman A, Benson P. Anthropology in the clinic: The problem of cultural competency and how to fix it. *PLoS Med.* 2006; 3(10):1673–1676. http://dx.doi.org/10.1371/journal.pmed.0030294.
3. Taylor JS. Confronting "culture" in medicine's "culture of no culture." *Acad Med.* 2003;78(6):555–559. http://journals.lww.com/academicmedicine/Abstract/2003/06000/Confronting__Culture__in_Medicine_s__Culture_of_No.3.aspx.

Cultural competency 105

4. DeRosa P. Social change or status quo? Approaches to diversity training. ChangeWorks Consulting Web site. http://changeworksconsulting.org/Div.Approaches -11.21.0.pdf. Published 2001. Accessed May 24, 2016.

5. US Department of Health and Human Services, Office of Minority Health. *National Standards for CLAS in Health and Health Care: A Blueprint for Advancing and Sustaining CLAS Policy and Practice.* Rockville, MD: US Department of Health and Human Services; 2013. https://www.thinkculturalhealth.hhs.gov/pdfs /EnhancedCLASStandardsBlueprint.pdf. Accessed July 4, 2016.

6. Jacobs CG; US Department of Health and Human Services, Office of Minority Health. National standards for culturally and linguistically appropriate services in health care: Ensuring health care quality for all. http://www.diversityconnection.org /diversityconnection/leadership-conferences/2012%20Conf%20Docs/Enchancing _Health_Care_with_CLAS.pdf. Published 2012. Accessed July 4, 2016.

7. Castro FG, Barrera M Jr, Holleran Steiker LK. Issues and challenges in the design of culturally adapted evidence-based interventions. *Annu Rev of Clin Psychol.* 2010;6:213–239.

8. Institute of Medicine. *Crossing the Quality Chasm: A New Health System for the 21st Century.* Washington, DC: National Academies Press; 2001.

9. Institute of Medicine. *Unequal Treatment: Confronting Racial and Ethnic Disparities in Health Care.* Washington, DC: National Academies Press; 2002.

10. The Joint Commission. *Advancing Effective Communication, Cultural Competence, and Patient- and Family-Centered Care: A Roadmap for Hospitals.* Oakbrook Terrace, IL: The Joint Commission; 2010. http://www.jointcommission.org/assets /1/6/ARoadmapforHospitalsfinalversion727.pdf. Accessed July 6, 2016.

11. National Alliance for Hispanic Health. *A Primer for Cultural Proficiency: Towards Quality Health Care Services for Hispanics.* Washington, DC: National Alliance for Hispanic Health; 2001.

12. Lauderdale J, Miller J. Standards of practice for culturally competent nursing care: A request for comments. *Transcultural.* 2009; 20(3):257–269.

13. American Psychological Association. Guidelines on multicultural education, training, research, practice, and organizational change for psychologists. *Am Psychol.* 2003;58:377–402.

14. National Association of Social Workers. *NASW Standards for Cultural Competence in Social Work Practice.* Washington, DC: National Association of Social Workers; 2001. https://www.socialworkers.org/practice/standards/naswculturalstandards.pdf. Accessed July 6, 2016.

15. Council of National Psychological Associations for the Advancement of Ethnic Minority Interests. *Guidelines for Research in Ethnic Minority Communities.* Washington, DC: American Psychological Association; 2000.

16. Wallerstein N, Duran B. Community-based participatory research contributions to intervention research: The intersection of science and practice to improve health equity. *Am J of Public Health.* 2010;100(S1):S40–46.

17. Israel BA, Shulz A, Parker EA, Becker AB. Review of community-based research: Assessing partnership approaches to improve public health. *Annu Rev of Public Health.* 1998;19:173–202.

18. Fadiman A. *The Spirit Catches You and You Fall Down: A Hmong Child, Her American Doctors, and the Collision of Two Cultures.* 1st ed. New York: Farrar, Straus, and Giroux; 1997.

19. Gregg J, Saha S. Losing culture on the way to competence: The use and misuse of culture in medical education. *Acad Med.* 2006;81:542–547.

20. Boutine-Foster C, Foster JC, Konopasek L. Physician, know theyself: The professional culture of medince as a framework for teaching cultural competence. *Acad Med.* 2008;83:106–111.

106   *Public health research methods for partnerships and practice*

21. Betancourt JR, Green AR. Linking cultural competence training to improved health outcomes: Perspectives from the field. *Acad Med.* 2010;85:583–585.
22. Corbie-Smith G, Thomas SB, St George DMM. Distrust, race, and research. *Arch Intern Med.* 2002;162(21):2458–2463.
23. George S, Duran N, Norris K. A systematic review of barriers and facilitators to minority research participation among African Americans, Latinos, Asian Americans, and Pacific Islanders. *Am J Public Health.* 2014;104(2):e16–e31.
24. Truog RD, Kesselheim AS, Joffe S. Paying patients for their tissue: The legacy of Henrietta Lacks. *Science.* 2012;337(6090):37–38.
25. Marmot M, Friel S, Bell R, Houweling TAJ, Taylor S. Commission on Social Determinants of Health. Closing the gap in a generation: Health equity through action on the social determinants of health. *Lancet.* 2008;372:1661–1669.
26. Baum FE, Bégin M, Houweling TA, Taylor S. Changes not for the fainthearted: Reorienting health care systems toward health equity through action on the social determinants of health. *Am J Public Health.* 2009;99(11):1967–1974.
27. Olavarria M, Beaulac J, Bélanger A, Young M, Aubry T. Organizational cultural competence in community health and social service organizations: How to conduct a self-assessment. *J Cult Divers.* 2009;16(4):140–150.
28. Ngo-Metzger Q, Telfair J, Sorkin DH et al. Cultural competency and quality of care: Obtaining the patient's perspective; 2006. http://www.commonwealthfund .org/~/media/files/publications/fund-report/2006/oct/cultural-competency-and -quality-of-care—obtaining-the-patients-perspective/ngo-metzger_cultcompqua litycareobtainpatientperspect_963-pdf.pdf. Common Wealth Fund, Publication #963. Accessed May 23, 2016.
29. Castro, FG, Barrera M Jr, Martinez CR Jr. The cultural adaptation of prevention interventions: Resolving tensions between fidelity and fit. *Prev Sci.* 2004;5(1):41–45.
30. Resnicow K, Baranowski T, Ahluwalia JS, Braithwaite, RL. Cultural sensitivity in public health: Defined and demystified. *Ethn Dis.* 1999;9(1):10–21.
31. Barrera M, Castro FG, Stryker LA, Toobert DJ. Cultural adaptations of behavioral health interventions: A progress report. *J Consult Clin Psychol.* 2013;81(2):196–205.
32. Office of Minority Health. History of the Office of Minority Health. http://www .minorityhealth.hhs.gov/omh/browse.aspx?lvl=2&lvlid=1. Updated February 25, 2016. Accessed July 13, 2016.
33. Braveman PA, Kumanyika S, Fielding J et al. Health disparities and health equity: The issue is justice. *Am J Public Health,* 2011;101:S149–S155. doi:10.2015 /AJPH.2010.300062.
34. World Health Organization. Social determinants of health. http://www.who.int /social_determinants/en/. Accessed July 14, 2016.
35. Ford CL, Airhihenbuwa C. Critical race theory, race equity, and public health: Toward antiracism praxis. *Am J Public Health.* 2010;100:S30–S35. doi:10.2015 /AJPH.2009.171058.
36. Rajaram SS, Bockrath S. Cultural competence: New conceptual insights into its limits and potential for addressing health disparities. *J Health Dispar Res Pract.* 2014;7(5):82–89.
37. Greenwald AG, Krieger LH. Implicit bias: Scientific foundations. *California Law Rev.* 2006;94(4):945–967.
38. Penner D, West G, Albrecht D, Markova T. Aversive racism and medical interactions with black patients: A field study. *J Exp Soc Psychol.* 2010;46:436–440.
39. Betancourt JR, Green AR, Carrillo JE, Park ER. Cultural competence and health care disparities: Key perspectives and trends. *Health Affairs.* 2005;24(2):499–505.
40. Johnson R, Saha S, Arbelaez JJ, Beach MC, Cooper LA. Racial and ethnic differences in patient perceptions of bias and cultural competence in health care. *J Gen Intern Med.* 2004;19(2):101–110.

Cultural competency   107

41. Paasche-Orlow MK, Wolf MS. The causal pathways linking health literacy to health outcomes. *Am J Health Behav.* 2007;31(suppl 1):S19–S26.
42. Thomas SB, Quinn SC, Butler J, Fyer CS, Garza MA. Toward a fourth generation of disparities research to achieve health equity. *Annu Rev Public Health.* 2011;32:399–416. doi:10.1146/aannurev-publhealth-031210-101136.

CULTURAL COMPETENCE RESOURCES

- For more information and ideas on the implementation of all components of Culturally and Linguistically Appropriate Services (CLAS), visit https://www.thinkculturalhealth.hhs.gov/.
- For more information on culturally and linguistically appropriate communication: http://www.jointcommission.org/assets/1/6/EffectiveCommunicationResourcesforHCOsrevised.pdf
- US Department of Health & Human Services, Outreach Activities & Resources. Multicultural Resources for Health Information: https://sis.nlm.nih.gov/outreach/multicultural.html
- National Center for Cultural Competence, Georgetown University, Center for Child and Human Development: https://nccc.georgetown.edu/curricula/resources.html
- Principles and Recommended Standards for Cultural Competence Education of Health Care Professionals: https://www.mghihp.edu/sites/default/files/about-us/diversity/principles_standards_cultural_competence.pdf
- Community Tool Box. Section 7: Building Culturally Competent Organizations: http://ctb.ku.edu/en/table-of-contents/culture/cultural-competence/culturally-competent-organizations/main
- Public Health Critical Race Praxis: http://www.publichealthcriticalrace.org/
- Cultural Bridges to Justice: http://www.culturalbridgestojustice.org/resources/written/level-playing-field

---

Activity

Group activity 1

Materials: note cards, paper tablets, pencils, pens, color stickers, action plan template.

This is a small group activity that can be used to assist with group discussion and decision-making on issues related to diversity and cultural competence. The activity is particularly useful for those individuals who have

108 *Public health research methods for partnerships and practice*

not felt that they were able to have a voice or speak out. The group should divide into smaller groups of 3 to 5 individuals and select a recorder for the group. Each member of every group will receive six colored stickers to be used later.

The small group will discuss ways to increase acceptance of diverse religious views and practices (any open-ended topic related to diversity and cultural competence can be substituted). Each person will individually brainstorm ideas on the topic. Allow approximately 5 to 7 minutes for individuals to brainstorm. Each member of the group will share the ideas developed (one response per person each time). As ideas are shared, thoughts may be clarified, but members should not criticize the materials being shared. All ideas shared should be recorded. After all ideas are shared, each member votes by placing dots by their favorite suggestions. Each group will share their top two ideas based on the vote.

The small groups will reconvene into the larger group. Each small group will present their ideas. Questions may be asked to clarify ideas, but ideas may not be criticized. At the end of the process, the group will use their remaining three dots to identify their favorite ideas. This portion of the activity should require 25 minutes.

The larger group will again be divided. Three groups will be formed, and each will discuss one of the three ideas selected to move forward. The groups will select a chairperson and a recorder and work to complete an action plan associated with the idea assigned (Table 5.1). Each group can share its action plan (approximately 5 minutes). Take 35 minutes for this portion of the activity.

Action plan template

Purpose: To work together to improve diversity and cultural competence within the organization or agency.

Group activity 2

Materials: case studies, flip chart, markers.

This is a small group activity to allow discussion on how researchers, community members, and health practitioners should critically think through engagement with culturally diverse communities. Each group will receive one of the five case studies and answer the accompanying questions. Each group will report back to the larger group after 15 to 25 minutes of discussion.

Feedback from the outside group members is encouraged for richer discussion on cultural competence in research and health practices. During the large discussion, the facilitator should reiterate the principles of cultural competence and the CLAS Standards.

Table 5.1 Planning table for group/community diversity and inclusion

	Goal	Objective	Method	Responsible party	Timeline	Measure
Group Idea	Example Increased awareness and acceptance of religious diversity among partners	Meeting times do not conflict with religious observances Events and activities do not conflict with religious observances	Check all currently scheduled meetings and events for conflicts that affect participation Create a calendar of religious observations to consult prior to scheduling	Chairpersons of partnership and/ or committees and events	Next meeting or one month	Changes in participation by diverse religious background Changes in complaints related to religious conflicts

Source: Coats JV, Stafford JD, Sanders Thompson V, Johnson Javois B, Goodman MS, *J Empir Res Hum Res Ethics*, 10(1):3–12, 2015.

Note: Developed based on CLAS Standards.

110   *Public health research methods for partnerships and practice*

Case study #1: "Research-fatigued community"

A group of public health researchers from one of the state's universities wants to develop a diabetes intervention for a community in the northwest part of the state. Historically, this area has some of the worst health outcomes in the state with high rates of obesity, hypertension, heart disease, diabetes, kidney failures, and premature deaths. It is a heavily researched area that has seen very little progress from past projects and interventions conducted over the years. In many of the instances, researchers outside the state came into the community and did not hire local people to help coordinate research efforts or did not take the time to learn about the community or speak to community leaders. Furthermore, most of the findings from the research projects have never been shared with the community, and the community has not seen the benefits and success of interventions or whether the findings could have been used to improve community health. The community has become very weary with researchers and, recently, has not been very welcoming to them.

1.   What should the university researchers be aware of about the community?
2.   How should the university researchers approach the community?
3.   Who should the university researchers work with to gain trust in the community?

Case study #2: "Rich in community, low on resources"

Lily is a small town about two hours away from the nearest city. It was once a booming agriculture community. When agriculture became more mechanized, manufacturing became the main industry. Today, most of the factories have closed and have moved out of the state and overseas. The heart of the community is an open space with a park that has been neglected; the park is near some unoccupied lots. Lily has seen an increased rate of obesity, especially in its children ages 5 to 8. Some of the teachers at the elementary school want to revitalize the park area and create a community garden and a quarter-mile walking track in the unused lots. The new space would allow the community to come together to exercise, buy fresh produce from the garden, and have family picnics. The teachers have partnered with the county health departments to host a community forum to gauge the interest of the community and determine next steps for the project. Almost every person in the community attended the meeting, and it was decided that a CAB should be created to steer the project. Below are some of the resources identified in the community.

1.   Who should sit on the community action board? Who do you think are the top 5 persons who need to sit on the board?
2.   What are the community's greatest resources or partnerships?
3.   What other programs would be culturally relevant to the community's issue with childhood obesity?

RESOURCES IN THE COMMUNITY

- Park area and adjacent lots
- Mr. Smith—*still farms his family land*
- Mayor—*promotes healthy lifestyles in the city*
- High school art teacher
- Mr. Reed—*owns a construction site*
- Mamma G—*well-respected elder who is like the mother of Lily*
- Pastor of the oldest church in Lily
- City councilman
- Elementary PTO president
- Police officer
- Fireman
- Bank owner
- County health department
- Doctor of health clinic
- Nurse practitioner of clinic
- Local restaurant owner
- PE teacher at the elementary school
- 4-H Club staff
- State representative

Case study #3: "Cultural considerations for social marketing"

A new refugee community has been growing in the lower region of the state. Dr. Moore, the local health center's OB/GYN, has seen an alarming number of cervical cancer cases in the refugee community and has found national statistics to support what she has seen. She wants to develop a social marketing campaign for the women to adhere to screening recommendations. Dr. Moore has reached out to a local organization that works with the refugee community and provides a number of services related to housing, finance, and health. The director of the organization explained to Dr. Moore that the refugee community has a low literacy rate not only in English but in their native language too. The community has a strong patriarchal society and believes the family is more important than self. Dr. Moore found this information very helpful and hopes to use it for the cervical cancer screening campaign.

1. What are the cultural factors that Dr. Moore should be aware of before working with the refugee community?
2. How would you advise Dr. Moore in crafting her cervical cancer screening campaign?

112   *Public health research methods for partnerships and practice*

3. While considering the low literacy rate in English and the target population's native language, how can Dr. Moore share her message on the importance of cervical cancer screenings?

Case study #4: "A culture of sickness"

Plato County Health Department is located a few miles from a Native American reservation. While providing health screenings at a health fair on the reservation, Kathy, the health department's nurse practitioner, saw an alarming number of patients who had high blood pressure, high glucose levels, and BMIs in the overweight and obese categories. Kathy began talking with the health fair's organizer, Rosa, to understand the unconcerned responses given to her when she provided the results. Rosa explained that many of the community members have accepted obesity and diabetes as a normal part of life, believing that at some point everyone will end up with diabetes. Because of this, Rosa wanted to host the health fair to begin changing this attitude in the community. Kathy wants to partner with Rosa to help change this "culture of diabetes" and improve health outcomes in the reservation.

1. Discuss how the "culture of diabetes" can affect health outcomes, health promotion, and education activities.
2. What are some of the historical contexts Kathy should be aware of before engaging in a partnership with Rosa?
3. What approaches should be taken to develop a health promotion program for the community?

Case study #5: "Changing demographics"

A new manufacturing plant has opened in a rural town. Since the plant's opening, the town has seen an increase in its Latino/Hispanic population. Historically, the community has consisted of residents with English as the primary language spoken. The English proficiency of the new Latino/Hispanic population ranges from English proficient to limited English proficient (LEP). At the local health clinic, the staff has adapted by asking the Latino/Hispanic population to bring their own interpreters such as a child, a coworker, or a community member. Sometimes, the front staff will tell the Latino/Hispanic patients that they need to bring their own interpreter before beginning service without asking language preference. Recently, the clinic's manager has acquired a Spanish language line, but it slows down the pace of the clinic. The staff has also begun to use Google translate and other Internet translation services to communicate with the patients.

1. What are some of the harmful implications than can happen with the current language services the clinic is offering?

2. What are some possible strategies or policies that the clinic manager could put into action to address the language service challenges that the clinic is now facing?
3. How can the clinic involve the Latino/Hispanic community in assisting with improving services to this population?

SELF-ASSESSMENT—WHAT DID YOU LEARN?

1. _____ is a set of behaviors, attitudes, and policies that enable researchers and practitioners to work and communicate effectively with diverse populations.
   a. Cultural competency
   b. Family health history
   c. Bedside manner
   d. Ethics

2. Cultural competency will result in _____.
   a. Improved communication
   b. Trust
   c. Patient compliance
   d. All of the above

3. Why do we need cultural competency in health?
   a. To keep government funding for the hospital
   b. Because it is mandated by federal law
   c. Because everyone has a right to health care that addresses unique needs
   d. None of the above

4. Cultural competency does NOT include _____.
   a. Valuing diversity
   b. Managing the dynamics of difference
   c. Ability to conduct self-assessment
   d. Narrow-mindedness

5. A physician is thought to be culturally competent if he or she _____.
   a. Speaks the language of the patient
   b. Sees patients of more than one race or ethnicity
   c. Provides an interpreter for patients
   d. Puts aside personal biases and considers each patient as an individual

114 *Public health research methods for partnerships and practice*

6. Cultural competency can occur on the _____ level.
   a. Individual
   b. Structural
   c. Organizational
   d. All of the above

7. What is culture?
   a. Thoughts, actions, beliefs, and values of a group
   b. Thoughts, actions, beliefs, and values of an individual
   c. Where a group came from
   d. Where an individual comes from

8. In order to acquire cultural competence, we must make fluid policies and practices.
   a. True
   b. False

9. Racially and ethnically diverse populations do NOT experience barriers to quality health care.
   a. True
   b. False

10. The CLAS standards were written to be consistent with and support other national health policies, including the Affordable Care Act.
    a. True
    b. False

11. Culturally competent researchers are responsible for assuring that _____.
    a. Appropriate theories, valid assessment tools, and research methods are used
    b. Participants receive enough money for completing surveys
    c. That every participant gets better after receiving the treatment being evaluated
    d. All of the above

12. Which steps are recommended when evidence-based interventions are adapted to be culturally appropriate?
    a. Information gathering
    b. Preliminary design and testing
    c. Intervention refinement and trial
    d. All of the above

6 Health literacy

Kimberly A. Kaphingst

LEARNING OBJECTIVES

- Define health literacy.
- Understand the limited health literacy perspective.
- Describe the associations between health literacy and health outcomes.
- Describe health literacy on a national scale.
- Discuss current research on health literacy.

SELF-ASSESSMENT—WHAT DO YOU KNOW?

1. What are the components of health literacy?
2. What are the effects of health literacy on health-related knowledge and outcomes?
3. Name and describe a health literacy assessment tool.

Introduction

In the past two decades, health literacy has received increasing attention as a critical determinant of health. This chapter will introduce the concept of health literacy and present data on levels of health literacy in the United States, as well as disparities in health literacy across population subgroups. The effects of health literacy on health-related knowledge, use of health services, and health-related outcomes will be presented. The chapter will then describe various assessments available to measure health literacy and recommendations for developing and evaluating written information for individuals with varying levels of health literacy. Finally, current research on health literacy and genomics will be described as a research example.

Definition of health literacy

More than simply health-related reading skills, health literacy is now thought to be composed of multiple domains of communication skills. Although different definitions of the construct of health literacy exist, the Institute of Medicine (IOM) described *health literacy* as the degree to which individuals can obtain, process, and understand basic health information and services needed to make appropriate health decisions.[1] The Patient Protection and Affordable Care Act of 2010, Title V, expanded this to define *health literacy* as "the degree to which an individual has the capacity to obtain, communicate, process, and understand basic health information and services to make appropriate health decisions."[2] The IOM operationalized health literacy as having the following components: conceptual and cultural knowledge, oral literacy (i.e., listening and speaking skills), print literacy (i.e., reading and writing skills), and numeracy (i.e., quantitative skills).[1]

Levels of health literacy in the United States

In 2003, the United States Department of Education conducted a nationally representative household assessment of more than 19,000 adults (defined as individuals 16 years of age or older); the assessment included items designed to measure health literacy.[3] These data revealed that about 36% of US adults have limited health literacy and are likely to face some difficulties with literacy tasks in the health care setting, such as reading educational brochures and prescription labels, completing forms, speaking with health care providers, and making health care decisions. The national assessment further highlighted disparities in health literacy across population subgroups. White and Asian/Pacific Islander adults had higher average health literacy than Black, Hispanic, American Indian/Alaska Native, and multiracial adults. Older adults (i.e., adults aged 65 years of age and older) had lower average health literacy than younger adults. Those with higher educational attainment had higher average health literacy than those with lower educational attainment.[3] These national data, therefore, suggest that considering limited health literacy will be important to efforts to address health disparities in the United States.

Effects of health literacy

Research studies have shown that health literacy has wide-ranging impacts on health-related knowledge, use of health services, and health-related outcomes.[1,4] More specifically, prior research has shown that individuals with limited health literacy have, on average, less health-related knowledge across a variety of health domains, lower use of preventive health services, and poorer self-reported health.[1,4] In addition, older adults with limited health literacy are more likely to die from all causes than older adults with higher health literacy.[3] Previous research studies have shown that individuals with limited health literacy are more likely to make medication errors and less likely to know how to manage their health problems.[5-7] In a study of 208 primary care patients with type 2 diabetes in a medically underserved population, Fan and colleagues[8] found that patients with limited health literacy had increased unintentional nonadherence to medications compared with patients with adequate health literacy; however, intentional medication nonadherence was not related to health literacy in this study. Patients with limited health literacy may have difficulty understanding medical information and may lack the self-efficacy (i.e., confidence in one's skills) to be actively involved in their own health care.[9,10] Due to the stigma that can be associated with limited health literacy, some patients may also experience feelings of shame, thereby not discussing their difficulties within the health care system or not seeking assistance when needed.[11,12]

Prior research studies have also suggested that health literacy impacts provider-patient communication.[13-15] One context in which this has been examined is the effect of health literacy on the decision-making process (e.g., the process of making treatment decisions in a clinical appointment).[9,16] In a study of 576 primary care patients from a medically underserved population, Seo and colleagues[17] found that those patients with adequate health literacy were almost twice as likely than those with limited health literacy to prefer an active role in decision-making. The authors suggested that patients with limited health literacy may be unaware of their options to participate in decision-making, instead believing that their providers know the best course of action. They recommended that providers should clearly provide contextual information and available options to patients as part of decision-making processes, as improved communication may facilitate patients' informed decision-making. While some patients may ultimately prefer to leave decisions to their providers, they may still want to be engaged in the decision-making process.[18] However, research on the relationship between health literacy and decision-making preferences is limited.[9,16,19,20] Most prior studies have been framed around disease-specific contexts;[9,10,16,20-24] have largely examined white, highly educated, and female populations;[9,10,19,20,23-26] or have not specifically assessed patients' preferences for how they would like to make decisions.[10,24-26] Therefore, examination of decision-making preferences among medically underserved groups is particularly needed as research suggests that shared decision-making interventions may provide greater benefits for disadvantaged groups.[17,27]

It is critical to highlight that the effects of health literacy on individuals' health knowledge, use of health services, and health outcomes are thought to be based on interactions between patients' skill levels and the demands of health care and social systems.[1,28] Previously, patients' skills have received more attention in health literacy research and practice than have attributes of health care organizations. A 2012 report from the IOM Roundtable on Health Literacy drew new attention to the importance of examining the attributes of a health-literate organization (i.e., an organization that makes it easier

118   *Public health research methods for partnerships and practice*

for people to navigate, understand, and use information and services to take care of their health).[29] Organizational attributes include having a respectful health care environment and having quality provider-patient communication. However, little research has compared the relative importance of patients' health literacy skills and organizational attributes in shaping patient-reported outcomes of care.

Prior work has suggested that patients' interactions with health care staff are important to their outcomes,[30,31] and having a respectful workforce that avoids stigmatizing patients with limited health literacy has been identified as a key attribute of health-literate organizations.[29] However, little is known about the importance of frontline staff members, such as front desk staff, as part of a health-literate workforce. Front desk staff have been described as the face of a health care setting, strongly informing patients' impressions of the organization.[32] These staff members have many important roles, including helping patients to access health care, to complete medical and insurance forms, to make appointments, and to obtain prescriptions. Some attention has been given to the importance of training staff in communication skills.[33,34] However, few studies have focused specifically on training staff in organizational attributes important to health literacy, such as the creation of a respectful and shame-free environment.[29,35,36] The findings from an ethnographic research study showed the important role that receptionists play in quality and safety of repeat prescribing of medications in general practice,[37] and authors of an intervention study examined the effects of health literacy training of office staff on their knowledge and intentions.[35]

The quality of provider-patient communication is another attribute of health-literate organizations suggested to affect patient outcomes.[13,29,38–40] Many aspects of provider-patient communication may be important to this attribute of a health-literate organization. For example, patient question asking can enhance patient satisfaction and recall of information provided during an appointment.[41] Prior research has shown that interventions that improve patients' question asking—such as providing patients with a list of questions that they can ask or with a training to improve their communication skills—can increase adherence to treatment recommendations and other medical outcomes.[40,42–45] Outside of the research setting, the importance of patient engagement and question asking has also been emphasized by health educators and others working in the field of health literacy.[36,46,47]

In a study conducted with a randomly selected statewide sample of 3,358 English-speaking adult residents of Missouri, Kaphingst and colleagues[28] examined the impact of patients' health literacy and the attributes of a health-literate organization on two patient-reported outcomes: whether respondents reported knowing more about their health and whether they reported making better choices about their health following their last doctor visit. The authors found that, in a multivariable logistic regression model controlling for self-reported health, having a personal doctor, number of chronic conditions, health insurance, and sociodemographic characteristics, respondents who had

Health literacy 119

a good front desk experience were 2.63 times as likely (95% confidence interval [CI]: 2.12, 3.26) and those who brought questions were 1.73 times as likely (95% CI: 1.32, 2.28) to report knowing more about their health after seeing a doctor. In a second multivariable model controlling for the same variables, respondents who had a good front desk experience were 1.58 times as likely (95% CI: 1.27, 1.96) and those who brought questions were 1.68 times as likely (95% CI: 1.30, 2.17) to report making better choices about their health after seeing a doctor. Patients' health literacy skills were not associated with either outcome. Therefore, the results of this study indicated that the attributes of a health care organization may be more important to patient knowledge and health behavior outcomes than patients' health literacy skills. The authors commented that these findings support and focused research to examine the effects of health care system organizational attributes on patient outcomes and to develop system-level interventions that might improve patient health.[28]

The findings from the study by Kaphingst and colleagues support the concept that key attributes of a health-literate organization potentially impact patient-reported outcomes of care. An important next step is to examine, how these organizational variables affect patient care. For example, is the effect of experiences with front desk staff on patient-reported outcomes due to specific interactions with front desk staff, frustration with the larger health care system, or a combination?[28] One mechanism by which interactions with front desk staff might impact patient outcomes is suggested by the finding that having a good front desk experience was a stronger predictor of learning from a doctor visit than of making better choices after the visit. A possible explanation for this finding is that a person's emotional response to a negative front desk experience might adversely affect the person's ability or motivation to process information in a doctor's visit occurring just after this experience.[28]

The results also highlight the importance of patient engagement in the medical encounter through bringing questions to the visit. Although interventions to encourage patient question asking (e.g., a list of questions to ask) have not always affected patient behaviors,[46] some studies have shown that patient question asking can affect patient knowledge, satisfaction, adherence to recommendations, and the quality of provider-patient interactions.[43,44,48] Patients with limited health literacy have a complex array of communication challenges,[15] which could impact their interactions with providers.[14,46,49,50] The findings from Kaphingst and colleagues suggest that patient engagement through question asking is important for patients with varying levels of health literacy skills,[28] supporting a universal approach of encouraging all patients, not just those with limited health literacy skills, to bring questions to doctor visits.[36,47]

Measurement of health literacy

A number of different measures of health literacy have been developed. These measures can be divided into two types: objective measures that ask

120 *Public health research methods for partnerships and practice*

respondents to complete a series of health literacy tasks and subjective measures that ask them to self-report their level of skills. No true "gold standard" measure exists, although the Test of Functional Health Literacy in Adults (TOFHLA)[51] is often used as such.[52] Because the full version of the TOFHLA requires 22 minutes to complete, a shorter version is often used, the Short Test of Functional Health Literacy in Adults (S-TOFHLA).[53] The S-TOFHLA is comprised of two multiple-choice reading comprehension passages.[54] In each passage, every 5th to 7th word is deleted; patients must choose from among four choices the word that best completes the sentence, a method called a modified Cloze procedure.[55] The S-TOFHLA is a timed test with a maximum of 7 minutes to complete; scores range from 0 to 36. The results are generally categorized into the following categories: adequate health literacy (S-TOFHLA score > 22), marginal health literacy (score 17–22), or inadequate health literacy (score 0–16). The S-TOFHLA is primarily a test of reading comprehension, although a numeracy (i.e., number skills) component is available.

Another common objective health literacy measure is the Rapid Estimate of Adult Literacy in Medicine (REALM).[56,57] In the full version of the REALM, patients are asked to read aloud a list of 66 health-related words and are scored on the number of words pronounced correctly. Shorter versions of the REALM are often used, such as the Rapid Estimate of Adult Literacy in Medicine-Revised (REALM-R).[58] For the REALM-R, patients are asked to read a list of eight health-related words and are scored on the number of words pronounced correctly. For the REALM-R, a score of 6 or less is generally considered to be limited health literacy. The REALM and REALM-R are considered to be measures of word recognition, which is related to reading comprehension.[52] A third commonly used objective health literacy measure is the Newest Vital Sign (NVS), a health literacy screener.[59] The NVS is based upon a nutritional label that is given to participants to view. Patients are verbally administered six questions about the label. A correct score of 4 to 6 is considered adequate health literacy, 2 to 3 is considered possible limited health literacy, and 0 to 1 is considered high likelihood of limited health literacy.[59] The NVS assesses numeracy skills and document literacy skills.

However, these measures have some time and staffing limitations that limit the feasibility of their use in fast-paced clinical settings, including the time required for the assessments and the requirement for verbal administration by trained staff. Therefore, subjective assessments, often called Single Item Literacy Screener (SILS) items, have been developed. SILS items are self-administered brief screening questions.[60–62] For example, common items are the following: (1) "How often do you have problems learning about your medical condition because of difficulty understanding written information?" (2) "How confident are you filling out forms by yourself?" and (3) "How often do you have someone (like a family member, friend, hospital/clinic worker, or caregiver) help you read hospital materials?"[61] In a study analyzing data

Health literacy 121

from patients in an urban academic emergency department (425 patients) and a primary care safety net clinic (486 patients), Goodman and colleagues[63] showed that two of the SILS combined with basic patient demographic information (i.e., age, gender, race) significantly improved the ability to identify patients with inadequate health literacy compared with demographic information alone.

The choice of best health literacy measure to use depends upon factors such as the mode of administration, educational topic, whether self-reported skills are of interest, and time available. Because the S-TOFHLA, REALM, and NVS require in-person administration, they are generally not appropriate for use in questionnaires to be completed by telephone, online, or on paper. SILS items can be administered across different modes of administration because these items do not require a person to administer them. Studies focused on nutrition might use the NVS, which is based on a nutritional label. SILS items assess self-reported skills, whereas the other measures are based on actual literacy tasks. The time required to administer the measures varies, with the S-TOFHLA generally requiring the most time. Pilot testing the measures with a target audience can assist in the selection of the best measure.

Recommendations for materials development

In order to meet the needs of patients with varying health literacy levels, a number of recommendations have been made for the development of written materials. The use of plain language, or strategies focused on clear and simple communication,[64] may improve comprehension of written information. For example, various recommendations have been made for the use of plain language strategies in developing informed consent forms.[65,66] The National Institutes of Health recommends writing consent documents at an eighth-grade reading level.[67] Other guidelines have emphasized the use of plain language strategies such as providing graphics and images to supplement text, presenting topics in a clear and descriptive way, and providing adequate white space throughout the document.[66,68]

Doak et al.[69] developed a series of guidelines for the design of health-related materials to improve their readability, describing optimal strategies for organization, writing style, and layout of health information. These guidelines address the following:

1. Content (i.e., evident purpose, content about behaviors, limited scope, summary or review included),
2. Literacy demand (i.e., reading grade level, use of active voice, use of common words, providing context first, use of headers and "road signs"),
3. Graphics (i.e., purpose shown in cover graphic, type of graphics, relevance of illustrations, explanations for lists and tables, captions for graphics),
4. Layout and typography factors,

122 *Public health research methods for partnerships and practice*

5. Learning stimulation and motivation (i.e., use of interaction, behaviors modeled, motivation addressed), and
6. Cultural appropriateness (i.e., match in logic, language, and experience to audience; appropriate cultural images and examples).

These guidelines can assist both in the development of new materials and in the assessment of existing written materials.[70,71]

Research example: Health literacy and genetics

The health literacy framework has been used to conduct research in a number of areas of health. A recent area of interest has been in the use of new genetic technologies. This section will describe research on health literacy and genetics, organized according to the IOM's components of health literacy. Much of the research conducted in this area has examined conceptual knowledge related to genetics.[72] These prior studies have found substantial gaps in genetics-related knowledge in the general public.[73] For example, qualitative research has shown that although individuals may be familiar with genetics-related terms, they have limited understanding of the underlying concepts.[74–76] Results from larger quantitative studies support this conclusion about gaps in knowledge. In a telephone survey conducted with 1,009 adults,[77] the authors found that although most respondents were aware of the connection among genes, inheritance, and disease risk, significantly fewer understood the biological mechanisms underlying these relationships. Haga and colleagues[78] found that 300 adults from the general public had higher knowledge about inheritance and causes of disease than they had biological knowledge about genes, chromosomes, and cells. However, research on knowledge about genetics that is conducted among medically underserved populations and patient populations with limited health literacy is still scant.

Although the question of how health literacy affects written and oral communication of genetic information has received less attention than levels of genetic knowledge in the public, a few prior studies have examined this issue. In a study conducted with 163 posttreatment breast cancer patients, Lillie and colleagues[79] found that, after reading written information about a genetic test, individuals with lower health literacy had lower recall of the information and lower preference for active participation in decision-making about the test. In a subsequent study, the research team found that health literacy impacted how women interpreted visual risk information about recurrence.[80] In their work on oral communication, Erby and colleagues developed a genetics-related word recognition measure called the Rapid Estimate of Adult Literacy in Genetics (REAL-G), based on the REALM described previously in the chapter.[57,81] The authors found that individuals with lower REAL-G scores had lower knowledge scores after viewing videotaped genetic counseling sessions, suggesting less learning from verbally presented genetic information.[81] This research team also found that more difficult oral language during a genetic counseling session was associated with less patient satisfaction.[82] These prior studies have, therefore, indicated that individuals with limited health literacy may understand less from written and oral communication about genetic information and may engage less in discussions with health care providers about the information.

The increasing importance of genetic information in clinical care heightens the need to examine how individuals understand and communicate about this information. On the basis of a conceptual framework of genetics-related health literacy, Kaphingst and colleagues[72] examined whether health literacy was related to knowledge, self-efficacy, and perceived importance of genetics, family health history, and communication about family health history in a medically underserved population.[72] The sample was composed of 624 patients at a primary care clinic at a large urban hospital. About half of participants (47%) had limited health literacy as assessed by the REALM-R; 55% had no education beyond high school, and 58% were black, 32% were white, and 10% other race. In multivariable models, limited health literacy was associated with lower genetic knowledge ($\beta = -0.55$; SE = 0.10, $p < 0.0001$), lower awareness of family health history (odds ratio [OR] = 0.50; 95% CI = 0.28, 0.90, $p = 0.020$), greater perceived importance of genetic information (OR = 1.95; 95% CI = 1.27, 3.00, $p = 0.0022$), but lower perceived importance of family health history information (OR = 0.47; 95% CI = 0.26, 0.86, $p = 0.013$) and more frequent communication with a doctor about family health history (OR = 2.02; 95% CI = 1.27, 3.23, $p = 0.0032$). These findings highlight the importance of considering domains of genetics-related health literacy (e.g., knowledge, oral literacy) in developing educational strategies for genetic information.[72]

Conclusions

Research has shown health literacy to be an important determinant of individuals' health-related knowledge, utilization of health care, and health outcomes. This chapter summarized the state of this evidence and described approaches to measurement of health literacy, and development and evaluation of written materials. The usefulness of the health literacy framework was presented in a case study of current research on genomics and health literacy. This chapter has also summarized a number of areas in which additional research is needed. In particular, research is needed to better understand the health-literate attributes of health care organizations and how intervention approaches can modify these attributes to improve the health of patients. Continuing to expand this area of research is critical to moving the understanding of health literacy and its impact on health forward.

124 *Public health research methods for partnerships and practice*

References

1. Nielsen-Bohlman L, Panzer AM, Kindig DA, eds. *Health Literacy: A Prescription to End Confusion.* Washington, DC: National Academies Press; 2004.
2. What is health literacy? Centers for Disease Control and Prevention Web site. http://www.cdc.gov/healthliteracy/learn. Accessed January 27, 2017.
3. Kutner M, Greenberg E, Jin Y, Paulsen C, White S. *The Health Literacy of America's Adults: Results from the 2003 National Assessment of Adult Literacy.* Washington, DC: National Center for Education Statistics; 2006.
4. Berkman ND, Sheridan SL, Donahue KE et al. *Health Literacy Interventions and Outcomes: An Updated Systematic Review.* Rockville, MD: Agency for Healthcare Research and Quality; 2011. Evidence Report/Technology Assessment 199.
5. Berkman ND, Sheridan SL, Donahue KE, Halpern DJ, Crotty K. Low health literacy and health outcomes: An updated systematic review. *Annu Intern Med.* 2011;155(2):97–107.
6. Gazmararian JA, Williams MV, Peel J, Baker DW. Health literacy and knowledge of chronic disease. *Patient Educ Couns.* 2003;51(3):267–275.
7. Miller DP Jr, Brownlee CD, McCoy TP, Pignone MP. The effect of health literacy on knowledge and receipt of colorectal cancer screening: A survey study. *BMC Fam Pract.* 2007;8:16.
8. Fan JH, Lyons SA, Goodman MS, Blanchard MS, Kaphingst KA. Relationship between health literacy and unintentional and intentional medication nonadherence in medically underserved patients with type 2 diabetes. *Diabetes Educ.* 2016; 42(2):199–208.
9. Mancuso CA, Rincon M. Asthma patients' assessments of health care and medical decision making: The role of health literacy. *J Asthma.* 2006;43(1):41–44.
10. Peek ME, Wilson SC, Gorawara-Bhat R, Odoms-Young A, Quinn MT, Chin MH. Barriers and facilitators to shared decision-making among African-Americans with diabetes. *J Gen Intern Med.* 2009;24(10):1135–1139.
11. Easton P, Entwistle VA, Williams B. How the stigma of low literacy can impair patient-professional spoken interactions and affect health: Insights from a qualitative investigation. *BMC Health Serv Res.* 2013;13:319.
12. Parikh NS, Parker RM, Nurss JR, Baker DW, Williams MV. Shame and health literacy: The unspoken connection. *Patient Educ Couns.* 1996;27(1):33–39.
13. Schillinger D, Piette J, Grumbach K et al. Closing the loop: Physician communication with diabetic patients who have low health literacy. *Arch Intern Med.* 2003;163:83–90.
14. Schillinger D, Bindman A, Wang F, Stewart A, Piette J. Functional health literacy and the quality of physician-patient communication among diabetes patients. *Patient Educ Couns.* 2004;52:315–323.
15. Williams MV, Davis T, Parker RM, Weiss BD. The role of health literacy in patient-physician communication. *Fam Med.* 2002;34(5):383–389.
16. DeWalt DA, Boone RS, Pignone MP. Literacy and its relationship with self-efficacy, trust, and participation in medical decision making. *Am J Health Behav.* 2007;31(suppl 1):S27–S35.
17. Seo J, Goodman MS, Politi M, Blanchard M, Kaphingst KA. Effect of health literacy on decision-making preferences among medically underserved patients. *Med Decis Making.* 2016;36:550–556.
18. Politi MC, Dizon DS, Frosch DL, Kuzemchak MD, Stiggelbout AM. Importance of clarifying patients' desired role in shared decision making to match their level of engagement with their preferences. *BMJ.* 2013;347:f7066.
19. Goggins KM, Wallston KA, Nwosu S et al. Health literacy, numeracy, and other characteristics associated with hospitalized patients' preferences for involvement in decision making. *J Health Commun.* 2014;19(suppl 2):29–43.

Health literacy 125

20. Naik AD, Street RL, Jr., Castillo D, Abraham NS. Health literacy and decision making styles for complex antithrombotic therapy among older multimorbid adults. *Patient Educ Couns.* 2011;85(3):499–504.
21. Aboumatar HJ, Carson KA, Beach MC, Roter DL, Cooper LA. The impact of health literacy on desire for participation in healthcare, medical visit communication, and patient reported outcomes among patients with hypertension. *J Gen Intern Med.* 2013;28(11):1469–1476.
22. Kumar R, Korthuis PT, Saha S et al. Decision-making role preferences among patients with HIV: Associations with patient and provider characteristics and communication behaviors. *J Gen Intern Med.* 2010;25(6):517–523.
23. Lillie SE, Brewer NT, O'Neill SC et al. Retention and use of breast cancer recurrence risk information from genomic tests: The role of health literacy. *Cancer Epidemiol Biomarkers Prev.* 2007;16(2):249–255.
24. Peek ME, Odoms-Young A, Quinn MT, Gorawara-Bhat R, Wilson SC, Chin MH. Race and shared decision-making: Perspectives of African-Americans with diabetes. *Soc Sci Med.* 2010;71(1):1–9.
25. Barton JL, Trupin L, Tonner C et al. English language proficiency, health literacy, and trust in physician are associated with shared decision making in rheumatoid arthritis. *J Rheumatol.* 2014;41(7):1290–1297.
26. Katz SJ, Lantz PM, Janz NK et al. Patient involvement in surgery treatment decisions for breast cancer. *J Clin Oncol.* 2005;23(24):5526–5533.
27. Durand MA, Carpenter L, Dolan H et al. Do interventions designed to support shared decision-making reduce health inequalities? A systematic review and meta-analysis. *PloS One.* 2014;9(4):e94670.
28. Kaphingst KA, Weaver NL, Wray RJ, Brown MLR, Buskirk T, Kreuter MW. Effects of patient health literacy, patient engagement and a system-level health literacy attribute on patient-reported outcomes: A representative statewide survey. *BMC Health Serv Res.* 2014;14:475.
29. Brach C, Keller D, Hernandez LM et al. *Ten Attributes of Health-Literate Health Care Organizations.* Washington, DC: Institute of Medicine of the National Academies; 2012.
30. Redling R. Improving customer service. It's not just what's in the box. *MCMA Connex.* 2003;3(7):36–41.
31. Brand R, Cronin J, Routledge J. Marketing to older patients: Perceptions of service quality. *Health Mark Q.* 1997;15(2):1–31.
32. Hadley H. Patient satisfaction in the patient-centered practice. *Conn Med.* 2008; 72(5):313–314.
33. Rowan K. Monthly communication skill coaching for healthcare staff. *Patient Educ Couns.* 2008;71(3):402–404.
34. Hart CD, Drotar D, Gori A, Lewin L. Enhancing parent-provider communication in ambulatory pediatric practice. *Patient Educ Couns.* 2006;63(1–2):38–46.
35. Mackert M, Ball J, Lopez N. Health literacy awareness training for healthcare workers: Improving knowledge and intentions to use clear communication techniques. *Patient Educ Couns.* 2011;85(3):e225–e228.
36. Weiss B. *Health Literacy and Patient Safety: Help Patients Understand.* Chicago, IL: American Medical Association Foundation; 2007.
37. Swinglehurst D, Greenhalgh T, Russell J, Myall M. Receptionist input to quality and safety in repeat prescribing in UK general practice: Ethnographic case study. *BMJ.* 2011;343:d6788.
38. Stewart M. Effective physician-patient communication and health outcomes: A review. *CMAJ.* 1995;152(9):1423–1433.
39. Stewart M, Brown J, Boon H, Galajda J, Meredith L, Sangster M. Evidence on patient-doctor communication. *Cancer Prev Control.* 1999;3(1):25–30.

126 *Public health research methods for partnerships and practice*

40. Kaplan S, Greenfield S, Ware J, Jr. Assessing the effects of physician-patient interactions on the outcomes of chronic disease. *Med Care.* 1989;27(suppl 3):S110–S127.
41. Thompson SC, Nanni C, Schwankovsky L. Patient-oriented interventions to improve communication in a medical office visit. *Health Psychol.* 1990;9(4):390–404.
42. Post D, Cegala D, Wiser W. The other half of the whole: Teaching patients to communicate with physicians. *Fam Med.* 2002;34(5):344–352.
43. Cegala D, Marinelli T, Post D. The effects of patient communication skills training on compliance. *Arch Fam Med.* 2000;9(1):57–64.
44. Roter D. Patient participation in the patient-provider interaction: The effects of patient question asking on the quality of interaction, satisfaction, and compliance. *Health Educ Monogr.* 1977;5(4):281–315.
45. Butow P, Dunn S, Tattersall M, Jones Q. Patient participation in the cancer consultation: Evaluation of a question prompt sheet. *Annu Oncol.* 1994;5(3):199–204.
46. Galliher JM, Post DM, Weiss BD et al. Patients' question-asking behavior during primary care visits: A report from the AAFP National Research Network. *Annu Fam Med.* 2010;8:151–159.
47. Health literacy universal precautions toolkit. Agency for Healthcare Research and Quality Web site. https://www.ahrq.gov/professionals/quality-patient-safety /quality-resources/tools/literacy-toolkit/index.html. Accessed January 27, 2017.
48. Lewis C, Pantell R, Sharp L. Increasing patient knowledge, satisfaction, and involvement: Randomized trial of a communication intervention. *Pediatrics.* 1991; 88(2):351–358.
49. Ishikawa H, Yan E. The relationship of patient participation and diabetes outcomes for patients with high vs. low health literacy. *Patient Educ Couns.* 2011;84(6):393–397.
50. Katz M, Jacobson T, Veledar E, Kripalani S. Patient literacy and question-asking behavior during the medical encounter: A mixed-methods analysis. *J Gen Intern Med.* 2007;22(6):782–786.
51. Parker RM, Baker DW, Williams MV, Nurss JR. The Test of Functional Health Literacy in Adults: A new instrument for measuring patients' literacy skills. *J Gen Intern Med.* 1995;10:537–541.
52. Mancuso JM. Assessment and measurement of health literacy: An integrative review of the literature. *Nurs Health Sci.* 2009;11:77–89.
53. Baker DW, Williams MV, Parker RM, Gazmararian JA, Nurss J. Development of a brief test to measure functional health literacy. *Patient Educ Couns.* 1999;38(1):33–42.
54. Baker DW, Williams MV, Parker RM, Gazmararian JA, Nurss JR. Development of a brief test to measure functional health literacy. *Patient Educ Couns.* 1999;38:33–42.
55. Taylor W. "Cloze procedure": A new tool for measuring readability. *Journalism Q.* 1953;30:415–433.
56. Davis TC, Crouch MA, Long SW et al. Rapid assessment of literacy levels of adult primary care patients. *Fam Med.* 1991;23(6):433–435.
57. Davis TC, Long SW, Jackson RH et al. Rapid Estimate of Adult Literacy in Medicine: A shortened screening instrument. *Fam Med.* 1993;25:391–395.
58. Bass PF III, Wilson JF, Griffith CH. A shortened instrument for literacy screening. *J Gen Intern Med.* 2003;18(12):1036–1038.
59. Weiss BD, Mays MZ, Martz W et al. Quick assessment of literacy in primary care: The newest vital sign. *Annu Fam Med.* 2005;3(6):514–522.
60. Chew LD, Bradley KA, Boyko EJ. Brief questions to identify patients with inadequate health literacy. *Fam Med.* 2004;36(8):588–594.
61. Chew LD, Griffin JM, Partin MR et al. Validation of screening questions for limited health literacy in a large VA outpatient population. *J Gen Intern Med.* 2008;23(5):561–566.

Health literacy 127

62. Wallace L, Rogers E, Roskos S, Holiday D, Weiss B. Brief report: Screening items to identify patients with limited health literacy skills. *J Gen Intern Med.* 2006;21(8):874–877.

63. Goodman MS, Griffey RT, Carpenter CR, Blanchard M, Kaphingst KA. Do subjective measures improve the ability to identify limited health literacy in a clinical setting? *J Am Board Fam Med.* 2015;28:584–594.

64. Eagleson R. Short definition of plain language; 2014. http://www.plainlanguage.gov/whatisPL/definitions/eagleson.cfm. Accessed January 27, 2017.

65. Jefford M, Moore R. Improvement of informed consent and the quality of consent documents. *Lancet Oncol.* 2008;9(5):485–493.

66. Ridpath JR, Wiese CJ, Greene SM. Looking at research consent forms through a participant-centered lens: The PRISM readability toolkit. *Am J Health Promot.* 2009;23(6):371–375.

67. Cordasco KM. Obtaining informed consent from patients: Brief update review. In: *Making Health Care Safer II: An Updated Critical Analysis of the Evidence for Patient Safety Practices.* Rockville, MD: Agency for Healthcare Research and Quality; March 2013: Chapter 39. Evidence Reports/Technology Assessments, No. 211. https://www.ncbi.nlm.nih.gov/books/NBK133402/. Accessed February 19, 2017.

68. Schnitzer A, Rosenzweig M, Harris B. Health literacy: A survey of the issues and solutions. *J Cons Health Internet.* 2011;15(2):164–179.

69. Doak CC, Doak LG, Root JH. *Teaching Patients with Low Literacy Skills.* 2nd ed. Philadelphia, PA: J.B. Lippincott Company; 1996.

70. Lachance C, Erby LH, Ford BM, Allen VC, Kaphingst KA. Informational content, literacy demands, and usability of websites offering health-related genetic tests directly to consumers. *Genet Med.* 2010;12(5):304–312.

71. Kaphingst KA, Rudd RE, DeJong W, Daltroy LH. Literacy demands of product information intended to supplement television direct-to-consumer prescription drug advertisements. *Patient Educ Couns.* 2004;55(2):293–300.

72. Kaphingst KA, Blanchard M, Milam L, Pokharel M, Elrick A, Goodman MS. Relationships between health literacy and genomics-related knowledge, self-efficacy, perceived importance, and communication in a medically underserved population. *J Health Commun.* 2016;21(suppl 1):58–68.

73. Lea DH, Kaphingst KA, Bowen D, Lipkus I, Hadley DW. Communicating genetic information and genetic risk: An emerging role for health educators. *Public Health Genomics.* 2011;14(4–5):279–289.

74. Mesters I, Ausems A, De Vries H. General public's knowledge, interest and information needs related to genetic cancer: An exploratory study. *Eur J Cancer Prev.* 2005;14:69–75.

75. Catz DS, Green NS, Tobin JN et al. Attitudes about genetics in underserved, culturally diverse populations. *Commun Genet.* 2005;8:161–172.

76. Lanie AD, Jayaratne TE, Sheldon JP et al. Exploring the public understanding of basic genetic concepts. *J Genet Counsel.* 2004;13(4):305–320.

77. Molster C, Charles T, Samanek A, O'Leary P. Australian study on public knowledge of human genetics and health. *Commun Genet.* 2009;12(2):84–91.

78. Haga SB, Barry WT, Mills R et al. Public knowledge of and attitudes toward genetics and genetic testing. *Genet Testing Molecular Biomarkers.* 2013;17(4):327–335.

79. Lillie SE, Brewer NT, O'Neill SC et al. Retention and use of breast cancer recurrence risk information from genomic tests: The role of health literacy. *Cancer Epidemiol Biomarkers Prev.* 2007;16(2):249–255.

80. Brewer NT, Tzeng JP, Lillie SE, Edwards AS, Peppercorn JM, Rimer BK. Health literacy and cancer risk perception: Implications for genomic risk communication. *Med Decis Making.* 2009;29:159–166.

128 *Public health research methods for partnerships and practice*

81. Erby L, Roter D, Larson S, Cho J. The Rapid Estimate of Adult Literacy in Genetics (REAL-G): A means to assess literacy deficits in the context of genetics. *Am J Med Genet.* 2008;146A:174–181.
82. Roter DL, Erby LH, Larson S, Ellington L. Assessing oral literacy demand in genetic counseling dialogue: Preliminary test of a conceptual framework. *Soc Sci Med.* 2007;65(7):1442–1457.
83. National Institutes of Health, Office of Communications and Public Liaison. *Achieving Quality and Effectiveness in Health Communication.* Bethesda, MD: National Institutes of Health; 2016. https://www.nih.gov/institutes-nih/nih-office-director/office-communications-public-liaison/clear-communication/clear-simple. Accessed January 27, 2017.
84. Use the nutrition facts label. National Heart, Lung, and Blood Institute Web site. https://www.nhlbi.nih.gov/health/educational/wecan/eat-right/nutrition-facts.htm Updated February 13, 2013. Accessed September 28, 2016.

Activity

When creating print materials, it is important to consider the audience and how to communicate the information most effectively. The provided checklist details the components of four principles for developing a plain language material.[83]

Consider the nutrition label (https://www.nhlbi.nih.gov/health/educational/wecan/eat-right/nutrition-facts.htm),[84] go through the checklist, and, using examples from the nutrition label, decide whether each principle on the checklist is reflected. For each principle, give an example of (1) why the nutrition label met the criteria on the checklist or did not meet the criteria on the checklist, and (2) a recommendation of how the nutrition label could be improved to better meet the needs of a person who may have limited reading and communication skills.

BOX 6.1   CHECKLIST FOR EASY-TO-UNDERSTAND PRINT MATERIALS

PRINCIPLE 1: CONTENT/STYLE

- The material is interactive and allows for audience involvement.
- The material presents "how-to" information.
- Writing reflects peer language whenever appropriate to increase personal identification and improve readability.
- Words are familiar to the reader. New words are defined clearly.
- Sentences are simple, specific, direct, and written in the active voice.
- Each idea is clear and logically sequenced (from the reader's perspective).

- There are a limited number of concepts in each piece.
- The writer uses concrete examples rather than abstract concepts.
- Text highlights and summarizes important points.

PRINCIPLE 2: LAYOUT

- The material uses advance organizers or headers.
- Headers are simple and close to text.
- Layout balances white space with words and illustrations.
- Text features both upper- and lowercase letters.
- Underlining or bold formatting—not caps—provides emphasis.
- The font selection (design, size) is easy to read. Opt for a 12-point font or larger size.

PRINCIPLE 3: VISUALS

- Visuals are relevant to text, meaningful to the audience, and logically located.
- Illustrations and photographs are simple and free from clutter and distraction.
- Visuals use age-appropriate images.
- Illustrations show familiar images that reflect cultural context.
- Visuals (graphics, photos) have captions written with active verb constructions. Each visual is illustrative and is directly related to 1 message.
- Visual elements (e.g., photographs without background detail, shaded line drawings, and simple line drawings), are shown to be appropriate and conducive to information retention in pre-testing with the audience.
- Cues (e.g., circle or arrows) highlight key information.
- The color palette is appealing to audience members during pretesting.

PRINCIPLE 4: READABILITY

- Readability analysis has been carried out to determine reading level.

(Adapted from Clear & Simple. National Institutes of Health. https://www.nih.gov/institutes-nih/nih-office-director/office -communications-public-liaison/clear-communication/clear-simple.)

SELF-ASSESSMENT—WHAT DID YOU LEARN?

1. What is health literacy?
   a. Ability to read brochures about health
   b. Ability to read medicine bottles
   c. Ability to read and understand scholarly medical journals
   d. Ability to understand and use basic health information in order to make appropriate health decisions

2. Health literacy affects a person's ability to _____.
   a. Fill out complex forms
   b. Engage in self-care and chronic disease management
   c. Share personal information, such as health history
   d. All of the above

3. Most Americans have _____ health literacy.
   a. Proficient
   b. Intermediate
   c. Basic
   d. Below basic

4. Which is NOT an assessment of health literacy?
   a. REALM
   b. NVS
   c. TOFHLA
   d. NHANES

5. Health literacy depends on _____.
   a. Solely the patient's literacy level
   b. Solely the physician's ability to communicate
   c. Both the patient and the physician
   d. None of the above

6. About _____ of adults in the United States have limited health literacy.
   a. 50%
   b. 25%
   c. 36%
   d. 80%

7. Providing patients with a list of questions can increase adherence to treatment recommendations and other medical outcomes.
    a. True
    b. False

8. Lower health literacy is associated with all of the following EXCEPT _____.
    a. Low health knowledge
    b. Poorer self-reported health
    c. Lower rates of hospitalization
    d. Less uses of preventative health services

9. Which of the following is not a plain language strategy?
    a. Providing graphics and images to supplement text
    b. Presenting topics in a clear and descriptive way
    c. Providing adequate white space throughout the document
    d. Standard presentation of statistical data

10. Patients with limited health literacy are more likely to participate in health decision-making.
    a. True
    b. False

7 Evidence-based public health

Sandra C. Hayes

LEARNING OBJECTIVES

- Define evidence-based public health.
- Describe key sources and types of evidence.
- Describe public health programs or policies that are based on strong or weak evidence.
- Describe some of the barriers to evidence-based decision-making in public health practice.

SELF-ASSESSMENT—WHAT DO YOU KNOW?

1. What are some different types of evidence?
2. What is the purpose of using evidence-based public health methods?
3. What types of evidence are characterized as strong in evidence-based public health?

What is evidence-based public health?

Evidence-based public health (EBPH) has been defined as "the development, implementation, and evaluation of effective programs and policies in public health through the application of principles of scientific reasoning, including systematic uses of data and information systems, and appropriate use of behavioral science theory and program planning models."[1] EBPH is a term used to describe the methodology that is used by public health practitioners to evaluate the effectiveness of public health programs, practices, and policies. Evidence-based public health can also support the decision to choose a specific course of action and determine how resources should be distributed.[2]

EBPH has its origins in clinical epidemiology and evidence-based medicine. *Clinical epidemiology* is the application of the principles and methods of epidemiology to conduct, appraise, or apply clinical research studies focusing on prevention, diagnosis, prognosis, and treatment of disease. *Evidence-based medicine* is the intentional use of modern, best evidence in making patient care decisions. Public health professionals began to use EBPH during the 1970s and 1980s out of the concern that expert reviews and recommendations from expert panels frequently failed to include relevant studies and produced suboptimal conclusions. These reports and studies did not demonstrate which aspects of health care practices were associated with better health outcomes.[2]

Why is EBPH important?

EBPH is important because it can be used to make decisions based on data that demonstrate which strategies work, that increase the likelihood of successful programs and policies being implemented, that improve workforce productivity, and that lead to more efficient allocation and utilization of public and private resources.[1,3,4] Some of the primary characteristics of EBPH include the following: (1) utilization of the best available data to make decisions, (2) implementation of a system to utilize data and information systems, (3) application of models that often have a foundation in behavioral science theory, (4) engagement with the community in the decision-making and assessment process, (5) inclusion of the use of sound evaluation to determine whether program objectives have been achieved, and (6) dissemination of what is learned to key stakeholders and decision makers.[5] EBPH is used in different ways. Practitioners use it for program planning and internal policies, local managers use it to make decisions about which programs to support, and senior managers within government and health care organizations use it to set priorities and make policy and funding decisions.[6] Figure 7.1 displays the process of evidence-based practice.

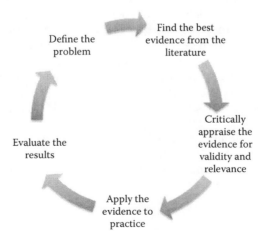

Figure 7.1 Process of evidence-based practice. (Adapted from Sackett, DL et al., *J R Soc Med.*, 88(11):620–624, 1995; Sibbald, WJ, *Crit Care Clin.*, 14(3):549–558, 1998.)

134   *Public health research methods for partnerships and practice*

Using data and information systems systematically

The first step in the EBPH process is to define the problem. This is done using a validated community health assessment tool. Validation involves establishing that the instrument produces data that are reliable and true. The information gathered from the needs assessment allows the public health program or policy to be tailored and implemented in a way that increases the likelihood of achieving the desired outcomes.

The community needs assessment, the most common tool used to identify community health needs, is the initial interaction with the community. It creates a clear, mutual plan of action between the practitioner and community. The community health assessment, in combination with a thorough review of the scientific literature, can be used to identify interventions, programs, and policies that have been effective in addressing the identified needs, available resources, and existing gaps. It also outlines the indicators that should be tracked to determine whether and how the public health program or policy contributed to change. Because a large amount of data is collected during the assessment process, it is important for practitioners to know how to synthesize, interpret, and evaluate the data in order to identify the best available evidence.

Making decisions using the best available data

Peer-reviewed studies

One strategy for selecting evidence is to search for *peer-reviewed studies*. The term "peer-reviewed" refers to information that has been reviewed by peer researchers in the field before the information is published, usually in a journal. Different scientific disciplines have different mechanisms for determining which journals are legitimately peer reviewed. The basic criterion is that there is a standardized method of peer review before a manuscript goes to publication. Typically, the journal editor will assign a manuscript to a small group of individuals who have been recognized as experts in the relevant field. The reviewers evaluate the manuscript submission and provide detailed criticism of the paper along with a recommendation to reject, accept with major revisions, accept with minor revisions, or accept as is. It is rare to get an "as is" acceptance in the first round of manuscript review.

When sources of information are being sought, considerations must be made regarding the quality of the sources, even among peer-reviewed journals. It is important to understand that some peer-reviewed journals do not hold the same weight as others in the scientific community. Small or obscure journals may follow the rules and gain recognized peer-reviewed status but may have a low bar for acceptance because they are desperate for submissions. Therefore, an important consideration in determining the quality of the source is the knowledge of where the paper was reviewed and published. In addition, the potential bias of peer reviewers might be a factor in the sources

Evidence-based public health   135

that are available. Peer reviewers may be biased against studies that contradict their own research or personal beliefs. Therefore, they may tend to select studies in their favored direction and may be hesitant to accept a submission that directly contradicts something they have published.

Data collection tools

Data collection tools may be quantitative or qualitative. These tools can be customized to depict the specific needs of a community, to create new sources of data, and to obtain data that may already exist. Examples of data collection tools include telephone, mail, online, or face-to-face surveys that collect self-reported data from community members. The types of questions, descriptions, advantages, and disadvantages of each can be found in Table 7.1.

Sources of public health data include health data tools and statistics, data from local public health departments (e.g., vital statistics, county health rankings, and disease registries), and data from the United States Census Bureau. These sources of data are expounded upon below.

- *Health Data Tools and Statistics:* This data portal was created through a collaboration of U.S. government agencies, public health organizations, and health sciences libraries and provides links to health statistics and datasets as well as resources to support data collection.
- *NHANES:* The survey is a series of studies designed to assess the health and nutritional status of adults and children in the United States. It is unique in that it combines interviews and physical examinations.
- *NHIS:* The survey data cover a broad range of health topics and are collected through personal household interviews. Survey results have been instrumental in providing data to track health status, health care access, and progress toward achieving national health objectives.
- *Local, state, and national public health agencies:* Local health departments are city, county, metropolitan, district, and tribal government agencies. There are approximately 2800 local health departments across the United States.[7] Every day, local health departments work to protect and promote health and well-being for all people in their communities. Data obtained from local public health departments include vital statistics, county health profiles, and disease registries.
- *U.S. Census Bureau:* Health statistics are very important in measuring the nation's overall health status. The Census Bureau provides accurate, detailed, and up-to-date statistics—covering people and businesses—relating to health in America.

Monitoring the health status of populations is a core function of all public health agencies but is particularly important at the municipal and community levels, where population health data increasingly are used to drive public health decision-making and community health improvement efforts.

Table 7.1 Types of survey questions with advantages and disadvantages

Type	Description	Advantages	Disadvantages
Closed-ended questions	Closed-ended questions limit the answers of the respondents to response options provided on the questionnaire	Time-efficient. Responses are easy to code and interpret. Ideal for quantitative research	Respondents are required to choose a response that may not exactly reflect their answer. The researcher cannot further explore the meaning of the responses
Open-ended questions	There are no predefined options or categories included. The participants should supply their own answers	Participants can respond to the questions exactly as they would like to answer them. The researcher can investigate the meaning of the responses. Ideal for qualitative research	Time consuming. Responses are difficult to code and interpret
Matrix questions *(Also referred to as the Likert scale)*	Matrix questions are also closed-ended questions but are arranged one under the other, such that the questions form a matrix or a table with identical response options placed on top	They are quick and economical to administer and score They are easily adapted to most attitude measurement situations They provide direct and reliable assessment of attitudes when scales are well constructed They lend themselves well to item analysis procedures	Results are easily faked where individuals want to present a false impression of their attitudes (this can be offset somewhat by developing a good level of rapport with the respondents and convincing them that honest responses are in their best interests) Intervals between points on the scale do not present equal changes in attitude for all individuals (i.e., the differences between "strongly agree" and "agree" may be slight for one individual and great for another)

(Continued)

Table 7.1 (Continued) Types of survey questions with advantages and disadvantages

Type	Description	Advantages	Disadvantages
			Internal consistency of the scale may be difficult to achieve (care must be taken to have unidimensional items aimed at a single person, group, event or method)
			Good attitude statements take time to construct (it is usually best to begin by constructing several times as many attitude statements as you will actually need, then selecting only those that best assess the attitude in question)
Contingency questions	Questions that need to be answered only when the respondent provides a particular response to a question prior to them are called *contingency questions*. Asking these questions effectively avoids asking people questions that are not applicable to them	Detailed data may be obtained from a specific subgroup of the population	Data only apply to a specific subgroup

138 *Public health research methods for partnerships and practice*

Unfortunately, most local health jurisdictions lack important data for developing population health profiles, such as data on chronic disease prevalence, quality of life, functional status, and self-perceptions of health status. In addition, data on important determinants of health, including health behaviors and access to health care services, are rarely available locally.[8]

Data on the important determinants of health are frequently collected in national and state surveys (e.g., the NHIS and the BRFSS) and provide critical information to assess progress toward achieving state and national health objectives. The surveys rarely serve local data needs, however, because of insufficient sample size and lack of flexibility to address local health issues.

Qualitative methods

Qualitative methods can help to provide a comprehensive snapshot of a community by answering the "how" and "why" of an issue. (See Chapter 11 for an extensive discussion of qualitative methods.) Examples of qualitative data collection methodology include simple observation, interviews, focus groups, photovoice, community forums, and listening sessions. This methodology involves the verbatim creation of transcripts, the development of data-sorting categories, and iterative sorting and synthesizing of data to develop sets of common concepts or themes.[9]

Quantitative methods

Quantitative methods in evidence-based public health (i.e., data in numerical quantities) can take many forms, ranging from scientific information in peer-reviewed journals, to data from public health surveillance systems, to evaluations of individual programs or policies.[5,10] (See Chapter 10 for a discussion of quantitative methods.)

There are advantages and disadvantages of each data collection method. No single source of data is best. Most often, strategies that utilize both qualitative and quantitative methods are needed to fully understand a problem and its best potential solutions.[11] Clinicians, agency heads of health and social services agencies, and community members can all serve as key informants or participants in group discussions.

Applying program-planning frameworks (that often have a foundation in behavioral science theory)

The most successful public health interventions are supported by an evidence-based health behavior theory. Health behavior theories are grounded in an understanding of health behaviors and the context in which they occur. Therefore, interventions to improve health behavior must be created and implemented with a clear knowledge of relevant theories of behavior change and the ability to apply them appropriately.

Evidence-based public health 139

The science and art of using health behavior theories reflect a combination of approaches, methods, and strategies from social and health sciences. Collectively, this broad range of perspectives from social and behavioral sciences are referred to as "social and behavioral science theory."[12,13] Some common health behavior theories and models are included in Table 7.2.

The logic model as a planning tool

The logic model is an important planning tool in EBPH. Logic models provide a graphic way to incorporate the concepts of health behavior theories. They visually demonstrate the association between program activities and their intended short-term objectives and long-term goals. The logic model is important because it summarizes key program elements, explains the rationale behind program activities, clarifies intended outcomes, and provides a communication tool.

Engaging the community in assessment and decision-making

Community engagement has been defined over the last two decades in several different ways.[14] One definition of *community engagement* is "the process of working collaboratively with relevant partners who share common goals and interests."[15] It involves "building authentic partnerships, including mutual respect and active, inclusive participation; power sharing and equity; mutual benefit or finding the 'win-win' possibility" in the collaborative project.[16] The emphasis on community engagement acknowledges that communities have important knowledge and valuable experience to add to public stakeholder discussions. (Also, see Chapters 1 and 3 for discussions of community engagement.)

Community-based participatory research (CBPR) is an evidence-based public health tool that involves a partnership of researchers and community members and a willingness to expand or reframe research questions to increase their relevance to community members. CBPR builds long-term relationships that outlast any specific research project; these relationships form the foundation of a sustained conversation that includes two-way communication and shared decision-making.

Conducting sound evaluations to determine programmatic success

Evaluation is used to answer questions about program effectiveness, implementation, and outcomes.[17] Evaluation should begin when a community assessment is initiated and continue across the life of a program to ensure proper implementation of the program or intervention. *Formative, process, impact*, and *outcome* evaluation are four basic types of evaluation used to assess success in achieving program objectives.

140 *Public health research methods for partnerships and practice*

Table 7.2 Common health theories and models[a]

Theory/model	Description	Key constructs
Individual		
Health belief model	For people to adopt recommended physical activity behaviors, their perceived threat of disease (and its severity) and benefits of action must outweigh their perceived barriers to action	Perceived susceptibility Perceived severity Perceived benefits of action Perceived barriers to action Cues to action Self-efficacy
Stages of change (transtheoretical model)	In adopting healthy behaviors (e.g., regular physical activity) or eliminating unhealthy ones (e.g., watching television), people progress through 5 levels related to their readiness to change—pre-contemplation, contemplation, preparation, action, and maintenance. At each stage, different intervention strategies will help people progress to the next stage	Pre-contemplation Contemplation Preparation Action Maintenance
Interpersonal		
Social learning/ social cognitive theory	Health behavioral change is the result of reciprocal relationships among the environment, personal factors, and attributes of the behavior itself. Self-efficacy is one of the most important characteristics that determine behavioral change	Self-efficacy Reciprocal determinism Behavioral capability Outcome expectations Observational learning
Theory of reasoned action	For behaviors that are within a person's control, behavioral intentions predict actual behavior. Intentions are determined by two factors— attitude toward the behavior and beliefs regarding other people's support of the behavior	Attitude toward the behavior Outcome expectations Value of outcome expectations Subjective norms Beliefs of others Desire to comply with others

(Continued)

Evidence-based public health 141

Table 7.2 (Continued) Common health theories and models[a]

Theory/model	Description	Key constructs
Theory of planned action	People's perceived control over the opportunities, resources, and skills needed to perform a behavior affect behavioral intentions, as do the two factors in the theory of reasoned action	Attitude toward the behavior Outcome expectations Value of outcome expectations Subjective norms Beliefs of others Desire to comply with others Perceived behavioral control
Community level		
Community organization model	Public health workers help communities identify health and social problems, and they plan and implement strategies to address these problems. Active community participation is essential	Social planning Locality development Social action
Ecological approaches	Effective interventions must influence multiple levels because health is shaped by many environmental subsystems, including family, community, workplace, beliefs and traditions, economics, and the physical and social environments	Multiple levels of influence Intrapersonal Interpersonal Institutional Community Public policy
Organizational change theory	Certain processes and strategies might increase the chances that healthy policies and programs will be adopted and maintained in formal organizations	Definition of problem (awareness stage) Initiation of action (adoption stage) Implementation of change Institutionalization of change
Diffusions of innovation theory	People, organizations, or societies adopt new ideas, products, or behaviors at different rates, and the rate of adoption is affected by some predictable factors	Relative advantage Compatibility Complexity Trialability Observability

[a] The examples of individual, interpersonal, and community-level theories of models of health behavior have been summarized from the following source: U.S. Department of Health and Human Services, *Physical Activity Evaluation Handbook*, Department of Health and Human Services, Centers for Disease Control and Prevention, Atlanta, GA, 2002, Appendix 3, p. 43. (http://www.cdc.gov/nccdphp/dnpa/physical/handbook/pdf/handbook.pdf)

142 *Public health research methods for partnerships and practice*

Formative evaluation is conducted to decide whether an element of the intervention (e.g., materials, messages) is feasible, appropriate, and meaningful for the target population.[18] For example, a quality improvement intervention allows patients at a primary care practice to obtain laboratory results through a secure Web portal. As part of a formative evaluation, a finding might be that patients either were not notified when their laboratory results became available or had difficulty logging into the portal. Formative evaluations provide findings such as these to practices and program sponsors on an ongoing basis, along with specific recommendations on how to improve patient access. In this example, this information could be used to refine the intervention by sending e-mail alerts to patients when new lab results are entered.[19]

Process evaluation assesses whether a program is being implemented in accordance with the established work plan, rather than the effectiveness of that program.[18] Process evaluation is important to help distinguish the causes of poor program performance. For example, was the program a bad idea, or was it a good idea that could not reach the standard for implementation set by the program? In all cases, process evaluations measure whether actual program performance was faithful to the initial plan. Such measurements might include contrasting actual and planned performance along all or some of the following:[20]

- The locale where services or programs are provided (e.g., rural, urban).
- The number of people receiving services.
- The economic status and racial/ethnic background of people receiving services.
- The quality of services.
- The actual events that occur while the services are delivered.
- The amount of money the project is using.
- The direct and in-kind funding for services.
- The staffing for services or programs.
- The number of activities and meetings.
- The number of training sessions conducted.

Impact evaluation assesses whether program objectives are being met and may reflect changes in knowledge, attitudes, behavior, or other intermediate outcomes. Validity (the extent to which a measure accurately captures what it is intended to capture) and reliability (the likelihood that the instrument will get the same result time after time) are important criteria for measures used in impact evaluation.[21] Impact evaluation can be critical in assisting administrators and legislators in making policy and funding decisions.

Evidence-based public health 143

Outcome evaluation provides long-term feedback on changes in health status, morbidity, mortality, or quality of life that can be attributed to an intervention.[11] Depending on the stage of development of the program and the purpose of the evaluation, outcome evaluations may include any or all of the outcomes in the sequence, including the following:[20]

- The changes in people's attitudes and beliefs.
- Changes in risk or protective behaviors.
- Changes in the environment, including public and private policies, formal and informal enforcement of regulations, and influence of social norms and other societal forces.
- Changes in trends in morbidity and mortality.

Disseminating what is learned to key stakeholders

Dissemination of findings is often overlooked. However, it is imperative for practitioners to share results with stakeholders, decision makers, and community members. Dissemination may take the form of formal written reports, oral presentations, publication in academic journals, or placement of information in newsletters or on Web sites.

Dissemination of information helps to address important questions. For example, what is the likely disease burden that might be prevented or reduced? Which programs and policy options are likely to result in meaningful improvements in health? How will the benefits be distributed among the affected groups? Which potential solutions are appropriate and feasible for a specific situation, considering the fit between strategy and the community context, political and technical feasibility, and cost and cost-effectiveness? Public health has the potential to inform these decisions but requires the use of evidence-based research techniques at every stage, from production of primary studies to synthesis of results across studies and then to translation of research-tested findings into effective community action. For the health of the public to be protected and improved, interventions that are based on the best available scientific evidence must be created and implemented; the existing scientific evidence base must continually be improved and expanded; and the use of the best available, science-tested programs and policies must be promoted.[22]

Levels of evidence

The levels of evidence illustrate how the relative weight of available evidence can be attributed to a particular study design. Typically, the higher a methodology is ranked (Figure 7.2), the more robust it is expected to be. On one end of the spectrum lies meta-analysis, a quantitative review synthesizing the results of a number of similar trials to produce a result of higher statistical power. Meta-analysis is thought to provide a high level of evidence. At the

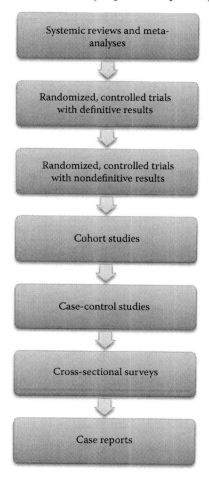

Figure 7.2 Hierarchy of evidence. (Adapted from Guyatt, GH et al., *JAMA.*, 274:1800–4, 1995.)

other end of the spectrum lie observational studies, thought to provide the weakest level of evidence. Common evidence-based public health resources can be found in Table 7.3.

Concerns

Although the hierarchy presented in this text is widely accepted within the scientific community, some concerns exist regarding how the evidence is ranked. Studies should be selected with ethical considerations in mind. For example, in accordance with the hierarchy of evidence, randomized studies are considered

Evidence-based public health 145

Table 7.3 Common evidence-based public health resources

Resource	Description
The Cochrane Public Health Group (CPHG)	The CPHG, formerly the Health Promotion and Public Health (HPPH) Field, aims to work with contributors to produce and publish Cochrane reviews of the effects of population-level public health interventions
Evidence for Policy and Practice Information and Coordinating Centre (EPPI-Centre)	The EPPI-Centre is part of the Social Science Research Unit (SSRU), Institute of Education, University of London. The EPPI-Centre was established in 1993 to address the need for a systematic approach to the organization and review of evidence-based work on social interventions
Guide to Community Preventive Services (*Community Guide*)	Developed by a nonfederal Community Preventive Services Task Force (Task Force), appointed by the Director of the Centers for Disease Control and Prevention (CDC). This group was convened in 1996 by the Department of Health and Human Services to provide leadership in the evaluation of community, population, and health care system strategies to address a variety of public health and health promotion topics
National Registry of Evidence-Based Programs and Practices (NREPP)	NREPP is a searchable database of interventions for the prevention and treatment of mental and substance use disorders. The Substance Abuse and Mental Health Services Administration (SAMHSA) developed this resource to help people, agencies, and organizations implement programs and practices in their communities

most robust. However, it would, in many cases, be unethical to perform an RCT to assess risk factor exposure. In this case, a cohort study would be necessary to determine whether a participant has been exposed by chance or personal choice. There has also been debate about where different methodologies are located within the hierarchy. For example, the RCT has traditionally been regarded as the most objective method of removing bias and producing comparable groups, but the technique is often slow and expensive; it produces results that are difficult to replicate in everyday practice. The strength of a study is influenced by how robust the study design is. Therefore, a robust observational study may provide more compelling evidence about a treatment compared to a poorly designed RCT. The hierarchy focuses largely on quantitative methodologies. However, in some cases, a qualitative study design may be more appropriate.

How does EBPH practice differ from evidence-based medical practice?

Important differences can be observed between evidence-based approaches in medicine and those in public health. First, the type and volume of evidence

146 *Public health research methods for partnerships and practice*

differ. Medical studies of pharmaceuticals and procedures often rely on RCTs including individuals, the most scientifically rigorous of epidemiologic studies. In contrast, public health interventions are usually based on data from cross-sectional studies, quasi-experimental designs, and time-series analyses. These studies sometimes lack a comparison group and require more caveats when interpreting the results.

Many RCTs have been used to investigate the effectiveness of medical treatments.[23] However, fewer studies have been performed on the effectiveness of public health interventions because they are difficult to design, and often results derive from natural experiments.[1,24] Although EBPH has adopted the term *intervention* from clinical disciplines, in public health, we seldom have a single "intervention" but rather a program that involves multifaceted approaches to address an issue within a community. Large community-based trials can be more expensive to conduct than randomized experiments in a clinic. Population-based studies generally require a longer time period between intervention and outcome. For example, a study on the effects of smoking cessation on lung cancer mortality would require decades of data collection and analysis. Contrast that with treatment of a medical condition (e.g., an antibiotic for symptoms of pneumonia), which is likely to produce effects in days or weeks, or even a surgical trial for cancer with endpoints of mortality within a few years. In addition, the formal training of persons working in public health is much more variable than that in medicine or other clinical disciplines.[25]

Future of EBPH

The future of EBPH rests in improving the quality of the evidence base, doing a better job of engaging communities to assist in developing policies and programs, and increasing community involvement. Community involvement in EBPH is most likely to be achieved through CBPR and the establishment of CABs. In addition, there must be efforts to improve public health assessment methodology.

Conclusions

EBPH continues to evolve. The successful implementation of EBPH practice is both a science and an art. EBPH is built on epidemiologic, behavioral, and policy research, which shows the magnitude of a public health problem and the interventions that are likely to be effective in addressing the problem. EBPH involves knowing which information is important to a particular stakeholder at a particular time. Unlike solving a math problem, significant decisions in public health must balance science and art because rational, evidence-based decision-making often involves choosing a single alternative from among a set of rational choices.

Evidence-based public health   147

BOX 7.1   EVIDENCE-BASED PUBLIC HEALTH RESOURCES

- **Guide to Community Preventive Services**
  http://www.thecommunityguide.org/
- **Healthy People 2020 Evidence-Based Resource Tool**
  http://healthypeople.gov/2020/implement/EBR.aspx
- **Healthy People 2020 Interventions and Resources**
  http://www.healthypeople.gov/2020/TopicsObjectives2020/
- **The Campbell Collaboration**
  http://www.campbellcollaboration.org/
- **Clinical Practice Guidelines (AHRQ)**
  https://www.ahrq.gov/professionals/clinicians-providers
  /guidelines-recommendations/index.html
- **The Cochrane Library**
  http://www.thecochranelibrary.com/view/0/index.html
- **Cochrane Public Health Group**
  http://ph.cochrane.org/finding-public-health-reviews
- **Centers for Disease Control and Prevention**
  - *National Health Interview Survey*
    https://www.cdc.gov/nchs/nhis/index.htm
  - *National Health and Nutrition Examination Survey*
    https://www.cdc.gov/nchs/nhanes/index.htm
- **Partners in Information Access for the Public Health Workforce**
  https://phpartners.org/health_stats.html
- **United States Census Bureau**
  http://www.census.gov/topics/health.html

References

1. Brownson RC, Baker EA, Leet TL, Gillespie KN. *Evidence-Based Public Health.* New York: Oxford University Press; 2003.
2. Secretary's Advisory Committee on National Health Promotion and Disease Prevention Objectives for 2020. Healthy People Web site. https://www.healthypeople .gov/2020/about/history-development/Secretary%E2%80%99s-Advisory -Committee. Accessed October 15, 2016.
3. Hausman AJ. Implications of evidence-based practice for community health. *Am J Community Psychol.* 2002;30:453–467.
4. Kohatsu ND, Melton RJ. A health department perspective on the Guide to Community Preventive Services. *Am J Prev Med.* 2000;18:3–4.
5. Brownson, RC, Fielding, JE, Maylahn, CM. Evidence-based public health: A fundamental concept for public health practice. *Annu Rev Public Health.* 2009;30:175–201.

148 *Public health research methods for partnerships and practice*

6. Jackson SF, Edwards RK, Kahan B, Goodstadt M. Canadian Consortium for Health Promotion Research. An assessment of the methods and concepts used to synthesize the evidence of effectiveness in health promotion: A review of 17 initiatives; 2001. http://sites.utoronto.ca/chp/CCHPR/synthesisfinalreport.pdf. Accessed November 20, 2016.
7. National Association of County and City Health Officials. NACCHO press kit. http://archived.naccho.org/press/upload/NACCHO_Press_Kit_June_15_Finalv2.pdf. Accessed November 23, 2016.
8. Simon PA, Wold CM, Cousineau MR, Fielding JE. Meeting the data needs of a local health department: The Los Angeles County Health Survey. *Am J Public Health.* 2001;91(12):1950–1952.
9. Hesse-Biber S, Leavy P. *The Practice of Qualitative Research.* Thousand Oaks, CA: Sage Publications; 2006.
10. Chambers D, Kerner J. Closing the gap between discovery and delivery. Paper presented at: Dissemination and Implementation Research Workshop: Harnessing Science to Maximize Health; March 26, 2007; Rockville, MD.
11. Jacobs JA, Jones E, Gabella BA, Spring B, Brownson RC. Tools for implementing an evidence-based approach in public health practice. *Prev Chronic Dis.* 2012;9:110324. doi: http://dx.doi.org/10.5888/pcd9.110324.
12. Glanz K, Bishop DB. The role of behavioral science theory in the development and implementation of public health interventions. *Annu Rev Public Health.* 2010;31:399–418.
13. Glanz K, Rimer BK, Viswanath K. *Health Behavior and Health Education: Theory, Research, and Practice.* 4th ed. San Francisco, CA: Jossey-Bass; 2008.
14. Centers for Disease Control and Prevention. *Principles of Community Engagement.* 1st ed. Atlanta, GA: CDC/ATSDR Committee on Community Engagement; 1997.
15. Tindana PO, Singh JA, Tracy CS et al. Grand challenges in global health: Community engagement in research in developing countries. *PLoS Medicine.* 2007;4(9):e273. doi:10.1371/journal.pmed.0040273.
16. Zakus JD, Lysack CL. Revisiting community participation. *Health Policy Plan.* 1998;13:1–12.
17. Shadish WR. The common threads in program evaluation. *Prev Chronic Dis.* 2006;3(1):1–5. http://www.cdc.gov/pcd/issues/2006/jan/05_0166.htm.
18. Thompson N, Kegler M, Holtgrave D. Program evaluation. In: Crosby RA, DiClemente RJ, Salazar LF, eds. *Research Methods in Health Promotion.* San Francisco, CA: Jossey-Bass; 2006: 199–225.
19. Genonnotti K, Peikes D, Wang W, Smith J. Formative evaluation: Fostering real-time adaptions and refinements to improve the effectiveness of patient-centered medical home interventions; 2013. https://pcmh.ahrq.gov/sites/default/files/attachments/FormativeEvaluation_032513comp.pdf. Accessed February 1, 2017.
20. Centers for Disease Control and Prevention. Introduction to program evaluation for public health programs: A self-study guide; 2011. https://www.cdc.gov/eval/guide/index.htm. Accessed November 23, 2016.
21. Nelson DE, Holtzman D, Bolen J, Stanwyck CA, Mack KA. Reliability and validity of measures from the Behavioral Risk Factor Surveillance System (BRFSS). *Soz Praventivmed.* 2001;46(suppl 1):S3–42.
22. Fielding JE, Briss PA. Promoting evidence-based public health policy: Can we have better evidence and more action? *Health Affairs.* 2006;25(4):969–978.

Evidence-based public health   149

23. Cameron C, Fireman B, Hutton B et al. Network meta-analysis incorporating randomized controlled trials and non-randomized comparative cohort studies for assessing the safety and effectiveness of medical treatments: Challenges and opportunities. *Syst Rev.* 2015;4:147.
24. Oldenburg BF, Sallis JF, French ML, Owen N. Health promotion research and the diffusion and institutionalization of interventions. *Health Educ Res.* 1999;14:121–30.
25. Tilson H, Gebbie KM. The public health workforce. *Annu Rev Public Health.* 2004;25:341–56.

Activity

This activity takes about 15 minutes.

Break the class into groups of 4 to 5 members each. Each group should examine a summary of data used to determine a service or intervention recommendation relevant to the public health issue or community issue of interest. Given existing data, participants discuss how culture, community resources, preferences, and norms might affect the implementation of an evidence-based intervention. Recommendations for future research should be considered.

An edited data summary from the Community Guide is provided below.

CARDIOVASCULAR DISEASE PREVENTION AND CONTROL: SELF-MEASURED BLOOD PRESSURE MONITORING INTERVENTIONS FOR IMPROVED BLOOD PRESSURE CONTROL

A total of 52 studies were conducted around the world: United States (23 studies), Europe (18 studies), Canada (6 studies), Australia (2 studies), Brazil (2 studies), and South Korea (1 study).

Randomized controlled trials (49 studies)

Nonrandomized studies (3 studies) in which self-measured blood pressure interventions were compared with usual care.

Common limitations affecting this body of evidence were the loss to follow-up, insufficient descriptions of the intervention, substantial differences between intervention and comparison groups at baseline, and outcomes that were not clearly defined. Only 3 studies included more than 500 patients.

All patients who received self-measured blood pressure monitoring interventions were trained to use blood pressure monitors provided by the programs, and they measured their blood pressure at home. Patients' blood pressure readings were delivered to health care providers during medical visits as self-recorded readings (23 studies), through electronic transmissions sent directly from blood pressure devices to central databases that providers could access (15 studies), or by mail (5 studies).

150   *Public health research methods for partnerships and practice*

Included study populations consisted primarily of adults aged 18 to 64 years with an even distribution of men and women. Among the 40% of included studies that reported race/ethnicity, populations primarily identified as white/Caucasian (median proportion: 72%; 15 studies). Two studies in which 75% or more of the patients identified as African American showed favorable blood pressure outcomes, indicating that self-measured blood pressure monitoring interventions when combined with additional support can be effective in this population.

Thirty-six studies reported that all patients had uncontrolled blood pressure at baseline. In the six studies that included patients whose blood pressure was controlled at baseline, further improvements in blood pressure were shown at follow-up, indicating that self-measured blood pressure monitoring interventions also help patients adhere to treatment when their blood pressure is under control. Four studies that targeted populations who had both high blood pressure and diabetes had greater improvements in blood pressure compared to overall findings, suggesting effectiveness among populations with comorbidities.

(From Community Preventive Services Task Force. Cardiovascular disease prevention and control: self-measured blood pressure monitoring interventions for improved blood pressure control. https://www.the communityguide.org/sites/default/files/assets/CVD-Self-Measured-Blood -Pressure_4.pdf. Updated July 5, 2016. Accessed January 31, 2017.)

SELF-ASSESSMENT—WHAT DID YOU LEARN?

1. _____ public health is the implementation of effective public health programs and policies through application of principles of scientific reasoning.
   a. Evidence-based
   b. Data-based
   c. Hypothesis-based
   d. Reasoning-based

2. Which of the following is NOT an outcome or purpose of evidence-based public health?
   a. Improves the outcome and utilization of available resources
   b. Gains conclusive and indisputable answers to public health questions

Evidence-based public health 151

    c. Allows research to connect to the actual implementation of public health
    d. Has the potential to increase knowledge about practice

3. Which of the following is a type of evidence?
    a. Program evaluations
    b. Scientific findings in an academic journal
    c. Personal experience
    d. All of the above

4. Community assessment tools used to identify the public health problem should _____.
    a. Be short
    b. Address the biological, physical, and social environment
    c. Be validated tools
    d. Include an inventory of community resources

5. Evidence is NOT _____.
    a. Subject to strict and rigorous rules
    b. Pieces of information or knowledge on which a conclusion can be based
    c. Cumulative and time-sensitive
    d. Relative to time and place and subject to new discoveries

6. Evidence-based public health integrates _____ _____ to improve the health of populations.
    a. Science and community preference
    b. Science and medicine
    c. Community preference and medicine
    d. Community preference and opinion

7. A randomized controlled trial (RCT) is considered stronger evidence on which to base a public health decision than _____.
    a. A case study
    b. A cross-sectional study
    c. A systematic review
    d. All of the above

8. There are no differences between evidence-based public health and evidence-based medical practice.
    a. True
    b. False

152 *Public health research methods for partnerships and practice*

9. The four basic types of evaluation used over the course of evidence-based public health practice include _____.
   a. Formative, impact, outcome, organizational
   b. Formative, process, community, outcome
   c. Process, outcome, impact, policy
   d. Formative, process, impact, outcome

8 Program planning and evaluation

Kristen Wagner, Sha-Lai Williams,
and Vetta Sanders Thompson

LEARNING OBJECTIVES

- Develop a public program or intervention.
- Develop SMART goals for programs and projects.
- Identify culturally competent evaluation approaches.
- Understand the importance of evaluation.
- Develop logic models.

SELF-ASSESSMENT—WHAT DO YOU KNOW?

1. What does SMART stand for?
2. What are the components of a logic model?
3. What is program evaluation?
4. Why is it important to evaluate your program?
5. What are some standard types of program evaluation?

Introduction

The field of public health contributes to the well-being of individuals, families, and communities through the delivery of evidence-based programs and services. Public health programs are structured activities developed for certain populations with specific goals in mind. Program activities may cover a range of services designed to monitor health conditions, empower people through health education programs, advocate for policies that support the health status of individuals and communities, or create opportunities for equitable access to needed health services.

Effective programs are a result of an intentional procedure that engages stakeholders in an iterative process that combines planning and evaluation tasks. A needs assessment typically starts the process by identifying problems. The assessment phase is followed by a design process that identifies change strategies,

154   *Public health research methods for partnerships and practice*

inputs needed to implement the strategies, and the articulation of intended program outcomes that are measured using relevant evaluation methods. This chapter will focus on the steps involved with developing effective, evidence-based programs and ways that evaluation can be used to regularly monitor program effectiveness and ensure that people who need the services receive them.

Program planning processes

Program planning and evaluation go together. At the beginning stage of program planning, you will specifically describe the problem that you are trying to address and the actions or activities that will take place to address that problem. Once you have described your program in detail, you will select evaluation measures that will allow you to collect the data needed to demonstrate the impact of your program. Although there is an order to these planning steps, it is important to consider the connection between program implementation and evaluation from the start. We describe, in the following, the steps involved in a full program cycle.[1]

Engaging stakeholders

The first step of the process is to develop a plan to engage stakeholders. Not only should stakeholders be engaged at the beginning of the process, but space should also be reserved for their voice throughout the entire planning and evaluation cycle. Stakeholders provide critical information from a client perspective regarding the accessibility of programs and services, the relevance of program activities to client needs, and cultural relevance of services and education programs to the target population. Integrated stakeholder involvement means greater buy-in and improvement of program sustainability by providing credibility to the program.[1,2] Engaging stakeholders through the entirety of the program planning process, including evaluation, can increase the likelihood that the data collected are important to the community and can be used to advocate for both sustainability of the program and the possibility of scaling up the program (see Chapter 1 for more information).

Identifying and prioritizing problems to address

Identifying a clear problem with a specific focus is the first step toward designing an effective program. The more clearly you define the issue in terms of duration, scope, and frequency, the more detailed and relevant your program design will be.[3] Knowing how long a problem has persisted provides some information about the complexity of an issue and the type of program needed to adequately address it. Identifying the scope of the problem will help you to focus your efforts on the populations most affected (e.g., a particular age group, racial or ethnic group, geographic region) and will result in more targeted, relevant program implementation. The frequency of a problem is

Program planning and evaluation   155

another important consideration. Is the problem chronic (ongoing and persistent, such as obesity), episodic (an outbreak of flu at a daycare center), or in a state of emergency (crisis)? The urgency with which services are delivered and strategies for implementation may vary based on your frequency determination. For example, an effort to reduce uncontrolled type 2 diabetes among African American women requires program strategies that are different from efforts to control flu outbreaks at a preschool, and still different strategies and activities from those that are needed to address the need for clean water after the devastation of a hurricane.

Reviewing existing data and evidence-based approaches

Increasingly, public health is focused on the implementation of evidence-based programs and services. Once you have identified the problems of importance to your community and set your priority, it is important to review the literature to determine how others have addressed this problem and what interventions have evidence to support their use.[1,4] For the purposes of program planning, systematic reviews and meta-analyses that provide an overview and synthesis of all studies on a specific topic are preferred to single studies. These data sources have information about interventions and programs that have a strong evaluation history (for more information, refer to Chapter 7). Once you identify the best-known approaches to solving the issue, you can adapt your program to the needs of your clients and community, considering the availability of resources. The Community Guide and Cochrane Database are good sources when looking for evidence-based programs (see also the resource list in "Where to Go for More Information" at the end of this chapter).

Visualizing your program

When you have invested time to engage stakeholders and to identify promising program models, your excitement and momentum will likely grow. It can be tempting to jump right into program implementation. However, it is important to remember that program implementation is a process, one that must be carefully planned and monitored if you are to accomplish your goals. Before you start to design a program, it is important to know why you are doing what you are doing and what you hope to accomplish. Take time to describe what your proposed program will do, the desired change to be achieved, and who will benefit from this change. Jumping right in with implementation and leaving too much to chance can easily lead to becoming sidetracked and losing sight of your vision for the program.[5] To visualize your program, use a logic model to map out the tasks and resources needed to accomplish your goals. Time invested in these steps during the planning process will increase the likelihood of quality programming and outcomes achievement. Program success—even short-term, incremental success—will help you to promote the program to consumers, community partners, other supporters, and decision makers.

156 *Public health research methods for partnerships and practice*

Specifying expected resources, activities, and anticipated outcomes

The nuts and bolts of making your program vision a reality requires you to clearly map out the resources needed to implement program activities in order to achieve your anticipated outcomes. To create this program map, you will need specific details in the following three areas: (1) the resources and raw materials needed (e.g., funding, facilities, equipment, material resources, and staff), (2) how these resources will be used (i.e., how these resources will directly support program activities), and (3) what will be accomplished when the program is completed (i.e., the results you expect to see).

Logic model development

A logic model is a tool used to systematically capture a program's vision and to provide a roadmap for the people responsible for implementation. Before a logic model is prepared, it is important that the program team articulates the mission, vision, and goals of the program. Once the overall vision of the program is established, the details of implementation can be mapped out. The logic model includes a comprehensive description of all program components, including activities, responsibilities, time frames, and outcomes, but breaks the program plan down into manageable parts.

The logic model is a series of if-then statements that illustrate how program activities may lead to desired outcomes.[6] Consider the old adage "An apple a day keeps the doctor away." In this scenario, your input is the apple. Your activity is to make sure that apples are made accessible to people in poor health, with the desired outcome being that their health will improve. An outline of a logic model is included in Table 8.1.

Resources and inputs

The inputs you invest in your program will likely be a combination of existing resources and those you still need to acquire or develop. For example, current staff and space may be assigned to implement and accommodate program services. However, you may need to seek funding, develop community partnerships, or recruit volunteers to ensure successful delivery of your community change effort. Be sure to include all conceivable resources needed during this planning phase so that the program does not fall short during implementation.

Activities

A description of program activities should include a list of tasks that will be undertaken in order to achieve the intended outcomes. This section is the cornerstone of your program plan and should include substantial detail regarding specific activities that will be implemented and who will be responsible

Program planning and evaluation 157

Table 8.1 The logic model: a series of "if-then" statements

Resources/ inputs	Activities	Outputs	Outcomes
(IF you have resources/ inputs, THEN you can run your program)	(IF you have access to resources, THEN you can accomplish your activities)	(IF you can accomplish these activities, THEN you will have delivered the services you planned)	(IF you delivered the services as planned, THEN there will be benefits for clients, communities, systems, or organizations)
Some examples			
Staff Money Research Equipment Facilities	Training Education Outreach Vaccinations Support groups	No. of people reached No. of people served No. of people vaccinated No. of providers who established a reminder system	Short term: people are more aware of the benefits of vaccination Intermediate: communities have access to vaccination services Long term: people seek out vaccination boosters over the life course

for the implementation of each task. As part of your program roadmap, it is important to list activities in the order in which they should be implemented and to include when each activity should begin and end to establish clear timelines that can be measured. For example, a series of activities might include the following: identifying medical clinic partners, identifying health needs of participants, matching participants to appropriate clinic and scheduling appointments, and following up with medical clinic partners to confirm that appointments were kept. In addition, personnel and staffing needs must be considered. In the previous example, who is responsible for matching participants to the appropriate clinic and scheduling appointments? Who will follow up to determine whether appointments were kept? Are new staff required to do the tasks, or can existing staff be trained and reassigned?

Outputs

Outputs are measures of your process. These measures help to track progress of program tasks involved in implementation and include indicators that signal the completion of outlined activities. Accomplishment of these milestones is a good indicator that the program is moving forward toward outcomes and larger program goals. For example, in a colorectal cancer screening program, you may count the number of senior living residents who attend a screening education session or track the number of residents who use navigation services

158 *Public health research methods for partnerships and practice*

to obtain screening. In another example, an awareness-raising campaign may be used to consider the new populations reached through a health marketing campaign. Documentation of these outputs may be found in administrative records such as intake or attendance sheets or as indicators on a project planning calendar. These indicators can also be included in the output statements.

Outcomes

Outcomes are the changes that you expect for the stakeholders as a result of program activities. Therefore, there should be a clear connection between the planned activities and the expected outcomes.[1] For example, if you plan to implement a community education program, you may anticipate an increase in knowledge, behaviors, or both. Programs that increase access to services may lead to improved health status. Typically, outcome measures are short term and are selected based on what can realistically be achieved within a program or fiscal year. It is important not to overpromise in this area. Be realistic about your available resources and what research evidence says about the time needed to create change in the chosen program area. For example, in the colorectal screening program mentioned previously in this chapter, the outcomes that might be measured are how many residents actually complete colorectal cancer screening and what percentage of residents meet standards for screening adherence. These metrics would be reviewed annually to provide a guidepost for program progress toward long-term goals.

An example of a logic model for a nutrition-related community health program is provided in Table 8.2.[7]

SMART goal development

Once your logic model is complete, you will embark on the process of goal development. In this process, you will translate program components and ideas outlined in the logic model to concrete terms that are measurable and results oriented. Goals provide a focal point for the change effort and should be identified during the program-planning phase to provide clear direction for the allocation of resources and program activities. When developing SMART (specific, measurable, attainable, relevant/realistic, and time framed) goals, determine (1) who or what you are collecting information about, (2) the desired result (e.g., increase, decrease, or some other result) compared to the status at baseline (the beginning), (3) what is intended to change, and (4) when you expect the desired effect to be achieved (Table 8.3). Established theory and promising practices are often used to design programs and craft appropriate goals. If you have not already explored relevant theories and programs, now is the time to do so to ensure that your goals are relevant and realistic.[8]

Once you have determined these goal components, you are ready to develop your SMART goals. SMART goals are defined in Table 8.4, which also includes guiding questions.

Table 8.2 Example of a logic model

Objectives	Activities	Inputs/resources	Outputs	Outcomes	Indicators/data
	(what we do to achieve objectives/ goals)	(human, financial, technology, and other resources needed for activities)	(products of activities that lead to specified outcomes)	(short-, medium-, and long-term desired results)	(indicators to measure implementation, progress, and success)
Improve health status among children age 5–12 from low-income families living in food desert.	• Community farmers' market • Health screenings • Nutrition education • "Produce prescription" for garden items	• Land and gardening supplies • Funding for produce vouchers • Medical volunteers • Farmers' market partner	• Project partners confirmed • 20% of eligible families enrolled in program • 10% of enrolled families participate in full screening and education offerings	Short term: • Parent nutrition knowledge increases • Children increase exercise through gardening activities Long term: • Child health status (obesity, diabetes, etc.) improves	• Enrollment records • "Produce prescription" voucher tracking • Pre/post parent nutritional knowledge assessment • Pre/post health screening data

160   *Public health research methods for partnerships and practice*

Table 8.3 Considerations in developing SMART goals[a]

Subject of data collection	Desired result compared to beginning	Area to be impacted	Time span or period of achievement
Participants/ individuals	-Increased -Decreased	-Knowledge -Awareness	-By the end of year 1
Organizations	-Improved -Modified	-Behavior	-By the end of year 2
Entities/ institutions	-Adopted -Enforced	-Policies	-July 2020

[a] The content of the table can be interchangeable. For example, goals for participants may include improving or modifying a behavior by July 2020.

Table 8.4 Questions that help to define SMART goals

Letter	Representation of letter	Questions
S	Specific	-Is the goal concrete and well defined? -Does it communicate what you would like to see happen? -Does the goal indicate WHAT change will occur and WHO will benefit from the change?
M	Measurable	-Can we track the results of our actions as we progress toward achieving the goal? -How will we know change has occurred?
A	Attainable	-Can we get it done in the proposed time frame? -Do we have the resources needed to achieve this goal in a specific time frame? -Is the goal set too high or low? -Are there any barriers?
R	Relevant (goals are results oriented)	-Do we have the resources to get the job done? -Do we have what is needed to achieve this goal?
T	Time bound	-When do you plan to start work toward this goal? -Have we set a deadline for achieving this goal?

Writing SMART goals well takes practice to ensure that they are specific, measurable, attainable, relevant, and time bound. When developing SMART goals, it is a good idea to engage both program staff and stakeholders in this process. Including a diverse set of perspectives in this process will help to refine the goals and ensure that they are relevant to the population that is to be served. A clearly stated goal identifies the outcome to be achieved, who will benefit from the intervention, and a time boundary for achieving the intended results. It is important to note that SMART goals do not include

Program planning and evaluation 161

how the goal will be achieved. That information should be in the logic model and connected to the intended outcomes.

Specific

The specificity of the goal statement should identify the change that is expected as a result of the program and who or what group will experience the change. This is a good time to review the activities and outputs included in the logic model and to articulate a goal that can realistically and directly result from these efforts. The second area of specificity identifies what individuals, groups, or communities will experience or how they will benefit from changes resulting from program activities.

Measurable

The measurements specified for each goal should be based on research evidence regarding reasonable expectations for change given program activities that will be delivered to a particular population. The specific criterion used to measure results will depend on the type of data that will be used to demonstrate success. If the goal is to enroll more people in a health program, the measure may be "a total of 150 individuals will participate in the program by the end of year 1" or, perhaps, "participation in the program will increase by 50% within 1 year of program implementation." The first goal may be appropriate for a new program starting with no participants, whereas the second goal may be more appropriate for an existing program that is adding new outreach activities to expand participation. Some goals may be measured using a standardized scale. In that case, the goal might state, "to increase health literacy by an average of 15% based on the Newest Vital Signs."

Attainable

If you are embarking on the development of a new program, it is likely that you believe that all of your goals are attainable. It is important to take a step back and do a realistic assessment of your program (mapped out in the logic model) to make sure that you have set a goal that can actually be achieved. For the goal, assess whether you have enough of the necessary resources and whether the time frames will realistically allow you to achieve your goal. Also, consider any challenges that the program may face that would inhibit progress toward your stated goal, and make adjustments as necessary.

Relevant

Once you have determined that a goal is attainable, you should assess the relevance of your stated goal to the larger vision and purpose of your program. Does the goal address the problem identified earlier in the planning process?

162 *Public health research methods for partnerships and practice*

Does the goal reflect the desired change you want to make through the program activities? Would the stated goal realistically result from the activities outlined in the logic model? You should also consider whether it is important and relevant to the stakeholders.

Time bound

When setting a time frame for your goal, consider when you can reasonably expect to see measurable results. Deadlines create focus, set priorities, and prompt action. Ideally, if you can establish a time frame for achieving the goal, you should state this in terms of the month and year in which it will be achieved. Another way to specify the time frame is in terms of time elapsed from the start of the program—for example, "within six months of the program start" or "by the end of program year 1." If you use general time specifications during the planning phase, it is a good idea to update the time frame with specific dates once the program begins. This level of detail will help to drive program progress and keep it on track. Table 8.5 shows an example of a SMART goal in development.

Copies of the logic model and SMART goals should be shared with all stakeholders to keep them informed about program plans and to maintain their support and buy-in.

Developing your evaluation plan

If you have followed the steps previously described, you have made it nearly to the end of the planning cycle. You have engaged stakeholders; identified a problem the program will address; mapped out the resources, activities, and outputs that will result in the desired change; and articulated the SMART

Table 8.5 Example of the development of a SMART goal

SMART letter representation	*Relevant question*	*Response*
Specific	What do I want to do?	Improve home safety for older adults
Measurable	How much and how often will I do it?	In 25% of homes with older adults, safety equipment will be provided
Attainable	How will I do it?	Install grab bars in bathtubs
Realistic	Can I do it? Do I have the resources?	Strong community volunteer base and local construction company donor will provide supplies and labor
Time framed	When will I do it?	Bars will be installed within 1 year (by December 2017)

SMART goal: By December of 2017, 25% of neighborhood homes inhabited by residents 65 years or older will have bathtub grab bars.

Program planning and evaluation   163

goals you intend to achieve. Now, it is time to put the final step in place to systematically collect program information and evaluate the efforts so that you and the stakeholders are able to verify the success of the program that you have taken so much time to design and implement.

What is program evaluation?

Program evaluation is the systematic collection of information on the activities and outcomes of a program to assess effectiveness, accessibility, and quality of personal and population-based services.[9] In other words, evaluation helps us to identify what the program does well, why it works, or why health changes are not occurring as expected. Evaluation may focus on the implementation of a program (e.g., process, activities, and outputs) or on program outcomes (i.e., did you achieve the goals related to knowledge, awareness, behavior, or policy changes?).

Why is program evaluation important?

Program evaluation takes a lot of work and investment. It is an opportunity for a program team to reflect on what has gone well and what could be improved in all phases of a program, from design to service delivery, and eventually, consumer outcomes. Through program evaluation processes, you will be able to do the following:

- Document what was done.
- Demonstrate effectiveness.
- Identify gaps and clarify the type and quantity of resources required to achieve desired outcomes.
- Identify areas for program improvement (inclusivity of populations in need, strategies to increase participation, efficiency of delivery, effectiveness of communication strategies, etc.).
- Advocate for policy improvements.
- Contribute to a broader knowledge base toward theory development and intervention effectiveness.

Taking time to evaluate the program process and outcomes provides numerous benefits for the change effort and stakeholders. First, evaluation data provide information about modifications that are needed or that can be made to sustain or expand program success.[10] The process of evaluation also provides an opportunity for increased communication among service providers and between providers and stakeholders. In addition to identifying areas for program improvement, compilation of evaluation data offers a chance to highlight program successes. Finally, the combination of program implementation results and stakeholder outcomes can demonstrate need and can

164 *Public health research methods for partnerships and practice*

mobilize citizen and political will to take action and address the needs associated with the change effort.

Process and outcome evaluation

There are two types of evaluation approaches to consider at this stage in the planning (process and outcome evaluation). Process evaluation is used to systematically document and track the implementation of program activities, knowledge that is important to consider as you work to continually improve the program. Outcome evaluation has a slightly different focus, as it centers on the measurement of program effects such as changes in knowledge, skills, attitudes, and behaviors as demonstrated by program participants. This type of evaluation provides a way to find out whether the project has achieved the desired objectives.

Process evaluation requires a data tracking system of the program activities to indicate that each task has been completed, the timing of completion is on track, the necessary resources were acquired, the target population is being reached, and challenges encountered along the way that either slowed progress of these tasks or prevented them from being carried out have been accounted for. In other words, process evaluation data can help you to determine whether a program is being carried out appropriately.[11] In the interest of continually improving program design and delivery, this information will be invaluable. Furthermore, the outputs and outcomes included in the logic model can be dependent upon the completion of these activities. If a process outcome is not achieved, it does not mean that stakeholder outcomes are no longer possible or that the program will fail. However, it is important to regularly review process outcome data and adjust programming accordingly to maximize the potential for the achievement of stakeholder outcomes.

Outcome evaluation refers to the systematic process of measuring change experienced by program participants and broader stakeholders. Data can be collected to measure stakeholder outcomes in a number of ways. For example, if the intended change is behavioral, you may ask participants to report their own behaviors at the beginning and end of a program period to see whether change has occurred. Participants may report behaviors using self-report measures and charts, diaries, or data recording technology such as pedometers, telephone applications, or other devices. Observations from a service provider, family member, or some other observer may be paired with the self-report to assess for consistency in reporting. Outcomes may also be obtained through review of medical, social service, or other records.

Selecting an evaluation method

As you begin to design the evaluation, be clear about the purpose of the evaluation and how the data will be used. What questions are you trying to

Program planning and evaluation 165

answer? Before you select an evaluation method, it is important to reflect on a number of critical questions:[8]

1. What is important to the team?
2. What is important to the community?
3. What is important to the funders?
4. How do you define success?

Answers to these questions may be found in a variety of sources, including in the program's mission statement, in the goals and objectives in the logic model, in the strategic plan, or in a grant application. Once you have answered these questions, consider the following as well:

- Which method will get the most useful information to key decision makers?
- Which method will collect information in the most cost-effective manner?
- Which method will gather information in a reasonable and realistic way?

Remember to involve stakeholders as much as possible in the evaluation design process (e.g., identifying goals, defining success, selecting indicators, and designing methods) to ensure that those whose lives have the potential to benefit from the program have a voice in the design, implementation, and monitoring processes.[9,12]

Examples of quantitative methods
- Demographic data
- Questionnaires with response scales
- Survey
- Pre/posttests
- Secondary data sources/administrative data

Examples of qualitative methods
- Open-ended questionnaires
- Diaries and journals
- Interviews (key informant)
- Focus groups
- Direct observations

Quantitative and qualitative data

There are two forms of data you may decide to collect: quantitative and qualitative data. Quantitative data, or information, can be measured in numbers such as the percentage of respondents in a survey or ratings on a scale. Qualitative data are in narrative form and may describe a range of outcomes that include experiences, behaviors, opinions, and knowledge. Quantitative

166 *Public health research methods for partnerships and practice*

data can describe the change that occurred, whereas qualitative data provide contextual information about why the change may or may not have occurred. In many cases, a mixed-methods approach that utilizes both quantitative and qualitative data is valuable (for more detailed descriptions of quantitative and qualitative data see Chapters 10 and 11).

Program design and evaluation considerations

Several important questions should be asked as you engage in program design and plan the evaluation:[8]

- Do outcome indicators already exist in current organizational data collection processes such as intake forms, community demographics, and other sources of information?
- Who will conduct the evaluation? Can it be easily incorporated into existing worker tasks?
- When and where will evaluation activities be conducted?
- How will the data be collected?

Often, evaluation falls short in the program planning and implementation process because answers to these questions are not fully developed and incorporated into program activities. Evaluation is an essential, informative task that will both sustain and improve the change effort.

Culturally competent and inclusive program design and evaluation processes

Inclusive program and evaluation designs that respect cultural viewpoints and experiences throughout the planning cycle are essential to the effectiveness of public health programs. Cultural competency within these processes requires careful consideration of a number of factors:[13,14]

- Consider whether hypotheses take into account cultural or ethnic differences across the participant group.
- Consider whether data collection methods are culturally appropriate, and consider the cultural contexts of the respondents.
- Consider how different methods may work in various cultures.
- Consider participatory approaches to evaluation that democratize knowledge by including stakeholders in all evaluation processes, from design and implementation to data interpretation.
- Consider potential language barriers that may pose challenges to understanding the evaluation questions. Check the wording of the questions—are they simple and easily understood by all? Refrain from using abbreviations or unconventional phrases.

Program planning and evaluation   167

- The use of multiple methods within an evaluation design may improve cultural appropriateness of the evaluation. Check to see whether question responses can be directly compared with existing information.

Working with research partners and consultants

In an effort to build theory and compile more comprehensive knowledge on the scope and effectiveness of public health interventions, it is increasingly common for practitioners to partner with evaluation researchers and consultants. These partnerships can face numerous challenges related to differences in treatment approaches, service delivery, and desired outcomes. Therefore, if you plan to collaborate with a researcher or evaluation consultant, it would be worthwhile to address the following issues early in the collaboration process:[15]

- Establish equal partnerships. Design an evaluation process that represents the goals of all partners, requires equitable investment, values the knowledge domains, and benefits all collaborative partners equally. Partnerships with researchers can increase the chances of receiving funding for evaluation efforts. However, such resources should be distributed among the research team and the project team, and—in the case of participatory evaluation processes—also stakeholders, for their contributions to the process.
- Develop both sustainable relationships and an exit strategy. Long-term partnerships between programs and research teams are ideal to sustain the feedback mechanism between evaluation and program planning. Partners should consider the intended timeline of the collaboration and how the relationship will affect service provision. Thus, they should develop an exit plan if the partnership is intended to last for only a limited period of time. These discussions should include ownership of the data, how they will be used, and long-term storage of the data, along with publication and authorship considerations.

Making sense of evaluation data

Evaluation data analysis

Evaluation data analysis is not as complicated or sophisticated as it sounds. It is the process of looking at the data to determine the progress of the program goals and objectives. Did the efforts improve outcomes, did you make or miss the targets, or is the progress about the same? Evaluation data can help you to identify program strengths and weaknesses. You can compare data over time to identify trends or gaps in stakeholder outcomes or program processes (see Chapters 10 and 11). The key to good data analysis is selecting the correct indicators and measures and matching the analyses to the data.

168   *Public health research methods for partnerships and practice*

Interpretation of findings

Regardless of the type of evaluation measures you use and the data collected, it is important that the results are interpreted accurately and not inflated to improve the reputation of the organization. To assure an accurate interpretation of the findings, a few considerations are in order: (1) data source quality (how honest or accurate are self-reported or observational data? Was technology used appropriately?), (2) question clarity (is there information on the reliability and validity of the questionnaire or survey used? Are they written at the correct literacy level for the target population?), (3) possible respondent or selection bias (only highly motivated individuals participate), and (4) consistency of data over time and across respondents.

Using data to inform program design and implementation

Evaluation is an important part of the program planning and implementation process. It is a quality improvement mechanism that can ensure that you are delivering effective programming to the community and meeting the expectations of the stakeholders. Therefore, it is essential that evaluation data are translated in an understandable format and shared with all stakeholders.

There are several possible forms of dissemination. The team should consider town hall meetings, community forums, reports, peer-reviewed articles, and professional and/or scientific conferences.

Writing evaluation reports

The accuracy and detail of the evaluation reports are just as important as the accuracy with which you designed the evaluation plan and interpreted the evaluation data. The consumers, collaborators, funders, and other interested people will want to know how successful you were at achieving the goals and affecting change in the community. Some may even want to replicate the program and will be looking for a detailed account of the planning process and outcomes. Therefore, the reports should include the following:

- Month and year baseline, follow-up data collection, or both.
- A description of the units of measurement the data represent.
- The total number of participants involved, along with the percentage and direction of change.
- Results presented in a comparable context when possible (e.g., results compared to last year, changes in the program compared to national results, etc.).

Program planning and evaluation   169

- Charts and graphs when possible and relevant. The audience may be more likely to pay attention to a line on a graph than what you have included in a page-long narrative.
- Accurate results that are not inflated, even if the data indicate that no change occurred. For all results, provide a possible explanation for the results, given all available data.
- Explanations for a "no-change" result. Possible reasons for a "no change" result may be that you were not using the correct indicators for the intended outcome, environmental changes in other programs or the larger community shifted and affected results of the program, or that no change is actually better than recent trends of negative changes. However, if a "no change" result is an accurate reflection on the quality of the program, share a plan for program changes that will more likely result in the intended outcomes over the coming year.

Conclusions

Public health programs provide valuable resources to individuals, groups, and communities. For continued positive effects in areas of health monitoring, service delivery, knowledge building, and advocacy, it is important that program designers take time to engage stakeholders in systematic problem identification, program design, monitoring, and evaluation processes. Whether you are a program administrator, project director, service worker, or community member, you want the programs you are involved with to be well designed, well managed, and responsive to community need. A variety of tools have been developed to aid these program-planning tasks. A logic model provides a visual map of the program idea that outlines program activities and actors, resources needed for implementation, desired outcomes, and evaluation criteria to measure program impact and success. The logic model provides a way to communicate the program vision with the project team, stakeholders, partners, and funders. In addition, the logic model provides a framework that, when reviewed regularly, guides program review, modifications, and continual improvements. Once you have planned the program, you will turn the attention to articulating program goals to guide the change effort. Using the SMART goals framework, you will develop goals that are specific, measureable, achievable, relevant, and time bound. This level of detail in the goal-setting process is much more likely to lead to successful change. If the procedures outlined in this chapter are followed, you will have the necessary ingredients to plan, implement, and evaluate a strong community change program.

170 *Public health research methods for partnerships and practice*

> **WHERE TO GO FOR MORE INFORMATION**
>
> - **Program planning**
>   Community Toolbox: Developing an Intervention: http://ctb.ku.edu/en/developing-intervention
>   United Way Strengthening Families Toolkit: http://strengtheningfamilies.unitedway.org/evaluating_steps.cfm
>   W. K. Kellogg Foundation Logic Model Development Guide: http://www.wkkf.org/resource-directory/resource/2006/02/wk-kellogg-foundation-logic-model-development-guide
> - **Developing an evaluation plan**
>   Better Evaluation: Tools for Participatory Monitoring: http://www.betterevaluation.org/search/site/?f[0]=bundle%3Aresources&f[1]=im_field_approaches%3A1273
>   Community Toolbox: Evaluating the Initiative: http://ctb.ku.edu/en/evaluating-initiative
>   Comprehensive List of Evaluation Resources: https://www.cdc.gov/eval/resources/
>   Racial Equity Evaluation Tools: https://www.racialequitytools.org/evaluate
> - **Evidence-based practices**
>   Cochran Collaboration Database: http://www.cochrane.org/
>   Healthy People 2020: https://www.healthypeople.gov/2020/tools-resources/Evidence-Based-Resources
>   Public Health Foundation: Community Guide: http://www.phf.org/programs/communityguide/Pages/default.aspx
>   SAMHSA Evidence-Based Practices Web Guide: https://www.samhsa.gov/ebp-web-guide

References

1. Keller LO, Schaffer MA, Hoagberg BL, Strohschein S. Assessment, program planning, and evaluation in population-based public health practice. *J Public Health Manag Pract*. 2002;8(5):30–43.
2. Scarinci IC, Moore A, Benjamin R, Vickers S, Shikany J, Fouad M. A participatory evaluation framework in the establishment and implementation of transdisciplinary collaborative centers for health disparities research. *Eval and Prog Plann*. 2017;60:37–45.
3. Delbecq AL, Van de Ven AH. A group process model for problem identification and program planning. *J Applied Behav Sci*. 1971;7(4), 466–492.
4. Brownson RC, Fielding JE, Maylahn CM. Evidence-based public health: A fundamental concept for public health practice. *Annu Rev Public Health*. 2009;30:175–201.
5. Weinbach RH, Taylor LM. *The Social Worker as Manager: A Practical Guide to Success*. 7th ed. Boston: Pearson, MA; 2014.

Program planning and evaluation 171

6. Schell SF, Luke DA, Schooley MW et al. Public health program capacity for sustainability: A new framework. *Implementation Science.* 2013;8(15). http://implementationscience.biomedcentral.com/articles/10.1186/1748-5908-8-15.
7. George DR, Rovniak LS, Dillon J, Snyder G. The role of nutrition-related initiatives in addressing community health needs assessments. *Am J Health Ed.* 2017;48(1):58–63.
8. Glanz K, Bishop DB. The role of behavioral science theory in development and implementation of public health interventions. *Ann Rev Public Health.* 2010;31:399–418.
9. Lavinghouze SR, Snyder K. Developing the evaluation plans: A critical component of public health program infrastructure. *Am J Health Educ.* 2013;44(4), 237–243.
10. Pluye P, Potvin L, Denis LP. Making public health programs last: Conceptualizing sustainability. *Eval Program Plann.* 2004;27:121–133.
11. Saunders RP, Evans MH, Joshi P. Developing a process-evaluation plan for assessing health promotion program implementation: A how-to guide. *Health Promo Pract.* 2005;6(2):134–147.
12. Guijt I. Participatory approaches. *Methodological Briefs: Impact Evaluation.* 2014;5: UNICEF Office of Research. http://devinfolive.info/impact_evaluation/img/downloads/Participatory_Approaches_ENG.pdf. Accessed March 7, 2017.
13. Eizenberg E, Benitez L, Lamb M, Saegert S, Hsieh TS. Participatory evaluation: How it can enhance effectiveness and credibility of nonprofit work. *Nonprofit Quarterly.* 2004. https://nonprofitquarterly.org/2004/03/21/participatory-evaluation-how-it-can-enhance-effectiveness-and-credibility-of-nonprofit-work/.
14. Chouinard JA. The case for participatory evaluation in an era of accountability. *Am J Eval.* 2013;34(2):237–253.
15. Coburn CE, Penuel WR, Geil KE. A strategy for leveraging research for educational improvement in school districts. William T. Grant Foundation white paper; January 2013. http://learndbir.org/resources/Coburn-Penuel-Geil-2013.pdf. Accessed March 1, 2017.

Activity

Directions: Your senior living community's health committee has decided to focus on cancer screening this year. Discuss the cancers of interest and their relevance to seniors in your community, as well as the existence of and guidelines for screening. Select the focus and activities regarding the cancer(s). Please, develop two to three SMART goals for the year, and record them in the table below. Indicate how the goals meet SMART criteria. Select at least one of the goals, and complete the logic model below. (30 minutes)

SMART Goals

	Specific	Measurable	Achievable	Realistic	Time bound
Goal 1					
Goal 2					
Goal 3					

172 *Public health research methods for partnerships and practice*

Logic model

Objectives	Activities	Inputs/ resources	Outputs	Outcomes	Indicator/data
	(what we do to achieve objectives/ goals)	(human, financial, technology, or other resources needed for activities)	(products of activities that lead to specified outcomes)	(desired short-, medium-, and long-term results)	(indicators to measure implementation, progress and success)
1.					
2.					

SELF-ASSESSMENT—WHAT DID YOU LEARN?

1. A program evaluation is meant to _____.
   a. Secure funding for a program
   b. Improve program effectiveness
   c. Identify new program ideas
   d. Prove program success or failure

2. A needs assessment is used to identify and measure the level of unmet need within an organization or a community.
   a. True
   b. False

3. _____ evaluation tracks the progress of program activities, whereas _____ evaluation assesses population changes such as health status, service access, and knowledge.
   a. Formative, summative
   b. Process, outcome
   c. Objective, comprehensive
   d. Formative, comprehensive

4. Which is a tool used to allow visualizations of the relationships between the components and outcomes of a program?
   a. Logic model
   b. Strategic model
   c. Improvement model
   d. Standardization model

Program planning and evaluation 173

5. What kind of goals should you develop for programs and projects to maximize their effect?
   a. Short-term goals
   b. Long-term goals
   c. SMART goals
   d. RIGHT goals

6. Which is NOT a benefit of evaluation?
   a. Increased communication
   b. Increased funding
   c. Identification of methods that are effective
   d. Identification of lessons learned

7. Each of the following is a characteristic of SMART goals except _____.
   a. Specific
   b. Realistic
   c. Tangible
   d. Achievable

8. Including stakeholders in your planning and evaluation processes will strengthen your program design and outcomes.
   a. True
   b. False

9. Logic models are _____.
   a. Flow charts that depict program components
   b. Diagrams to assist in project communication
   c. Flow charts that align program resources with community needs
   d. Diagrams that create decision trees to aid program planning

10. Which of the following are goals used to select evaluation method(s)?
    a. Deliver the most useful information to key decision makers
    b. Obtain information in the most cost-effective manner
    c. Obtain information in a reasonable and realistic way
    d. All of the above

9 Research methods

Bettina F. Drake, Danielle M. Rancilio, and Jewel D. Stafford

---

LEARNING OBJECTIVES

- Define research.
- Describe the steps of the research process.
- Identify and explain research methodology.
- Identify appropriate research methods and techniques.

SELF-ASSESSMENT—WHAT DO YOU KNOW?

1. At what point in the research process should you formulate your hypothesis?
2. What needs to be established before causality between an exposure and an outcome can be proven?
3. What is bias?

Introduction

The research process can seem somewhat challenging at first, but once you begin to understand the steps, it becomes a way of systematic thinking that helps to answer questions and address complex problems. The overall aim of this chapter is to enable you to have a general understanding of research. You will learn the following:

1. Why research is important.
2. The important characteristics of research.
3. The various types of research that exist.

The quality and strength of a research study and the corresponding results are based on several ideas.

- Past research informs new research. We are able to come up with new research questions based on prior research findings.
- Reproducibility is a sign of reliable science. If the research question is tested over and over with the same results, we are able to have a higher level of confidence that the results are accurate.
- The generalizability of the study findings needs to be understood. Findings or conclusions from your study may be applied only to the community at large if the participants in the study are similar (in age, gender, health status, or other factors important to the research question) to the broader community that the results should impact.
- Investigating a research question often generates new questions. Research findings may or may not reveal what was expected, leading to more questions that need to be investigated. Additionally, research results may lead us to ask, "Why are we seeing these results?"
- The research is conducted for the betterment of society. As researchers, we hope that our research findings can be used to help the community that the research is based upon. On a larger scale, researchers aspire to be able to disseminate their research to other communities and better the world as a whole.

What is research?

Merriam-Webster's Collegiate Dictionary formally defines *research* as "a careful or diligent search; studious inquiry or examination; or the collection of information about a particular subject."[1] However, in a broader sense, research is really the process of observing and gaining new knowledge about anything. For example, this process can include a person, place, thing, event, span of time, and other observable phenomena. Researchers gather, examine, and use the information that is collected to provide new knowledge or ideas on a certain subject. Research is used for a wide variety of daily activities. Medical research is probably the first example that comes to mind for most people when talking about research. However, research is used for predicting the weather, crop production, and traffic patterns. Even your favorite stores use research to provide the items that you buy every day.

The *scientific method* is important when preparing to do research. It allows the researcher to investigate and examine a certain subject in a systematic manner and helps prevent *bias* and other outside influences during the research process.[2]

176 *Public health research methods for partnerships and practice*

BOX 9.1   WHAT IS BIAS?

Bias is a systematic error in the study design, data collection process, or data analysis, which can change the results of a study.[3]

The scientific method is defined by the following steps:[2]

1. Observe and gather information.

    Sample questions: What is your research subject? What do you already know about it?
2. Define the research question.

    What do you want to know about the subject?

    Example question: Do stricter gun laws lower violence in inner city communities?
3. Form a hypothesis.

    A hypothesis is an educated guess using the knowledge that you collected while observing and gathering information on the subject. Often a hypothesis is formed using an "if-then" statement.

    Example hypothesis: *If* there are stricter gun control laws in place, *then* gun violence in the inner city will lessen.
4. Perform experiment, and collect data.

    This is one of the most important steps in the research process. During this step, your hypothesis is tested. During most experiments, a step-by-step procedure is followed. This ensures that nothing is changed except what you are testing. These steps are then followed to collect the data.
5. Analyze data.

    This is the "number-crunching" step. During this step, the data are organized and prepared for statistical analysis.
6. Interpret data, and draw conclusions.

    Summarize your results. Do your results from the data analysis support your prediction in your hypothesis? On the basis of your results, you can either reject or fail to reject your hypothesis.

    Example concluding question: With the stricter gun laws in place, did inner city gun violence lessen?
7. Publish results.

    Share your findings.
8. Refine and retest.

    Did your results support your hypothesis? If so, that is great, and you have supported your original hypothesis. Nonetheless, it is important to keep in mind that if the experiment is repeated it is possible that you will obtain different results that will lead you to reject the hypothesis.

Did you reject your hypothesis? If so, some experiments may stop at this point. However, in order to seek more answers, a researcher may continue investigating the research subject. On the basis of the outcome from the previous experiment, the researcher will form a new hypothesis to test and begin the experiment process all over again.

BOX 9.2   USING RESEARCH IN DAILY LIFE ACTIVITY

The research process applies to many situations in our daily lives. Whether buying an item, searching for a school, or investigating a problem in our community, we use research to gather information and make decisions based on the evidence we find. We will use the following case study to examine the research process.

Jennifer's Story:
Jennifer and John met in college. They have been dating seriously for approximately 4 months and are very much in love. Just before spring break, John proposed to Jennifer, and she accepted. Jennifer wanted to take John to her parents' house and inform them of the good news. Her parents, however, have never met John before and know nothing about him. Her parents, Gloria and Henry, only know that John lives in Columbia, MO. Henry has always been a little overprotective of his daughter and wants to know more about John to figure out whether he is a good man for his daughter.

Ask yourself the following questions:

1. If you were Henry, what steps would you take to find information about John?
2. How could you determine whether John is a good match for Jennifer?
3. What sources of information would you use to gather facts and collect verifiable evidence?
4. Who would you talk to in order to obtain information about John?
5. What might cause Henry to make an incorrect conclusion about his daughter's marriage?
6. What are some things we can do to avoid obtaining inaccurate information?

The source of research questions

Careful observations and formulating questions are integral steps in the research practice. Conducting research means that we are gathering facts and information to answer our question. The research process begins with a question: What would you like to know or study? Usually this question emerges from a topic of interest or an identified concern or problem that requires further investigation. The question has to be narrow enough to be tested in a research study. Perhaps you have had a question about a trend or pattern that you observed that you might want to explore further, such as breast cancer mortality rates among African American women. Research questions may come from the following sources:

- Community concerns
- Researchers
- Previously conducted research
- Grant funders
- Observation
- Personal experience
- Discussion with colleagues and other experts

Before generating a research question, complete the following steps:

1. Do some preliminary thinking and searching to narrow your topic.
2. Consider the outcome that interests you.
3. Consider the components that impact the outcome of interest.
4. State your hypothesis.

Generating a research question is the first step to developing the answer. The questions in the research process have to be tested. Researchers often make predictions or educated guesses about their topic of interest. How can we provide a scientific explanation about what will occur in our research project? As noted in the section on the scientific method, an educated guess or tentative answer to the research question is called a hypothesis. Formulating a hypothesis involves making a statement, which clearly states the cause and effect relationship between a set of *variables* or *observations*.[3] Formulating a hypothesis occurs before the collection of data and/or the research project.

Independent and dependent variables

Variables are the observations or characteristics that will be measured in the research process or experiment. To better understand how variables are measured, we have to define the types of variables in the research project. *Independent variables* are units of observation that are manipulated or changed in some way. The outcome of the change measured is called the *dependent variable*.[4] For example, if you are studying the effectiveness of a new training program on student levels of achievement, characteristics of the training program would be the independent variables, and the measure of achievement is the dependent (outcome) variable. Subsequent to collecting and analyzing this information, the researcher will use these observations to describe the relationship between or among the variables, draw conclusions, and publish results of the research project. The following list includes an example of a testable research question, a hypothesis, a dependent variable, and an independent variable:

- *Testable research question:* Is tobacco smoking associated with cancer?
- *Hypothesis:* Tobacco smoking affects cancer.
- *Dependent variable:* Cancer diagnosis.
- *Independent variable:* Smoking status or frequency/duration of smoking.

Hypotheses must be stated in a way that can be easily measured and that answers the original research question, provides predictions about the research outcome, and is based on existing knowledge. Testing the hypothesis involves formulating the hypothesis, data collection, and data analysis to confirm the hypothesis. *Data* is the word that researchers use for information that is collected during research. Data can be numbers, words, or symbols.

The hypothesis does not have to be "proven." The researcher confirms the hypothesis through observations or data collection. Observations can be expressed as verbal descriptions (qualitative data) or statistics (quantitative data). Scientific observation relies on accuracy and the ability to be replicated. If the observations are tested, verifiable, and confirmed by others, they can be considered a factual basis of scientific knowledge. The last but important step of the scientific method involves presenting your findings. When you have finished gathering your data, you have to form a conclusion about what you found. This is accomplished through analysis and will help determine whether your research confirms your original question.

Research settings

Research is conducted in a variety of settings. It can be done within a laboratory, school, community health center, hospital, government agency, or nongovernmental organization. It can be done over the telephone, on the Internet, by mail, or in person. Where and how research is done depends on the investigator, the population being sampled, and the question being asked.

The type of research determines research settings, the populations being studied, and how the data are best collected.

180　*Public health research methods for partnerships and practice*

What is an association?

In answering a research question, you are determining whether there is a relationship (*association*) between an exposure and an outcome in a population of people. If an association is present, when someone is exposed, the disease may occur more or less frequently. An association does not mean causation. There are nine criteria of causality that should be considered for the association between the exposure and outcome of your research question.[5] All criteria do not need to be met to support a causal relationship.

The nine criteria for causality include the following:[5]

1. *Temporal relationship:* The design of the study should assess an exposure that occurs before the outcome.
2. *Strength of association:* A strong statistical measure of association should exist between the exposure and outcome.
3. *Dose-response relationship:* This relationship is present when the disease is more likely to occur based on a higher level/rate of exposure. For example, people who smoke 1, 2, or 5 packs of cigarettes a day are progressively more likely to be diagnosed with lung cancer.
4. *Consistency:* Researchers of other studies in which they assess your research question have found similar results.
5. *Consideration of alternate explanations:* The association between the exposure and outcome is not due to other factors. It is necessary to consider multiple hypotheses before making conclusions about causality.
6. *Experiment:* The outcome can be prevented by an appropriate experimental regimen.
7. *Specificity:* This is established when a single cause (exposure) produces a specific effect, for example, a certain disease. Because diseases or other outcomes have multiple factors that influence their development, it is often unlikely to find a one-to-one, cause-effect relationship between an exposure and an outcome.
8. *Coherence:* The association should align with existing research knowledge. Ask, "Does this fit within what we already know about this exposure and outcome?"
9. *Biologic plausibility:* The association agrees with what we already know about how a disease or specific health outcome and exposure work in the body.

In public health research studies, researchers do not determine the cause of a disease in a given individual; instead, they determine the relationship or association between a specific exposure and the *frequency* (number of people with the disease) in a population. Because of this, researchers do not predict with their studies the exact cause of the disease in every individual. In addition, because an association is found in the study sample does not mean it is

Research methods   181

true in the general population. The degree to which your study sample represents the general population is the amount of *external validity* your research results will have. With good external validity, the associations found in your study can be applied to the broader population. *Internal validity* is determined by how well the study was designed to ensure that accurate measures of the exposure and outcome variables were gathered.

How data are gathered

Data can be gathered by a researcher through a variety of routes. The simplest way to collect data is through observation, which involves watching the study subject and noting the observations (this research approach is called ethnography). Data can also be collected through talking in person or over a phone conversation (interview). Depending on the study, a researcher may ask whether he or she has permission to record the verbal interview to ensure that no answers are missed or that the data can be extracted at a later point. Some questionnaires or surveys used to gather data are mailed or e-mailed to research participants, but due to the indirect contact with this method, it may pose a problem with survey response rates. With the increase in technology capabilities, more and more research studies are using Internet-based surveys that can be completed on a desktop, laptop, tablet, or even a cell phone.

Quantitative vs. qualitative

Two types of data exist: *quantitative*, which deals with numbers, and *qualitative*, which deals with descriptions.[6] (See Chapters 10 and 11 for more details regarding the types of data.) Quantitative data are most often collected in the form of a survey or through clinical records. Some examples of these data are lengths, weights, and numbers of times that an event occurs. Sometimes, quantitative data can measure the degree of a qualitative variable. For example, on a scale of 1 to 5, how effective do you think gun control laws are, 1 being extremely effective and 5 being not very effective at all. Qualitative data deal with descriptions that can be observed but not measured. These studies involve thoughts, ideas, opinions, and various discussion topics. Sometimes qualitative data are then used to develop a quantitative survey instrument. Depending on your research question, you might collect just one type of data (quantitative or qualitative) or both (mixed-methods).

Data collection methods

Surveys

Surveys can be used to ask questions in a variety of formats to obtain information. These questions might be about demographics, such as age, sex, or

182 *Public health research methods for partnerships and practice*

race, or they might be informational. For example, "At what age did you start smoking?" is informational. Most surveys are composed of closed-ended questions that have a set multiple choice response options (e.g., Yes/No, True/False, or Likert scale options [Strongly Disagree to Strongly Agree]). Surveys are usually a cost-effective form of research and can be adapted to address a broad array of research questions. They can be administered face to face, by mail, using the Internet or e-mail, or over the phone (including texting). Some limitations of survey studies exist.[7] Studies that use surveys require special skills in sampling and proper question design in addition to analysis to prevent bias and any confusion or misinterpretation of the questions or answers (discussed more in Chapter 10). Surveys may also give you background information for the problem, but they may not always uncover the true answer to the problem being investigated, and the underlying factors or causes might not be captured.

Clinical records

Reviewing clinical records is another way to collect data. Clinical records allow researchers to obtain detailed medical information on a population of people. This form of data collection eliminates any errors that might occur with participant recall of medical information and history. The downside to reviewing clinical records is that this can often be time-consuming, access to records may be complicated or difficult, and information may not be recorded in a systematic way.

Focus groups or interviews

A focus group is a group of people who are asked about their perceptions, opinions, beliefs, and attitudes towards a service, concept, or idea. This type of data collection is used to uncover reasons or insights, to learn about attitudes, and to develop interventions. For this kind of study, the interviewer follows a structured or semi-structured interview guide. The facilitator asks an initial question and then follows discussion with probing follow-up questions, with most of these questions being open ended.

Primary vs. secondary data

Primary data

Primary data are data that are collected for the very first time. Primary data are the data that the researcher observes or gathers from participants for the purpose of answering a specific research question.[8] Table 9.1 summarizes the advantages and disadvantages of primary data.

Table 9.1 Advantages and disadvantages of primary data

Advantages	Disadvantages
Applicable and usable for research question	Expensive
Accurate and reliable—can answer direct research questions	Not immediately available—takes time to define problem, sampling frame, method, and analysis
Up-to-date	Not as readily accessible

Secondary data

Table 9.2 Advantages and disadvantages of secondary data

Advantages	Disadvantages
Inexpensive	Frequently outdated (e.g., census data collected every 10 years)
Easily accessible	Potentially unreliable
Immediately available	Potential lack of variables
Provides essential background and help clarifying research question	Potential lack of data (i.e., no data available or very difficult to obtain)

Secondary data are data that have already been gathered. These data are usually composed of published information available from other sources, which can be internal or external to the organization of the researcher.[8] Table 9.2 summarizes the advantages and disadvantages of secondary data.

Examples of secondary data sources:

- Census, American Community Survey
- Behavioral Risk Factor Surveillance Survey (BRFSS)
- Youth Risk Behavior Surveillance System (YRBS) CDC Fact Finder
- Surveillance, Epidemiology, and End Results (SEER) Program
- Missouri Health Assessment

Figure 9.1 is a flow chart for describing different types of data.

How to design a study

After developing your research question and hypothesis, it is time to decide on the type of study that will answer the research question. The first step in designing a study is determining how big the gap is between what you currently know and what you want to know. Often this is determined by collecting information from previously conducted studies on the frequency or amount of the disease or outcome in your population of interest. *Incidence rate* is one measure of disease frequency that measures the number of new cases of the disease in a population over a period of time. This differs from *prevalence*

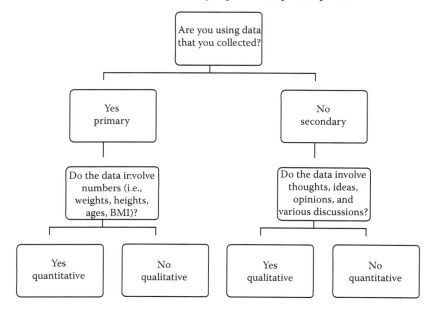

Figure 9.1 Flow chart on types of data.

rate, which is used to assess the total amount of people with the disease over a period of time. For diseases with a long duration such as diabetes or heart disease, the prevalence of the disease may be higher than the incidence of disease over the same period of time. The mortality rate, or the number of people who have died from the disease, has an impact on the prevalence. As people die, they are no longer in the pool of individuals who contribute to the prevalence rate. These rates are important to understand how common the disease is in your population and how often people die from the disease, which will play a role in deciding which study design to use.

Conclusions

Research is used every day and can be seen in many different forms. The observations and data collected during the research process allow us to answer questions, make decisions, and may even lead to more unanswered questions. Therefore, research is conducted in a systematic way to prevent bias or outside influences from skewing the data and results. Data can be quantitative or qualitative. Researchers may also use previously collected data (secondary data) to answer new questions they might have. Data are used to determine whether an association exists between an exposure and an outcome, also known as the independent and dependent variables. From the results of the data collection and analysis, a researcher will determine whether an association exists to either reject or fail to reject his or her research hypothesis. Because of research, many environmental, occupational, and medical advances have been made. With continued research, further advances will be made in the future.

References

1. *Merriam-Webster's Collegiate Dictionary*. 11th ed. Springfield, MA: Encyclopaedia Brittanica; 2003.
2. Vacc N, Loesch LC. *Professional Orientation to Counseling*. Philadelphia, PA: Taylor & Francis; 2013.
3. Creswell JW. *Research Design: Qualitative & Quantitative Approaches*. Los Angeles, CA: Sage Publications; 1994.
4. Penslar R, Porter J. *Institutional Review Board Guidebook*. Rockville, MD: Office for Human Research Protections, US Department of Health & Human Services; 2001.
5. Szklo M, Nieto FJ. *Epidemiology: Beyond the Basics*. 3rd ed. Burlington, MA: Jones & Bartlett Learning; 2014.
6. Last JM. *A Dictionary of Epidemiology*. New York, NY: Oxford University Press; 2001.
7. Merrill RM. *Introduction to Epidemiology*. 7th ed. Burlington, MA: Jones & Bartlett Learning; 2017.
8. Sahu SK, Singh TJ. *Research Methodology*. Agra, India: SBPD Publications; 2016.

Summary activity

You may have questions about ways to improve the activities, services, or policies at your organization.

Example 1: As a worker for a community-based organization, you *observe* an increased rate of obesity among Black teens in the community high school. Your agency decides to apply for grant funding to implement a new program teaching adolescents about proper nutrition and physical activity. How will you get the information (evidence) to demonstrate that obesity is a problem in your community?

Example 2: A new smoking cessation program had been implemented at the local community college. After a year, you would like to know whether the program is effective. How will you go about determining this?

Example 3: During a community forum, many community members stated that the high breast cancer rates are due to the toxic waste dump? How will you prove or disprove their claims?

186 *Public health research methods for partnerships and practice*

BOX 9.3 COMMON TERMS IN RESEARCH

A *population* is a group of people meeting specific criteria to which results can be generalized. The focus of your population can be a specific age, gender, race, or other factor. It is important that your population not be too limited, as this might lead to bias.

A *sample* is a smaller selection of the population. Samples represent the population, but in more manageable numbers than are in the whole population.

Bias is a systematic favoritism in research that can happen during data collection but also during the selection process for the population sample. Usually, bias does not happen on purpose; it can happen by accident. To help prevent bias, researchers often use random selection.

Random selection is the process of selecting people to participate in a study at random so that the study will not be biased. Another way to prevent bias is to have a larger sample size.

Sample size is the number of participants involved in a study. A sample size can be small, involving just a few people, or large and include millions of people. The larger your sample size, the less likely you are to have a selection bias.

Variables are measurable quantitative or qualitative values that either change or cause the change of another variable. Two types of variables are relevant to the process of developing a research study.

- The *independent variable*, or exposure, is observed and is not changed by the experiment.
- The *dependent variable*, or outcome, is caused by or changed by another factor.

EXAMPLE: In the example of our hypothesis in the "What is Research" section of the chapter, "If there are stricter gun control laws in place, then gun violence in the inner city will lessen," stricter gun laws would be our independent variable, and inner city gun violence would be our dependent variable.

SELF-ASSESSMENT—WHAT DID YOU LEARN?

1. Research is _____.
   a. Systematic
   b. Intensive
   c. Designed to increase knowledge
   d. All of the above

2. What is the first step of research methodology?
   a. Designing the research study
   b. Selecting the sample
   c. Collecting data
   d. Formulating a research question

3. You should formulate your hypothesis _____.
   a. Before you collect your data
   b. After you collect your data
   c. After you analyze your data
   d. It does not matter when you formulate your hypothesis.

4. Which is NOT a criterion for causality?
   a. The relationship is consistent when replicated.
   b. A dose-response relationship.
   c. The exposure occurs before the outcome.
   d. The relationship is the opposite of what is currently believed.

5. Sample size refers to _____.
   a. The number of participants involved in the study
   b. The dosage of the medication being administered in the study
   c. The group of people who are eligible to enter the study
   d. The number of people who respond to recruiting materials

6. What is bias?
   a. Systematic favoritism in the data collection process
   b. Assigning participants randomly to two or more different groups
   c. Process of selecting people fairly to participate
   d. A connection or link between the outcome and the exposure

10 Quantitative research methods

Melody S. Goodman and Lei Zhang

LEARNING OBJECTIVES

- Identify strengths and weaknesses of quantitative methods.
- Describe stages of questionnaire design.
- Identify sampling methods.
- Understand usefulness of statistics in health research.
- Understand p-values and odds ratios.

SELF-ASSESSMENT—WHAT DO YOU KNOW?

1. List three types of sampling that can be used to recruit participants into a study.
2. How would you design a questionnaire to evaluate a program?
3. What is an odds ratio?

Introduction

Although many people approach quantitative methods with trepidation because of a fear of math, most of them have the basic math and critical thinking skills to design and conduct quantitative analysis. If you can do some basic math (add, subtract, multiple, divide, take square roots, and raise to second and higher powers) with a calculator or with statistical software, you have the basic skills to conduct quantitative analysis. You do not need to know high-level statistics, as most researchers consult a biostatistician for their advanced research. However, you do need to know enough to communicate with quantitative researchers (e.g., epidemiologists and biostatisticians) in order to understand, learn from, and use your data.

We know that most people do not like numbers, but really what have numbers done to you for you not to like them? Numbers are persuasive and can create change, which is why it is important to understand them. They can be

Quantitative research methods 189

used for good or bad, but with some basic knowledge no one will be able to get one past you. You need to understand the methods used to get the numbers before making any decisions about whether to trust them. Statistics can be persuasive and can change how people see things. We often see many negative statistics about certain groups (e.g., black males, LGBTQ) in the media, but it is important to know that for every negative statistic that exists there is a positive one. The message is all about the perspective and how the numbers are used to tell the story.

BOX 10.1 CHANGING PERSPECTIVE USING STATISTICS

Statistics can change your perspective. We often hear negative statistics about black people, but here are some positive ones.

- Four out of 5 black fathers living with their children read to them.
- Black fathers aged 15 to 44 had the highest rates of helping children with homework and taking them to and from activities of any race.
- Of black fathers aged 15 to 44 who live with their children, 80% bathe, dress, diaper, or help their child use the toilet daily—highest of any race.
- Ninety percent of young black adults aged 25 to 29 have completed high school or its equivalent—the same as the national average.
- Black high school graduates are three times more likely to be in college or employed than unemployed.

(From Jackson DZ. The positive numbers about young black men. Boston Globe. *http://www.bostonglobe.com/opinion/2015/02/22/the -positive-numbers-about-black-men/0TcPR1Hhn8Yf0yuVoWZxfJ /igraphic.html?p1=Article_Graphic. Accessed: January 30, 2017.)*

Statistics are used in quantitative analysis, and their use is both an art and a science. The science is based on mathematical and statistical theory, but these only yield numbers. How one interprets those numbers in the context of the data is an art. Rosner[1] defines *statistics* as "the science whereby inferences are made about specific random phenomena on the basis of relatively limited sample material," and Ross[2] defines statistics as "the art of learning from data" and states that "it is concerned with the collection of data, their subsequent description, and their analysis, which often lead to the drawing of conclusions." Most of the statistical theories we use are based on *probability* (the likelihood of something happening or being the case). Although some

190 *Public health research methods for partnerships and practice*

rare events may occur, the likelihood of occurrence for certain events should be based on large sample statistics.

BOX 10.2 "LUCKY GRANDMA" EXAMPLE OF RARE EVENTS

What if someone told you, "Statistics say smoking cigarettes can kill you, but my grandmother smoked three packs a day since she was 20 and she died at age 103." On the basis of probability, we know that even if an event is rare, it can occur.

Let's do some math. Suppose that the probability of living until age 103 for someone who smokes three packs a day from age 20 is 1 in 10,000 and that in the US population there are 1,000,000 people who have smoked three packs a day since age 20.

In this case, you would expect $1,000,000 \times 1/10,000 = 100$ people to live until age 103 and the other 999,900 to die before age 103.

Conclusion: This was one lucky grandma, as our calculation shows that most (99.99%) people who smoke at this rate will not live to age 103.

Some people may think that quantitative analysis happens at the end of a research study once the data are collected, but a good quantitative research study makes plans for the analysis before the data collection. As in community-academic partnerships, the key to success in research is having a good team. Study design is a key skill of epidemiologists and biostatisticians; you will want people with these skills at the table as you begin to design your study.

BOX 10.3 QUOTE FROM SIR RONALD A. FISHER

"To consult the statistician after an experiment is finished is often merely to ask him to conduct a post mortem examination. He can perhaps say what the experiment died of."

Here are some considerations to make before you start your study:

- What measures will you use for data collection?
- Are these measures created by your research team, or have they been used in previous studies?
- Are the measures validated? If so, in which populations?
- How many participants are needed for your study to have meaningful quantitative differences?

Quantitative research methods 191

You should start with a pilot study to see whether any issues exist with survey administration or data collection that need to be resolved. Many people want to skip the pilot phase, and this can be detrimental to the research study. If there is something wrong with your survey, it is best to catch any issues after just a few surveys are administered instead of after all the data have been collected. Once your data are collected, there is no type of quantitative or statistical analysis that can resolve major issues related to study design, survey administration, respondent comprehension, or other issues with survey items. After you have collected or extracted the data for your study, quantitative analyses are used to describe the data, test hypotheses, examine associations, and test for statistically significant differences among subpopulations.

Quantitative analysis is based on the idea that phenomena can be quantified (i.e., measured and expressed numerically) and involves the analysis of numerical data. Burns and Grove[3] describe the analysis of numerical data as "a formal, objective, systematic process in which numerical data are utilized to obtain information about the world." *Hypotheses* are statements that we make about the possible relations between variables or differences between groups (e.g., Do patients treated with drug A show greater improvement than those treated with drug B? Does drug C affect men and women differently? What are the barriers to accessing mammography in a community?). Quantitative analysis has several weaknesses and can be complemented by qualitative research. When the methods are combined, the resulting approach is referred to as *mixed-methods research*. Mixed-methods approaches are often used in public health research. However, quantitative methods are considered the gold standard in medically orientated research.

Although quantitative approaches are not useful in all situations, when used appropriately, they can help examine important questions. Many people will say that they do not like numbers. However, most of them have an implicit awareness of scales and can understand an element of value attached to a quantity. Quantitative methods can be used to describe characteristics, evaluate outcomes, and test research hypotheses. It is important to have a strong study design (e.g., survey questionnaire, recruitment, data collection, and analysis), as statistical estimation relies on quality data collected on large samples using structured data collection tools.[4] As described in Chapter 9, a strong design follows the scientific method, aims to reduce bias through data collection and analysis, and obtains a representative sample of the population with results that are generalizable.

Quantitative approaches have several strengths, as they enable the examination of structures and processes that are both directly observable (e.g., height, weight, blood pressure, cholesterol) and not directly observable (e.g., beliefs, well-being, pain, satisfaction, stress, discrimination) but are well suited for quantitative description. These approaches allow for the examination of change over time (concepts can be measured and directly compared to a previous time point) and associations between two or more factors. A major strength of quantitative data is that they can be used to create visual images (e.g., graphs,

192   *Public health research methods for partnerships and practice*

maps, figures, tables). Quantitative data also allow for a breadth of coverage in a large population, which can be used to generalize and make predictions.

Despite several strengths of quantitative approaches, there are some weaknesses. Quantitative approaches are only applicable to measurable phenomena. Although quantitative analysis allows for the examination of change over time, it is often difficult to study processes or dynamic phenomena using static snapshots at multiple time points. Quantifying factors often simplifies and compresses the complex reality, and, in many cases, the whole may not be equal to the sum of its parts. In other words, analysis may lack depth and be relevant to only part of a whole. In addition, defining anything, especially humans, in terms of numbers is risky when there is a lack of detailed narrative. Descriptions of actors' perspectives, intentions, motivations, and meanings are difficult given their inherently qualitative nature. Using quantitative methods for such factors requires extensive knowledge on the subject in order to ask the "correct" questions.

In many situations, a mixed-methods approach is best, as it allows for combinations of quantitative and qualitative methods of measurement within a single study, making it possible for a wider range of information to be obtained. This enables the research team to use the best combination of methods to address a question (e.g., closed- and open-ended survey questions) and obtain the information needed.

Sampling methods

Sampling consists of selecting part of a population to observe so that one may estimate the characteristics of that entire population. A *population* is the total collection of elements about which we make inferences. The list of the total elements is called the *sampling frame*. A *census* study includes all the elements in the population, but a sample does not. For example, in 2015, to estimate the prevalence of obesity among Mississippi public school (K-12) students, researchers from the University of Southern Mississippi surveyed 5,222 students from a total of 478,056 students enrolled in public schools. In this case, the sample consisted of the 5,222 students, and the population included all the enrolled students.[5] It is unnecessary and too costly to collect information from all the public school students; a sample can be obtained that is representative of the population. The sample can be used to make inferences about the population from which it was drawn.

A good sample is a miniature of the population, and it can represent the characteristics of that population. In general, a good sample should be free of selection bias and measurement bias. *Selection bias* occurs when there is a gap between the target population and the sampled population. For example, when we study tobacco consumption in a rural county using a telephone survey, the estimates from this study could be biased, as a sizable percentage of the households do not have telephones. *Measurement bias* occurs when there is a difference between the measurement and its true value. For example, during an obesity study, the scale could erroneously add 2 pounds to the weight

Quantitative research methods   193

of every student if it has an incorrect setting or is not placed on a hard or even surface. Both selection bias and measurement bias must be considered and minimized in the design stage of the survey.

Methods of sampling

Probability samples assign a known and nonzero chance of selection for each element in the sampling frame. The probability of selection of each component does not have to be equal. For example, the Mississippi Pregnancy Risk Assessment Monitoring System (PRAMS) oversamples mothers having very-low-birth-weight babies, as this is a small group among all mothers who have had recent deliveries. This overrepresentation means that the mothers in this small group have higher chances of selection than any other mothers but provides a sufficient sample from this subpopulation to allow for inferences about this group and comparisons to other mothers.[6]

- A *simple random sample* (SRS) is the simplest form of a probability sample. In an SRS selection, each element in the population has an equal chance of being selected. Selecting an SRS is accomplished by using a table of random numbers, listed in appendices of many statistical textbooks; or by using statistical software, such as IBM Statistical Package for Social Sciences (SPSS). Random number tables contain digits that have no patterns in layout regardless of rows, columns, or diagonals. SRS is the foundation for more complex sampling designs. However, because of difficulty in identifying every member of the population in very large samples, the pool of available participants becomes biased; therefore, researchers rarely use SRS to conduct large population-based surveys.
- A *systematic sample* is often used as a proxy for SRS when no list of the population exists or when the list is in roughly random order. In systematic sampling, an element of the population is selected by beginning with a random start, and then a sampling fraction to select every kth element is used until the required sample size is reached. For example, in the 2013 Mississippi Worksite Survey, researchers used systematic sampling to investigate type and size of the worksites associated with their health policies in addition to their health promotion and education-related activities. Researchers surveyed 600 from a total of 3,600 worksites. The sampling fraction is $k = 6$ (3,600/600; use the next integer if this cannot be fully divided). If we arbitrarily use 7 as the random start, then the worksites listed as numbers 7, 13, 19, 25, 31, 37, 43, and so on will be in the sample. The advantages of the method are that it is simple to design and easy to use. However, bias could occur if the population list has a hidden order or has a monotonic (consistent) trend.[7]
- The *stratified sample* process is to divide the population into subpopulations that share at least one common characteristic (e.g., males/females;

field workers/office workers) called *strata*, then to select a sufficient number (sample size large enough for us to be reasonably confident that the stratum represents the subpopulation with the characteristic) of elements from each stratum using SRS. Stratified sampling is often used when one or more of the strata in the population have a low incidence relative to the other strata (e.g., used to oversample minority populations in national surveys) and can reduce sampling error. For example, the Mississippi PRAMS used stratified sampling.

- In a *cluster sample*, the population is divided into groups called *clusters*, in which each element of the population can be assigned to only one cluster. The researcher randomly selects clusters to include in the sample. In 1-stage cluster sampling, all of the elements within selected clusters are included in the sample. In 2-stage cluster sampling, an SRS of elements within the clusters is selected. Cluster sampling does not generate estimates that are as good as those from random and stratified sampling and should only be used when the population consists of natural clusters (e.g., households on a street, schools in a town, counties within a state). For the Youth Risk Behavior Surveillance System (YRBSS), each state, territorial, tribal, and large urban school district employs a 2-stage cluster sample design to produce a representative sample of students in grades 9 through 12 in its jurisdiction.[8]

- *Nonprobability sampling* techniques use the subjective judgment of the research team to select participants instead of using random selection (probability sampling).

  - *Convenience sampling* (volunteer) is a nonprobability recruitment approach that can be used in exploratory research when the researcher is interested in getting an inexpensive approximation of the truth. This can provide an estimate of the results, without expending the time or incurring the costs required to collect a random sample. As the name implies, participants in the sample are selected because they are convenient.

  - *Quota sampling* is the nonprobability equivalent of stratified sampling. As with stratified sampling, the researcher identifies the strata and their proportions as they are represented in the population. Then, convenience sampling is used to select the required number of subjects from each stratum. This process differs from stratified sampling process, in which the strata are filled using random sampling.

- A *purposive sample* is a nonprobability sample that is selected based on one or more traits of the population and the objective of the study. For example, we may want to examine treatment for African American lesbian women who have breast cancer. In order to be in our study, a woman must have all three traits (African American, lesbian, breast cancer diagnosis). Even in a breast cancer treatment clinic, it may be hard to identify patients with all three traits, and many patients would have to be screened

Quantitative research methods 195

in order to get a sample with a decent size. In situations like this, other recruitment approaches may work better.

- The *snowball sampling* technique is a special nonprobability method that can be used when the desired sample characteristic is rare and when it may be extremely difficult or cost prohibitive to locate respondents from the target population. This sampling technique relies on referrals from initial participants to generate additional participants based on their membership in the target population. Although this approach can dramatically lower search cost, it comes at the expense of introducing bias because it reduces the likelihood that the sample will represent a good cross section from the population, as participants are likely to suggest members of the target population similar to themselves.

In a complex survey, sample members do not have an equal probability of being selected. There are many types of complex sampling schemes (e.g., stratification, clustering, oversampling, multistage sampling). Those discussed in this chapter are just a few. It is important to note that when a sample is complex, statistical estimation and analysis are also more complex. If you decide that a complex survey design is appropriate for your project, consult a biostatistician who can help you to design the study and conduct the analysis. Most complex designs use weighting to ensure that the sample is adjusted to reflect the population. It is important to use appropriate statistical techniques that adjust for the complex survey design. Most statistical software programs can be used to conduct this type of analysis (e.g., SUDAAN, SAS, Stata).

Despite the potential complexity of sampling designs, several reasons exist to consider a complex sampling design for a study. Complex sample designs can be more cost-effective and can improve the precision of estimates when compared with an SRS. Given how tight research budgets tend to be these days, this is an effective way to reduce the cost of a survey. In addition, complex samples can be used to ensure sufficient representation of small subpopulation groups (e.g., racial/ethnic minorities, LGBTQ) in the final sample and to gain access to difficult-to-access sampling frames (e.g., school children, patients). It would be hard to sample school children without first sampling schools or to sample patients without first sampling hospitals and community health centers. These designs ensure sufficient sample sizes for subgroups to make comparisons between groups by key demographic factors (e.g., race, gender, age, education, income).

Data

BOX 10.4   QUOTE FROM W. EDWARDS DEMING

"In God we trust. All others must bring data."

---

196 *Public health research methods for partnerships and practice*

Several methods exist for obtaining data for quantitative analysis. Data can be obtained through primary data collection (e.g., survey, systematic observation, experimental designs and intervention studies) or from secondary sources (e.g., medical records, text, previous survey). *Primary data* are data collected by the research team for a specific purpose. *Secondary data* are pre-existing data collected for some other purpose that can be used by the research team to address their questions. Since secondary data are collected for some other primary purpose, analysis is limited by the variables that are available and by how they were collected, measured, and categorized for the primary purpose.

Quantitative data can come in a variety of forms, but most will have a data matrix composed of two components: the observation unit and variables. The *observation unit* can be an individual, group (e.g., family, household, couple, math class), institution (e.g., school, business, municipality), text (e.g., newspaper article, novel), or event or activity (e.g., war, strike, revolution). A *variable* is an observable and measurable characteristic of an observation unit that varies across different units. For example, variables for individuals may include height, weight, or diabetes diagnosis; household may include annual income, number of adults, number of children, or type of housing; school variables may include size, funding amount, or graduation rate; newspaper variables may include number of words, reads, or social media shares/likes; and strike variables might include number of picketers, number of people crossing a picket line, or length of strike.

A data matrix is the starting point for quantitative analysis. In the data matrix, each observation unit occupies one row, and each variable occupies one column. Figure 10.1 is an example of a data matrix. The first column

ID #	Q1	Q2	Q3	Q11	Q12	Q13
816	M	N	B	1	1	1
888	F	Y	W	1	.	1
221	F	N	W	1	.	2
808	F	N	B	1	0	4
781	F	N	B	0	.	3
635	F	N	B	1	0	3
978	F	N	W	0	.	2
135	F	N	B	1	.	2
728	M	N	W	0	.	4

Figure 10.1 Sample data matrix. ID: participant identification number; Q1: question 1 and contains text responses, Q2: question 2 and contains text responses, Q3: questions 3 and contains text response, Q11: question 11 and contains numeric responses, Q12: question 12 which contains numeric and missing responses and Q13: question 13 and contains numeric responses.

contains participants' ID numbers, the second column corresponds with Question 1, and the last column corresponds with Question 13. This information may be clear for any user. However, there should always be a codebook for a data matrix that defines the question that was asked and what the values for each variable mean (see Box 10.5).

BOX 10.5 EXAMPLE OF A CODEBOOK

Variable Name	Question Text	Response Codes
Q1	What is your gender?	F=Female M=Male
Q2	Are you Hispanic or Latino?	Y=Yes N=No
Q3	What is your race?	B=Black W=White

In the data matrix in Figure 10.1, some of the variables are characters (Q1, Q2, Q3) whereas others are numbers (ID, Q11, Q12, Q13). The "." in Q12 indicates a missing response.

Survey methods

Survey research utilizes a structured questionnaire in which the same questions are posed to each person. Surveys can be administered in different formats (e.g., postal mail, e-mail, Internet polls, text message, face-to-face interviews, telephone interviews). However, some research questions are not suited for survey research. Surveys are commonly used in public health to understand attitudes, opinions, and beliefs concerning health-related issues. They can also be used to examine characteristics of populations regarding health-related topics (e.g., drug use patterns, utilization of healthcare) and to collect information about the demographic characteristics (e.g., age, gender, race, education, income) of a population. Survey results can be used to test hypotheses and examine associations among factors. Surveys can be used to ask a lot of questions efficiently and can sample large populations at a low cost.

A major limitation of using surveys in research and evaluation is the potential for response bias, in which respondents provide untruthful or misleading responses that can often be based on social desirability. In addition, self-reported data are fallible because they are based on the respondent's knowledge and recall ability. Surveys also have the potential for many other forms of bias, including sampling, coverage, measurement, and nonresponse bias.

198 *Public health research methods for partnerships and practice*

- *Sampling and coverage bias* occurs when some members of the intended population are less likely to be included in the sample than others. This can lead to a sample that is not representative of the population of interest.
- *Measurement bias* can cause systematic errors in the data that result from poorly measuring the concepts and/or careless data collection. For example, the survey interviewer might ask about drug use but does not give the proper time frame and collects utilization before the period of interest, causing an overestimation of the utilization rate.
- *Nonresponse bias* occurs when people who respond to the survey are systematically different in a meaningful way from nonresponders. This is often a problem with postal mail surveys in which respondents are sent a survey in the mail and must complete it and return it via postal mail. Suppose that you conduct such a survey in Florida and you find that retirees are more likely to respond than those currently in the workforce. In this case, the survey would have nonresponse bias.

When developing a study, you want to choose a design that has the potential to limit any bias that may occur.

Questionnaire design

Six stages are necessary for a quality survey questionnaire:

1. Determine the aims of the questionnaire.
2. Select the appropriate question styles.
3. Design questions.
4. Pilot test questions.
5. Revise questions.
6. Administer the questionnaire.

Stage 1: Determining the aims of the questionnaire

In this initial stage, you should start by writing down the purpose of the survey. Identify the research questions, target population, hypotheses, and the type of information you will need. It is important to consider how the information will be used when designing the survey. With this information in mind, an overall questionnaire plan or outline should be developed. The research team should write a detailed list of the information to be collected and the concepts to be measured in the study. This list should then be translated into measurable variables. The analysis plan should state each variable's role in the analysis (e.g., predictor, outcome, confounder). A *predictor variable* is a variable that is being measured in a research study in order to observe the effect on the outcome variable. The *outcome variable* is the variable of interest in a research study. A *confounding variable* is associated with both the exposure

Quantitative research methods   199

(predictor) and the outcome variables, which can lead to bias if not included in the examination of the relationship between the predictor and the outcome.

A review of the literature is often necessary to determine whether there are existing validated survey items to measure the concepts in your survey. Validated measures should be used on surveys whenever possible. Be sure to use items in the exact form in which they are validated. If items are changed, or only a subset of items are used, previous validation does not necessarily hold. Using validated items not only saves survey development time, but also allows for comparison to other surveys that have used the same items. However, there are many cases in which the survey is measuring something specific to your organization or project, or items may not have been validated in the population that you plan to survey. In these instances, it is necessary to develop your own survey items or to modify existing items from other instruments.

Stage 2: Selection of appropriate question style

The type of information that you wish to collect will determine the type of question style that is suitable, but questions come in two general formats: open ended and closed ended. *Open-ended questions* allow respondents to formulate their own answers, and *close-ended questions* provide respondents with a number of alternative answers from which to choose. Responses come in two general formats: *exclusive answer* (only one possible answer) and *nonexclusive answer*, which allows for more than one response to a question (e.g., check all that apply).

BOX 10.6   EXAMPLES OF OPEN- AND CLOSED-ENDED QUESTIONS

- Open format
  - What are the main sources of stress in your life?
  - How many children do you have?
- Closed format
  - What is your race?
    - Answer options: black, white, Native American, Asian, other
  - How many children do you have?
    - Answer options: 0, 1, 2+

Stage 3: Survey instrument and question design

Before you develop the survey instrument, it is important to determine the mode of survey administration (e.g., face-to-face interviews, telephone interviews, self-completed questionnaire, computer-assisted approaches), as some question formats are appropriate only in some instances (e.g., verbally administered). Regardless of the mode of administration, you want your survey instrument to be easy for respondents to complete.

For paper surveys, this means having ample white space and room to write answers. This allows respondents to clearly see each question's response options (if applicable) and to have room to mark or write a clear and complete response. For web-based surveys, you want to make sure that surveys are easily viewed on a computer screen or mobile device and that they do not have too many questions per screen that require participants to scroll to complete. In addition to having a survey that is visually appealing to the respondent, you want to ask questions that are clear and concise and that obtain the information that you are looking to collect. Whereas respondents should be allowed to skip any questions to which they do not want to respond, a good survey will have the most important questions first and will not take too long to complete. Here are some key points to remember:

- Participants are most likely to skip questions near the end of the survey if it is too long.
- Do not start a survey with sensitive questions, or people might not want to continue with the survey.
- Place the most important items in the first half of the survey to increase response rates on the important measures even if the survey is only partially completed.
- Make sure that survey directions are clear and that there is a natural flow between questions.
- Define key and/or confusing terms.
- Keep participant recall to a minimum (ask about the recent past).

When validated questions are not available or appropriate for your survey, you will have to develop your own questions. Several elements should be avoided when developing survey questions:

- *Leading questions* that encourage or prompt the desired answer should be avoided. When conducting a program evaluation, you may be tempted to ask questions such as, "Did you like the program?" This is a leading question because it leads the respondent to feel like it is prompting for a "yes" response, which could bias respondents to be more favorable about the program than a revised version of this question such as, "What are your thoughts on the program?"
- *Ambiguous questions* should be avoided. These are questions that can be interpreted in more than one way, or the questions are vague or general such as, "Did you like school?" This can be an ambiguous question because it is unclear whether this is about elementary school, high school, or secondary education.

Quantitative research methods 201

- *Double-barreled questions* involve more than one issue but only allow for one answer (e.g., Did you find the program interesting and useful?). What if the respondent found the program useful but not interesting or vice versa; he or she is allowed only one answer. Double-barreled questions should be separated into two questions. In this case, the questions would be the following: (1) "Did you find the program interesting?" and (2) "Was the information provided during the program useful to you?"

Do not use complex vocabulary, jargon, or acronyms without definitions (e.g., Do you plan to attend the APHA annual meeting?). It is not clear from the question that APHA is the American Public Health Association. You also want to avoid long, complex questions that require definitions, use a patronizing tone, or ask offensive questions. For close-ended questions, ensure that the response options are appropriate for the survey question. If you use a paper survey that has multiple pages, be sure to number the pages and include the participant's ID number on each page in case the pages get separated.

**BOX 10.7 MAKING SURE QUESTIONS
AND ANSWER OPTIONS MATCH**

Make sure that question and answer options match. Below is an example of nonmatching question and answer options and how we could fix them:

- Bad: Have you had pain in the last week? (1) Never, (2) Seldom, (3) Often, (4) Very often
- Fix: How often have you had pain in the last week? (1) Never, (2) Seldom, (3) Often, (4) Very often

---

A high-quality survey instrument is both valid and reliable. There are several types of validity that are important to consider (e.g., internal, external, criterion, construct).

- *Internal validity* refers to how well an experiment is done and whether it avoids confounding; internal validity allows for the inference about causal relationships between variables.
- *External validity* refers to the generalizability to a larger population or even a different population or setting. Is what you found on the survey applicable to the "real" world and generalizable beyond the sample of survey respondents?
- *Criterion validity* assesses whether a measure reflects a certain set of abilities and can be established in two ways: *concurrent validity*, comparing the measure to an established measure (gold standard), or *predictive validity*, testing the measure over a period of time.
- *Construct validity* is the degree to which a survey tool measures what it claims to be measuring.

202 *Public health research methods for partnerships and practice*

A reliable instrument will have consistent measurements of the same thing over time. For example, a nurse uses a pain survey with a patient, and on the basis of his response she decides to check back on him in 15 minutes and uses the same tool to reassess his pain. If there is no change in the patient's condition or treatment, a reliable tool will indicate the same level of pain as the previous measurement.

Once your survey is developed, you should pilot test the survey (stage 4) in the target population. This will allow you to identify questions that need revision, questions that can be removed, and those that should be added (stage 5). At this point, you should ensure that terms used in the survey are clear to respondents or determine whether they require additional definition. Administer the revised survey to a sample of the target population (stage 6), analyze the resulting data, and report the results of the analysis

The success of a survey is based on the response rate. To enhance the response rate, be sure to reduce participant burden when creating the survey tool. If possible, offer an incentive for participation; make clear to the participants the purpose and importance of the survey and what the information will be used for.

Analyzing survey data

In an analysis of survey data, an initial step is to examine the demographic characteristics of the respondents. It is also important to keep track of the nonresponders so that you can compare their characteristics to those of the respondents. This will allow you to determine whether any nonresponse bias exists. When it is not possible to track nonresponders, you can compare late responders to early responders and see whether there are differences. Whereas this is situation dependent, it has been suggested that the late responders will be more like the nonresponders than the early responders.[9] The next step is to examine the descriptive statistics for each of the survey questions. Important questions should be summarized and reported in a meaningful way using figures, tables, maps, or a combination where appropriate. Besides analysis of descriptive statistics, researchers often conduct in-depth analysis and test hypotheses related to the research questions. This will be presented in more detail in this chapter's section on hypothesis testing.

Graphic methods

Graphic displays provide a quick overall impression of the data, which is sometimes difficult to obtain with numeric measures. Making a good graphic or tabular display requires that the material be as self-contained as possible and that it is understandable without the need for additional text. These attributes require clear labeling, including the title, units, and axes on graphs or figures. The statistical terms used in tables and figures should be well defined. Keep in mind these important attributes of good displays.

Bar graphs provide a pictorial representation of a frequency distribution for either nominal or ordinal data. This is a widely used approach for displaying group data. However, the sense of the actual sample points in the respective groups is lost. Figure 10.2 is a bar chart for the type of health insurance among participants in the 2012 NHANES National Youth Fitness Survey (NNYFS). In this figure, we can see that most respondents have private insurance, and Medicaid is the second most common type of insurance among this sample.

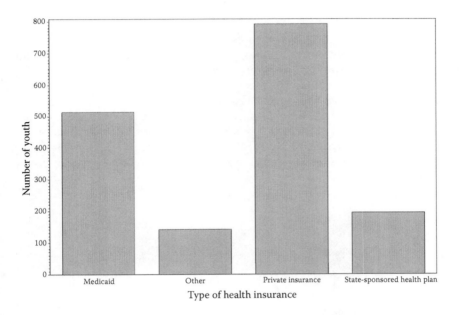

Figure 10.2 Bar chart of type of health insurance for 2012 NNYFS participants. NNYFS:NHANESNationalYouthFitnessSurvey;NHANES:NationalHealthand Nutrition Examination Survey.

BOX 10.8 EXPLANATION OF DATA USED TO CREATE FIGURE 10.2

The data used to create Figure 10.2 come from the National Health and Nutrition Examination Survey (NHANES), specifically the NHANES National Youth Fitness Survey (NNYFS) of 2012. The variable represented in the bar chart comes from the Health Insurance Questionnaire section of NNYFS. Health insurance information was collected by trained NHANES interviewers and was collected in the participants' homes using a computer-assisted interview process. The "other" category

204 *Public health research methods for partnerships and practice*

> of health insurance includes participants who did not say they were covered by private insurance, Medicaid, or a state-sponsored health plan; "other" also includes having no coverage.
>
> *(From National Health and Nutrition Examination Survey, National Youth Fitness Survey, Centers for Disease Control and Prevention, National Center for Health Statistics; 2012. https://wwwn.cdc.gov/Nchs/Nhanes/Search/Nnyfs12.aspx.)*

Histograms depict the frequency distribution of continuous data and are the most commonly used type of graph. The pictorial image allows the viewer to determine whether the data are symmetric or skewed, to determine which values have high levels of frequency, and to examine the spread of the data for the presence of gaps or outliers (some data values that are far from most of the others). Figure 10.3 is a histogram of waist circumference (cm) for the 2012 NNYFS participants. In this figure, we can see that the data are skewed, with most of the observations between 50 and 70 centimeters.

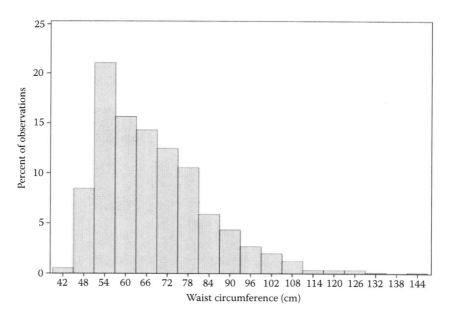

Figure 10.3 Histogram displaying the distribution of waist circumference (cm) for 2012 NNYFSparticipants.NNYFS:NHANESNationalYouthFitnessSurvey;NHANES: National Health and Nutrition Examination Survey.

> **BOX 10.9 EXPLANATION OF DATA USED TO CREATE FIGURE 10.3**
>
> The data used to create Figure 10.3 come from the National Health and Nutrition Examination Survey (NHANES), specifically the NHANES National Youth Fitness Survey (NNYFS) of 2012. The variable represented in the histogram comes from the body measurements section of the NNYFS. The waist circumference of participants (aged 3 to 15 years) was measured by a trained health technician and measured in centimeters.
>
> *(From National Health and Nutrition Examination Survey, National Youth Fitness Survey, Centers for Disease Control and Prevention, National Center for Health Statistics; 2012. https://wwwn.cdc.gov/Nchs/Nhanes/Search/Nnyfs12.aspx.)*

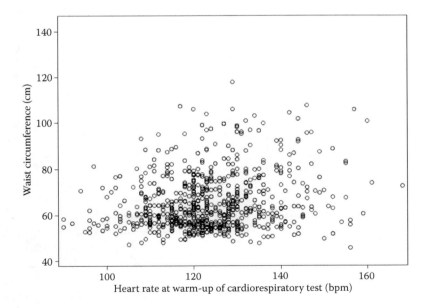

Figure 10.4 Two-way scatterplot of waist circumference by heart rate at warm-up of cardiorespiratory test for 2012 NNYFS participants. BPM: beats per minute; NNYFS: NHANES National Youth Fitness Survey; NHANES: National Health and Nutrition Examination Survey.

206   *Public health research methods for partnerships and practice*

Two-way scatterplots are used to depict the relationship between two continuous variables. Each point on the graph represents a pair of values. Figure 10.4 is a two-way scatterplot of waist circumference by heart rate at warm-up of the cardiorespiratory test for the 2012 NNYFS participants. Each point on the scatterplot represents each participant in the sample and their corresponding heart rate and waist circumference. Scatterplots will display a trend in the relationship between the two variables (if one exists) and can be used to identify points that are potential outliers in the data. Figure 10.4 does not show a clear relationship between heart rate and waist circumference. A few points are potential outliers, as most of the data are clumped together, and there are a few points with high heart rates and others with high waist circumferences.

**BOX 10.10   EXPLANATION OF DATA
USED TO CREATE FIGURE 10.4**

The data used to create Figure 10.4 come from the National Health and Nutrition Examination Survey (NHANES), specifically the NHANES National Youth Fitness Survey (NNYFS) of 2012.[1] The y-axis variable in the scatterplot comes from the body measurements section of the NNYFS. This variable, waist circumference, is the same variable used in Figure 10.3. The variable on the x-axis, heart rate at warm-up of cardiorespiratory test, comes from the cardiorespiratory endurance section of the NNYFS. Participants aged 6 to 11 years old participated in this examination. The warm-up heart rate was measured at the end of the 1-minute warm-up portion of an exercise test completed on a treadmill and was presented in beats per minute (bpm). The heart rate was measured using an automated monitor. The abdomen and thorax of the participant was connected to the monitor using four electrodes. Trained examiners conducted the test and monitored participants.

(From National Health and Nutrition Examination Survey, National Youth Fitness Survey, Centers for Disease Control and Prevention, National Center for Health Statistics; 2012. https://wwwn.cdc.gov/Nchs/Nhanes/Search/Nnyfs12.aspx.)

Geographic information system (GIS) maps are being used more often in public health research because they are an excellent way to display spatial and geographical data. Figure 10.5 is a GIS map of Suffolk County, MA, that shows the proportion of white population by zip code with each shade representing a tertile of percentages (<33%, 33%–66%, 67%+).

Quantitative research methods 207

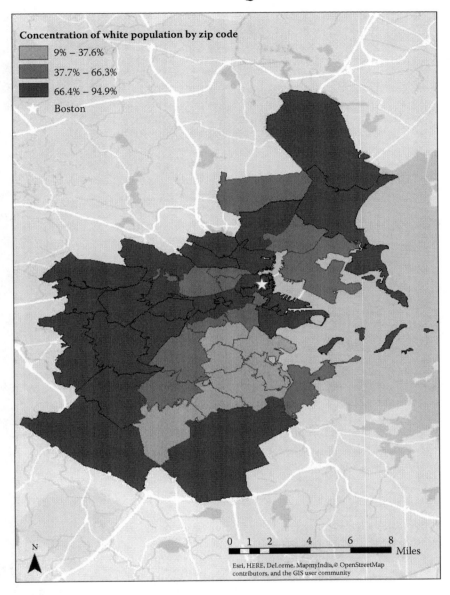

Figure 10.5 White population percentage by zip code in Suffolk County, MA. The darker gray scale indicates a higher percentage White population. The white star on the map represents the approximate center of Boston, MA. (From 2013 ACS 5 year estimates: United States Census Bureau. American Community Survey 2013: Total Population by Race. http://www.social explorer.com/tables/ACS2013_5yr/R11382873?ReportId=R11382873. Accessed April 4, 2017.)

208   *Public health research methods for partnerships and practice*

BOX 10.11   EXPLANATION OF DATA USED TO CREATE FIGURE 10.5

Figure 10.5 displays a map made using ArcGIS, a geographic informa-tion system. Within the figure, the concentration of white populations by zip code in Suffolk County, MA, is presented in three categories, each depicted by a varying color, from light gray to dark gray to black. The city of Boston is represented by a white star for a reference point. The population data come from the U.S. Census Bureau's 2013 American Community Survey 5 year estimates. On the map, there are a scale bar and a north arrow on the lower edge, in addition to the legend in the upper left corner, which are always included on a map.

(From United States Census Bureau. American Community Survey 2013: Total Population by Race. http://www.socialexplorer.com/tables/ACS2013_5yr /R11382873?ReportId=R11382873. Accessed April 4, 2017.)

Hypothesis testing

Statistical significance

Following the sampling methods and data collection procedures discussed in previous sections, we reject or fail to reject a hypothesis on the basis of sample statistics. If we have a good reason—usually through statistical testing—to believe the estimate from the sample differs from the measure of that population not by chance alone, then the difference has *statistical signif-icance*, or the difference is statistically significant. Many researchers drop the word "statistically" and just refer to this difference as significantly different.

The definition of hypothesis test

A hypothesis is a statement about one or more populations. The purpose of hypothesis testing is to aid researchers in reaching a conclusion concerning a population by examining a sample from that population. In classical tests of significance, two types of hypotheses are used. The *null hypothesis* proposes no difference or relationship between the variables of interest. It is used for testing, and usually denoted as H_o. A second or *alternative hypothesis* contra-dicts H_o and states that there is a difference or relationship. The alternative hypothesis is also known as the research hypothesis, often denoted as H_a.[10] It is the conjecture or supposition that motivates the research. We set up the null and alternative hypotheses in this way as it allows for the use of statistics to lead to proof by contradiction.

Quantitative research methods 209

Rules for setting up a hypothesis testing

The null hypothesis is listed and presented before an alternative hypothesis. However, when we construct hypotheses, we usually start with the alternative hypothesis as it is related to the research questions. We put what we hope or what we expect from the research in H_a. As H_o and H_a should include all possible situations, it is not difficult to set up H_o after H_a is developed. In addition, H_o should contain the statement of equality. For example, we want to conduct research on diabetes prevalence related to the racial disparity in Missouri. The research question is that the prevalence of diabetes for African American adults is different (e.g., higher or lower) from the prevalence for white adults in Missouri. This statement should be H_a, as it is what we expect from the findings of the research. There are three possible situations. The prevalence of diabetes for African American adults could be higher, lower, or equal to prevalence for white adults. On the basis of the rules for setting up hypotheses, we can set the null hypothesis (H_o) as the following: the prevalence of diabetes for African American adults is the same as the prevalence for white adults in Missouri. The hypothesis can be reworded as the following:

Null hypothesis (H_o): No significant difference exists in the prevalence of diabetes between African American adults and white adults in Missouri.
Alternative hypothesis (H_a): A significant difference exists in the prevalence of diabetes between African American adults and white adults in Missouri.

The alternative hypothesis includes two possible situations: the prevalence of diabetes for African American adults is either higher or lower than the prevalence for white adults in Missouri. This is a nondirectional test, which is also referred to as a *2-tailed test*. Sometimes, researchers prefer to conduct a directional, or a *1-tailed test*. The following example shows hypotheses in a 1-tailed test:

Null hypothesis (H_o): The prevalence of diabetes among African American adults is lower or equal to the prevalence of diabetes among white adults in Missouri.
Alternative hypothesis (H_a): The prevalence of diabetes among African American adults is higher than the prevalence of diabetes among white adults in Missouri.

Steps for hypothesis testing

Researchers often use the following steps for hypothesis testing: (1) set up the hypothesis, (2) calculate the test statistics, (3) state the decision rule, (4) calculate critical value of the test statistics, and (5) draw a conclusion. However, when we use the statistical software for data analysis, we often skip steps 3 and 4.

210 *Public health research methods for partnerships and practice*

Level of significance

The *level of significance* is a probability that one rejects a true null hypothesis. It is often denoted as α. Many researches use 0.05 as the level of significance. This states that researchers are comfortable being incorrect in their conclusions about the hypothesis 5% of the time, which means that, on average, we draw correct conclusions 95% of the time.

P-values and statistical significance

The p-value is the probability of obtaining the observed estimate (or one that is even more extreme) under the null hypothesis. It is the probability that the observed difference seen in the data is caused by chance alone. The p-value does not provide information about the magnitude of the difference, and it implies statistical significance but not practical relevance. Just because something is statistically significant does not make it scientifically meaningful. The practical relevance is often assessed through the evaluation of effect size. A detailed discussion on the evaluation of effect size can be found elsewhere.[11–14]

We evaluate the p-*value* relative to the *a priori* selected level of significance α (e.g., 0.05). The level of significance is set before the data analysis begins and should not be changed based on the results. If the p-value is less than α, the null hypothesis is rejected, and the results are significant. It suggests that the results of the study could not have occurred by chance alone—something must be going on. If the p-value is greater than α, we fail to reject the null hypothesis, and the results are not significant. The possible reasons could include differences due to chance, a sample size that is too small, low incidence of the test result, or too much variability in the observed variable.

We technically "fail to reject" the null instead of "accept" the null hypothesis. It is argued that a null hypothesis can never be proven and, hence, cannot be "accepted." We can only reject or fail to reject a null hypothesis. Despite the very real statistical difference in these terms, some people use the less formal terminology of "accept." However, to accept the null hypothesis is a completely different thing than failing to reject it and often comes with a much higher probability of error.

To evaluate hypotheses, we need to take a sample and evaluate whether the sample is more consistent with the null hypothesis or with the alternative hypothesis. For example, to test the null hypothesis "There is no significant difference in the prevalence of diabetes between African American adults and white adults in Missouri," we use the data from the BRFSS.[15,16] In 2014, the diabetes prevalence for Non-Hispanic African Americans in Missouri was 18.0% (95% CI: 13.6–22.4%); comparatively, the diabetes prevalence among white adults in Missouri was 10.1% (95% CI: 9.1–11.0%). We conducted a chi-square test using the BRFSS dataset and found that the p-value was less than 0.05, so we rejected the null hypothesis and concluded that there is a significant difference in the prevalence of diabetes between African American adults and white adults in Missouri.

When interval estimates are available in addition to the point estimates, instead of running a statistical test, researchers can evaluate a null hypothesis by just comparing the two interval estimates. If the intervals do not overlap, researchers can reject the null hypothesis. For example, the two intervals for African Americans (13.6–22.4%) and whites (9.1–11.0%) do not overlap; hence, the null hypothesis is rejected. However, using comparison of the intervals to evaluate a null hypothesis is conservative and may not warrant researchers to fail to reject a null hypothesis even when the two intervals overlap.

We use statistics to discover whether two variables are associated. If they are, we investigate how strongly they are associated and whether chance can explain the observed association. Statistics are primarily designed to assess the role of chance in association, but having association cannot constitute proof of a causal relationship. This is especially true for cross-sectional studies (measurement at one point in time) such as BRFSS.

Odds ratio

The odds ratio (OR) measures the association between an exposure and an outcome. It gives the odds that a specific outcome will occur given a particular exposure, compared to the odds that the outcome will occur without the exposure. It is commonly used in case-control studies. In rare diseases, the risk of disease in the population can be estimated using the odds ratio.

Computing an odds ratio

If we denote, respectively, a and b as the number of people having and not having the disease given a particular exposure, and c and d as the number of people having and not having the disease without the exposure, then the odds of disease in those with risk factor is a/b, and the odds of the disease without the risk factor is c/d (Table 10.1).

We calculate the OR using the formula below:

$$OR = \frac{a}{b} \div \frac{c}{d} = \frac{ad}{bc}$$

Table 10.1 Standard 2×2 table for exposure and disease

	Disease (cases)	No disease (controls)
Exposure	a	b
No exposure	c	d

212 *Public health research methods for partnerships and practice*

OR is also referred to as the *cross-products* ratio. It is the product of the main diagonal (supports the null hypothesis of an association) divided by the product of the off diagonal.

Interpreting odds ratios

ORs assess the risk of a particular outcome or disease if a certain factor or exposure is present. They answer the question of how much more or less likely it is that someone who is exposed to the factor under study will develop the outcome as compared to someone who is not exposed. When the OR is less than 1, then the event is less likely to happen; when the OR is greater than 1, then the event is more likely to happen. Specifically,

- OR < 1, exposure is associated with lower odds of disease/outcome/event.
- OR = 1, exposure is not associated with disease/outcome/event.
- OR > 1, exposure is associated with higher odds of disease/outcome/event.

Odds ratio example

Suppose that a researcher conducted a case-control study to investigate the association between smoking and lung cancer. The findings were recorded in a 2×2 table shown in Table 10.2.

On the basis of the OR formula, we calculate

$$\text{OR} = \frac{ad}{bc} = \frac{175 \times 940}{825 \times 60} = \frac{164,500}{49,500} \approx 3.32$$

In accordance with the calculation, a person who smokes is 3.32 times more likely to develop lung cancer, as compared to a person who does not smoke. In addition, we often obtain the 95% confidence interval for the OR using statistical software. For example, we can use the SPSS crosstab procedure to obtain its 95% CI (2.44, 4.52). The number 1 is not in the interval, so we can conclude that smokers have significantly higher odds of developing lung cancer.

Table 10.2 Standard 2×2 table for smoking (exposure) and lung cancer (disease)

Smoking status	Lung cancer	No lung cancer
Smoker	*a = 175*	*b = 825*
Nonsmoker	*c = 60*	*d = 940*

Quantitative research methods 213

Adjusted odds ratios

When we calculate the ORs while controlling for the covariates (other than the risk factor), the ORs are known as *adjusted odds ratios*. For example, in a study to investigate whether heavy smoking and binge drinking are associated with school violence while controlling for students' gender, race, and grade, Zhang and Johnson[17] found the adjusted OR for carrying a weapon was 1.80 (95% CI: 1.42, 2.28) for heavy smokers and 3.01 (95% CI: 2.41, 3.76) for binge drinkers (Table 10.3). In other words, students who are heavy smokers are 1.8 times more likely and binge drinkers are about 3 times more likely to carry a weapon on school property. In addition, the number 1 is not in the 95% CIs so both heavy smoking and binge drinking are significantly associated with school violence.

Table 10.3 Adjusted odds ratio for violence-related behaviors on school property by selected factors, Mississippi, 1993–2003

Characteristic	Carried a weapon odds ratio (95% CI)	Threatened or injured odds ratio (95% CI)
Gender		
Male	4.04 (3.01–5.43)	1.37 (1.14–1.65)
Female	1.00 (referent)	1.00 (referent)
Race		
White/Non-Hispanic	1.23 (0.96–1.59)	0.52 (0.42–0.64)
Black/Non-Hispanic	1.00 (referent)	1.00 (referent)
Grade		
9th	1.24 (0.92–1.66)	1.97 (1.54–2.52)
10th	1.49 (1.09–2.06)	1.33 (1.02–1.73)
11th	1.25 (0.95–1.65)	1.33 (1.00–1.76)
12th	1.00 (referent)	1.00 (referent)
Heavy smoking		
Yes	1.8 (1.42–2.28)	1.9 (1.43–2.53)
No	1.00 (referent)	1.00 (referent)
Binge drinking		
Yes	3.01 (2.41–3.76)	2.03 (1.62–2.54)
No	1.00 (referent)	1.00 (referent)

Abbreviation: CI, confidence interval.

214 *Public health research methods for partnerships and practice*

**BOX 10.12 EXPLANATION OF DATA
USED TO CREATE TABLE 10.3**

The data used to create Table 10.3 come from the 1993–2003 Mississippi Youth Risk Behavior Surveillance System (YRBSS). The adjusted odds ratios were obtained from two separate binary logistic regressions. The outcome variables a student carrying a weapon, or being threatened or injured. The two factors of interest were heavy smoking and binge drinking. The three covariates were students' gender, race, and grade level. The survey used complex sample design with weighting, and analysis used SUDAAN.

(From Zhang L, Johnson WD. Violence-related behaviors on school property among Mississippi public high school students, 1993–2003. J Sch Health. 2005;75(2):67–71. doi:10.1111/j.1746-1561.2005.tb00013.x.)

Conclusions

Quantitative methods are used quite often in public health research because they can be used to demonstrate a need, evaluate an intervention or program, or propose a new point of view. Using quantitative methods, we can examine whether two or more variables are associated. If so, how strongly are they associated, and can this association be due to chance alone? We can also examine differences in subpopulations on the basis of demographic characteristics. Other than in the gold-standard, double-blind, randomized controlled trial, statistics cannot constitute proof of a causal relationship. However, such data can provide strong evidence and can be used to create change in policies and programs, to demonstrate a need in a community or population, or to examine differences in outcomes among subpopulations.

References

1. Rosner B. *Fundamentals of Biostatistics*. 8th ed. Pacific Grove, CA: Brooks Cole Education; 2015.
2. Ross SM. *Introductory Statistics*. 2nd ed. Burlington, MA: Elsevier Academic Press; 2005.
3. Burns N, Grove SK. *The Practice of Nursing Research: Conduct, Critique & Utilization*. 4th ed. Philadelphia, PA: Saunders; 2001.
4. Polit DF, Beck CT, Hungler BP. *Essentials of Nursing Research: Methods, Appraisal, and Utilization*. Philadelpha, PA: Lippincott; 2001.
5. Kolbo J, Zhang L, Werle N et al. Overweight and obesity prevalence and trends among Mississippi public school students: A decade of data between 2005 and 2015. *J Miss State Med Assoc*. 2016;57(10);310–317.
6. Mississippi State Department of Health, Office of Health Data and Research. Mississippi Pregnancy Risk Assessment Monitoring System (PRAMS) surveillance report, 2011. http://msdh.ms.gov/msdhsite/_static/resources/6859.pdf. Published 2015. Accessed February 20, 2017.

Quantitative research methods 215

7. Cooper DR, Schindler PS. *Business Research Methods*. 12th ed. New York, NY: McGraw-Hill; 2014.
8. Brener ND, Kann L, Shanklin S et al. Methodology of the Youth Risk Behavior Surveillance System—2013. *Morb Mortal Wkly Rep*. 2013;62(RR01):1–23. https://www.cdc.gov/mmwr/preview/mmwrhtml/rr6201a1.htm.
9. Moser C, Kalton G. *Survey Methods in Social Investigation*. 2nd ed. London, UK: Heinemann; 1971.
10. Agresti A, Finlay B. *Statistical Methods for the Social Sciences*. 4th ed. Harlow, UK: Pearson; 2009.
11. Ferguson CJ. An effect size primer: A guide for clinicians and researchers. *Prof Psychol Res Pract*. 2009;40(5):532–538.
12. Nakagawa S, Cuthill IC. Effect size, confidence interval and statistical significance: A practical guide for biologists. *Biol Rev*. 2007;82(4):591–605.
13. Olejnik S, Algina J. Measures of effect size for comparative studies: Applications, interpretations, and limitations. *Contemp Educ Psychol*. 2000;25(3):241–286.
14. Sullivan GM, Feinn R. Using effect size—or why the p value is not enough. *J Grad Med Educ*. 2012;4(3):279–282.
15. National Center for Health Statistics. Behavioral Risk Factor Surveillance System documentation; 2001. http://www.cdc.gov/brfss/about.
16. Behavioral Risk Factor Surveillance System (BRFSS) Survey Data, Centers for Disease Control and Prevention; 2004. www.cdc.gov/BRFSS. Accessed February 20, 2017.
17. Zhang L, Johnson WD. Violence-related behaviors on school property among Mississippi public high school students, 1993–2003. *J Sch Health*. 2005;75(2):67–71. doi:10.1111/j.1746-1561.2005.tb00013.x.

Activity

You work at a local community-based organization that has a mission to make school food options healthier. Your organization has been asked for its official stance on diet colas.

You have 24 hours to come up with an official position, and you only have information from the nutrition labels (provided below), which you were able to quickly pull from the Internet. Your organization decides to do a quantitative analysis of nutritional information, and your team is in charge of coming up with the analysis plan. Use the information provided to answer the following questions.

1. What data elements (variables) would you pull from the nutrition labels? How would these variables be measured? Fill in the table below.

Variables	Measured

2. What would your data matrix look like?
3. What information would you compare among products?
4. What hypotheses would you test?

216   *Public health research methods for partnerships and practice*

5. What additional information would you like to have to conduct your analysis?
6. Based on the information you have discovered, is your organization pro diet cola or anti diet cola? Explain.

Nutrition Labels and Ingredient Lists of Four Sodas	
BRAND A COLA	*BRAND A DIET COLA*
Nutrition Facts	**Nutrition Facts**
Serving Size 1 Can (12 fl oz)	Serving Size 1 Can (12 fl oz)
Amount Per Serving	**Amount Per Serving**
Calories 150　　　Calories from Fat 0	**Calories** 0　　　Calories from Fat 0
% Daily Value*	**% Daily Value***
Total Fat 0g　　　**0**%	**Total Fat** 0g　　　**0**%
Cholesterol	Cholesterol
Sodium 30 mg　　　**1**%	**Sodium** 35 mg　　　**2**%
Total Carbohydrates 41g　**14**%	**Total Carbohydrates** 0g　**0**%
Dietary Fiber 0g　　　**0**%	Dietary Fiber 0g　　　**0**%
Sugars 41g	Sugars 0g
Protein 0g	**Protein** 0g
Not a significant source of other nutrients	Not a significant source of other nutrients
*Percent Daily Values are based on a 2,000-calorie diet	*Percent Daily Values are based on a 2,000-calorie diet
INGREDIENTS: Carbonated water, high fructose corn syrup, caramel color, sugar, phosphoric acid, caffeine, citric acid, natural flavour	INGREDIENTS: Carbonated water, caramel color, aspartame, phosphoric acid, potassium benzoate (preserves freshness), caffeine, citric acid, natural flavor, acesulfame potassium

Quantitative research methods 217

BRAND B COLA	
Nutrition Facts	
Serving Size 1 Can (12 fl oz)	
Amount Per Serving	
Calories 140	Calories from Fat 0
	% Daily Value*
Total Fat 0g	**0%**
Cholesterol	
Sodium 45 mg	**2%**
Total Carbohydrates 39g	**13%**
Dietary Fiber 0g	**0%**
Sugars 39g	
Protein 0g	
Not a significant source of other nutrients	
*Percent Daily Values are based on a 2,000-calorie diet	
INGREDIENTS: Carbonated water, high fructose corn syrup, caramel color, phosphoric acid, natural flavors, caffeine	

BRAND B DIET COLA	
Nutrition Facts	
Serving Size 1 Can (12 fl oz)	
Amount Per Serving	
Calories 0	Calories from Fat 0
	% Daily Value*
Total Fat 0g	**0%**
Cholesterol	
Sodium 40 mg	**2%**
Total Carbohydrates 0g	**0%**
Dietary Fiber 0g	**0%**
Sugars 0g	
Protein 0g	
Not a significant source of other nutrients	
*Percent Daily Values are based on a 2,000-calorie diet	
INGREDIENTS: Carbonated water, caramel color, aspartame, phosphoric acid, potassium benzoate (to protect taste), natural flavors, citric acid, caffeine	

SELF-ASSESSMENT—WHAT DID YOU LEARN?

1. Which of the following is NOT a type of sampling?
   a. Snowball
   b. Convenience
   c. Stratified
   d. Broad

2. _____ is the probability that the observed difference is caused by chance.
   a. *t*-test
   b. Kappa
   c. *P*-value
   d. Chi square

218 *Public health research methods for partnerships and practice*

3. A mixed methods approach can lead to a stronger overall study because _____.
   a. A wider range of information is obtained
   b. More precise data points are obtained
   c. More people are willing to participate
   d. None of the above; mixed methods never lead to a stronger study

4. If a p-value is less than alpha, you should _____.
   a. Fail to reject the null hypothesis and conclude that the results of your study are not due to chance alone
   b. Fail to reject the null hypothesis and conclude that the results of your study are due to chance alone
   c. Reject the null hypothesis and conclude that the results of your study are not due to chance alone
   d. Reject the null hypothesis and conclude that the results of your study are due to chance alone

5. Quantitative research is aimed at _____ a research hypothesis.
   a. Developing
   b. Testing
   c. Describing
   d. Explaining

6. _____ means that each member of a population has an equal and known chance of being selected.
   a. Quantitative data
   b. Random sampling
   c. Convenience sampling
   d. Probability

7. A weakness of quantitative research is that it _____.
   a. Has a lower credibility compared to qualitative research
   b. Simplifies complex reality
   c. Is difficult to make predictions
   d. Makes analyzing larger datasets difficult and time consuming

8. What question style allows respondents to formulate their own answers on a questionnaire?
   a. Open format
   b. Closed format
   c. Exclusive format
   d. Non-exclusive format

9. _____ is the measure that gives the likelihood that an outcome will occur given a particular exposure.
   a. Frequency
   b. Chi square
   c. *P*-value
   d. Odds ratio

10. When determining the aim of a questionnaire, you should do all of the following except _____.
    a. Write down the purpose of the study
    b. Identify hypotheses
    c. Pilot test questions
    d. Identify the type of information you will need

11 Roles, functions, and examples of qualitative research and methods for social science research

Keon L. Gilbert and Susan Mayfield-Johnson

LEARNING OBJECTIVES

- Describe qualitative research.
- Describe how qualitative methods are used in social science research.

SELF-ASSESSMENT—WHAT DO YOU KNOW?

1. What are qualitative methods?
2. What are the characteristics of three qualitative models that are appropriate for public health?
3. How might qualitative methods differ from quantitative methods?

Introduction

One of the greatest challenges that we have with understanding social phenomena is the idea of finding "meaning." We expend a considerable amount of energy trying to ascertain the meaning of behavior, thoughts, ideas, and various social interactions in social science research. We rely on different sources of information or data to provide us with evidence about the social phenomena we are trying to understand. However, constraints are encountered when building this evidence base. Time, cost, social problem to be investigated, stakeholders involved, and intended beneficiaries are all factors to consider when deciding on the kinds of data to collect and the methods by which these data should be collected. Two broad forms of research exist: qualitative and quantitative. Quantitative research is often lauded as the higher-ranked form because it is viewed as being more objective. (See Chapter 10 for a more thorough definition of *quantitative research methods* than is provided in this chapter.) However, qualitative research is viewed as being more reflexive, as relying on the construction of knowledge by interpreting meaning from experiences and various

Roles of qualitative research and methods for social science research 221

contexts. Part of this reflexive characteristic is acknowledging that researchers' experiences and personalities can influence and bias research processes.[1]

Researchers such as Creswell[2] suggest that to make claims about *what* knowledge is (ontology), we must try to explain *how we know* what knowledge is (epistemology), the *values* ascribed to knowledge (axiology), *how knowledge is described* verbally and in written format (rhetoric), and the *procedures or processes* used to study knowledge (methodology). Qualitative research as a method to achieve these aims is often viewed as nontraditional but naturalistic and can be conducted within a well-designed, well-informed process that provides credible evidence for understanding social phenomena.[3]

What is qualitative research?

Several definitions of qualitative research exist that center around research or the production of results that are not statistical or quantified.[3-5] These definitions also suggest that the research procedures take place within natural settings, contexts, or in the environment (social or physical) of those participating in the research. Qualitative research is designed to capture the lived experiences of people through storytelling, observing their behaviors, documenting social movements, and understanding how social interactions and social relationships shape attitudes, thoughts, opinions, and behaviors. This form of research also takes into account the nature of the environment and how it may shape these attitudes and behaviors within and across different environments. Qualitative methods take broader forms such as narratives, case studies, ethnographies, or developing theory—or frameworks by which we can explain a social phenomenon. This differs from quantitative research in that it provides a broader context by which we can understand data from the voices, pictures, documents, and material culture of participants. Quantitative research usually takes the form of experiments, surveys, and other methods by which we can count or quantify a phenomenon by the use of variables, treatments, and repeated measures.

We do not always have to select one method over the other. Qualitative and quantitative research can be combined in what is commonly referred to as *mixed-methods*[2] or *integrated research*. The idea of incorporating both methodologies arises from the strengths and limitations of each method. One method or research process cannot fully capture the social phenomenon being studied, and research may be enhanced by the use of both methodologies. In using both methods, each helps to inform the other and enhances research findings.

These methods can be used sequentially, meaning that one method is used to elaborate or expand the findings from the previously used method. An illustration of this may be conducting a survey of how men access or acquire health information. Your survey may only provide you with responses such as 35% of men access/acquire information using the Internet, 35% access/ acquire health information from their physician, and yet another 30% access/

222　*Public health research methods for partnerships and practice*

acquire health information from family and friends. These results do not tell you why they prefer these modes of access for acquiring information. You may decide to host a focus group with men to further explore what their reasons or motivations are for accessing/acquiring information in those ways and how that information is used.

Alternatively, quantitative and qualitative methods may be used concurrently, or at the same time, to collect data about a public health issue. The data are then analyzed independently but used in a combined way to explain the public health issue being investigated. You may find a large sample of men and ask several questions about how they access or acquire health information, and you may simultaneously engage smaller groups of men in focus groups. The focus groups allow the researcher to explore more in depth how each type of access is used by men and to ask how that information may be used differently, as well as the benefits and limitations of accessing information in those ways. As the researcher, you may compare these results in your reporting to tell a more robust story about how men access and acquire health information and why they make those choices.

Different types of data provide an opportunity for *triangulation*. Researchers can triangulate within each method and across two or more approaches. For qualitative research, this may involve conducting participant observations within a religious setting such as a church, synagogue, or mosque to understand the role these settings play in structuring the transmission of health promotion information. The researcher may make several visits to these religious settings to document or capture events, activities, speeches, sermons, and readings that may influence health behaviors. A second method may be used, such as interviews, to speak with individuals who attend or belong to that church, synagogue, or mosque. This method allows the researcher to ask participants directly how the setting structures opportunities for health promotion activities to take place. Using these two qualitative methods provides a sense of how the religious setting structures the delivery of health promotion messages and how people may respond to those messages in their daily lives. These two methods, combined, provide a greater sense of the influence and role of religious settings in health promotion that cannot be achieved with a single method. Triangulation across methods may be achieved using quantitative and qualitative methods sequentially or concurrently as described previously. Given the various types of data that are collected that fit within a qualitative research modality, it is important to consider the purpose of collecting those data to identify the right method (quantitative vs. qualitative) and the procedure by which the data are collected.

Qualitative data collection methods

A wide range of qualitative procedures can be used to collect qualitative data. The type of method depends on the main questions that need to be answered, as well as other potential constraints, which include time and cost.

Roles of qualitative research and methods for social science research   223

The research question should drive the selection of the method(s) employed as a way to make the best use of resources and to avoid burdening research participants. The next several sections will describe commonly used qualitative methods and the characteristics of each.

Primary method: Interviews

With the explosion of reality TV and the focus on people's experiences, interviewing has pervaded our culture. Everyone wants their "5 minutes of fame," but interviewing as a data collection technique in social science research requires systematic focus and methodological procedures or steps.

What is an interview?

Interviewing is a process in which a researcher and a participant engage in conversation focused on questions related to a research study. The most common form of an interview is the person-to-person encounter in which one person elicits information from the other. Groups or collective formats can also be used to obtain data, but we most commonly think of an interview as a person-to-person discussion. The main purpose of an interview is to obtain a special kind of information. We interview people to find out things from them that we cannot directly observe. We cannot observe feelings, thoughts, and intentions. We cannot observe behaviors that took place at some previous point in time. We cannot observe situations that preclude the presence of an observer. We cannot observe past events that we cannot replicate (or don't want to—like a massive school shooting). We cannot observe how people have organized the world and the meaning they attach to what goes on in the world. We have to ask people questions about those experiences and hope that they share their viewpoint.[5] The purpose of interviewing, then, is to allow us to enter into the other person's perspective.

Interview categories

Interviews can be categorized in a number of ways. The most common way is by the amount of structure that is applied to the research design or approach. Interviews are usually catalogued into the following design formats: highly structured, semistructured, or unstructured/informal.[5,6] *Highly structured interviews* include specific wording and order. Wording of the questions is predetermined and cannot be changed. The order of the question series is established in advance and does not deviate in format. This type of interview is also known as an *oral survey*. In many qualitative studies, highly structured interviews are usually used to obtain demographic data. Examples of highly structured interviews include census bureau surveys and marketing surveys. *Semistructured interviews* have an interview guide with structured interview questions, but there is flexibility in how the question

224   *Public health research methods for partnerships and practice*

may be asked, wording of the question, order, and format. The largest part of the interview is guided by a list of questions or issues to be explored with specific data required from the person being interviewed; however, there is no predetermined wording or order. Finally, *unstructured or informal interviews* are more like a conversation with exploratory questions. There is not a definitive structure or order to the questions, and the goal is usually to learn from the interview to formulate questions for later use. Unstructured or informal interviews are often used when the researcher does not know enough about the phenomenon to ask relevant questions, and they are primarily implemented or used in case studies, participant observations, and ethnographic studies.

Interview questions

An interviewer can ask several types of questions to stimulate responses from a participant.[7] Background or demographic questions are the first type. Background or demographic questions are ones related to the participant's demography (data about the characteristics of a population). Some examples might include age, income, education, health insurance status, etc., of the person being interviewed to supply contextual history relevant to the research study. Not all interviews require demographic information; it is relevant only if it is needed for the research study.

Knowledge questions are usually asked to elicit a participant's actual factual knowledge about a situation or experience. They are most helpful in providing elements to paint or illustrate a particular circumstance. *Experience and behavior questions* aim at the specifics of what a person does or did—his or her behaviors, actions, and activities. For example, in a study of leadership exhibited by hospital administrators, one could ask, "Tell me about a typical day at work; what is the first thing you are likely to do in the morning?" Experience and behavior questions provide details about the circumstance. *Opinion and values questions* include items related to the researcher's interest in a person's beliefs or opinions, or what he or she thinks about something. After asking the question of hospital administrators mentioned previously in this paragraph, a researcher might ask an opinion or value question such as, "What is your opinion regarding whether administrators should also be leaders?"

Feeling questions tap the affective dimension of human life. In asking feeling questions, the interviewer is looking for adjective responses like *happy, afraid, anxious, intimidated, confident,* or other words that describe feelings experienced by the participant. They are often worded as "How do you feel about...?" They help to qualify emotional sensations and reactions. Finally, *sensory questions* are similar to experience and behavior questions, but they are used to elicit more specific data about what was seen, smelled, heard, tasted, and touched. In the hypothetical study on hospital administrators mentioned previously, a sensory question might be, "What was the best

Roles of qualitative research and methods for social science research   225

advice you heard from your colleagues to help you prepare for the job of running a hospital?"

We often think that asking "why" is a great way to learn about a phenomenon; however, it is not a recommended type of question. Why questions tend to be speculative about causal relationships and can lead to dead-end responses. Consider the following example. A researcher questions a child in kindergarten in a physical activity study about her favorite time at school. She says, "Recess." The researcher asks, "Why do you like recess?" Her answer is that she can go outside and play on the swings. You ask, "Why do you like to go outside?" She answers, "That is where the swings are! Duh!" Instead, the "why" question can be rephrased into one of the categories listed previously to provide more detailed content.[6] For example, the researcher could ask an experience or behavior question like, "Tell me about what you like to do at recess." The main point here is that you do not have to ask "why" to make an open-ended question.

In addition, other types of questions are helpful in eliciting information in interviews: hypothetical, devil's advocate, ideal positions, and interpretive.[7] *Hypothetical questions* ask what the respondent might do, or what it might be like in a particular situation. Hypothetical questions usually begin with "what if" or "suppose." If I were conducting a study about displaced workers in a training program, an example might be, "Suppose it was my first day in this training program. What would it be like?"

Devil's advocate questions ask the respondent to consider an opposing view or explanation to a situation. It requests that the person being interviewed challenge his or her initial perspectives. The previously mentioned displaced workers who are in a training program might be asked the devil's advocate question, "Some people would say that people who lost their jobs did something to bring about their firing. What would you tell them?"

Ideal position questions ask respondents to describe an ideal situation. Continuing with the example of the displaced workers in a training program, we might ask the ideal position question, "Would you describe what you think the ideal training program would look like?" Finally, *interpretive questions* happen when a researcher advances tentative explanations or interpretations of what the respondent has been saying, and the researcher asks for a reaction. An example is the following: "Are you finding returning to college as an adult a different experience from what you expected?"

Good interview questions are ones that are open ended and that yield descriptive data, including stories about the phenomenon. The more detailed and descriptive the data obtained are, the better. Phrases that help to set up a good interview and yield rich data may start with the following phrases:

- Tell me about a time when…
- Give me an example of…
- Tell me more about that…
- What was it like when…

226 *Public health research methods for partnerships and practice*

When developing interview questions, it is virtually impossible to specify all of the questions ahead of time because they are dependent on how the participant answers the lead question. Having probes or follow-up questions can be as simple as seeking more information or clarity about what a person has said about who, what, when, and where. The researcher can ask the respondent to provide this additional information.

Interview questions to avoid

Although some types of questions elicit rich and detailed information, some questions should be avoided in interviews.[7] One type of question to avoid is one where multiple questions are asked in one question. This is a question that is actually several questions, and respondents cannot and do not answer all of the questions. The following is an example of multiple questions posed in one question that might be applied (in error) in the previous example of displaced workers in a training program: "How do you feel about the instructors, the assignments, and the schedule of classes in the work training program?" This type of question asks the respondent to answer too many items at once. Instead, break down the questions and ask them one by one.

Leading questions reveal a bias or an assumption that the researcher is making, which may not be held by the participant. These types of questions set the respondent up to accept the researcher's point of view. An example might include, "What emotional problems have you had since losing your job?" This question reflects an assumption on the part of the researcher that someone who loses his or her job may have emotional problems. This view or attitude may not be shared by the respondent, but the respondent may try to answer the question using speculative causal relationships or assumptions about the researcher's motives.

Finally, many people who develop interviews try to avoid yes-or-no questions. Although some people want to know about a specific phenomenon and ask a yes-or-no question, yes-or-no questions offer an easy way out and can shut down the flow of information. At the very least, they slow the exchange between the interviewer and the respondent. A researcher asks, "Do you like the program?" This type of question requires a yes-or-no answer. Instead, the researcher should ask, "What do you like about the program?" or "How have you found the experience of returning to school?" The latter questions prompt the participant to explain with more detail about the experience.

Primary method: Focus groups

When people think of focus groups, most people think about advertising, public relations, and product testing. However, there is another side to focus groups that receives less attention. It is the one that is focused on research to assess community needs, help design interventions, evaluate policies, pilot test data collection instruments, or help to understand and even explain

Roles of qualitative research and methods for social science research   227

quantitative findings. *Focus groups* are a way of getting individuals together to discuss a specific set of questions to elicit group information on a specified topic. Several core features make focus groups distinct.

Characteristics of focus groups

Focus groups are not just a group of people getting together to talk about a certain topic. That would be a discussion group. Focus groups have more rigor and structure to them than discussion groups, and Krueger articulates that focus groups have certain distinctive characteristics.[8] One characteristic is that focus group questions are focused, meaning that questions are carefully sequenced so that they focus more on key topics of the study. The questions progressively direct participants into discussing the topic in greater detail and with more depth. In interviews, the researcher may ask the most significant questions first or use an informal or unstructured research design approach. These are not strategies that are appropriate for focus groups.

Another characteristic of a focus group is that there is no push for agreement. Focus groups are unique in that the goal is not about reaching a single solution or negotiation. While it is a noteworthy goal to develop consensus or compromise, it is not the intention of a focus group. Focus groups are conducted to gather a range of attitudes, opinions, and experiences, and the unique perceptions and occurrences are valuable to the group processes.

The environment of a focus group should be comfortable, nonthreatening, and permissive. The moderator or facilitator of a focus group should be recognized as an individual who is open to hearing all points of view and who states that there are no right or wrong answers to the questions. Participants may have differing opinions, and these differences are valuable to gaining information about the focus group topic. The moderator/facilitator should also provide a set of ground rules for the focus group discussion so that all participants feel comfortable and respected in providing what they think and how they feel. The focus group should be held in a place that is convenient and comfortable to all participants.

The participants who are invited to the focus group are homogeneous in the sense that they have something in common regarding certain factors that are of interest to the researchers. Focus groups use a purposeful sample composed of information-rich participants on a specific topic to foster a sense of commonality that results in greater sharing of insights on a particular phenomenon. It is this homogeneity that provides individuals comfort with other like people and fosters thoughtful listening and responses that result in greater sharing of insights.

Another characteristic of a focus group is that group size should be reasonable. The size of a focus group can range from as few as 5 to as many as 12. The size depends on the background of the participants, the topic, and the expertise of the moderator. The larger focus groups tend to work better with topics that do not evoke strong emotional attachments. Smaller focus groups

228 *Public health research methods for partnerships and practice*

are recommended for topics that might be viewed as sensitive or personal or when the participants have considerable experience and expertise with the topic. The richness of a focus group comes from the details and explanations of participants' comments and having adequate time for participants to engage in discussion.

Each focus group should have a skilled moderator.[9] Skillful moderators make facilitation look easy. They are friendly and open, and they engage participants, making them feel welcome and relaxed. They give a thorough introduction to help individuals feel comfortable to engage in the focus group process, and they move smoothly from one question to another. They have a set of questions and get through all of the questions in the allotted time. They get people to share their views freely, and they know when to ask for more information. A focus group works well when participants build on each other's comments rather than continually responding directly to the moderator.

Patterns and trends are examined across the groups to ensure that the analysis fits the study. Identifying patterns and trends across the groups and deriving meaning from the discussion is one of the most time-consuming aspects of focus group research. It should be systematic in that it follows a prescribed plan in a consistent way and can be verified by others who review the process.

Developing focus group questions

When you decide that a focus group is the right approach for your research design, you need to take a few steps in order to develop your focus group questions.[10] Develop questions that address the purpose of your study. Although this seems obvious, there are a few instances when people get caught up in developing what would be fun and whimsical questions that do not address the overall purpose of the study. Identify questions that will produce useful and rich information. Questions should be conversational and easy-to-understand. What we mean is that you should ask questions in a way that encourages participants to talk to each other and use language that the participants would use. Avoid jargon or language that may only be common in a particular field of study.

Aim for the right number of questions. Although there should not be too many questions, too few questions will not allow for ample discussion and depth of a subject. A good number of questions is usually around 10 to 14, with appropriate probing questions utilized throughout the discussion, but the number does depend on the subject, the participants, and the sensitivity of the topic. Make sure to sequence the questions so that they set the stage for conversation, and then focus the questions to get to the most important topics. Finally, participation in a focus group is extremely important. The purpose of the focus group is to have participation and dialogue from respondents on a variety of questions related to a certain topic. Do not be hesitant in including activities, techniques, or strategies in the design of questions to get people more actively engaged in the conversation during the focus group.

Roles of qualitative research and methods for social science research 229

Activities may include having respondents draw a picture of an ideal situation, brainstorming topics to a question, listing factors that are important, sorting through pictures to illustrate emotion, arranging figures in an organization design, or mapping out health resources in a community.[9] These types of activities can be useful in allowing participants to stretch their imagination and creativity while simultaneously categorizing aspects that may be critical to analysis.

Characteristics of good focus group questions

As with interview questions, there are guidelines for developing appropriate focus group questions.[10] Seek to have open-ended questions that provide powerful information and can get participants to talk about the phenomenon of interest. Avoid dichotomous questions that would end in a yes-or-no response. You want people to describe a certain situation, recall the emotions they felt, or develop an opinion and provide detailed rationales for their decision. Questions that instinctively have a yes-or-no answer should be avoided. In addition, asking "why" is rarely recommended. Instead, ask about attributes and/or influences to the question. *Attributes* are characteristics or features of the topic question whereas *influences* are items that prompt or cause action.

Think back questions are often used in focus groups to take people back to an experience, to have participants revisit the phenomenon, and to get them to provide descriptive sensory attributes or firsthand encounters. Strive for conversational questions. Ask questions in ways that encourage participants to talk to one another and build upon each other's stories. Also, employ questions that get participants actively involved with the dialogue. Apply some of the previous techniques described, and include reflection, examples, choices, ratings, drawings, or brainstorming in suitable sections of the focus groups to maximize participatory efforts. Focus the questions so that there are a particular order and sequence that make the focus group flow from one topic to another, from general to specific, and from beginning to end—in a way that makes sense to both moderator and participants. Be cautious of serendipitous questions, questions that occur by chance or discovery in a happy or beneficial way. Save these types of questions for the end of the focus group discussion.

When developing your focus group question list, use different types of questions in particular areas. The *opening question* serves as an icebreaker to get the group talking. This might include going around the group to ask the participants to identify their name and the city in which they live. The introductory question usually focuses the conversation on the topic of choice and begins to direct people's attention and ideas. The *transition questions* allow for movement between distinct sections of the focus group to get to the key questions. *Key questions* are the questions that are of great importance in a focus group. This is the information that is being sought on the focus group topic. Key questions are used to collect rich description, insight, and examples. To finish

230 *Public health research methods for partnerships and practice*

the discussion, *ending questions* are utilized to wrap up the dialogue, have participants make recommendations, and ensure that all participants were heard during the discussion.[9]

Steps in planning a focus group

Focus groups should be planned out in stages.[10] The first step is to decide whether a focus group is appropriate. Clarify the purpose of the study. Focus groups work well for understanding how people see needs or assets in their community. They also work well when people need to explore an idea, behavior, product, or service. Focus groups are not appropriate for getting people to come to a consensus or compromise on a particular need or topic. They are also not suitable to teach or test knowledge or skills. If this is the purpose for the focus group, another method should be investigated or considered.

The second step in this process is to decide whom to involve in the focus group. Deciding whom to invite to participate in the focus group discussion is imperative. You need to decide what types of people have the experience or characteristics that will allow for them to provide rich and meaningful information on the study topic. As previously discussed, participants invited to a focus group should be homogeneous and have something in common about the topic to be examined.

After you have developed the purpose of the focus group and have decided on a topic, the third step would be to listen and get advice from your target audience. Identify a few individuals who are representative of your focus group participants. Discuss the study with them, ask questions about the focus group topic, question wording and language, and ask about appropriate time and location. Try to ascertain how to identify and locate people with the characteristics you are looking for in your focus group. Finally, determine what it would take to get people to come and participate in the focus group.

The fourth step would be to put your thoughts and ideas into writing. Develop a written plan for the design, implementation, and evaluation of the focus group. Developing a plan compels you to arrange your concepts in a logical order and allows others to review your plan and offer constructive suggestions for improvement. Your written plan should include a statement of purpose; the number of groups and participants; and a list of potential questions, timeline, budget, and evaluation plans.

Primary method: Photovoice

Photovoice is a way for community members to take and share photographs that express the strengths and needs of their community. It is a participatory tool based on health promotion principles and the theoretical literature for education for critical consciousness, feminist theory, and a community-based approach to documentary photography.[11] It is designed to help raise the consciousness of community members. Photovoice is a form of participatory

Roles of qualitative research and methods for social science research   231

action research, and it can be used as a qualitative research method. It is a creative tool that allows community individuals to have a voice and express their everyday realities through pictures to formal policy makers and leaders.

Photovoice background and conceptual framework

Defined as "a process by which people can identify, represent, and enhance their community through a specific photographic technique,"[12] photovoice engages community participants in photographing their everyday health and work realities and further emphasizes the goals of involving community members by taking pictures, telling their stories, and informing policy makers about issues of concern at the grassroots level.[13] Photovoice facilitates the possibility of perceiving the world from the viewpoint of the people who lead lives that are different from those traditionally in control of the means for imaging the world.[11] Thus, this approach to participation respects the knowledge from the participants as an essential source of expertise. It confronts a fundamental research problem in that what professionals, researchers, specialists, and outsiders think is important may completely fail to match what the community thinks is important. Furthermore, the images produced and the issues discussed by the participants may help stimulate policy and social change.

The method is designed to enable people to create and discuss photographs as a means of catalyzing community change and looking at root causes to problems. By using cameras, community members document the reality of their lives. By sharing and talking about their photographs, they use the power of the visual image to communicate about their life experiences and perceptions. As they engage in a group process of critical reflection, participants may discuss individual change, community quality of life, and policy issues. The immediacy of the visual image creates evidence and promotes a vivid participatory means of sharing expertise and knowledge.

Rationale for photovoice

Photovoice has three main goals: (1) to enable people to record and reflect their community's strengths and concerns through taking photographs; (2) to promote critical dialogue and knowledge about important personal and community issues through discussion of their photographs; and (3) to reach policy makers.[12,13] There are a number of reasons why photovoice can be a particularly powerful way to approach empowerment and advocacy. The Community Toolbox at the University of Kansas shares several reasons why one should utilize the photovoice method.[14] For instance, the rewards of taking photographs are immediate. In our modern times, a camera, especially a digital one, produces instant results and encourages participants to continue taking other pictures. Another reason noted is that photography can be fun and creative. For many vulnerable people, survival is the ultimate goal

232 *Public health research methods for partnerships and practice*

when they live in extreme and difficult conditions. The opportunity to create a visual element can be a powerful and fulfilling experience that can transcend the normality of everyday existence. It can also open the door to unexplored and hidden talents a person did not know he or she had. Also, taking pictures of familiar scenes and people can change the way people view their social and physical environment. When people are forced to think about how they want to picture the scenes they are taking, participants may start to view those landscapes differently and contemplate changes.

Basic photography is easy to learn and accessible to almost everyone. Anyone who can see and hold a camera can take pictures. Although every picture may not be artistically exceptional, it can still tell a story. A picture can have meaning and be a powerful display of someone's ideas, thoughts, or perceptions. Photovoice utilizes these pictures to make a statement. You may have heard that "a picture is worth a thousand words." Being able to see what someone else sees is more powerful than an explanation. Effective advocacy conveys a need for change, and photos are visual illustrations that make a far better case than words alone. In fact, images can be understood regardless of language, culture, or other factors. It is difficult to argue about a situation when there is a visual display to the contrary. Policy makers cannot deny the reality of a photograph when it is starkly apparent. When faced with photos of actual conditions, policy makers must acknowledge reality.

Photovoice methodology

The selection and use of photovoice can be applied to a variety of settings. It is most successful as a method when one of the following conditions is present: (1) it is used to change people's opinions about themselves and their environment, (2) a group's situation needs to be highlighted (like the plight of a neighborhood after a natural disaster), (3) a specific problem needs to be publicized, (4) change is necessary and photovoice can help inform policy makers, (5) policy makers need to be held accountable, (6) a community assessment is needed or in progress, or (7) there is a need for documentation or data collection for an evaluation of an intervention or program.[14]

The photovoice methodology begins with a topic of interest and posing questions. For the CRFT program, the topic was social capital. Two primary questions on social capital were posed: What impacts the health of your community (social capital)? How does this reflect community needs? A photovoice training was conducted with the CRFT Fellows to introduce participants to the method. It also allowed for a discussion of the theoretical foundation and purpose for the research study, addressed any questions, and provided an opportunity for obtaining informed consent. It also included a discussion on how to use a camera, ethics and power, ways of seeing photographs, and personal safety. Fellows were allowed 2 weeks to collect photographs.

Each fellow selected a picture for the community photo exhibit that was to take place at the graduation ceremony. A sample discussion group with

Roles of qualitative research and methods for social science research   233

the CRFT Fellows was conducted during their training sessions with pictures they selected. This discussion group was conducted so that the meaning of the image was contextualized within the group discussion. The SHOWED question outline was followed.[11–13] SHOWED represents *see, happening, our, why, empowered, do*; SHOWED questions are the following:

1. What do you *see* in this picture?
2. What is *happening* here (the problem)?
3. How does this problem relate to *our* lives?
4. *Why* do these problems exist?
5. How can we become *empowered* by our new knowledge and understand-ing of these problems and why they exist?
6. What can we *do* to address these problems?

Each CRFT Fellow followed the SHOWED question guide outlined in a handout to explain the reasons for taking the picture and the picture's signifi-cance. From SHOWED questions and group discussions, a caption to high-light the picture's significance was developed. At the graduation ceremony, photovoice pictures were prominently displayed with captions for a commu-nity photo exhibition.

Reporting qualitative findings

Most researchers and audiences are more versed in understanding quantita-tive research than qualitative research. Qualitative research involves finding the right structure and format to report findings in a meaningful way that conveys the organization of the study design, the methods used to collect the data, and the analysis and interpretation of those data. Often qualita-tive research is criticized when compared to quantitative research because of its smaller sample size. However, qualitative research does not have the goal of being representative in the same way but to be reflective of a par-ticular issue or population under study. Thereby, qualitative researchers have to be mindful of how they describe how data are collected, why the sample that was engaged was selected, and how they help to answer the research question under investigation. It is imperative to avoid (when neces-sary) making quantitative statements about qualitative results. These are not studies that should be about the accounting or numerical representation of findings—but reporting of the collective experiences of the population that was selected. Often, summaries of findings and quotations are used to illustrate the main themes or concepts conveyed by research participants. Data are also explained by providing the context and including the role of the researcher in order to be transparent about how the data were obtained, analyzed, and reported.

234　*Public health research methods for partnerships and practice*

Conclusions

Qualitative studies are uniquely powerful in their ability to tell the stories of groups that may go unrecognized in quantitative research methods. The richness of data that emerges from qualitative research methods helps to expand upon issues that researchers are interested in studying. Qualitative methods, like quantitative methods, must be considered with great sincerity and should not be treated as a second-class methodology or approach. Within the qualitative research toolkit, there is a range of options, as described previously, that can be integrated together or combined with quantitative research methods to investigate social issues. Qualitative research is more than a mere aggregation of anecdotes, stories, and images, but a collection of experiences, systematically collected from research participants to convey the broader meaning of a pressing social issue or public health challenge.

Comparing qualitative and quantitative research methods

Quantitative research methods (see Chapter 10) and qualitative research methods can complement each other nicely in mixed-methods research approaches, or they can be best applied alone. The method—either one type or both together—depends on the research questions to be addressed. Table 11.1 shows various aspects of the two research methods that researchers can use to determine which method might be more appropriate, if not both. The table shows the following for each method: purpose, conceptual basis, functional role, approaches, and the role of the researcher.

Table 11.1 Qualitative research vs. quantitative research[15–17]

Aspect of method	Qualitative research	Quantitative research
Purpose	• Construct historical and social contexts • Generate/build theory • Build concepts • Provide meaning/interpretation	• Conduct empirical observation • Measure • Test/verify theory • Test hypothesis
Conceptual basis	• Assumes a dynamic reality based on lived experiences • Assumes multiple realities that are continually changing based on individual interactions and interpretation • Focuses on complex and transactional issues • Develops theory	• Assumes a fixed and measurable reality • Focuses in a concise and narrow way • Tests theory

(Continued)

Roles of qualitative research and methods for social science research   235

Table 11.1   (Continued) Qualitative research vs. quantitative research[15–17]

Aspect of method	Qualitative research	Quantitative research
Functional role	• Provides narratives of lived experiences • Provides meaning for cultural and social norms • Explains social phenomenon from perspective of those affected • Centers on people, engages interactively • Contextual • Explores, discovers, constructs	• Provides description of participants that can be used to assess experiences, attitudes, perceptions, and behaviors • Describes, explains, and predicts • Tests hypotheses • Examines cause and effect • Makes predictions
Approaches	Words and narrative analysis • Narrative research • Ethnographies • Case studies • Data reported in the language of the information • Data collected through conversations, observations, or existing text • Data analyzed for major themes • Inductive reasoning used to synthesize data • Open-ended questions	Numbers and statistical analysis • Experimental • Nonexperimental • Data analyzed through numerical comparisons and statistical inferences • Data reported through statistical analysis • Data collected through counting/measuring things • Deductive reasoning used to synthesize data • Closed-ended questions • Specific variables examined
Researcher's role	• Usually immersed "in the field," conducting interviews and observing and recording behaviors • May change research design as the study progresses • May change the type of data collected as the study progresses	• Operates as observer or recorder; not a participant • Designs all aspects of the study before collecting data • Knows in advance what data will be collected

Sources: Johnson, B., Christensen, L., *Educational Research: Quantitative, Qualitative, and Mixed Approaches*, Sage Publications, Thousand Oaks, CA, 2008; Lichtman, M., *Qualitative Research in Education: A User's Guide*, Sage Publications,Thousand Oaks, CA, 2006; Minichiello, V. et al., *In-depth Interviewing: Researching People*, Longman Cheshire Pty Ltd, Hong Kong, 1990.

References

1. Ritchie J, Lewis J, McNaughton Nicholls C, Ormston R. *Qualitative Research Practice: A Guide for Social Science Students and Researchers*. Thousand Oaks, CA: Sage Publications; 2014.

236 *Public health research methods for partnerships and practice*

2. Creswell JW. *Research Design: Qualitative, Quantitative, and Mixed Methods Approaches.* Thousand Oaks, CA; Sage Publications; 2003.
3. Denzin N, Lincoln YS. *The SAGE Handbook of Qualitative Research.* Thousand Oaks, CA: Sage Publications; 2005.
4. Ulin PR, Robinson ET, Tolley EE. *Qualitative Methods in Public Health: A Field Guide for Applied Research.* San Francisco, CA: Jossey Bass; 2005.
5. Strauss J, Corbin A. Grounded theory research: Procedures, canons, and evaluative criteria. *Qualitative Sociology,* 1990;13(1):3–21.
6. Morse JM, Richards L. *Read Me First for a User's Guide to Qualitative Methods.* Thousand Oaks, CA: Sage; 2002.
7. Merriam SB, Associates. *Qualitative Research in Practice: Examples for Discussion and Analysis.* San Francisco, CA: Jossey-Bass; 2002.
8. Krueger RA. *Developing Questions for Focus Groups.* Thousand Oaks, CA: Sage; 1998.
9. Krueger RA, Casey MA. *Focus Groups: A Practical Guide for Applied Research.* 4th ed. Thousand Oaks, CA: Sage; 2009.
10. Krueger RA, Casey MA. Focus group interviewing. In Wholey J, Hatry H, Newcomer K, eds. *Handbook of Practical Program Evaluation.* San Francisco, CA: Jossey-Bass; 2010:378–403.
11. Wang C. Photovoice: A participatory action research strategy applied to women's health. *J Womens Health.* 1999;8:185–192.
12. Wang C, Burris MA. Photovoice: Concept, methodology, and use for participatory needs assessment. *Health Educ Behav.* 1997;24:369–387.
13. Wang C, Burris MA. Empowerment through photo novella: Portraits of participation. *Health Educ Q.* 1994;21:171–186.
14. Community Toolbox, Work Group for Community Health and Development at the University of Kansas. Implementing photovoice in your community. http://ctb.ku.edu/en/table-of-contents/assessment/assessing-community-needs-and-resources/photovoice/main. Accessed February 3, 2017.
15. Johnson B, Christensen L. *Educational Research: Quantitative, Qualitative, and Mixed Approaches.* Thousand Oaks, CA: Sage Publications; 2008.
16. Lichtman M. *Qualitative Research in Education: A User's Guide.* Thousand Oaks, CA: Sage Publications; 2006.
17. Minichiello V, Aroni R, Timewell E, Alexander L. *In-depth Interviewing: Researching People.* Hong Kong: Longman Cheshire; 1990.

SELF-ASSESSMENT—WHAT DID YOU LEARN?

1. Qualitative research attempts to answer the _____ of a situation.
   a. Who
   b. What
   c. When
   d. Where

2. Which of the following is NOT a type of formal interview?
   a. Structured
   b. Semistructured

Roles of qualitative research and methods for social science research   237

   c. Unstructured
   d. All of the above are a form of formal interview

3. Qualitative research examines phenomena mostly through _____.
   a. Numbers
   b. Sounds
   c. Words
   d. Statistics

4. In qualitative research, it is best to avoid _____.
   a. Leading questions
   b. Open questions
   c. Fixed questions
   d. Complex questions

5. What is a key informant?
   a. A group member who helps the researcher gain access to relevant people/events
   b. A senior level member of the organization who refuses to allow researchers into it
   c. A participant who appears to be helpful but then blows the researcher's cover
   d. Someone who cuts keys to help the ethnographer gain access to a building

6. The flexibility and limited structure of qualitative research designs are advantages because_____.
   a. The researcher does not impose any predetermined formats on the social world
   b. They allow for unexpected results to emerge from the data
   c. The researcher can adapt their theories and methods as the project unfolds
   d. All of the above

7. Qualitative research prefers _____ rather than _____ questions.
   a. Multiple choice, fixed
   b. Multiple choice, open-ended
   c. Fixed, multiple choice
   d. Open-ended, multiple choice

238 *Public health research methods for partnerships and practice*

8. What is a "probing question"?
   a. One that inquires about a sensitive or deeply personal issue
   b. One that encourages the interviewee to say more about a topic
   c. One that asks indirectly about people's opinions
   d. One that moves the conversation on to another topic

9. Why is it helpful to prepare an interview guide before conducting semistructured interviews?
   a. So that the data from different interviewees will be comparable and relevant to your research questions
   b. So that you can calculate the statistical significance of the results
   c. In order to allow participants complete control over the topics they discuss
   d. To make the sample more representative

10. Which is an example of a qualitative research question?
    a. How many adults have been to the emergency room in the past year?
    b. Why are levels of asthma higher in one group than another?
    c. Which drug is more efficacious?
    d. What is the biggest indicator of obesity?

12 Research ethics

Aimee James and Anke Winter

LEARNING OBJECTIVES

- Define research ethics and bioethics.
- Compare and contrast clinical ethics versus research ethics.
- Identify examples of unethical practices in research.
- Understand ethical theories and professional ethical duties.
- Identify historical milestones in ethics.
- Understand the *Belmont Report*.
- Understand institutional review board (IRB) protocol review standards.

SELF-ASSESSMENT—WHAT DO YOU KNOW?

1. Why is it important for participants to make a free and informed choice regarding whether to participate in a study?
2. List some vulnerable populations that are protected during scientific research.
3. What is an IRB, and what is its role?
4. What are the components of the Responsible Conduct of Research?

Introduction: What do we mean by *research ethics*?

You have probably heard about research ethics, but what does that really mean? How is that different from other descriptions of ethics, or is it different at all? When it comes down to *research ethics*, we are talking about norms and standards about how researchers conduct their work—searching for knowledge, truth, and accurate representations of data. However, we are also talking about issues of respect, trust, collaboration, human rights, health and

240   *Public health research methods for partnership and practice*

safety of research participants, social responsibility, and public accountability for our research, results, and reporting. These issues apply to any type of research. *Bioethics*, on the other hand, usually refers to biological research or research applied to medicine. When people are talking mostly about ethics regarding patient care, they are talking more about *clinical ethics*. There are similarities amongst all of these concepts, but we are focusing on the specific area of research ethics. Researchers follow specific rules and regulations as part of their professional norms. Some—if not many—of these policies are a direct result of instances in which researchers acted poorly or potentially harmed research participants.

BOX 12.1 CASE EXAMPLE

Chris has designed a smoking cessation intervention and will conduct a research study to evaluate the intervention at a community center. The intervention is evidence based, meaning that it is based on best practices supported by data, and it has been shown to work in other populations. To advertise the study, Chris and the research assistants posted signs around the community center and asked staff there to tell people about the study. Pat works at the community center and is very excited to hear about the study. Pat wants to help Chris recruit and has already identified several people who smoke who could be approached about participating. There will be two groups in the study—an intervention group and a delayed intervention group—so that Chris can compare the results.

Think about each person's role: Chris, Pat, people who use the community center, and people who end up participating. As you read through the chapter, think about the kinds of research ethics concerns that apply to each of these groups. Think about the following questions:

- Does everybody at the center have an equal chance to participate?
- Are there privacy concerns that should be addressed in the recruitment and the intervention processes?
- What do you think of the study design?
- What are some ways to adequately protect participants?
- Does anyone have undue influence on participant selection and enrollment?

Historical milestones in research ethics

Before the 20th century, no federal regulations existed that could ensure the protection and welfare of research participants. The ethical conduct of research was primarily subject to the individual conscience, professional codes of conduct, and laws and customs of the society and government.[1] Historical

Research ethics 241

events in the 20th century led to the establishment of federal rules and regulations in the United States that inform our code of research conduct to date.[2] In the following paragraphs, we will briefly discuss some of the key historical milestones and their relationship to current regulations and practices in the United States. We have limited the discussion of historical milestones to those most relevant to the content and context of this chapter.*

Nuremberg Code (1948)

During World War II, German physicians and administrators conducted medical experiments on thousands of concentration camp prisoners. These torturous experiments were performed without the consent of the subjects and often resulted in death or permanent harm. On December 9, 1946, in Nuremberg, Germany, an American military tribunal opened criminal proceedings against 23 leading German physicians and administrators for their willing participation in war crimes and crimes against humanity. As a direct result of the so-called Doctors' Trial, the Nuremberg Code was established in 1948.[3] The Nuremberg Code was the first international document to outline research principles that are centered on the research subject—as opposed to the physician—and to focus on the protection of subjects' human rights.[4] As one of the key principles, the Nuremberg Code includes a requirement that "the voluntary consent of the human subject is absolutely necessary" (Principle 1) as well as a right of the subject to withdraw from participation in an experiment (Principle 9).[5] In addition to advocating voluntary participation and informed consent, the Nuremberg Code includes principles regarding quality standards of experiments and safeguards. Although the Nuremberg Code did not carry the force of law, it is considered one of the most important documents in the history of research ethics because of its profound influence on the adoption of informed consent as a basic requirement of medical research.[5]

Declaration of Helsinki (1964)

In 1964, the World Medical Association established the Declaration of Helsinki, a statement developed for the medical and clinical research community regarding ethical principles for medical research involving human subjects.[6] The statement built on the principles of the Nuremberg Code and defined rules for "research combined with clinical care" and "non-therapeutic research." Since its publication, the declaration has been an international standard reference for rules of conduct of research involving human beings and has been revised several times, most recently in 2013.[6] The declaration

---

* For more extensive information, see the National Institute of Environmental Health Sciences research ethics timeline: http://www.niehs.nih.gov/research/resources/bioethics/timeline/.

242   *Public health research methods for partnership and practice*

introduced the concept of research protocols (detailed written plans of all research procedures) and review of those protocols by an independent committee. This concept provided the foundation for oversight of research through the institutional review board (IRB) system in the United States and research ethics committees in other countries.

Tuskegee syphilis study (1932–1972)

In 1932, the United States Public Health Service in collaboration with Tuskegee Institute initiated a study called the "Tuskegee Study of Untreated Syphilis in the Negro Male."[7-9] The goal of the study was to record the natural history of syphilis. Six hundred low-income African American males from Macon County, Alabama, were included in the study and monitored for 40 years. Among the participants, 399 had syphilis, and 201 were free of the disease. The men with syphilis were mostly at late stages of the disease at the start of the study. The participants were told that they were treated for "bad blood," a term thought by investigators to be used by the community to describe syphilis. However, available sources differ on whether local people really used this term, and if so, what it meant and what the investigators thought it meant. Men in the study were not told specifically that they had syphilis. The men received free medical exams, free meals, and burial insurance for their participation in the study. In 1972, an Associated Press article and its related public outcry led to the appointment of an advisory panel to review the study. Following the recommendations of the panel, the study was stopped in 1972.[7,10] Several ethical concerns were identified. First, there was no evidence of informed consent. The men were not properly informed about the purpose of the study, their disease status, and associated risks and benefits of participating in the study. Men were treated for minor medical ailments but not for their syphilis. When the study began, treatment for syphilis was questionable, lengthy, and risky. Even after penicillin, an effective antibiotic treatment for syphilis, became widely available, the study continued without providing adequate treatment to the participants. Furthermore, the advisory panel concluded that the potential knowledge to be gained was sparse compared to the risks associated with study participation.[8,10] The legacy of the Tuskegee experiment has had a substantial impact on research activities, diminishing potential participants' trust of researchers and their willingness to participate. It also impacted policies for the protection of research participants.

The National Research Act (1974) and the Belmont Report (1979)

Largely due to publicity of the Tuskegee experiment, the National Research Act of 1974 was passed.[10,11] The National Commission for the Protection of Human Subjects of Biomedical Research and Behavioral Research was established through the National Research Act. The Commission's task was to identify basic ethical principles for the conduct of biomedical and behavioral research involving human subjects and to develop guidelines for the implementation of those principles. The Belmont Report, published in 1979, summarizes the basic ethical principles identified by the Commission and provides guidelines that should assist in resolving ethical problems surrounding the conduct of research with human subjects.[12] Three basic principles—respect for persons, beneficence, and justice—were established in the Belmont Report and are the foundation of many regulations involving human subjects to date.

Federal Policy for the Protection of Human Subjects ("The Common Rule") (1991)

The Federal Policy for the Protection of Human Subjects, developed based on the Belmont Report and widely referred to as "The Common Rule," provides rules and regulations for the protection of human subjects.[13] In 1991, the policy became law and was adopted by several federal agencies in the United States. With few exceptions, it applies to most federally funded and regulated research activities as well as research activities carried out at single institutions and research collaborations across institutions.[14] The Common Rule defines key terms such as *research*, *human subject*, and *minimal risk* and the type of research that is subject to the regulations. It further mandates the oversight of research activities through an IRB to ensure compliance with the federal policy and the protection of the human research participant's rights and welfare. Other main elements of the Common Rule include requirements for informed consent and for the protection of vulnerable research subjects.[13] As of 2017, efforts are under way to revise the Common Rule, which has not been substantially revised since 1981. Proposed revisions aim to address changes that have occurred in the constantly evolving research landscape over the past decade and that could not have been addressed at the time of initiation, such as analysis of biospecimens (i.e., material taken from the human body such as human tissue and blood), use of electronic clinical information, and real-time data from mobile devices.[15,16]

The three basic principles of the Belmont Report and their translation into research practice

As noted previously, the Belmont Report established three fundamental ethical principles: respect for persons, beneficence, and justice.[12] We will briefly discuss these principles and their translation into research practice.

Respect for persons

According to the Belmont Report, respect for persons addresses at least two ethical convictions: individuals should be treated as autonomous agents, and persons with diminished autonomy are entitled to protection.[12] In the context of a research study, an autonomous person is an individual capable of

244 *Public health research methods for partnership and practice*

understanding what he or she is being asked to do, can make a reasoned judgment about the consequences of study participation, and can make a free choice about whether to participate in a study.[17] Diminished autonomy can occur for various reasons. For example, a person with impaired cognitive abilities could be unable to make an informed decision. Diminished autonomy could also occur due to circumstances in which an individual's ability to make a free choice may be compromised (e.g., research conducted among prisoners). The informed consent process is key to ensure an individual's right to self-determination, and should be seen as an educational process during which the potential participant makes a free and informed choice about study participation.[18]

Key components of the process are information, comprehension, and voluntariness. It is important that adequate information about the purpose and nature of the study are provided and any risks or benefits and possible alternatives are disclosed to the potential study participant. The investigator needs to ensure that the information is provided in a format that is understandable to the study's audience and under circumstances that allow the participant to review the information, ask questions, and have time to consider participation. The informed consent statement should be written for the lay audience at an eighth grade reading level (i.e., avoid technical terms). The participation in a research study must be completely voluntary with a consent and decision process free of coercion and undue influence. In addition, the participant has to have the opportunity to withdraw from the study at any time and without facing any negative consequences. Additional protections must be in place for those individuals with diminished autonomy.[18] In addition to the informed consent process, the ethical principle of "respect for persons" entails the individual's right to privacy. It is, therefore, essential to implement safeguards for the protection of participants' privacy when conducting a research study.

Beneficence

The ethical principle of beneficence has been translated into two general rules: (1) do not harm and (2) maximize possible benefits and minimize possible harms.[12] In the research context, this principle translates into a careful consideration of the nature and scope of risks and benefits associated with the study and a systematic risk/benefit assessment. Furthermore, the results of the assessment should be communicated and shared with the potential research participants. The term *risk* refers to the possibility that harm may occur and that a variety of possible harmful events should be considered, including psychological harm, physical harm, legal harm, social harm, and economic harm (costs or excessive costs). Participation in some studies poses the risk of physical injury—for example, through the development of adverse reactions to medical procedures, drugs, or devices. Some studies may require the collection of sensitive information (e.g., social security number, information on drug/alcohol use, disease history) which, in case of a breach of confidentiality, can possibly have negative legal, social, and economic consequences. The term *benefit* refers to a positive outcome/value in relation to health or welfare. Risks associated with a study can range from minimal to significant.[12] Federal regulations define minimal risk as "the probability and magnitude of physical or psychological harm that is normally encountered in the daily lives, or in the routine medical, dental, or psychological examination of healthy persons."[13]

When evaluating the nature and scope of risks and benefits, it is essential to consider that risks and benefits of research can affect the individual participants, their families, and the society at large. The process of risk and benefit assessment includes different elements: (1) the consideration of risks and benefits at the individual participant level and (2) the consideration of the anticipated benefit of the research for the society through the knowledge gained as well as the loss of benefit for the society if the research is not conducted.[12] It is possible that a research study has no or little immediate benefits for the individual participant but holds the promise to have a beneficial effect for the society through the knowledge gained. However, it is crucial that the risks for the individual are reasonable and weighed against the anticipated importance of the knowledge to be gained.

Another important aspect is the minimization of the risk that individual subjects possibly may be exposed to by placing safeguards to reduce the chance of harmful events occurring. Examples of ways to minimize risk include a sound and scientifically justified rationale for the design and conduct of the research that considers previously published data (i.e., from animal studies and other studies involving human subjects) and alternative study designs and procedures; incorporation of adequate safeguards into the study design such as data safety and monitoring plans (i.e., describing appropriate collection, management, and quality assurance of data; reporting of adverse events to ensure participant safety) for interventional studies (e.g., clinical trials); inclusion of a trained research team with sufficient experience and expertise; and incorporating procedures to protect data confidentiality (e.g., limiting access to data, keeping data in safe and secure locations).

Justice

In the research context, the ethical principle of justice demands that the risks and benefits of research should be distributed fairly and equitably. It translates into the concept of fair and equitable subject selection and inclusion in the research study. For example, injustice occurs when the burden of research is carried only by selected populations while everyone can benefit from the results. Participant populations should not be selected based on their perceived social undesirability for research studies associated with high risks, nor should populations with perceived social desirability be selected for beneficial research or low-risk studies.[18] Injustice can also occur during the conduct of a study if study participants are not treated fairly because of existing social, racial, sexual, or cultural biases.

246 *Public health research methods for partnership and practice*

Protection of vulnerable populations

Vulnerable populations require special consideration and protection in research. Several circumstances or reasons can contribute to an individual's vulnerability and affect their ability to make an informed decision as well as a decision free of undue influence and coercion. For example, individuals with "diminished autonomy" are considered vulnerable (i.e., prisoners, institutionalized persons, children, people with cognitive impairments).[17] In addition, a person can be vulnerable because of their current health status (i.e., pregnant women, terminally ill patients). Social, educational, or economic disadvantages are other important factors that can contribute to an individual's vulnerability. Frequently considered vulnerable populations include but are not limited to the following: children, pregnant women, fetuses, prisoners, cognitively impaired persons, traumatized or comatose patients, terminally ill patients, older patients, employees, students, and minorities.[19] Federal regulations require that special considerations are given to the protection of particularly vulnerable subjects such as children, prisoners, pregnant women, mentally disabled persons, or economically or educationally disadvantaged persons.[19] Special provisions exist for research involving pregnant women, human fetuses and neonates, prisoners, and children.[13] The concept and definition of *vulnerability* in the research context have been controversial and frequently debated over the past decades.[20] Determining an individual's vulnerability simply because of membership in a group or population has been criticized, and alternative frameworks—for example, evaluating vulnerability based on an individual's characteristics in the context of the research study—have been proposed.[21,22]

Roles and responsibilities of the institutional review board

All U.S. institutions that participate in federally funded and regulated research have one or more IRBs to ensure the protection of human research subjects. The IRB reviews and approves research protocols and continues to oversee research activities once the research study is initiated.[13] IRBs must consist of at least five members with various backgrounds and expertise to provide adequate review of research projects. It is a researcher's duty to submit his or her research protocol for IRB review and study approval before initiation of a research study that involves human subjects. Criteria for IRB approval include minimization of risk, reasonable relation of risks and benefits, equitable selection of study participants, proper informed consent process and its documentation, adequate data monitoring and safeguards to protect the subject's privacy and maintain confidentiality, and adequate protection of vulnerable populations, if applicable. The IRB can require modifications to the research protocol if criteria are not met. After study initiation, the IRB continues to monitor the conduct of the research study and compliance to the study protocol. If a study requires protocol amendments, these need to be filed and approved before any change is implemented. Furthermore, unanticipated problems that may arise

Research ethics 247

during the conduct of the study, such as protocol deviations and problems that can harm subjects, must be reported to the IRB.[18,23]

Responsible conduct of research and research misconduct

Most federal agencies define research misconduct as "fabrication, falsification, and plagiarism" in proposing, performing, reviewing, or reporting research.[14] *Fabrication* means making up data or results and then reporting them as real data. *Falsification* means changing data or findings in ways that misrepresent what is actually happening in a study. Last, *plagiarism* involves taking someone's writing or ideas without giving credit or getting permission. However, there are research activities and actions that feel "wrong," but aren't necessarily "fabrication, falsification, and plagiarism" or are not outright violations of IRB standards. As part of the norms and standards of research and researcher behavior, the term *Responsible Conduct of Research* is far more encompassing and addresses a broad range of concerns.

Since the 2000s, organizations who oversee research, such as the NIH, have talked about responsible conduct of research. The Office of Research Integrity at the NIH works to reduce scientific misconduct by offering training and resources for both researchers and teachers and by investigating allegations of misconduct in federally funded research. Today, all research trainees who are supported by a federal grant (e.g., NIH or National Science Foundation) must demonstrate that they have received training in responsible conduct of research. Training includes teaching learners about research misconduct policies and the implications of a validated violation (for NIH-funded researchers, it can mean being barred from participating in any NIH-funded research for a period of time). For the purposes of this chapter, we will define general *scientific misconduct* as violations of the principles of responsible conduct of research.

Training in the responsible conduct of research includes several elements.[24] It is more than "just" an IRB concern or about making up data. Responsible conduct addresses how we collect data, keep track of it, and accurately report it. It continues through fair distribution of authorship (i.e., including those who did the work—and only those who contributed to a project) and the process of peer review by which research manuscripts are evaluated for publication and grant applications are evaluated for funding. We provide an overview of a few of these issues here.

Human subjects research and informed consent

We are focused here on public health and community-based research.* Informed consent, covered previously in this chapter, is an ever-present concern in our research: When is consent truly informed and voluntary?

---

* Here, we leave out the concerns around animal research and many areas of basic science.

248   *Public health research methods for partnership and practice*

Researchers work hard to tell participants "enough" about a study in ways they can understand and without overwhelming them. How well do we promote benefit and reduce risk to participants and ensure that burden—and benefits—of research are distributed fairly and equitably?

Safe laboratory and research practices

Whereas most of the chapter has focused on safety of research participants, attention also needs to be paid to the safety of research staff and investigators. In light of terrible accidents in university labs, there is increasing discussion about how to protect students and workers in labs across the country. What about researchers in community-based studies? Investigators need to think about where (and when) they are sending staff to collect data when they go into the field. If research assistants are being sent into risky situations (remember, they are often carrying gift cards and personal data, or interviewing people one-on-one in a closed room), are there adequate protections and precautions in place?

Data acquisition, management, and presentation

Researchers are obligated to collect data in accurate ways, to manage their data appropriately and safely, and to present them fairly. It goes beyond fabrication and falsification to also include careful attention to procedures to maximize the validity of data. For example, this means careful organization of data collection and storage so that surveys or samples are not mixed up or misplaced, and that data are entered with care and accuracy.

Conflict of interest

Researchers must pay attention to personal, professional, and financial conflicts of interest. Sometimes, we do this through study design factors such as blinding investigators to the condition or the hypothesis. We may use independent observers or monitors to keep our studies aligned with requirements. Financial conflicts of interest have been the source of much study and policy. Researchers and clinicians must report who they receive funding or payment from, and this may alert institutions to more carefully monitor a study with the potential for conflicts. Physicians may have conflicts of interest when they are leading a study and also recruiting patients for that study. Conflicts of interest are sometimes obvious, but often they are more unconscious processes that researchers and bodies that oversee research must be attuned to.

Collaboration

Collaboration in science is becoming more common. Researchers are encouraged to work in teams with their colleagues or to work with community

Research ethics   249

organizations and community members. However, doing so raises a number of issues: what are people's roles, who takes credit, who gets the resources and benefits, and who makes decisions? Researchers collaborating with industry need to pay particular attention to conflicts of interest.

Publication and authorship

Authorship is a common measure of productivity for researchers, but it is also about disclosing the activities and results of research. Responsible conduct in authorship means giving authors fair credit for their work. Responsible authorship is not just about making sure the people who wrote the manuscript are included as authors; it is also about making sure that there are not "gift authors" who did little for the study but are given credit as a nod to their seniority (an example would be a department chair requesting to be listed on a manuscript written by a junior faculty member even if he or she had nothing to do with the study or writing it up). For community-engaged research, maintaining standards of authorship may mean including community partners as authors, as representation of their contribution to the study and results.

Peer review processes

Most papers in scientific journals are *peer reviewed*. They are reviewed by other scientists to evaluate the integrity of the study and the soundness of results and conclusions. For peer review to work, reviewers need to be fair in their judgments even if they are working on competing studies. Reviewers also need to respect confidentiality, refrain from sharing the paper or findings with someone else, and avoid taking ideas from a paper for their own work. The same applies to grant applications.

Mentor–mentee relationships

Inherently, the relationships between mentee and mentors, students and teachers, or employees and supervisors are about power and resources. When it comes to mentees and students participating in research or developing their academic career, a mentor or supervisor holds a lot of power. Mentee–mentor relationships may involve issues of conflicts of interests (in whose best interest is the effort?), authorship (who gets credit?), and safety (what are mentees asked to do?).

Societal impact of research and the scientist as a responsible member of society

This final element encourages scientists to think about the broad impact of their research and of dissemination of research. Not only is it our responsibility to report results accurately, but it is our responsibility to help community

250   *Public health research methods for partnership and practice*

members understand the research findings and how they apply to them. As you can see, responsible conduct of research and research ethics are much more than just IRB concerns.

Ethical and not-so-ethical practice in research

We could spend pages and pages on examples of research misconduct. Our goal here is to provide an overview of some of the most notable cases and provide you with resources should you want to seek more information. Some of these examples are well publicized, but some we only learn about over time. In other instances, we see studies differently when we look back in light of historical experiences and different expectations about how research can—and should—be conducted.

Willowbrook Home for Children

Willlowbrook was a state boarding school in Staten Island, New York, for developmentally disabled children.[25,26] It was also the site of a number of research studies on hepatitis, starting in the 1950s. To understand the studies and the concerns, we must first understand the context. Hepatitis was a major concern at Willowbrook for both students and staff. Hepatitis is contagious, and most children became infected with the disease after coming to the school.* At the time, physicians observed that younger children had a milder version of the disease, and once they had been ill, they were either immune or did not have severe reactions if reinfected. A researcher from New York University School of Medicine, Dr. Saul Krugman, wanted to find ways to develop immunity in children who had not yet been infected. This could prevent the infections from spreading and reduce the burden of disease at the school.

Krugman conducted two main types of studies. Researchers obtained consent from the parents for their children's participation. In the first set of studies, some children received injections that aimed to create protective antibodies. Children in the control group did not receive such injections, and the research team observed who became ill with the disease. In the other studies, all new children were given protective antibodies; in some of these, a subset of children were deliberately exposed to the hepatitis virus to directly test their immunity. In these studies, children participating in the study were housed in a special part of the facility to prevent accidental exposure to other infections.

Over the course of the studies, important information was learned. Researchers were among the first to determine that there are different types of

---

* Reports indicate that the principal investigator believed that most children became infected. Other sources estimate that the percentage was lower.

Research ethics 251

hepatitis (types A and B; hepatitis C was discovered later) and that they were spread differently and had different symptoms. The antibody injections were effective against cases of hepatitis A. Researchers also found that children deliberately given the virus generally had milder cases. Additionally, the rate of hepatitis at the school was reduced significantly (an 80% to 85% reduction according to some reports), due to both vaccination and better health care of children.

Even at the time, there were questions raised about the studies.[27,28] We can also look back at Willowbrook in light of the concepts of respect for persons, beneficence, justice, and fairness. In particular, questions have been raised about whether consent was truly informed and voluntary, whether it posed undue risk and burden on children who were doubly vulnerable due to their mental status, and whether researchers had a duty to improve the overall sanitary conditions at the school that contributed to the spread of hepatitis.

Research on infectious disease: A few examples and special considerations

Willowbrook is just one example of how difficult it is to study infectious diseases and test vaccines in real-world community settings. We can look back to the late 1800s to examine how theories of infectious disease were studied and how our approaches have changed.

In the 1800s, yellow fever was a dreaded disease. It could enter a city and decimate the population quickly and painfully, often killing entire families. Yellow fever reached across the Eastern coast and along the Mississippi, hitting cities like New Orleans multiple times, causing thousands of deaths each time.[29,30]*

Yellow fever was thought to spread through the air. Several physicians and researchers proposed the idea that yellow fever was spread by mosquitos, but the idea was roundly disparaged. With the looming threat of yellow fever across the United States in 1900, the surgeon general of the US Army moved to establish a board for the scientific study of infectious diseases, particularly yellow fever. The Yellow Fever Board was then established in Cuba, a country particularly hard-hit by the disease. With a dedicated team of researchers, the group conducted a series of studies on volunteer soldiers and on themselves to establish that mosquitos were indeed the vector for spreading this dreaded disease. Several of those who became ill, including Dr. Jesse Lazear (a researcher who exposed himself in order to test the hypothesis), died from

---

* In 1793, Philadelphia was the nation's capital with a population of 45,000. In October of that year, a yellow fever epidemic broke out, killing about 5,000 people and causing many (estimates around 17,000–20,000) to flee the city. This raised concerns about the safety of Philadelphia, and the city lost its bid to keep the capitol. Shortly after that, the US Capitol moved to Washington, DC.[32]

252 *Public health research methods for partnership and practice*

the disease. After this, mosquito eradication efforts helped curb the disease, with a final epidemic in New Orleans in 1905. A safe and effective vaccine was developed in the 1940s,* and cases are extremely rare these days. Still, no known effective cure exists for yellow fever.

Clearly, protections for human research participants were not yet enacted in the early 1900s when the yellow fever studies began. However, the case reverberates today in questions about study design, informed consent, voluntary participation, and balance of risk and benefit. First, early study efforts were underfunded and were not rigorously designed in a way that would convince skeptics of the hypothesis that the researchers posed.[31] Second, we must question how "voluntary" and "informed" participation was for the soldiers who participated in the yellow fever research, both because so few people believed the mosquito theory and because the participants' position as military personnel may have limited their ability to consent without undue influence. Third, the soldiers who participated in the study experienced little potential benefit, although the benefit to society in the end was significant. They were, however, paid what in today's dollars would be large sums of money.[31] On the other hand, in that era, how else could researchers have proven that mosquitos transmitted the disease? How else could they have begun a program to reduce exposure? Also, would paying participants less be more or less ethical?

We still have these debates today when trying to establish causes of disease and when testing vaccines. Although, today, we can identify viruses and pathogens and can study disease processes (to an extent) without intentionally exposing humans to them, we face ethical dilemmas along the way to eradicating disease in humans. Think about the recent outbreaks of Ebola, in which researchers and physicians had to balance the need to test vaccines and yet do *something* in the face of a dreadful and fast-spreading epidemic. We must grapple with and balance the urgent need to protect populations and not wait too long, with the concern—and potential negative outcomes—of moving along an unproven vaccine in a vulnerable population. Even now, as the Western hemisphere faces a surge in cases of the mosquito-borne Zika virus, we struggle with the research side of giving people accurate information and testing vaccines and treatments for disease. The Vaccine Research Center of the NIH initiated an investigation into a Zika vaccine in response to the outbreak. In the face of uncertain negative effects of Zika, early phase studies are underway to test the safety of candidate vaccines and whether they generate appropriate immune responses. These studies are underway in the United States and in South American countries affected by the virus. A next step could be to intentionally expose people to the virus to see whether the vaccine works.

---

* A vaccine was developed in 1936, but medical personnel later learned that it caused hepatitis.

Conclusions

Research ethics is a complicated area, and protections for research participants have come a long way over the last several decades. The field has moved from recommendations for practice to federally mandated oversight for institutions and individuals who receive federal funding. Institutions can be fined millions of dollars for violations of human subjects' protections. However, as noted in this chapter, many gray areas still exist in research ethics, and the discussion of research ethics and responsible conduct of research starts long before the study is planned and continues through analysis and dissemination of findings. Community representation and participation are essential to research studies. In addition, they can be incredibly helpful in ensuring that researchers consider different perspectives and understandings of research and that researchers and research studies remain relevant to and respectful of the communities affected by the work.

References

1. Schneider WH. The establishment of institutional review boards in the U.S. background history; 2005. http://www.iupui.edu/~histwhs/G504.dir/irbhist.html. Accessed August 4, 2016.
2. Resnik DB. Research ethics timeline (1932–present). http://www.niehs.nih.gov /research/resources/bioethics/timeline/. Accessed August 4, 2016.
3. Leaning J. War crimes and medical science. *BMJ Br Med J*. 1996;313(7070): 1413–1415.
4. *Trials of War Criminals Before the Nuernberg Military Tribunals under Control Council Law*. Vol. 2. No. 10. Washington, DC: US Government Printing Office; 1949:181–182. https://history.nih.gov/research/downloads/nuremberg.pdf. Accessed February 22, 2017.
5. Shuster E. Fifty years later: The significance of the Nuremberg Code. *N Engl J Med*. 1997;337(20):1436–1440.
6. World Medical Association. Declaration of Helsinki: Ethical principles for medical research involving human subjects. http://www.wma.net/en/30publications/10policies /b3/. Accessed February 20, 2017.
7. The Tuskegee timeline. Centers for Disease Control and Prevention Web site. http://www.cdc.gov/tuskegee/timeline.htm. Accessed August 4, 2016.
8. About the USPHS Syphilis Study. Tuskegee University Web site. http://www .tuskegee.edu/about_us/centers_of_excellence/bioethics_center/about_the_usphs _syphilis_study.aspx. Accessed August 4, 2016.
9. Jones JH. *Bad Blood: The Tuskegee Syphilis Experiment*. New York, NY: Free Press; 1981.
10. How Tuskegee changed research practices. Centers for Disease Control and Prevention Web site. http://www.cdc.gov/tuskegee/after.htm. Accessed August 4, 2016.
11. National Research Act, 42 USC§289*l*-1 (1974).
12. National Commission for the Protection of Human Subjects of Biomedical and Behavioral Research. *The Belmont Report: Ethical Principles and Guidelines for the Protection of Human Subjects of Research*; 1979. http://www.hhs.gov/ohrp/regulations -and-policy/belmont-report. Accessed February 20, 2017.
13. Protection of human subjects. *Fed Regist*. 2009;45(46):101–505. http://www .hhs.gov/ohrp/regulations-and-policy/regulations/45-cfr-46/index.html. Accessed February 20, 2017.

254 *Public health research methods for partnership and practice*

14. Karenman SG. *Teaching the Responsible Conduct of Research in Humans.* Rockville, MD: Office of Research Integrity. https://ori.hhs.gov/education/products/ucla/chapter2/page04b.htm. Accessed January 30, 2017.
15. Emanuel EJ. Reform of clinical research regulations, finally. *N Engl J Med.* 2015;363(1):151104140050005. http://www.nejm.org/doi/abs/10.1056/NEJMp151 2463.
16. Lo B, Barnes M. Federal research regulations for the 21st century. *N Engl J Med.* 2016;374(13):1205–1207.
17. Adams LA, Callahan T. Ethics in medicine. University of Washington School of Medicine Web site. https://depts.washington.edu/bioethx/topics/resrch.html. Accessed January 30, 2017.
18. Pimple KD. Protection of human subjects in non-biomedical research: A tutorial. National Ethics Center Web site. https://nationalethicscenter.org/resources/510/download/hspt-nbm.pdf. Accessed February 1, 2017.
19. Department of Health and Human Services. Special classes of subjects. In: *Institutional Review Board Guidebook.* http://archive.hhs.gov/ohrp/irb/irb_chapter6.htm. Accessed February 22, 2017.
20. ten Have H. Respect for human vulnerability: The emergence of a new principle in bioethics. *J Bioeth Inq.* 2015;12(3):395–408.
21. Welch MJ, Lally R, Miller JE et al. The ethics and regulatory landscape of including vulnerable populations in pragmatic clinical trials. *Clin Trials.* 2015;12(5): 503–510. http://ctj.sagepub.com/content/12/5/503.abstract.
22. Kipnis K. Seven vulnerabilities in the pediatric research subject. *Theor Med Bioeth.* 2003;24(2):107–120.
23. Department of Health and Human Services. Basic IRB review. In: *Institutional Review Board Guidebook.* http://archive.hhs.gov/ohrp/irb/irb_chapter3.htm. Accessed February 22, 2017.
24. National Institutes of Health. Update on the Requirement for Instruction in the Responsible Conduct of Research. Notice number: NOT-OD-10-019. https://grants.nih.gov/grants/guide/notice-files/NOT-OD-10-019.html. Accessed February 3, 2017.
25. National Institutes of Health. Willowbrook hepatitis experiments. In: *Exploring Bioethics.* Bethesda, MD: National Institutes of Health; 2009:1–4.
26. Krugman S, Ward R. Clinical and experimental studies of infectious hepatitis. *Pediatrics.* 1958;22(5):1016–1022.
27. Krugman S. Experiments at the Willowbrook State School. *Lancet.* 1971; 1(7706):966–967.
28. Goldby S. Experiments at the Willowbrook State School. *Lancet.* 1971;1(7702):749.
29. Crosby MC. *The American Plague: The Untold Story of Yellow Fever.* New York, NY: Berkley Publishing Group; 2007.
30. PBS. The great fever. http://www.pbs.org/wgbh/amex/fever/index.html. Accessed February 12, 2017.
31. Mehra A. Politics of participation: Walter Reed's yellow fever experiments. *AMA J Ethics.* 2009;11(4):326–330.
32. NCC Staff. How Philadelphia lost the nation's capital to Washington. *Constitution Daily*; 2016. http://blog.constitutioncenter.org/2016/07/how-philadelphia-lost-the-nations-capital-to-washington/. Accessed January 31, 2017.

Small group discussion questions

1. What do you think of the experiments at Willowbrook? Consider the concepts of beneficence, respect for persons, and justice, and discuss the pros and cons of the studies.

Research ethics 255

2. Think back to the case of Chris's smoking cessation study. Now that you've learned more about research ethics and responsible conduct of research, what factors should Chris consider when planning and implementing the study? Are there questions that the potential participants should ask before agreeing to participate? Take on different roles, and consider both the IRB and the ethical concerns in the study.

3. Conflicts of interest can cause a lot of concern. Some studies show that studies funded by the pharmaceutical industry are more likely to show that drug treatments have benefits, but other studies are not as clear. Using Chris and the smoking cessation study as an example, think about possible personal, financial, and professional conflicts of interest. Come up with examples of each and also a way that Chris or the study team could minimize these risks.

4. Describe some ways researchers may conduct research in the face of an outbreak of disease. Vaccines and treatments take decades to move from development through the process of safety testing and approvals before they become available to the public. Consider just how vulnerable someone is who has or is at risk of having a life-threatening illness. How do we as researchers approach informed consent, risks, and benefits in such a case? How soon is too soon, and how late is too late for testing potentially life-saving but unproven treatments or protocols? How can community partnerships help with that process?

5. It is the norm to offer a monetary payment to people who participate in a research study. Some people view this as an incentive, others as a reimbursement for time and hassle, and others as compensation for invasive or risky research practices. Sometimes, the amount is driven by the time a participant gives to a study, but sometimes it is driven by the reality of our budget. What is your stance on this? What is a fair amount to pay people? What do you think should go into these decisions? When is an amount so much that it is coercive and removes autonomy and choice?

SELF-ASSESSMENT—WHAT DID YOU LEARN?

1. The Nuremberg Code was developed in response to _____.
   a. Nazi experiments in concentration camps
   b. The Tuskegee syphilis study
   c. The Willowbrook hepatitis study
   d. Research conducted on prisoners in jail

2. Equitable subject selection _____.
   a. Is not necessary
   b. Means a researcher cannot have exclusion criteria

c. Means a researcher cannot involve vulnerable populations
d. Takes into account the purposes of the research and the setting it is conducted in

3. A researcher must get approval from which organization before enrolling the first participant in a study?
   a. IRB
   b. NIH
   c. CDC
   d. FDA

4. The Tuskegee syphilis study led to the development of _____.
   a. The Common Rule
   b. The Belmont Report
   c. The NIH
   d. The Nuremberg Code

5. The role of the IRB is to ensure all of the following EXCEPT _____.
   a. Participants are compensated.
   b. Risks to subjects are reasonable compared with benefits.
   c. Subject privacy and confidentiality are maintained.
   d. Informed consent is obtained.

6. Which of these includes the three basic ethical principles of the Belmont Report?
   a. Respect for persons, respect for country, and justice
   b. Respect for country, justice, and beneficence
   c. Beneficence, justice, and respect for persons
   d. Justice, beneficence, and equality

7. An investigator accepts authorship on a project that he or she did not work on. This is an example of what?
   a. Selection bias
   b. Scientific misconduct
   c. Uninformed consent
   d. Standards of practice

8. Which is NOT an example of a vulnerable population?
   a. Healthy women who are pregnant
   b. Prisoners
   c. Terminally ill persons
   d. None of the above. They are all considered vulnerable.

9. What is the process that ensures prospective participants make a free and informed choice about whether to participate in a study?
   a. Plain language explanation
   b. Verbal assent
   c. Informed consent
   d. Decision aid

10. Which is a duty of the IRB?
    a. Review the study and procedures and give the final approval or disapproval for the study
    b. Give the final approval or disapproval for the study
    c. Review the study and procedures, give the final approval or disapproval for the study, and provide review of the ongoing study
    d. Review the initial study and procedures and continue to review the ongoing study

13 Health services and health policy research

Kimberly R. Enard, Terri Laws, and Keith Elder

LEARNING OBJECTIVES

- Define health policy and health services research.
- Identify and develop relevant, well-framed health policy research questions.
- Describe public use and other common data sources for health policy research.

SELF-ASSESSMENT—WHAT DO YOU KNOW?

1. What is the relationship between health and health policy?
2. When is government intervention necessary in population health?
3. Name two goals of health services research.
4. What are the four core areas of health services research?

Introduction

BOX 13.1

"Appropriately configured and managed health systems provide a vehicle to improve people's lives, protecting them from the vulnerability of sickness, generating a sense of security, and building social cohesion within society; (policies) can ensure that all groups benefit from socioeconomic development, and they can generate the political support needed to sustain them."

Sir Michael Marmot (on behalf of the Commission on Social Determinants of Health).[1]

Health services and health policy research   259

According to the World Health Organization (WHO), health is "a state of complete physical, mental, and social well-being, not merely the absence of disease or infirmity."[2] Many people agree with this definition, in some form, as an important goal, but then several key questions arise.

- How do we achieve this goal for individuals and populations?
- What role should the government play in advancing this goal?
- How do we measure and monitor the extent to which this goal is being achieved over time?

The manner in which a society defines health is an expression of the values and the resources it is willing to bring to bear in order to optimize population health outcomes. However, a wide range of health processes and outcomes have been clearly linked to factors outside of the medical domain.[3–6] These links represent complex, multilevel pathways through which the health of individuals and populations may be shaped over the course of a single lifetime or across many generations.[3–7]

Social determinants of health

According to some estimates, health behaviors, genes, and biology together account for approximately 25% of population health, whereas the social determinants of health are responsible for influencing the balance of individual and population health.[8] The social determinants of health are the circumstances in which people are born, grow, live, work, and age. The fundamental drivers of these conditions include SES; attributes of the social, economic, physical, and built environments[3–6]; and cultural factors (e.g., religion, language, and relational patterns) that may modify risk behaviors associated with health threats.[9,10] A substantial body of literature points to the social determinants of health as major contributors to health disparities or systematic differences in health outcomes that are closely linked to race or ethnicity, SES, or other social disadvantages.[11,12]

Within the conceptual framework of the Commission on Social Determinants of Health, the health system is also conceptualized as a social determinant of health: health systems mediate differences in the consequences of illness by facilitating access to care, quality of care, and intersectoral collaboration focused on improving individual and population health.[7] This framework offers the perspective that the government is and should be very much involved in promoting population health, not just through health policy but through intersectoral public policies and systems. It emphasizes that every aspect of government may potentially affect health and, therefore, the policies of different departments and agencies within the government (e.g., health, education, housing, social services, labor, transportation) should be collaborative in nature in order to meet the interdependent and complementary challenges related to achieving population health goals.[7]

Role of health policy in influencing health

Federal, state, and local governments in the United States are charged with creating the conditions in which individuals and populations can achieve good health. The extent to which governments intervene in health care markets to protect or promote population health varies across states, counties, and local municipalities. When necessary, governments address these responsibilities through the formulation, implementation, and modification of health and other public policies, which are authoritative decisions, plans, and actions undertaken to achieve specific health-related goals and objectives within a society. Figure 13.1 illustrates the interdependent and cyclical relationships among health, health policy, and health services research that are discussed in this chapter. For example, government entities implement policies (e.g., levying taxes on private households and businesses) to address market failures that occur when competitive firms underproduce certain public or social goods, such as health care, education, and public housing.[13] The tax proceeds are then used to purchase the underproduced public goods: health insurance coverage (Medicaid) for children and elderly, blind, or disabled people with limited income and resources, or safety-net care delivered by hospitals, local health departments, and federally qualified health centers for low-income and other vulnerable populations who may otherwise have to forego needed health care. Government entities at various levels may also enact policies designed to promote or protect public health. These policies include, for example, initiatives to protect the environment, ensure safe food and water, control infectious diseases, support maternal and child health, and license and regulate the health insurance industry. Additionally, federal and state governments have intensified efforts over the past decade to improve health system performance by linking reimbursement policies for Medicare, Medicaid, and other public programs to outcomes related to the triple aim of improving patients' experiences of care, improving population health, and reducing per capita costs of health care.[14–16]

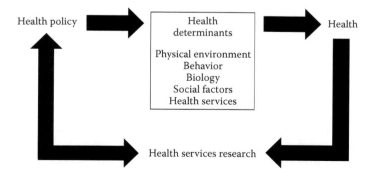

Figure 13.1 Relationship among health policy, health, and health services research.

Health services and health policy research 261

Forms and categories of health policies

Health policies are delivered in four basic forms: laws (e.g., the ACA enacted by Congress)[17]; rules and regulations (e.g., the final rule implementing Section 1557 of the ACA, issued by the Department of Health and Human Services, Office for Civil Rights, that prohibits discrimination on the grounds of race, color, national origin, sex, age, or disability in certain health programs and activities)[18]; operational decisions (e.g., Centers for Medicare and Medicaid Services' processes for reviewing and approving state proposals to expand access to Medicaid)[19]; or judicial decisions (e.g., the US Supreme Court's decision to make state Medicaid expansion optional under the ACA).[20,21] In addition, there are two major categories of health policies: allocative and regulatory.[21]

Allocative health policies

Allocative health policies may be distributive or redistributive.[21] For example, distributive health policies are those that facilitate funding for medical research, public health promotion, health care workforce training, and construction of health facilities.[21] In contrast, redistributive health policies are those that support means-tested public benefits programs that include Medicaid, the State Child Health Insurance Program (SCHIP), and Supplemental Security Income (SSI). Other health-related redistributive policies include Temporary Assistance for Needy Families (TANF), food stamps, and public housing programs.[21]

Regulatory health policies

Regulatory health policies include market-entry restrictions (e.g., licensing of health care providers); price-setting controls (e.g., limiting reimbursement rates to Medicare and Medicaid providers), health care delivery quality controls (e.g., Food and Drug Administration oversight of drugs, medical devices, equipment); market-preserving controls (e.g., antitrust regulations intended to ensure fair market competition and protect consumers from predatory business practices), and social regulation (e.g., public smoking bans).[21] Health and other public policies are integral components of the social determinants of health framework through their influence on individual and population health and the entire health system.

Setting the policy agenda

Indicators and studies

For a problem to make it onto the policy agenda, stakeholders must be convinced that some change is necessary, and it must be important and urgent in the eyes of policy makers.[21,22] Some problems emerge because certain

262 *Public health research methods for partnerships and practice*

data trends reach unacceptable levels, with an important systematic indicator clearly highlighting a growing crisis that needs to be addressed.[22] For example, high rates of health care-related bankruptcy in the United States were key drivers of health care reform legislation. Data demonstrating that people living in the United States have low life expectancy and high infant mortality rates—compared with people in other Organisation for Economic Co-operation and Development (OECD) countries, despite much higher health care spending in the United States (Table 13.1)—have also triggered demands to hold US health system providers accountable for delivering high-value health care.

These data are constantly being monitored by government and nongovernment actors, such as health services researchers working in academia, think tanks, and other agencies, and the data are flagged for review and possible action by policy makers and bureaucrats when trends in these data warrant further investigation.[21,22] Changes in specific data trends, however, do not always signal a problem; instead, such changes may point to the need for ongoing monitoring or more detailed analyses. For example, although the number of emergency department (ED) visits increased by 17.4% from 1991 to 2010, the number of EDs declined 10.6% during the same period (Figure 13.2). These data do not *necessarily* reflect a problem; one might assume that, despite closures, the remaining EDs are geographically accessible to patients who most need ED services and that sufficient capacity exists to serve the needs of those patients. However, published studies have demonstrated that EDs are more likely to close in safety-net hospitals located in areas with high community-level poverty, suggesting that the ED closures may influence disparities in access to care.[23–27] As part of quality improvement initiatives, other types of data, such as patient safety indicators,[28] may be used within individual hospitals, hospital systems, or regions to provide early warning signals

Table 13.1 Commonly cited health indicators

Country	Life expectancy at birth[a]		Infant mortality rate[b]	Health care spending (% of GDP)	Per capita health care spending[c]
	Males	Females			
Canada	76.7	82.0	5.3	9.2	$2,937
France	75.2	82.7	4.6	9.3	2,387
Germany	74.7	80.7	4.4	10.6	2,780
Japan	77.7	84.6	3.2	7.6	1,984
Sweden	77.4	82.0	3.4	8.4	2,270
United Kingdom	75.7	80.2	5.6	7.3	1,813
United States	74.1	79.5	6.9	13.1	4,540

Source: OECD Health Data 2010, Paris: Organisation for Economic Co-operation and Development, 2003.
[a] Age in years.
[b] Perinatal deaths per 1,000 live births.
[c] In purchasing power parity (PPP) dollars.

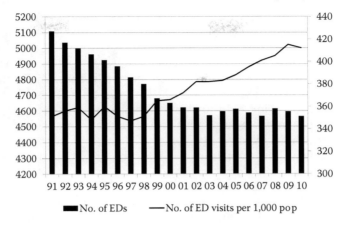

Figure 13.2 Emergency department access and utilization in the United States, 1991–2010. (From *American Hospital Association Annual Survey data*, National and State Population Estimates, U.S. Census Bureau, 2010.)

regarding hospital complications and adverse events after surgeries, procedures, and childbirth, *before* such events become problematic. Patients and families represent another important source of data and are increasingly being engaged both in identifying and reporting potential or real-time problems in clinical settings and in participating in patient-centered outcomes research initiatives. For example, the Patient-Centered Outcomes Research Institute (PCORI), authorized by Congress as part of the ACA in 2010, funds research that is designed to provide evidence to help people make better-informed health care decisions based on their needs, values, and preferences.[29] Since its inception, PCORI has undertaken several national research priorities, including addressing health care disparities through patient engagement.[30]

Focusing events, symbols, and metaphors

Indicators, however, are not always sufficient to capture the attention of policy makers. In fact, problems are not always apparent in data trends. To get the attention of policy makers, a focusing event, such as a crisis or disaster, or an emerging powerful symbol may be necessary. Although focusing events are less common in health care than in other industries, they do occur. The Ebola "scare" at Texas Health Presbyterian Hospital in Dallas, Texas, the first US city to grapple with the virus, prompted the development of several new policies and procedures to address infectious diseases, including the need for better infection control, triage practices, and communication in hospitals. News headlines in 2014 that "bad VA care may have killed more than 1,000 veterans," because of malpractice or lack of care from Department of Veterans Affairs (VA) medical centers triggered a political firestorm and demands for comprehensive analyses of health service delivery practices within that federal health system.[31] Under the Veterans Choice Program Authorized by Section 101 of the Veterans Access, Choice, and Accountability Act of 2014 (Pub. L. 113–146), the VA defined wait-time goals as "not more than 30 days from either the date that an appointment is deemed clinically appropriate by a VA health care provider, or if no such clinical determination has been made, the date a Veteran prefers to be seen for hospital care or medical services." The VA also conducted a nationwide audit to identify any inappropriate scheduling practices used by employees regarding Veteran preferences for appointment dates, reviewed waiting list management procedures, and took corrective action to address issues resulting from the audit. In Figure 13.3,[59] data trends show that the percentage of appointments scheduled over 30 days at VA facilities near Gainesville, Florida, improved from January 2015 through September 2016 but that they continue to exceed the VA's 30-day goal, reinforcing the message from the initial focusing event: wait times at VA facilities have improved, but some are still too long.

A powerful symbol or metaphor can be something that represents a mood, sense of unrest, or sense of frustration or anger that has taken root among a large (sometimes vocal but unheard) segment of society. In what is now considered a classic research article, physician and medical historian Vanessa Northington Gamble outlines a brief history of blacks' encounters with the US health care system. Among the events and social history she documents, the Tuskegee Syphilis Study is so widely known that it overshadows the rest of the history and acts as a metaphor for black mistrust of the health care system. (See Chapter 12 for an extensive discussion of the Tuskegee Syphilis Study.)

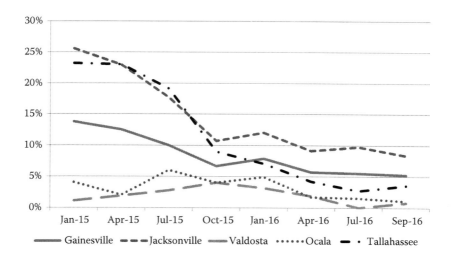

Figure 13.3 Veterans affairs appointment wait times greater than 30 days by selected Florida facilities, 2015–2016. (From Patient access data. Veterans Health Administration. http://www.va.gov/health/access-audit.asp.)

Health services and health policy research   265

As such, contemporary researchers continue to examine the study's legacy for its meaning and impact on health disparities experienced in the African American community decades after the study was publicly exposed in 1972.[32-34] In another example, when an unarmed black teenager, Michael Brown, was shot and killed by a white police officer in Ferguson, Missouri, in 2014, and a grand jury declined to charge the officer with murder, the hands-up sign became a national symbol of protest against racial profiling and systemic problems in law enforcement. As several similar crises occurred across the nation, the differential treatment of minorities in the criminal justice system gained traction as a policy matter, along with calls for more comprehensive data collection and reporting of factors related to disparities in the criminal justice system.

Feedback

Another way to identify and bring attention to particular problems or issues is through feedback about existing programs. This feedback comes in the form of systematic monitoring and reporting, evaluation studies (e.g., cross-sectional or longitudinal analyses of access to care/utilization, quality, or cost data), operational experience of bureaucrats and decision makers or, more commonly, complaints from individuals or groups to government agencies, legislators, and others. For example, errors in implementation of specific programs or policies, failure to meet stated goals and objectives, unfeasible program or policy costs, or unanticipated consequences may all provide feedback that a change in direction is needed. Continually scanning the environment for such scenarios and tracking related data are important activities because policy makers and other government actors not only take the temperature when policies are initially developed and implemented, but they also check for changes in public mood over time. Health services researchers therefore play an important role in gathering, cataloging, and correlating facts related to health problems and issues and in predicting which policy solutions are most feasible.

Ultimately, problems fade from view. This may occur, for example, when the growth rate of a problem levels off (possibly in response to an effective policy solution) or because people adapt, become desensitized, or lose interest in the problem. For example, prior to 1990, uninsured women, including disproportionate numbers of racial or ethnic minorities, were less likely than insured women to receive breast and cervical cancer screenings as recommended. To address disparities in access to breast and cervical cancer screenings, Congress passed the Breast and Cervical Cancer Mortality Prevention Act of 1990, which directed the CDC to establish the National Breast and Cervical Cancer Early Detection Program (NBCCEDP). The program provided low-income, uninsured, and underserved women access to timely breast and cervical cancer screening and diagnostic services. Overall, mammography screening rates improved for women 40 years and older (Figure 13.4[60]); cervical cancer screening rates for women 18 years and older also improved but later declined among some groups (Figure 13.5[61]). Improvements in screening rates

266 Public health research methods for partnerships and practice

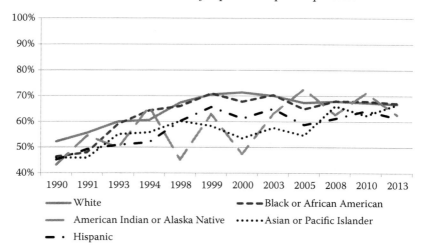

Figure 13.4 Percent of United States women aged 40 years and older who had mammogram within the past 2 years by race or ethinicity, 1990–2013 (selected years). (From CDC/NCHS, *National Health Interview Survey*, Health, United States, 2015.)

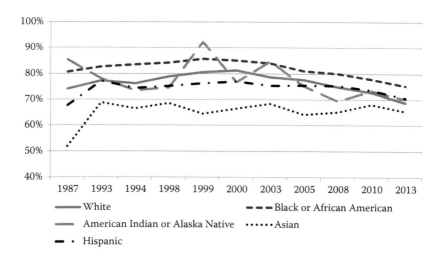

Figure 13.5 Percent of United States women aged 18 years and older who had pap smear within the past 3 years by race or ethnicity, 1987–2013 (selected years). (From CDC/NCHS, *National Health Interview Survey*, Health, United States, 2015.)

Table 13.2 Female cancer incidence and death rates[a]

Racial/ethnic group	Breast cancer		Cervical cancer	
	Incidence	Death	Incidence	Death
All	127.8	25.5	8.7	2.6
African American/Black	118.3	33.8	11.4	4.9
Asian/Pacific Islander	89.0	12.6	8.0	2.4
Hispanic/Latino	89.3	16.1	13.8	3.3
American Indian/Alaska Native	69.8	16.1	6.6	4
White	132.5	25.0	8.5	2.3

Source: National Cancer Institute, Cancer Health Disparities: Table 2. Female Breast Cancer Incidence and Death Rates and Table 3. Cervical Cancer Incidence and Death Rates.

[a] Statistics are for 2000–2004 and are age adjusted to the 2000 US standard million population and represent the number of new cases of invasive cancer (1) and deaths (2) per year per 100,000 women.

notwithstanding, many uninsured women who were screened and diagnosed with cancer were still unable to afford treatment. Feedback regarding the benefits and limitations of the program caused Congress to enact the Breast and Cervical Cancer Prevention and Treatment Act of 2000, which enabled states to offer women access to treatment through their state Medicaid programs if they were diagnosed with cancer in the NBCCEDP. As shown in Table 13.2,[62] however, disparities in cancer incidence and death rates persist. Death rates for breast and cervical cancers are highest among African American/Black women, despite their comparatively lower incidence of the disease, highlighting the need for continued focus in this area. Health services researchers, however, continue to monitor the environment for emerging health problems and focus attention on new issues through the publication of and dissemination of sound, empirical evidence.

Health services research

From 2000 to 2002, a series of groundbreaking reports by the IOM[35–37] sparked national debate and led to increased demands for accountability related to alarming problems concerning quality of care and disparities in care in the US health system. In response, Congress directed the Agency for Healthcare Research and Quality (AHRQ) to report annually[38,39] on these issues, specifically highlighting how health care quality and disparities have changed over time and where the need to improve health care quality and reduce disparities is greatest. The National Healthcare Quality and Disparities Reports,[39] which measure trends in effectiveness of care, patient safety, timeliness of care, patient centeredness, and efficiency of care are key reminders of the need for comprehensive health services research.

Health services research is a "multidisciplinary field of scientific investigation that studies how social factors, financing systems, organizational

268　*Public health research methods for partnerships and practice*

structures and processes, health technologies, and personal behaviors affect access to health care, the quality and cost of health care, and ultimately, our health and well-being."[40] The main goals of the field are to identify the most effective ways to organize, manage, finance, and deliver high-value health care; to reduce medical errors; and to improve patient safety.[41]

Core areas of health services research

The four core areas of health services research include access to care, quality of care, cost of care, and the evaluation of a service or technology. Effective access to care is a prerequisite to achieving high-value health care or delivering quality of care that produces the best health outcomes at the lowest costs of care.[42] Access-to-care measures typically include structural measures (e.g., having health insurance coverage or a usual source of care provider), patient assessments (e.g., self-reported access to care or delays in gaining access to needed services), and utilization (e.g., primary care visits, receipt of needed services).[42] In addition to examining these three major aspects of health services research, various types of evaluations of health services or technologies (e.g., cost-benefit, cost-effectiveness, comparative effective analyses) are increasingly used to inform health care decision-making. The goals of such analyses are to identify and provide evidence that will lead to the best allocation of limited health care resources.

Conceptualizing health services utilization

The social determinants of health framework referenced previously in the chapter represents one model that may be used to explain the fundamental relationships among health, health policy, and health services delivery; to define health-related problems and issues that exist within populations; and to inform the development of possible solutions that emerge as key targets for intervention. Other frameworks (e.g., Andersen Behavioral Model of Health Services Use,[43,44] the Outcome Model of Quality, or the Donabedian model,[45,46] as well as ecological, social-ecological, and biopsychosocial models[47,48]) are also used by health services researchers to better examine the pathways that exist among health, health policy, and health services delivery. The Andersen model,[43,44] for example, which is widely used in health services research, encompasses individual-level (predisposing, enabling, and need) as well as community-level (environmental and health system) characteristics to present a multilevel perspective of health behavior, utilization, and outcomes. A major strength of using conceptual models in health policy and health services research is that such frameworks not only clarify the problem or issue being examined but also help to predict which solutions, or interventions, may be most effective in addressing the problem, facilitating systematic measurement, and monitoring the solutions being implemented. Conceptual models also enable timely recognition of and response to changes in the environment (intended and unintended) that are associated with health and other public policies.

Health services and health policy research   269

Defining research questions

Before initiating new investigations, health services researchers must first identify a subject area of interest and define a significant problem to be examined within that area. A health services researcher who is interested in childhood asthma, for example, may first investigate the overall scope and magnitude of childhood asthma and, then, as part of the problem definition, consider the following questions:

- Who is affected by the problem?
- How are they affected?
- Why is the problem significant?
- Why does it demand immediate attention?

The next step is to examine existing literature, reports, and other available resources to gain a preliminary understanding of what other researchers interested in childhood asthma have already discovered. This process should include an examination of the research design, quality, and intervention features of studies that have already been conducted and an honest assessment of the new research contributions that are needed. Some new areas of research might be the following:

- Is there a specific area that has not yet been investigated?
- Would the field benefit from replicating a previous research question?

The next step is to focus the potential research question by asking a series of open-ended "how" and "why" questions. Examples include the following:

- Why are rates of childhood asthma higher in areas with high rates of population-level violent crime?
- How do practice-level variations in management of childhood asthma impact specific health outcomes (e.g., ED visits and hospitalizations)?

After the research question has been defined, it should be evaluated in accordance with criteria related to relevance and feasibility.

- Is the research question novel?
- Is it interesting?
- Does it address a gap in the literature or extend the literature, or does the research question simply retread old ground?
- Is this the right time for this question to be answered?

The research question should be narrow, focused, and measurable. In addition, the research question should be one that is feasible to address given the available data and proposed methodology and in light of time and resource

270 *Public health research methods for partnerships and practice*

constraints. In the end, it is crucially important to be sure that the research question passes the "so what" test. If the research question is answered, what difference will it make to the population it is intended to help? An important health services research question will not only define and measure facts about issues related to health services delivery, but it will also make a new and significant contribution to the field.

Data

Two types of data—qualitative or quantitative—may be used to conduct health services research. (See Chapters 10 and 11 for more extensive discussions of these types of data.) Qualitative data are traditionally descriptive in nature and captured in oral or written language or pictures (e.g., interviews, focus groups, ethnographies, content analysis of public records, media products, and published studies).[49] For example, a systematic review of peer-reviewed studies evaluating interventions to improve access to care for African American men is a type of qualitative research. An analysis of patients' comments—also qualitative research—regarding their experiences of care within a health system is considered critically important in the quality improvement field of health services research.

Most published health services research studies, however, use quantitative datasets. Quantitative data focus on the numerical measurement and analyses of relationships between variables. In health services research, the quantitative methods are generally used to examine the relationship between or among individuals or populations in the processes of care, morbidity, and mortality for numerous health conditions. Quantitative data used to conduct health services research are widely available from various private and public sources. Private data used commonly in health services research, for example, include proprietary hospital or health insurance administrative datasets. Many public datasets are available free of charge and may be downloaded from the Internet; other datasets are available for a fee. Many of these public datasets also have nonpublic confidential variables, such as geocodes, to facilitate the merging of more than one dataset. Nonpublic confidential variables may be available to health services researchers with permission under strict user guidelines.

BOX 13.2   PUBLIC USE AND OTHER COMMON DATA SOURCES FOR HEALTH SERVICES RESEARCH

- American Hospital Association Annual Survey: https://www.ahadataviewer.com/book-cd-products/AHA-Survey
- Behavioral Risk Factor Surveillance System (BRFSS): www.cdc.gov/brfss

---

- California Health Interview Survey (CHIS): http://healthpolicy.ucla.edu/chis
- California Office of Statewide Health Planning and Development (CA OSHPD): http://www.oshpd.ca.gov
- Centers for Disease Control and Prevention (CDC) National Center for Health Statistics FastStats: http://www.cdc.gov/nchs/fastats
- Centers for Medicare and Medicaid Services Research, Statistics, Data & Systems: https://www.cms.gov/Research-Statistics-Data-and-Systems/Research-Statistics-Data-and-Systems.html
- Commonwealth Fund Health System Data Center: http://datacenter.commonwealthfund.org
- Dialysis Facility Compare (DFC): https://data.medicare.gov/data/dialysis-facility-compare
- End-Stage Renal Disease Clinical Performance Measures Project (ESRD CPMP)
- Health Plan Employer Data and Information Set (HEDIS): http://www.ncqa.org/publications-products/data-and-reports
- Healthcare Cost and Utilization Project (HCUP): http://www.ahrq.gov/research/data/hcup
- HIV Research Network (HIVRN): https://cds.johnshopkins.edu/hivrn
- HIV/AIDS Surveillance System: http://www.cdc.gov/hiv/statistics/surveillance
- Medical Expenditure Panel Survey (MEPS): https://meps.ahrq.gov/mepsweb
- Medicare Current Beneficiary Survey (MCBS): https://www.cms.gov/Research-Statistics-Data-and-Systems/Research/MCBS
- Minimum Data Set (MDS): https://www.cms.gov/Research-Statistics-Data-and-Systems/Files-for-Order/Identifiable Data Files/LongTermCareMinimumDataSetMDS.html
- National Ambulatory Medical Care Survey (NAMCS)/National Hospital Ambulatory Medical Care Survey (NHAMCS): http://www.cdc.gov/nchs/ahcd
- National CAHPS Benchmarking Database (NCBD): http://www.ahrq.gov/cahps/cahps-database
- National Healthcare Safety Network (NHSN): http://www.cdc.gov/nhsn
- National Health and Nutrition Examination Survey (NHANES): http://www.cdc.gov/nchs/nhanes/about_nhanes.htm
- National Health Interview Survey (NHIS): https://www.cdc.gov/nchs/nhis

272 *Public health research methods for partnerships and practice*

- National Home and Hospice Care Survey (NHHCS): http://www.cdc.gov/nchs/nhhcs
- National Hospital Discharge Survey (NHDS): http://www.cdc.gov/nchs/nhds
- National Household Survey of Drug Abuse (NHSDA): http://www.samhsa.gov/data/population-data-nsduh
- National Immunization Survey (NIS): http://www.cdc.gov/vaccines/imz-managers/nis
- National Study of Long-Term Care Providers (NSLTCP): http://www.cdc.gov/nchs/nsltcp
- National TB Surveillance System (NTBSS): http://www.cdc.gov/tb/statistics
- National Vital Statistics System, Mortality (NVSS-M): http://www.cdc.gov/nchs/nvss/deaths.htm
- National Vital Statistics System—Linked Birth and Infant Death Data (NVSS-I): http://www.cdc.gov/nchs/nvss/linked-birth.htm
- Organisation for Economic Co-operation and Development (OECD) Health Statistics: http://www.oecd.org/els/health-systems/health-data.htm
- Outcome and Assessment Information Set (OASIS): https://www.cms.gov/Medicare/Quality-Initiatives-Patient-Assessment-Instruments/OASIS
- Sources for Data on Social Determinants of Health: http://www.cdc.gov/socialdeterminants/data/index.htm
- Substance Abuse and Mental Health Services Administration (SAMHSA) data collection: http://www.samhsa.gov/data
- Surveillance, Epidemiology, and End Results Program (SEER): http://seer.cancer.gov
- United States Renal Data System (USRDS): https://www.usrds.org

Although health services researchers are usually able to find datasets that are well suited to answer many of their research questions, other questions are harder to address because of data limitations. In a special issue of the journal *Health Services Research* published in 2010, one author noted, "perhaps more than any other infrastructure component, data define the possibilities and the limits of health services research."[50] In other words, the feasibility of conducting health services research depends largely on the availability of appropriate data, yet several challenges to utilizing such data exist. In order to support the increasing demand for health services research in the era of health reform, challenges related to data stewardship, privacy and confidentiality, data

Health services and health policy research 273

quality, data linkages, and the need to address measurement issues related to disparities, patient safety, chronic illnesses, value-based purchasing, and other emerging policies must be addressed.[50]

Conclusions

In the United States, federal, state, and local policies impact conditions of the social, economic, and physical environments that influence the health of individuals and populations. These policies include those that directly target access to care, quality of care, and value within the health system. Through its critical role in informing the formulation, implementation, and modification of health policies, health services research will continue to drive efforts aimed at improving individual and population health outcomes, which, in turn, can positively impact the overall social and economic performance of the nation, particularly in comparison with the performance of other highly developed societies.

References

1. Marmot M. Achieving health equity: From root causes to fair outcomes. *Lancet.* 2007;370(9593):1153–1163.
2. Callahan D. The WHO definition of "health." *Stud Hastings Cent.* 1973;1(3):77–87.
3. Braveman P, Egerter S, Williams DR. The social determinants of health: Coming of age. *Annu Rev Public Health.* 2011;32:381–398.
4. Braveman P, Gottlieb L. The social determinants of health: It's time to consider the causes of the causes. *Public Health Rep.* 2014;129(suppl 2):19–31.
5. Braveman PA, Egerter SA, Mockenhaupt RE. Broadening the focus: The need to address the social determinants of health. *Am J Prev Med.* 2011;40(1 suppl 1):S4–S18.
6. Woolf SH, Braveman P. Where health disparities begin: The role of social and economic determinants—And why current policies may make matters worse. *Health Aff (Millwood).* 2011;30(10):1852–1859.
7. World Health Organization. A conceptual framework for action on the social determinants of health. http://www.who.int/sdhconference/resources/Conceptual frameworkforactiononSDH_eng.pdf. Accessed September 12, 2016.
8. Social determinants of health: Know what affects health. Centers for Disease Control and Prevention Web site. http://www.cdc.gov/socialdeterminants/index .htm. Accessed September 12, 2016.
9. Idler EL. Religion: The invisible social determinant. In: Idler EL, ed. *Religion as a Social Determinant of Public Health.* New York, NY: Oxford University Press; 2014:1–23.
10. Ford J, Kadushin C. Between sacral belief and moral community: A multidimensional approach to the relationship between religion and alcohol among blacks and whites. *Sociological Forum.* 2002;17(2):255–279.
11. Braveman P. What are health disparities and health equity? We need to be clear. *Public Health Rep.* 2014;129(suppl 2):5–8.
12. Disparities. Healthy People 2020 Web site. https://www.healthypeople.gov/2020 /about/foundation-health-measures/Disparities. Accessed September 12, 2016.
13. McConnell C, Brue S, Flynn S. *Principles of Microeconomics.* New York, NY: McGraw-Hill; 2015.

274 *Public health research methods for partnerships and practice*

14. Working for quality: Achieving better health and health care for all americans. Agency for Healthcare Research and Quality Web site. http://www.ahrq.gov/work ingforquality/about.htm. Accessed September 12, 2016.
15. Berwick DM, Nolan TW, Whittington J. The triple aim: Care, health, and cost. *Health Aff (Millwood)*. 2008;27(3):759–769.
16. Hacker K, Walker DK. Achieving population health in accountable care organizations. *Am J Public Health*. 2013;103(7):1163–1167.
17. Patient Protection and Affordable Care Act, 42 USC §18001 (2010).
18. Section 1557: Protecting individuals against sex discrimination. US Department of Health and Human Services Web site. http://www.hhs.gov/civil-rights/for -individuals/section-1557/fs-sex-discrimination/index.html. Accessed September 9, 2016.
19. Rudowitz R, Musumeci MB. The ACA and Medicaid expansion waivers. The Henry J. Kaiser Family Foundation Web site. http://kff.org/medicaid/issue-brief /the-aca-and-medicaid-expansion-waivers/. Accessed August 31, 2016.
20. A guide to the Supreme Court's decision. The Henry T. Kaiser Family Foundation Web site. http://kff.org/health-reform/issue-brief/a-guide-to-the-supreme-courts -decision. Accessed August 31, 2016.
21. Longest BB. *Health Policymaking in the United States*. Chicago, IL: Health Administration Press; 2016.
22. Kingdon JW. *Agendas, Alternatives, and Public Policies*. New York, NY: Longman; 2003.
23. Hsia RY, Kellermann AL, Shen Y-C. Factors associated with closures of emergency departments in the United States. *JAMA*. 2011;305(19):1978–1985.
24. Hsia RY, Srebotnjak T, Kanzaria HK, McCulloch C, Auerbach AD. System-level health disparities in California emergency departments: Minorities and Medicaid patients are at higher risk of losing their emergency departments. *Ann Emerg Med*. 2012;59(5):358–365.
25. Hsia RY-J, Shen Y-C. Rising closures of hospital trauma centers disproportionately burden vulnerable populations. *Health Aff (Millwood)*. 2011;30(10):1912–1920.
26. Shen Y-C, Hsia RY. Changes in emergency department access between 2001 and 2005 among general and vulnerable populations. *Am J Public Health*. 2010;100(8):1462–1469.
27. Shen Y-C, Hsia RY, Kuzma K. Understanding the risk factors of trauma center closures: Do financial pressure and community characteristics matter? *Medical Care*. 2009;47(9):968–978.
28. Detection of safety hazards. Agency for Healthcare Research and Quality, Patient Safety Network Web site. https://psnet.ahrq.gov/primers/primer/24/detection-of -safety-hazards. Accessed September 9, 2016.
29. Patient-Centered Outcomes Research Institute. http://www.pcori.org/about-us. Accessed November 22, 2016.
30. Hasnain-Wynia R, Beal AC. Role of the patient-centered outcomes research institute in addressing disparities and engaging patients in clinical research. *Clin Ther*. 2014;36(5):619–623.
31. Devine C. Bad VA care may have killed more than 1,000 veterans, senator's report says. *CNN*. June 24, 2014. http://www.cnn.com/2014/06/24/us/senator-va-report. Accessed September 12, 2016.
32. Gamble VN. Under the shadow of Tuskegee: African Americans and health care. *Am J Public Health*. 1997;87(11):1773–1778.
33. Corbie-Smith G. Tuskegee as a metaphor. *Science*. 1999;285(5424):47; author reply 49–50.

34. Satcher, D. Tuskegee legacy: The role of the social determinants of health. In: Katz RV and Warren RC, eds. *The Search for the Legacy of the USPHS Syphilis Study at Tuskegee*. Lanham, MD: Lexington Books; 2011:41–47.
35. Institute of Medicine, Committee on Quality of Health Care in America. *Crossing the quality Chasm: A New Health System for the 21st Century*. Washington, DC: National Academies Press; 2001.
36. Kohn LT, Corrigan JM, Donaldson MS. *To Err is Human: Building a Safer Health System*. Washington, DC: National Academies Press; 2000.
37. Smedley BD, Stith AY, Nelson AR. Institute of Medicine, Committee on Understanding and Eliminating Racial and Ethnic Disparities in Health Care. *Unequal Treatment: Confronting Racial and Ethnic Disparities in Health Care*. Washington, DC: National Academies Press; 2003.
38. Kelley E, Moy E, Stryer D, Burstin H, Clancy C. The national healthcare quality and disparities reports: An overview. *Medical Care*. 2005;43(3):I-3–I-8.
39. National Healthcare Quality and Disparities Reports. Agency for Healthcare Research and Quality Web site. http://www.ahrq.gov/research/findings/nhqrdr /index.html. Accessed September 9, 2016.
40. Agency for Healthcare Research and Quality. An organizational guide to building health services research capacity. http://www.ahrq.gov/funding/training-grants /hsrguide/hsrguide.html. Accessed September 12, 2016.
41. AcademyHealth. Health services research methodology core library recommendation, 2007. US National Library of Medicine Web site. https://www.nlm.nih .gov/nichsr/corelib/hsrmethods.html. Accessed February 6, 2017.
42. Andersen RM, Davidson PL, Baumeisgter SE. Improving access to care in America. In: Andersen RM, Rice TH, Kominski GF, eds. *Changing the US Health Care System: Key Issues in Health Services Policy and Management*. 3rd ed. San Francisco, CA: Jossey-Bass; 2007:3–31.
43. Andersen RM. Revisiting the behavioral model and access to medical care: Does it matter? *J Health Soc Behav*. 1995;36(1):1–10.
44. Phillips KA, Morrison KR, Andersen R, Aday LA. Understanding the context of healthcare utilization: Assessing environmental and provider-related variables in the behavioral model of utilization. *Health Serv Res*. 1998;33(3 Pt 1):571.
45. Sollecito WA, Johnson JK. *McLaughlin and Kaluzny's Continuous Quality Improvement in Health Care*. Burlington, MA: Jones and Bartlett Publishers; 2011.
46. Donabedian A. Evaluating the quality of medical care. *Milbank Q*. 1966; 44(3):166–206.
47. Sallis JF, Owen N, Fisher EB. Ecological models of health behavior. In: Glanz K, Rimer BK, Viswanath K, eds. *Health Behavior and Health Education: Theory, Research and Practice*. San Francisco, CA: Jossey-Bass; 2008:464–485.
48. Engel GL. The need for a new medical model: A challenge for biomedicine. *Science*. 1977;196(4286):129–136.
49. Green J, Thorogood N. *Qualitative Methods for Health Research*. London, UK: Sage; 2013.
50. Pittman P. Health services research in 2020: Data and methods needs for the future. *Health Serv Res*. 2010;45(5 Pt 2):1431–1441.
51. Birnbaum H, White AG, Schiller M, Waldman T, Cleveland J, Roland C. Societal costs of prescription opioid abuse, dependence, and misuse in the United States. *Pain Med*. 2011;12(4):657–667.
52. Oderda G, Lake J, Rudell K, Roland C, Masters E. Economic burden of prescription opioid misuse and abuse: A systematic review. *J Pain Palliat Care Pharmacother*. 2015;29(4):388–400.

53. Rudd RA, Aleshire N, Zibbell JE, Gladden RM. Increases in drug and opioid overdose deaths—United States, 2000–2014. *MMWR Morb Mortal Wkly Rep.* 2016;64(50–51):1378–1382.
54. National Institute on Drug Abuse. Overdose death rates. https://www.drugabuse .gov/related-topics/trends-statistics/overdose-death-rates. Accessed November 22, 2016.
55. Responding To the opioid epidemic, the Surgeon General reaches out to prescribers. *KHN Morning Briefing.* August 26, 2016. http://khn.org/morning-breakout /responding-to-the-opioid-epidemic-the-surgeon-general-reaches-out-to-prescribers. Accessed November 22, 2016.
56. Zezima K. The nation's opioid crisis garners attention at party conventions. *Washington Post.* July 26, 2016. https://www.washingtonpost.com/politics/the -nations-opioid-crisis-garners-attention-at-party-conventions/2016/07/26/49b33554 -5339-11e6-bbf5-957ad17b4385_story.html. Accessed November 22, 2016.
57. Keith, T. Drug overdose, on the rise, cropping up as campaign issue [transcript]. *All Things Considered.* National Public Radio. May 28, 2015. http://www.npr.org /sections/itsallpolitics/2015/05/28/410306003/drug-addiction-on-the-rise-cropping -up-as-campaign-trail-issue. Accessed November 22, 2016.
58. Injury prevention and control: Opioid overdose. Centers for Disease Control and Prevention Web site. https://www.cdc.gov/drugoverdose/epidemic. Accessed November 22, 2016.
59. Patient access data. Veterans Health Administration Web site. http://www.va.gov /health/access-audit.asp. Accessed September 12, 2016.
60. Centers for Disease Control and Prevention, National Center for Health Statistics. Health, United States, 2015: With special feature on racial and ethnic health disparities. Table 70. Use of mammography among women aged 40 and over, by selected characteristics: United States, selected years 1987–2013. http://www.cdc .gov/nchs/hus/contents2015.htm#070. Accessed September 12, 2016.
61. Centers for Disease Control and Prevention, National Center for Health Statistics. Health, United States, 2015: With special feature on racial and ethnic health disparities. Table 71. Use of Pap smears among women aged 18 and over, by selected characteristics: United States, selected years 1987–2013. http://www.cdc.gov/nchs /hus/contents2015.htm#071. Accessed September 12, 2016.
62. National Cancer Institute. Cancer health disparities. Table 2. Female breast cancer incidence and death rates. https://www.cancer.gov/about-nci/organization/crchd /cancer-health-disparities-fact-sheet#q5. Accessed September 12, 2016.

Activity

Think about a contemporary health-related problem or issue of interest to you. Briefly review recently published studies, government or nongovernment reports and issue briefs, and news sources for more information about the identified problem or issue. Are there existing data trends relevant to this problem or issue that may be cause for concern? Are there focusing events, emerging crises, or symbols that may point to the urgency of the potential problem? Write a preliminary definition of the problem. As a health services researcher, what data sources and variables would you examine in order to evaluate and monitor this potential problem or issue?

Health services and health policy research 277

Example: Opioid overdose deaths

Published studies

- *Birnbaum et al.:* "Societal Costs of Prescription Opioid Abuse, Dependence, and Misuse in the United States"[51]
- *Oderda et al.:* "Economic Burden of Prescription Opioid Misuse and Abuse: A Systematic Review"[52]

Government reports

- *CDC:* "Increases in Drug and Opioid Overdose Deaths—United States, 2000–2014"[53]
- *National Institute on Drug Abuse:* "Overdose Death Rates"[54]

News sources

- *KHN Morning Briefing:* "Responding to the Opioid Epidemic, The Surgeon General Reaches Out to Prescribers"[55]
- *Washington Post:* "The Nation's Opioid Crisis Garners Attention at Party Conventions"[56]

Focusing events, emergency crises, and symbols

- *Celebrity deaths:* Prince, Heath Ledger
- *News headline:* "Drug Overdose, On the Rise, Cropping Up as Campaign Issue," with graphic "Drug Deaths Eclipse Traffic Fatalities in the U.S."[57]

Problem definition

- From 2000 to 2014, nearly half a million people died from drug overdoses, and more people died from drug overdoses in 2014 than in any previously recorded year.[58] These deaths are increasing among men and women, all races, and adults of nearly all ages. More than 6 out of 10 drug overdose deaths involve an opioid.[58] The number of opioid-associated overdose deaths (including those due to heroin and prescription opioid pain relievers such as oxycodone, hydrocodone, methadone, as well as fentanyl) has nearly quadrupled since 1999.[58] Prescription opioid pain relievers are a driving factor in the 15-year increase in opioid overdose deaths, which highlight the importance of safely managing prescribed opioid medications.[58]
- Several federal- and state-level policies have been suggested as possible solutions to address the prescription opioid epidemic, including the following: changes in opioid prescribing to reduce exposure to opioids, prevent abuse, and stop addiction; expanded access to evidence-based

278 *Public health research methods for partnerships and practice*

substance abuse treatment for people already struggling with opioid addiction; expanded access and use of naloxone—an antidote to reverse opioid overdose; federal or state prescription drug monitoring programs and databases; and improved detection of the trends of illegal opioid use by working with state and local public health agencies, medical examiners and coroners, and law enforcement.[58]

- *Example Research Question:* Is a statewide prescription drug monitoring program effective in decreasing the overall number of opioid prescriptions in the state?

Potential data sources

- Multiple cause-of-death mortality data from the National Vital Statistics System (http://www.cdc.gov/nchs/nvss/mortality_public_use_data.htm)
- Opioid overdose data (http://www.cdc.gov/drugoverdose/data/index.html)
- State-level health information exchange data
- State-level hospital discharge data

SELF-ASSESSMENT—WHAT DID YOU LEARN?

1. Which of these is NOT a goal for health services?
   a. Patient safety
   b. Efficiency
   c. Patient accumulation
   d. Timeliness

2. Whom should health policy research involve?
   a. Academic researchers alone
   b. Policy makers alone
   c. Academic researchers and policy makers together
   d. Academic researchers first, followed by approval by policy makers

3. Health policy research is _____.
   a. Method driven
   b. Number driven
   c. Problem driven
   d. Money driven

4. When is government intervention necessary in health policy?
   a. After market failure
   b. To protection of rights

Health services and health policy research   279

    c. To improve performance of programs
    d. All of the above

5. Health policy refers to _____.
    a. Decisions, plans, and actions that are undertaken to achieve specific health care goals within a society.
    b. The examination of the uses, costs, and outcomes of health services for populations.
    c. The examination of how disease, injury, and risk factors impact health at the population level.
    d. The leadership, management, and administration of public health systems.

6. The four core areas of health services research include access, cost, evaluation of impact, and which of the following?
    a. Public health
    b. Quality
    c. Technology assessment
    d. Efficacy

14 Developing a grant proposal

Jewel D. Stafford

LEARNING OBJECTIVES

- Understand grant guidelines and requirements.
- Understand the power of collaboration for grant writing.
- Develop specific aims.
- Understand components of a good grant proposal.
- Define a project, and develop a research plan.

SELF-ASSESSMENT—WHAT DO YOU KNOW?

1. What components are needed to apply for a grant?
2. Why is it important to think about the time frame of the grant?

Introduction

What is a grant proposal?

A grant proposal is a well-developed plan designed to address a specific problem or need.[1] For example, you may want to implement a training program to enhance the knowledge of community residents. Although you have a great idea, you may need additional human and financial resources to ensure that the program is successful. A great way to obtain this level of support for your program, research idea, or intervention is to write and submit a grant proposal. The grant proposal can be utilized to convince grant funders to support your research idea or program. Grant funders allocate funding with priority for well-written proposals that have the potential to generate high-quality outcomes. Researchers and community organizations can work together to develop a proposal to seek funding for a specific idea, community program, research project, or intervention.

Developing a grant proposal 281

The scientific investigation, or research process, can begin with grant funding, which at first can seem like a daunting task. The challenge lies in ensuring that the grant proposal ideas are aligned with the mission of the grant funder. Many federal government agencies and nonprofit organizations have specific funding priorities and designated grant funding for health programs, research ideas, training programs, and/or community initiatives.

Developing a grant proposal is an opportunity to select a specific funding opportunity with a targeted focus to support and advance your research agenda, examine a specific health problem, enhance community capacity to address challenges, and/or to evaluate the effectiveness of existing programs, services, and policies. Accomplishing this task will require considerable effort and collaboration, but receiving grant funding can be quite rewarding. Grants can provide much-needed funding for health promotion activities, thereby building community capacity and collaborations that solve complex health problems.

The grant proposal describes the tasks, activities, and approaches to accomplish research or program objectives.[2] In other words, the proposal is a detailed work plan that outlines how you will operationalize your ideas, test your research hypothesis, evaluate the effectiveness of the program, and answer your overall research question. The purpose of the proposal is to persuade the grant funder and reviewers that the intended (proposed) work plan can be achieved. Thus, it is important to select the most appropriate, valid methodology to obtain answers to your research question. Throughout the chapter, the following terms will be used to distinguish between a general proposal and a research grant proposal:

- *Proposal:* a strategic plan that is designed to address a specific problem and convince reviewers and potential collaborators to participate in the research activities, tasks, or initiatives.[3]
- *Grant proposal:* a comprehensive request for funding to support research activities, projects, and/or programs. The application has multiple components and specific criteria, and it is submitted to a local, state, or national agency.[3]

First things first: Why are you looking for a grant?

Local, state, and federal grant agencies can provide funding to conduct research, improve community conditions, address social justice challenges, and increase access to health, education, and social initiatives. Examples of grant-funded projects include but are not limited to the following:

- Developing a community-based intervention to reduce sexually transmitted infections among young adults 18 to 25.
- Examining the effectiveness of therapeutic models among homeless veterans.

282 *Public health research methods for partnerships and practice*

- Increasing access to health care among rural residents.
- Training community health workers on research methods.
- Building community capacity through the development of a community coalition.
- Determining effective protocols of cancer treatment in African American breast cancer patients.

Developing a grant proposal may also be in response to a request for proposal (RFP) or Request for Application (RFA) issued by the funder. A grant funding agency may issue RFPs to elicit and fund specific research projects to further its organizational mission whereas the RFA is a general announcement regarding funding opportunities and research areas. Although both provide guidelines and parameters, the RFP is a contract mechanism that describes the scope of work for the funding agency.

Grant proposals can vary depending on the funding agency, the purpose of the research project, and the expertise of the personnel who will undertake the research activity, project, or program. However, each research proposal must address the following:

- What are you proposing to accomplish through the grant?
- Why have you selected your proposed method, approach, or research project?
- How will you accomplish your goal?

Grant writing can be challenging at first, but answering these questions helps the grant reviewers, funders, and potential collaborators to understand the utility of the research proposal. Granting agencies want to fund research endeavors that will expand or contribute to the knowledge of the field, explore new ideas and paradigms, or establish best practices. Research investigators answering all three of the aforementioned questions can highlight the significance, impact, and uniqueness of the research project. In addition, each grant should be viewed as a building block to other potential grant opportunities. Why? Each project or research idea, specifically those ideas that involve community-university collaborations, should be framed with sustainability in mind. Therefore, each grant opportunity can serve as an incremental step to additional funding, research, and publication opportunities.

The grant cycle (Figure 14.1) is a helpful visual that shows the essential sequence of activities that takes place during the grant proposal process. Each of the components in the grant cycle has multiple steps to assist the research team with the planning and implementation process.[4]

So you want to write a grant…

Grant writing is a collaborative, strategic process that begins with an idea. The process may appear straightforward, but it requires time and preparation.

Developing a grant proposal 283

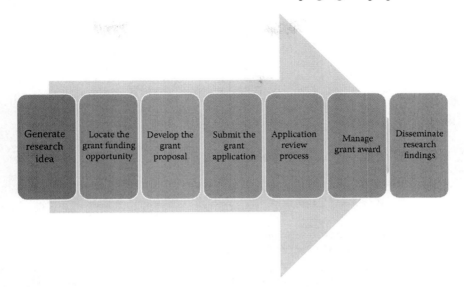

Figure 14.1 The grant cycle. (From Grant process overview, National Institutes of Health Web site, https://grants.nih.gov/grants/grants_process.htm, updated February 25, 2016, accessed December 15, 2016.)

The steps to writing a successful grant require a well-developed research idea, planning your intended research activities, aligning your research proposal within the objectives of the funding agency, and collecting relevant information that will meet grant application requirements.[3] Research proposals should address an identified need and area of interest and should clearly articulate the focus of the grant. The topic of interest in your grant application will help you to determine the type of grant you are looking for. Are you looking to conduct research, engage partners, build community capacity, develop a manuscript, host a conference, or conduct a health intervention? Grant funding agencies provide specific information on the types of grants they can fund and how they fit in with their overall mission.

Grant funding sources

A variety of grant funding sources exist for community-based health projects. Funding agencies have specific mechanisms to fund training, basic and applied research, pilot projects, and conferences.[5] The most common sources of funding fall within the following categories:

- *Federal agencies:* The governmental agencies that provide grant opportunities vary by department. HHS, for example, can support research and nonresearch funding for large agencies such as the NIH, the CDC, and the Health Resources and Services Administration (HRSA). Each

284 *Public health research methods for partnerships and practice*

of these agencies has reserved funding and specific eligibility criteria for public health professionals, researchers, and nonprofit organizations.

- *Foundations:* Foundations support projects, initiatives, and studies for individuals, nonprofit organizations, and various initiatives. They usually provide funding for those projects that are not typically covered by federal organizations. Some examples of such foundations are the Robert Wood Johnson Foundation, the Bill & Melinda Gates Foundation, and the W.K. Kellogg Foundation. Foundations are great sources of funding for small pilot projects, conferences, trainings, and innovative collaborations between academic and community-based partnerships. In 2014, the Foundation Center's directory included approximately 87,000 foundations with funding opportunities.[6] Additional funding sources may include professional societies such as the American Diabetes Association or the American Cancer Society.

Selecting the appropriate grant funding opportunity means that it fits within the scope of your project ideas and is aligned with your research interests. The focus of the grant may be too broad or too specific; there may be a need to tailor your original ideas to fit the requirements of the grant application. The goal of the grant proposal is to clearly articulate the unique qualities of the project idea, how your research team can complete the project activities, and organizational/institutional support that can provide the infrastructure to carry out the tasks and activities of the grant. If applicants have questions regarding their proposed ideas, it is a good idea to contact the program officer prior to the grant writing process. The program officer can provide key and insightful information about the funding agency's priorities, deadlines, upcoming webinars, and information sessions and whether the grant idea is aligned with the agency's funding opportunity. This step will save time and effort spent writing a grant that is later considered ineligible because it does not meet the funder's criteria.

After potential applicants develop their research idea and generate a hypothesis, they should identify the appropriate team members who can best support, advance, and provide expertise to carry out the research ideas. Selecting experienced researchers and collaborators can provide a diverse range of knowledge and skills, including identifying the most appropriate type of interventions, activities, and projects that can address and examine the research question. Grant funding agencies underwrite a variety of activities to support their mission and goals. Listed below are examples of the types of grants that organizations offer.

Types of grants

- *Research grants:* This type of grant provides funding for systematic scientific inquiry with a targeted research project, including, but not limited to, clinical trials and basic, observational, and pilot research studies.[4] The grant funding provides support for the personnel, equipment, and additional resources needed to carry out the research project.

Developing a grant proposal 285

- *Conference/Seminar grants:* Grant funding is allocated to provide support for conferences, workshops, and seminars.
- *Planning grants:* This type of grant provides funding to help organizations engage in collaborative planning activities.
- *Training grants:* Grant funding is allocated to provide research training and educational support for undergraduate, graduate, and/or doctoral students.

Finding the appropriate grant

Finding an appropriate grant is one of the key steps to ensuring that your project will have an opportunity to be reviewed and funded. As you embark on the journey of locating and applying to the grant funding agency, you should consider some questions. For example, are your research idea and expertise aligned with the mission, structure, and vision of the granting organization? What are the eligibility requirements? Does the grant organization have specific priorities? For example, the NIH is a large research organization, composed of 27 institutes and centers, of which 24 provide grant-funding opportunities. Each of the institutes has a specialized mission and priority area designed to provide funding to approximately 2,500 academic institutions each year.

With increased competition among prospective grantees to receive funding, it is imperative for grantees to search for and identify which granting organization is best suited for their research projects and endeavors. As you look for funding opportunities, be sure to investigate the Web site, and familiarize yourself with funding priorities, application details, eligibility requirements, and budgetary restrictions. Many organizations use their Web sites to release helpful tips in the form of frequently asked questions; they also might include webinars and meetings that detail best practices about their grant process. Researching the Web sites is a great way to stay updated on information about future funding opportunities, helpful tips for the grant process, templates, or examples of previously funded opportunities.

Searching grant databases or joining professional listservs to receive alerts about grant notifications is helpful. Professional organizations and collaborations with colleagues are also beneficial, as they will also provide relevant information regarding upcoming funding opportunities. Examples of grant databases include the following:

- *Foundation Center:* An online database that provides funding opportunities from foundations in the United States. (http://www.foundation -search.com)
- *Grants.gov:* An online database that provides information on federal granting organizations. (http://www.grants.gov/)

286 *Public health research methods for partnerships and practice*

- *New York Foundation for the Arts (NYFA):* An online database that provides grant information on a variety of fields and disciplines. (https://www.nyfa.org/)

Outline your plan of action

Once you have located the grant opportunity, begin early and read the grant instructions carefully. The RFP contains all the application guidelines, so use this as your roadmap. This will help you to develop timelines and respond to each of the required components of the grant opportunity. To this end, disseminate the grant RFP or opportunity to the proposed research team. Doing so can provide a collaborative approach to the development of the proposal. During this review of guidelines, you can also delegate the tasks to the members of the team with the relevant expertise.

Each grant has an assigned *principal investigator (PI)/project director (PD)* who will provide administrative oversight for the budget, timelines, planning, implementation, evaluation, and dissemination activities proposed. The PI's oversight extends to the data collection, analysis, and management procedures, and the PI ensures that ethical research protocols are followed. The PI also provides direction for the grant reporting activities to funders and departments within the organization to ensure the grant regulations and requirements are met. The *co-principal investigator* (co-PI) assists the PI in his or her role of "scientific, fiscal and administrative oversight" if the grant receives funding.[2] Each *co-investigator* collaborates with and assists the PI with conceptualization, development, and implementation of grant activities. The co-investigator is considered a part of the senior administrative team (key personnel) and designates a percentage of his or her time on the grant. The *project manager/study coordinator* assists with management and coordination of the grant activities under the supervision of the PI, including the hiring, training, and supervising of research staff. Additional responsibilities include coordinating the administrative logistics, monitoring project activities, providing technical assistance and regular correspondence, and maintaining consistent communication with grant team members. The *research assistants* provide support to the research team related to the assessment, development, and evaluation phases of the project. Responsibilities may include developing questionnaires, data collection, management, and analysis. Depending on the grant activities, several others may be included in the list of personnel (e.g., senior data analyst, health professionals, clinicians, CABs, community liaison, or student assistants).

Read the RFP, embrace the power of partnerships, and ask the following the questions:

- Does our research team have the expertise to accomplish the proposed tasks and activities?

Developing a grant proposal 287

- What will I need to fulfill the grant requirements (e.g., human resources, financial resources, community partnerships)?
- Who will need to come aboard? What community stakeholders should be involved?
- Where will the activities take place?
- Why is this an important issue, topic, or concern for our region?
- How will this move the field forward, advance science, and benefit the community?

Develop the timeline

Developing a grant proposal may take approximately 30 to 90 days, producing a proposal that may be 15 to 100 pages in length, depending on the grant application process. This can be an intensive task, so ensure that each of the research team members has agreed to their roles and responsibilities. If you are collaborating with organizations and agencies and letters of support or MOUs are required for the application, this information needs to be developed and set in place in accordance with the grant guidelines.

The timeline can be accomplished in a variety of ways. You can use the grant application deadlines as your guideposts for the timelines, work with your university/institutional grant office to help you establish grant timelines, or collaboratively set dates with your community organization and grant collaborators.

Contact the program staff

Grant organizations have program officials, staff, or officers to help applicants with the technical, programmatic, and structural components of the grant application process. Grant applicants should contact the program officer to ensure that their proposed goals are aligned with those of the RFP and the larger mission of the agency. Program officers can provide vital grant guideline information that will ensure a successful grant proposal. For example, they can emphasize what will receive funding and outline the types of projects that will not receive consideration. Some program officers provide guidance on the budget, specifically which budget items will not be allowed. For instance, some granting agencies may not fund refreshments or travel expenses. Depending on the type of project you are proposing, this may require you to secure and locate in-kind (contributed goods or services that are not charged to the budget of the grant) services or supplemental funding to ensure those expenses are covered even if not through the grant.[5]

Submit a letter of intent (when applicable)

Some funding agencies require a letter of intent (LOI) from prospective grantees to determine and prepare for the number of grant applicants. The

288 *Public health research methods for partnerships and practice*

LOI is designed to (1) provide a formal introduction to the proposed idea; (2) discuss the goal and specific objectives of the grant; (3) describe the research methods, team, and anticipated outcomes; and (4) describe how the organization's mission aligns with the funder's mission.

Grant proposal components

Grant proposals should be tailored to meet the requirements of the specific agencies, but there is key information that should be in each grant application. Each proposal should have a title page, abstract, the background and significance, the research design and methodology, specific aims of the project, the evaluation plan, SMART goals and objectives, budget and budget narrative, project narrative, and timeline.

Title page

The title page summarizes and provides highlights of the grant proposal. It includes the name of the PI and institutional and organizational affiliations. It also has official signatures. The title of the proposal should reflect the overall purpose and function of the proposed project. Some titles are used to illustrate the relationship between variables, whereas other titles relate directly to the RFP and the agency's mission. The following is an example of a title that might relate directly to an RFP: Community Alliance for Research Empowering Social Change (CARES), a community-based research training to address and examine suburban health disparities in Long Island, NY.

Abstract

The abstract is a summary of the proposed project, including background information, the research question, methodology, procedures, and activities that the research team will undertake to answer the research question. Grant funding agencies note their preferences for the length of an abstract, which can range from 250 to 500 words or can be a specified number of characters or lines.

Background and significance

The background and significance provide the introduction, purpose, and rationale for your proposed project. The section states why your project is innovative and how it will contribute to the body of scientific knowledge. This section highlights the importance of the literature review, as it details how your unique research project will address existing gaps, improve health outcomes, and/or advance the field of knowledge.

Developing a grant proposal   289

Research design and methodology

The research design and methodology section describes the procedures, experiments, and approach you will utilize to get results for the grant (e.g., host 15 meetings, conduct 3 focus groups, interview 17 participants, and collect 150 surveys). This is a key component of any proposal and can make or break a proposal during the review process. It is important to clearly state what you plan to do and how you plan to do it. Using a rigorous study design and data collection tools are vital for success.

Specific aims

The specific aims are the objectives of your research proposal and are based on your research hypothesis and methodology. The hypothesis and the specific aims are essential sections of the grant. The specific aims provide the objectives, whereas the hypothesis offers predictions about the independent and dependent variables, provides an answer to the research question, and is grounded in the literature. A solid hypothesis for the research study should lead the grant reviewers to specific aims. The specific aims provide the action steps for the grant and demonstrate that you and your research team have the capacity to accomplish your goals. Reviewers will link your specific aims with the research design and methods. Thus, in the section on specific aims, you will discuss what you are planning to accomplish during the grant period and how you will address each of your aims—the approaches that you will use. The page on specific aims usually contains an introductory paragraph that grabs the attention of reviewers by describing the goal, identifying an existing gap in knowledge, and describing how the research proposal will address a need and present the solution for the gap.[7]

BOX 14.1   EXAMPLE OF SPECIFIC AIM

Racial disparities persist among African American and Latino adults in the areas of teen pregnancy, obesity, and education. Traditional research approaches and community-level interventions aimed at addressing health disparities have often neglected the complex relationships among race, class, and public health that lead to behavioral risk factors that disproportionately impact communities of color. In our region, there are limited positive youth development programs to address these issues. Therefore, a new paradigm that includes these communities as fully engaged research partners to identify, explore, and address their identified needs will prove beneficial to reducing health disparities[8] through community outreach and information dissemination.

The focus of our program is to empower African American adolescents to make healthy decisions regarding their health, behaviors, and relationships. We propose to develop and implement interventions designed for African American youth in order to create a comprehensive and sustainable program to serve the needs of the adolescent population. We name this program the *St. Louis Healthy Adolescent Peer Education (SHAPE) program.*

We intend to achieve the following aims for the program:

Aim 1: Develop new and enhance existing academic-community partnerships that inform and guide community engagement strategies and outreach efforts. We will develop a community advisory board (CAB) with diverse membership of teens and community members to guide and inform community engagement, outreach, and dissemination efforts through region-specific and culturally appropriate plain language strategies.

Aim 2: Identify community health priorities and develop an action plan to address the priority areas using a community-driven approach. We will identify and address community health needs through a series of four mini-summits on adolescent health, forums designed to elucidate top areas of concern. We will also develop strategies to address social and behavioral risk factors that contribute to health disparities for teens in the region.

Aim 3: Educate stakeholders (community and academic) on CBPR approaches to address health disparities. We will educate and train community members on the role of CBPR in addressing community needs; we will also train academic researchers on CBPR, community engagement, and developing and sustaining academic-community partnerships through eight weekly sessions and three experiential workshops.

The proposed project is significant because it will be developed through a unique consortium of academic and community stakeholders to provide the necessary infrastructure for CBPR to reduce disparities within minority and underserved communities in St. Louis and to empower communities to participate in the research process as equal partners. Our approach is innovative because it will develop multiple pilot project proposals through partnerships to develop positive region-specific youth development interventions.

Developing a grant proposal   291

Evaluation plan

A comprehensive evaluation plan will allow funders to observe a clear blueprint explaining how you define success and how you will evaluate the effectiveness of the program or project. In this section, you will describe how they will evaluate the impact of the project. This includes a plan to measure the research project results and the expected outcome or achievement at the end of the grant-funding period. Engaging your stakeholders and receiving buy-in to develop your evaluation plan will prove beneficial to your grant proposal. It will demonstrate the collaborative process that will occur throughout the grant-funding period among the research team members.

The evaluation plan should be aligned with the grant proposal's specific aims and provide a clear set of measurable objectives.[7] These objectives are often referred to as SMART objectives, as indicated in the following list:[9]

- *Specific (and strategic):* Grant objectives that answer the question "Who?" or "What?"
- *Measurable:* Grant objectives that can be measured and that answer the question "How?"
- *Attainable:* Grant objectives that are realistic and can be achieved in a specific amount of time.
- *Relevant/realistic (results oriented):* Grant objectives that include the expected result within the availability of resources, knowledge, and time.
- *Time framed:* Goals that have a clearly defined time frame that includes a target or deadline date.

Grant applicants can provide SMART goals and objectives in their evaluation plan (Table 14.1). (See Chapter 8 for more information about SMART goals.)

The evaluation plan should detail how the research team will monitor and track activities, conduct the research protocols, perform data collection and analysis, and utilize other potential sources of data. The rationale for the selection of evaluation metrics should be clearly identified, as the evaluation metrics will be used at the end of the proposed project or program to demonstrate the effectiveness of the program and whether success has been achieved.

Table 14.1 Development of SMART goals

Who/what	Change/ desired effect	In what	By when
Participants	Increased	Knowledge	One year
Organizations	Decreased	Awareness	By year 2
Entities	Improved	Behavior	November 2017
Institutions	Modified	Policies	
	Adopted		
	Enforced		

292 *Public health research methods for partnerships and practice*

In this section, you want to explicitly detail the data collection methods and provide examples of evaluation tools, including surveys.

A conceptual model that graphically shows the integration of the project and the key measures of the evaluation will allow the funders to visualize your anticipated outcome. A logic model can provide a great visual picture that shows the grant activities, short-term and long-term goals, as well as the resources. It is a comprehensive description of the proposed research or program components set in a series of if-then statements. For example, if you have staff, then you can conduct the 8-week training for 20 participants and enhance their knowledge. To ensure that the project team can provide a visual representation of the evaluation plan, many grant funders request grant applicants to submit a logic model (see, for example, Table 14.2). Both formative and summative evaluation approaches for the overall grant can be used to assess the impact of the research project, and these evaluation approaches can be emphasized in the evaluation plan and illustrated in the logic model. (See Chapter 8 for more details about logic models.)

Project budget and budget narrative

The budget lists and details the costs associated with research activities. These items may include personnel (salaries and benefits), travel/mileage, meeting space, and equipment. The budget narrative gives a brief (i.e., less than a paragraph) rationale for each line item in the budget. The guidelines for the line items usually specify the resources the funding agency is willing to cover, so it is imperative to read the application thoroughly to ensure that you are including only budget items that the grant will cover. For example, some grants will not cover travel or refreshments. Therefore, when writing the proposal, consider how those gaps will be addressed. Additional considerations to include are the salaries and benefits of the personnel. It is important to include the increasing cost of inflation for the salaries and benefits. Direct costs in a budget may include

- Equipment.
- Supplies.
- Meetings.
- Printing and copying.

Project narrative

The project narrative is composed of all of the other components of the grant application required by the funding agency. It describes the proposed activities for the grant and is usually divided into subsections to provide a detailed, well-developed research plan that includes the research goals, hypothesis, methods, anticipated outcomes, evaluation plan, and ethical treatment for human subjects (if applicable). The grant should discuss previous studies and existing data on the topic to establish a baseline of the scientific knowledge

Table 14.2 Example of logic model[a]

Resources	Activities	Outputs	Outcomes	Impact/Goals
What existing resources are available? What resources do we need?	With these resources, we will conduct the following activities	These are the specific amounts of services we will provide. We will use this evidence to evaluate our progress	What difference is the program making?	These express the overall mission or purpose of the program
	Training	**Training**		
- Community partnerships - Community participants - Staff - Trainers - Equipment - Software - Facilities	- Develop training manual - Provide 8-week training to community members - Conduct research training workshops - Evaluate training program data - Submit IRB application - Present project findings at town hall meeting	- 8 weekly trainings - 3 research training workshops - 25 trained participants - 3 developed pilot projects - 25 fellows completing the training program	- Increased knowledge of community members of evidence-based research methods - Enhanced knowledge and understanding of research among the community - Engagement of community members and faculty members to participate in pilot research projects	- Build the infrastructure for community-engaged research that explores and addresses community health concerns - Develop evidence-based, culturally appropriate interventions - Improve community health outcomes through a community-partnered approach

[a] Project Goal: To develop community engaged research that explores and addresses community health concerns through engagement, training, and collaborative research projects.

on the subject. In this section, the grant writer defines the project through a well-defined incremental approach. The research goals and objectives of the grant should be stated explicitly. The goals are broad and provide a statement of what the grant, project, or program will accomplish.[9] In the logic model example, the goal is to develop community-engaged research through engagement, training, and collaborative research projects that explore and address community health concerns. The objectives are specific, measurable, concrete statements about how you will achieve your goals. If you are using descriptive statistics, providing training, or conducting focus groups, the rationale for the approach should be clearly defined. The description of the research goals should be innovative, evidenced based, and grounded in the literature. When writing this section, demonstrate competence, expertise, and previous experience with the research topic. Identify evidence-based approaches, know the experts, and cite their work.

The project narrative is a great opportunity to define and describe what makes this project unique and why it should receive funding. The narrative includes the inductive or deductive approaches to the research project with descriptions of the hypothesis, methodology, anticipated outcomes, and how success will be defined.[10] For example, what instruments or tools will be used in the data collection process? What software will be used for the data analysis? In addition, what is the sustainability plan? As previously mentioned, the grant is a stepping stone for accomplishing a larger vision that may be used to support other grant submissions or research activities or to address a major community need. Therefore, it is imperative for grant funders to see the sustainability plan, which ensures a return on their investment.

The grant must clearly identify the human subjects' protocols during the research project and the ethical considerations during the research process. These include the recruitment plan, informed consent procedures, data collection processes, as well as the plan to keep the data confidential. Grant writers should include information about the procedures for consulting with the IRB and how the applicant organization will adhere to responsible research conduct. Consulting with the IRB usually does not occur prior to the grant submission, but it is always a good idea to provide the IRB application status, especially if an application was submitted and is currently pending approval.

The human and financial resources that are necessary to carry out the project activities will be described in the project narrative as well. The project team, setting, and institutional resources utilized to ensure the success of the program are discussed to justify the approaches and to demonstrate that there is a well-developed strategy to operate the research grant activities. The contributions of collaborators and consultants—including their roles, skills, knowledge, and expertise—are also discussed as part of the project team.

The project narrative describes the feasibility of the research plan and the work that is to be completed in the amount of time allotted by the grant

Developing a grant proposal   295

Activity	2016								
	Apr	May	Jun	July	Aug	Sept	Oct	Nov	Dec
Organize Community Advisory Board (CAB)	X								
Schedule CAB meetings	X			X		X		X	
Meet key community leaders	X	X							
Meet with social service	X								
Schedule programs (ongoing)		X	X	X	X	X	X	X	X
Evaluate program									X

Figure 14.2 Sample grant timeline. ARCH indicates Aligning Research for Community Health; CAB, community advisory board; IRB, institutional review board; SHAPE, St. Louis Healthy Adolescent Peer Education.

funders. Some approximate guidelines for grant timelines to achieve specific outcomes are:

- *One-year grants:* plan and develop.
- *Two-year grants:* plan, develop, and implement.
- *Five-year grants:* assess, plan, develop, implement, evaluate, and disseminate.

Timeline

The timeline describes the activities, scope of work, and tasks that will be accomplished within the grant period. Examples of tasks and activities described in the timeline can include, but are not limited to, IRB approval, data collection, focus groups, training, recruitment, interventions, dissemination, data analysis, and grant reporting. The examples in Figure 14.2 illustrate three ways to demonstrate grant timelines.

Conclusions

Grant proposals may vary, but if the project can demonstrate relevance, innovation, contribution to the existing body of knowledge, and a compelling argument for your research with goals that align with the mission of the grant funder, you are headed in the right direction.[11] In this chapter, we have identified and discussed the essential elements to developing a proposal. These are guidelines; it is always recommended to read the grant funding application for more explicit details on how to submit a successful grant. Developing a strong proposal takes time, patience, and collaboration, so remember to start

296 *Public health research methods for partnerships and practice*

early, read the directions, and seek advice from experienced mentors who can offer feedback and suggestions for your proposal drafts prior to submission.

References

1. Gitlin LN, Lyons KJ. *Successful Grant Writing, Strategies for Health and Human Service Professionals*. 4th ed. New York, NY: Springer; 2013.
2. Grant process overview. National Institutes of Health Web site. https://grants.nih.gov /grants/grants_process.htm. Updated February 25, 2016. Accessed December 15, 2016.
3. Kumar R. *Research Methodology: A Step-by-Step Guide for Beginners*. London, UK: Pearson Education; 2005.
4. Carr CE. *The Nuts and Bolts of Grant Writing*. Thousand Oaks, CA: Sage Publications; 2014.
5. Dawes AJ, Maggard-Gibbons M. Writing a grant/obtaining funding. In: Chen HK, Kao LS, eds. *Success in Academic Surgery*. Cham, Switzerland: Springer; 2017:145–159.
6. Foundation Center statistics. Foundation Center Web site. http://foundationcenter .org/. Accessed January 30, 2017.
7. DePoy E, Gitlin LN. *Introduction to Research: Understanding and Applying Multiple Strategies*. St. Louis, MO: Elsevier Health Sciences; 2015.
8. Minkler M, Wallerstein N, Wilson N. Improving health through community organization and community building. In: Glanz K, Rimer BK, Viswanath K, eds. *Health Behavior and Health Education: Theory, Research, and Practice*. San Francisco, CA: Jossey-Bass; 1997:287–312.
9. Osman Z. Research proposal writing. *Current Ther Res*. 2016;78:S4.
10. Babbie ER. *The Practice of Social Research*. Scarborough, Canada: Nelson Education; 2016.
11. Staines GM. *Go Get That Grant!: A Practical Guide for Libraries and Nonprofit Organizations*. Lanham, MD: Rowman and Littlefield; 2016.

Activity 1: Analyze an abstract

Read the following abstract, and use it to answer the questions that appear afterward.

Introduction: African American seniors between the ages of 65 and 70 experience a disproportionate rate of diabetes. The purpose of this study was to translate the diabetes program curriculum to be age and culturally specific for African American seniors in the St. Louis region.

Methods: The research team conducted focus groups and interviews to discuss community members' perspectives of risk and protective factors that encouraged or were barriers to healthy behaviors. In total, 31 community members, aged 65 to 68 years old, participated in 4 focus groups and 10 individual interviews. Participants self-identified as educators, guardians, or retired residents. Researchers analyzed transcripts based on inductive methods of grounded theory.

Results: Data analysis showed that translation of the diabetes information was based on the lessons that incorporated cultural strategies for healthy behaviors such as faith and spirituality; improving knowledge and access to healthy foods; having interactive, hands-on learning activities for healthy lifestyles in the diabetes lesson plans; and using a group format to deliver the diabetes program lessons.

Developing a grant proposal 297

Table 14.3 Putting it all together: Developing a grant idea

What is the community need?

_____

_____

_____

What is the overall goal of the program that you would like to see funded?

_____

_____

_____

Objectives	Time frame	Personnel	Activity	Evaluation method
1.				
2.				

Project team:

_____

_____

_____

Budget

- ☐ Personnel:
- ☐ Equipment:
- ☐ Supplies
- ☐ Travel
- ☐ Other (in-kind resources, consultant fees, contracts, etc.)

Anticipated results (i.e., the intended outcomes):

_____

_____

_____

Conclusions: This culturally sensitive, equitable approach to the training program engaged community members to identify strategies inherent to their culture and environment, which could be effectively adapted by other communities.

Activity 1 Questions:

- What problem is this research study trying to address?
- What approach did they use to solve their problem?
- After using this approach, what did they uncover?
- What lessons did they learn after completing their study?

Activity 2: Develop a grant pitch

As a community-based organization, you notice an increased rate of obesity among black and Hispanic populations. Your agency decides to apply for

298 *Public health research methods for partnerships and practice*

grant funding to implement a new program teaching community members about nutrition and physical activity. The granting agency has convened a special review panel to hear your research idea on a specific health problem in your region. On the basis of your identified project idea to address the health problem, please answer the following questions to form a 2-minute pitch that

1. Demonstrates that you have identified the *public health problem* for your community.
2. Demonstrates that you have the *capacity* to use the grant money available to build sustainable community health projects in the region.

Developing your pitch will require you to think about and develop the framework for your grant idea. Review and complete Table 14.3 to demonstrate that your organization has an innovative, comprehensive grant idea that includes the public health problem/community need and the capacity to carry out the activities.

SELF-ASSESSMENT—WHAT DID YOU LEARN?

1. When grants are being reviewed by the funding agency, all of the following criteria are considered EXCEPT _____.
   a. Innovation
   b. Investigator qualifications
   c. Availability of funds
   d. Significance

2. The grant should discuss previous studies and existing data on the topic to establish a baseline of the scientific knowledge on the subject.
   a. True
   b. False

3. When considering applying for a grant, all of the following are important to consider EXCEPT _____.
   a. Where the activities outlined in the grant will take place
   b. Who you will need to work on the project
   c. How the work will benefit the field
   d. All of the above are important to consider.

4. Which is NOT a component of a grant application?
   a. List of academic journals to submit papers to
   b. Specific aims
   c. Letters of support
   d. Budget

Developing a grant proposal 299

5. A request for proposal (RFP) is a more general funding announcement than a request for application (RFA).
   a. True
   b. False

6. What are the specific aims?
   a. A detailed list of the costs associated with completing the research activities
   b. A description of the activities, scope of work, and tasks that will be accomplished within the grant period
   c. A summary of the proposed project, including background information, the research question, methodology, procedures, and activities the research team will undertake to answer the research question
   d. The objectives of the research proposal that are based on the research hypothesis and methodology

7. The primary responsibility of the principal investigator (PI) is

   _____.
   a. To manage hiring, training, and supervising of research staff
   b. To provide administrative oversight for the budget, time-lines, planning, implementation, evaluation, and dissemination activities proposed
   c. To provide evaluation support such as developing question-naires, data collection, management, and analysis
   d. To coordinate the administrative logistics, to monitor project activities, and to provide technical assistance and regular correspondence

8. One main question that a research proposal must address is the following: _____.
   a. Who inspired you to choose the research question or create the proposed project?
   b. What journals do you think would be interested in publishing your results?
   c. Why have you selected the proposed method, approach, or research project?
   d. Which project in the literature is your proposal most similar to?

9. The purpose of the evaluation plan section of a grant is
_____.
   a. To evaluate how previous research addressed the problem
   b. To detail the procedures, experiments, and approach you will utilize to get results for the grant
   c. To describe how you will measure the research project results and the expected outcome/achievement at the end of the grant
   d. To list the objectives of your research proposal based on your research hypothesis and methodology

10. The length of the grant determines whether the timeline should include information on how to assess, plan, develop, implement, evaluate, and disseminate results.
   a. True
   b. False

15 Changing health outcomes through community-driven processes
Implications for practice and research

Keon L. Gilbert, Stephanie M. McClure, and Mary Shaw-Ridley

LEARNING OBJECTIVES

- Describe history and principles of community organizing.
- Describe community organizing resources useful for public health initiatives.
- Identify and develop relevant, well-framed community organizing strategies.

SELF-ASSESSMENT—WHAT DO YOU KNOW?

1. What is community organizing?
2. What are the characteristics of two community organizing models appropriate for public health?
3. What is the primary purpose of a community advisory board?
4. What are the attributes of an action plan for organizing the community?

Introduction

The practice of community organizing around social, political, or economic issues is not a new concept. Formally aggregating civic groups, concerned community members, social and health service agencies, and policy makers to address chronic conditions entered the field of public health in the late 1980s and the early 1990s.[1,2] The change resulted from a perception that many public health interventions were not as effective as they could be because they had not fully engaged the populations they intended to serve. Moreover, community members working together is part of a longer tradition of place-referenced, cultural, affinity, or religious groups working separately and in partnership to identify and solve problems affecting them. These groups' interest in working with researchers, though not novel, has been a particular focus within the field

302 *Public health research methods for partnerships and practice*

of public health for some time.[3,4] The importance and necessity of working with community groups in various iterations has become a widely accepted value in public health research. This value stipulates that partnering with communities and community-based organizations, in particular helps to develop for interventions that are a better fit with community contexts and are, thus, more likely to be effective in improving a community's health outcomes.

Community organizing and development efforts can focus outwardly or inwardly on changing social systems, rules, norms, and laws or on changing the social acceptability of certain behaviors.[5] Rothman has identified three models or approaches to community development: locality development, social planning, and social action. Rothman's locality development places an emphasis on building community capacity by empowering the community to become the experts.[6] For example, individuals living with HIV or living in urban areas with high rates of HIV could be trained as community experts on planning and implementing a comprehensive needs assessment (CNA) that includes the voices of the affected community. The social planning model is heavily data driven (efforts are made to obtain multiple viewpoints on community issues, current status, and needs across many issues) and involves coordination of services. The community serves as a source of data and provides suggestions for how services should be coordinated or can be better coordinated to meet community needs.[7] An example of the social planning model is a gap analysis that utilizes multiple sources of client-level data, including satisfaction surveys completed by persons living with and otherwise affected by cancer who receive health services through an integrated care system. Satisfaction surveys, focus groups, and face-to-face interviews can provide researchers and practitioners with important information on acceptability, availability, and utilization of services to improve coordination, collaboration, and promotion of linkages within a community. These data are utilized along with epidemiological data that can help characterize conditions of interest on a population level. The combination of community-derived and epidemiological data provides a more complete picture of community health status than either data source alone, which can facilitate not only more effective intervention, but better policy development.

Grassroots organizing is fundamental to the social action model, which takes a bottom-up approach to community organizing. The Black Lives Matter movement is grassroots activism that originated in the African-American community to campaign against persistent racism and violence in communities of color.[8] Citizen engagement is seen as an integral first step in building community capacity and formalizing interorganizational networks such as community coalitions.

These three community development and organizing models provide important guidance in crafting functional and effective partnerships between researchers and community groups. They can enhance practices and efforts to coordinate services within communities, facilitate strategies to build and to sustain citizen participation, establish new social networks and improve

Changing health outcomes through community-driven processes 303

existing ones, change community norms, and enact community empowerment using community assets and strengths.

With an emphasis on broad and direct interaction with communities, these community development approaches tackle issues that are less robustly addressed by traditional community health approaches, such as a partnership between institutions or organizations with shared interests. Traditional efforts tended to focus on smaller, at-risk populations that have been historically neglected in the plans and priorities of single organizations or researchers at universities. The kinds of community organizing and partnerships needed to address setting-specific health concerns, like urban and rural health disparities, present unique challenges. Urban and rural contexts can benefit from health promotion activities with their rich array of social and human resources, ranging from networks of community organizations and foundations to formal and informal service providers, which become key resources for interorganizational health promotion efforts. However, if organizations who share health promotion interests and goals are primarily interested in retaining their autonomy, the potential benefit of their combined resources may not be realized.

Structuring community engagement processes

Enhancing relationships between academics and communities through structured engagement activities should be a major goal of community-based research enterprises and opportunities. Academic researchers and academic institutions who prefer to engage with communities using community-organizing approaches can utilize a variety of structured engagement activities. These include community coalitions, natural helper models, and CABs. Although each structure, individually, has its strengths and limitations, they can all be effective means by which communities initiate and facilitate identification of relevant issues, identify potential partners, and build mutually beneficial relationships with those partners. The long-term goal is to strengthen communities to reach their ability to initiate and facilitate activities to identify the issues they determine are relevant, to identify potential partners, and to work in partnership to address those issues.

Community coalitions

One highly regarded approach to community-driven health promotion processes is community health coalitions. Coalitions can be effective in health promotion for several reasons. As we begin to consider multifaceted approaches to health promotion and disease prevention, coalitions represent vehicles for carrying out those multifaceted approaches over the long term. Coalitions may also offer the best chance at progress toward redress of substantive and somewhat intractable public health issues such as tobacco, alcohol, and drug abuse; teenage pregnancy; and violence. For example, tobacco coalitions

304 *Public health research methods for partnerships and practice*

fought for indoor smoking bans. Community coalitions often follow an action set model and fulfill planning, coordinating, and advocacy functions by addressing key elements of a socioecological perspective, including working across multiple domains and changing communities through normative and system changes.[9]

Being part of a coalition enables organizations to become involved in new and broader issues without having the sole responsibility for managing or developing those issues. Coalitions can generate widespread public support for issues, actions, or unmet needs by increasing the "critical mass" behind a community effort, and thereby helping to achieve objectives beyond the scope of any one organization. As a direct result, sustainable capacity can be established to address community issues over the long term, such as coalitions that have focused on infant mortality. Entering into collaborative arrangements can mobilize more talents, resources, and options for influencing an issue than any single organization could and can minimize duplication of effort and services among organizations with similar objectives. Interorganizational collaboration can provide an avenue to recruit participants from diverse constituencies and take advantage of new resources in changing situations because they are flexible.[1,2,5]

Natural helper models

Within any given community, there is a cadre of individuals who provide informal assistance—tangible aid, emotional support, or informal advice. These individuals may work unobtrusively to ensure those in need are not stigmatized. They may attend meetings within and outside their community to be in the know and to voice the perspectives of their community. Such individuals have been called natural helpers[10] by public health researchers and practitioners, and have been recruited to serve as "lay health advisors" in a number of successful public health interventions. In many African American communities, natural helpers include church members, barbers, and beauticians; health promotion interventions have been developed that leverage the community connections and influence of these individuals. In Latino communities, persons filling the role of lay health advisors are often referred to as *promotores*. Because of their knowledge of and connections within their communities, the use of promotores is frequently built into efforts to improve adherence to health recommendations, increase appropriate rates of service utilization, enhance client and health provider communication, or improve access to services. There is a continuum of approaches and models that may be used when enlisting natural helpers or a lay health advisor—from student and adult volunteers to paid project employees in health care or community settings.[10] One example is the use of Youth Ambassadors as an integral part of the several efforts in Los Angeles to affect obesity there,[11] including the South LA (Los Angeles) Healthy Eating Active Communities[12,13] work to transform corner stores into locations that feature healthy food options. Some

Changing health outcomes through community-driven processes 305

of the most recent examples of paid lay health advisors involve health navigators, who work within health care settings to enroll eligible persons in insurance plans.[14] These health navigators played a significant role in the increased number of Americans with health insurance, whether obtained through the private market or through participation in Medicaid.[14]

Community advisory board

Although community input is essential to much of the work of public health, continuous pursuit of perspectives and insights on a population scale does not lend itself to timely and effective problem-solving. Putting together a CAB is one way of assuring community participation and retaining the ability to be relatively nimble and responsive to issues as they arise. CABs can be particularly beneficial to research efforts, as a well-chosen advisory board can help build or strengthen researcher-community relationships and collaborations. The structure of these boards can range from short-term, project-specific advisory boards to long-term boards that provide advice and guidance to a larger program of research or intervention. Quinn[15] proposes five functions of CABs:

- Act as a liaison between researchers and community.
- Represent community concerns and culture to researchers.
- Assist in the development of study materials.
- Advocate for the rights of research study participants.
- Consult with potential study participants to provide recommendations about research study enrollment.

In addition, CABs can serve to protect the interests of the community in light of the power imbalance that characterizes many academic-community partnerships. Many communities of color have been taken advantage of by researchers and academic research institutions, both public and private.[16] Advisory boards have emerged as one means by which more equitable relationships between communities and academic institutions may be fostered.

Building capacity for community change

Whether community collaboration is sought by one of the three means suggested above, or a combination of them, it is nearly always the case that time and effort must be devoted to capacity building in order for communities to benefit from academic-community partnerships in a substantive and sustained way. Jackson et al.[6] suggest that because community capacity tends to coalesce within existing organizations, a geographic approach to this asset may be useful. Mapping the geography of community capacity can be useful in assessing the potential for successful interorganizational collaboration: "Capacity is linked to the ability of a community to include and deal with a variety of conflicting factions that coexist within the same geographic area."[5]

306 *Public health research methods for partnerships and practice*

Being able to galvanize those factions in service to a shared goal is important to conducting research and enacting programs that have potential to benefit a broad swath of the community. Natural helpers and CABs provide representation at the grassroots and leadership levels, respectively, and help to ensure that interventions draw upon existing community assets, and meet the needs of the community, while remaining culturally sensitive and appropriate. Recognition of community assets and commitment to asset-based, community capacity building is of central importance, particularly for poor and minority communities, often viewed as being deficit ridden.[17] Paulo Freire has established a well-used model of critical consciousness that emphasizes community assets and meeting people and organizations at their level, by taking into consideration their cultural, social, and political environments to engage in meaningful dialogue and to build partnerships. This is a critical step in the needs assessment process.[18–20] Kretzman and McKnight[21] furthered the community asset approach, embodying Freire's work, to help move our understanding of the concept of functional communities. Functional communities are defined by possession of or access to material resources that serve as building blocks for assets, which can be mobilized and used to address the issues and concerns in order to foster change.[22]

Participation and membership in organizations

The communitarian approach dominates the discourse of social capital and public health, which largely focuses on participation in activities, civic participation, and trust in others.[23,24] At the core of the communitarian approach to social capital is the construct of participation. Participation, in many ways, is the driving force behind social capital in public health. Participation involves building trusting relationships within one's neighborhood, community, church, synagogue, voluntary association, civic group, or parent-teacher association (PTA). Coleman[25] suggested that participating in voluntary associations engages participants in processes that form social ties or strengthen their existing social ties. These ties provide the contexts for social support to operate, and for social networks to be formed or strengthened. There are several definitions of participation that will be discussed. The powerful role of participation has largely been discussed within the context of social capital in public health.[26–30] However, social capital involves an understanding of an individual's ability to participate or be active, which, in itself, can be an indicator of an individual's state of health. Participatory action, which undergirds community-driven processes, connects individuals and groups to others in either homogeneous or heterogeneous social networks, and, by virtue of their participation, may provide them access to social support.

Citizen participation is characterized by a strong participant base and by diverse networks that enable different interests to take collective action. When individuals understand that benefits override costs associated with participation, they become involved. The documented role of participation in health

Changing health outcomes through community-driven processes 307

promotion is evidence of the necessity for citizen involvement in defining and resolving needs.[18] Citizen involvement activities may not always be based upon a well-defined group identity, such as a religious-based group, or a group that is bound by a geographic barrier, such as a neighborhood. These activities may include voting, signing a petition, or attending a local school board, a city council meeting, or a range of other activities that help to provide a sense of community and social cohesion.[31,32]

The World Health Organization (WHO) Ottawa Charter for Health Promotion defines participation as a means of collective action illustrated by the "collective efforts by communities which are directed towards increasing community control over the determinants of health, and thereby improving health."[33] The Ottawa Charter further emphasizes:

> Health promotion works through concrete and effective community action in setting priorities, making decisions, planning strategies and implementing them to achieve better health. At the heart of this process is the empowerment of communities—their ownership and control of their own endeavors and destinies. Community development draws on existing human and material resources in the community to enhance self-help and social support, and to develop flexible systems for strengthening public participation in and direction of health matters. This requires full and continuous access to information, learning opportunities for health, as well as funding support.[33]

The Ottawa Charter helped to establish a global focus on participation, from which health promotion initiatives will focus on a continuum of efforts that will empower individuals, organizations, and communities as a whole. Participation within empowered communities creates an opportunity for individuals and organizations to provide social support for health to address conflict within communities and to continue to gain influence and control of the social determinants of health.[33] Public health's emphasis on a communitarian approach to social capital reflects the Ottawa Charter's focus on participation, as well as on community development efforts to engage communities in the process of improving health status. The Harlem Children's Zone Initiative is an example of the communitarian approach to improve the health and well-being of children and their families affected by high levels of school absenteeism due to asthma.[34]

Empowered individuals seek greater power and authority to affect change within their neighborhoods and communities. Their organized action leads to building sources of social capital that can be used to address future community issues. Baum and Ziersch[35] state that participation can range from consultation to structural participation, where lay persons are the main driving forces. This form of structural participation in civil society is crucial to concepts and measures embodied in social capital.[36] For policy makers and researchers, a concern exists regarding the extent of institutional support (e.g., state, nation) that is essential to maintain a civil society—a concern that

308 *Public health research methods for partnerships and practice*

is, perhaps, germane to the growing body of literature on links between social capital and policy.[36,37]

Like all of the mechanisms discussed, participation occurs within a community's particular social, political, and economic context, which may promote or dissuade participation. It is critical to be able to examine what people participate in, the depth of their involvement, the frequency of their involvement, and the geographical location (within or outside of one's neighborhood), or whether participation occurs in another community of identity. The benefits, values, opportunities, and stressors involved in participatory action are to be accounted for in measuring participation. The Ottawa Charter helped to develop an agenda for health promotion, the goal of which was to restore and enhance extrafamilial social relations and community capacity. This approach embodies and operationalizes participation, empowerment, and collective action, and is central to health promotion practice.[38] Social capital embraces all the social, collective, economic, and cultural resources to which a community has access. This reflects a community's potential for cooperative action to address local problems and to provide support for its members.

Lomas[39] states that the way we organize our society, the extent to which we encourage interaction, and the degree to which we trust each other are probably the most important determinants of health. Social capital is seen as an important facilitator of community self-help and is an outcome of community development, as it aids communities to work more easily to solve collective health and social problems.[38,40] The Putnam model of social capital incorporates the existence of community networks, civic engagement, local identity, and a sense of solidarity and equity with other community members, along with trust, reciprocal help, and support. Putnam, therefore, promotes community engagement as the primary mechanism for building better-educated, healthier, more politically involved communities, thereby producing a more democratic society.

Building community and organizational capacity

Organizations can avoid the risk of organizational mortality by forming interorganizational networks to remain innovative and aware of the changing sociopolitical climate and the changes in health status of community residents.[41,42] Community health partnerships are seen as one strategy to engage communities, using community members and organizations as an asset to provide solutions for health problems. The linkage between community capacity and health builds upon the recognition that the social, political, and physical environment, along with economic forces and social relationships, has an impact on health status. Therefore, improving health requires changing the broader community in which health disparities exist. One means of addressing health disparities is to enhance the organizational capacity of a community to address the factors contributing to poor health status.

Crisp, Swerissen, and Duckett[43] identified four approaches to building capacity: a top-down organizational approach, a bottom-up organizational

Changing health outcomes through community-driven processes 309

approach, a partnerships approach, and a community-organizing approach. A top-down organizational approach is established by executives and leaders of an organization, and they make decisions unilaterally that are then communicated to subordinates. This approach is unlike a bottom-up organizational approach that seeks input from all levels within an organization to ensure that the decisions or changes address some of their needs and concerns, and are feasible. The partnership approach seeks to, according to Crisp and colleagues,[43] "strengthen the relationships between existing organizations," whereas a community-organizing approach builds upon individual community members' formation of new organizations or joining with existing organizations. The authors describe providing resources (i.e., financial, other resources, or a combination) to organizations with the goal of enhancing the ability of organizations to identify, analyze, and address their needs with their own resources. This approach recognizes that communities have existing assets, in the form of individuals, networks, and organizations.

Green, Daniel, and Novick[44] suggest that partnerships, which might include universities, voluntary agencies, local government, civic groups, and others, are necessary for health promotion and disease prevention programs as well as research for several reasons:

- No one group has the resources, access, or sufficient trust to intervene on a broad array of social determinants of health in the community.
- "Shared commitment and planning to ensure the resources, mandate, reach and credibility contribute to sustainability."
- Partnerships help to avoid the narrow perspective that only one group would bring to research or program development.
- Partnerships can help to generate greater public awareness and support as well as create critical mass for action.
- Partnerships provide the breadth necessary to develop an ecological approach to health disparities.[44]

Organizations that reflect an enhanced sense of capacity should have an infrastructure that enables them to be responsive to the existing and emerging health issues of their community. Organizational capacity can be characterized and developed in several ways. First, organizations need a strong and transformative leadership base with the skills, relationships, and vision that can motivate individuals and organizations into a collective force for change.[1,2,45] Second, organizations need defined roles and formalized processes with clear guidelines for collaborative work.[9,46,47] Third, organizations need a well-designed system of communication that promotes information sharing and problem discussion and resolution.[1,2,9,46,48,49] Fourth, organizations need human and financial capital to perform collaborative work.[46,49] Fifth, organizations need to be adaptive in the sense that continuous learning occurs, using multiple sources of data to remain relevant to the changing contextual conditions of communities.[46,49]

Conclusions

The process of engaging communities should involve working together to create a context in which communities and academics work in full partnership. There is a range of tools that each can employ to ensure equitable engagement in the effort to collect, analyze, and use data appropriately to meet the needs of communities. This includes planning and executing interventions that address changes at multiple levels of communities' social ecology. A critical need exists to build sustainable relationships that may extend beyond a specific project so that these relationships become the foundation of efforts to address the fundamental causes of health concerns in a given community. However, health concerns can be prevented by building both the capacity of the community and the organizations that academics partner with in order to extend a community's ability to address issues over the long term.

One of the issues that requires greater attention is the evaluation of academic-community partnerships. The coalition literature provides some examples, and there is an emerging emphasis on measuring the effectiveness of partnership approaches as well. The goal in this chapter was to describe the processes by which communities can begin to better initiate and guide relationships with academics in order to engage in research endeavors that improve health outcomes. There is no shortage of social, economic, and health issues to address, but there is not always a clear path to knowing how to identify the necessary resources to address those issues. Partnership approaches are one option, not only with academic institutions, but also partnerships with local and state governments, the private sector, and health care institutions. The examples provided here are largely focused on academic-community partnerships, but the principles, functions, and processes described can be applied to a range of potential partnership approaches that allow communities to initiate and guide these relationships.

BOX 15.1   TOOLS AND RESOURCES

- Bolder Advocacy: http://www.bolderadvocacy.org/tools-for-effec tive-advocacy/evaluating-advocacy/advocacy-capacity-tool
- Social Planning and Research Council of British Columbia: http://www.sparc.bc.ca/community-capacity-building-tool
- Society for Public Health Education (SOPHE) Annual Advocacy Summit and Resolutions:
  - http://www.sophe.org/AdvocacySummit.cfm
  - http://www.sophe.org/Resolutions.cfm

References

1. Butterfoss FD, Goodman RM, Wandersman A. Community coalitions for prevention and health promotion. *Health Educ Res.* 1993;8(3):315–330. doi:10.1093/her/8.3.315.
2. Butterfoss FD, Goodman RM, Wandersman A. Community coalitions for prevention and health promotion: Factors predicting satisfaction, participation, and planning. *Health Educ Q.* 1996;23(1):65–79. doi:10.1177/109019819602300105.
3. Lasker RD, Weiss ES. Broadening participation in community problem solving: A multidisciplinary model to support collaborative practice and research. *J Urban Health.* 2003;80(1):14–47. doi:10.1093/jurban/jtg014.
4. Cheadle A, Senter S, Solomon L, Beery WL, Schwartz PM. A qualitative exploration of alternative strategies for building community health partnerships: Collaboration-versus issue-oriented approaches. *J Urban Health.* 2005;82(4):638–652. doi:10.1093/jurban/jti120.
5. Butterfoss FD, Kegler MC. Toward a comprehensive understanding of community coalitions: Moving from practice to theory. In: DiClemente R, Crosby RA, Kegler MC, eds. *Emerging Theories in Health Promotion and Practice and Research Strategies for Improving Public Health.* San Francisco, CA: Jossey-Bass; 2002:157–192.
6. Jackson SF, Cleverly S, Poland B, Burman D, Edwards R, Robertson A. Working with Toronto neighbourhoods toward developing indicators of community capacity. *Health Promot Int.* 2003;18(4):339–350. doi:10.1093/heapro/dag415.
7. Laverack G, Wallerstein N. Measuring community empowerment: A fresh look at organizational domains. *Health Promot Int.* 2001;16(2):179–185. doi:10.1093/heapro/16.2.179.
8. García JJL, Sharif MZ. Black lives matter: A commentary on racism and public health. *Am J Public Health.* 2015;105(8):e27–e30. doi:10.2105/AJPH.2015.302706.
9. Wandersman A, Valois R, Ochs L, De la Cruz DS, Adkins E, Goodman RM. Toward a social ecology of community coalitions. *Am J Heal Promot.* 1996;10(4):299–307. doi:10.4278/0890-1171-10.4.299.
10. Eng E, Rhodes SD, Parker E. Natural helper models to enhance a community's health and competence. In: DiClemente RJ, Crosby RA, Kegler MC, eds. *Emerging Theories in Health Promotion and Practice and Research.* San Francisco, CA: Jossey-Bass; 2009:303–330.
11. Kim S, Koniak-Griffin D, Flaskerud JH, Guarnero PA. The impact of lay health advisors on cardiovascular health promotion: Using a community-based participatory approach. *J Cardiovasc Nurs.* 2004;19(3):192–199. doi:10.5993/AJHB.24.1.7.
12. Samuels SE, Craypo L, Boyle M, Crawford PB, Yancey A, Flores G. The California Endowment's healthy eating, active communities program: A midpoint review. *Am J Public Health.* 2010;100(11):2114–2123. doi:10.2105/AJPH.2010.192781.
13. Cheadle A, Samuels SE, Rauzon S et al. Approaches to measuring the extent and impact of environmental change in three California community-level obesity prevention initiatives. *Am J Public Health.* 2010;100(11):2129–2136. doi:10.2105/AJPH.2010.300002.
14. Islam N, Nadkarni SK, Zahn D, Skillman M, Kown SC, Trinh-Shevrin C. Integrating community health workers within Patient Protection and Affordable Care Act implementation. *J Public Heal Manag Pr.* 2015;21(1):42–50. doi:10.1097/PHH.0000000000000084.Integrating.
15. Quinn SC. Protecting human subjects: The role of community advisory boards. *Am J Public Health.* 2004;94(6):918–922.
16. Passmore SR, Fryer CS, Butler J, Garza MA, Thomas SB, Quinn SC. Building a "Deep Fund of Good Will": Reframing research engagement. *J Health Care Poor Underserved.* 2016;27(2):722–740. doi: 10.1353/hpu.2016.0070.

312 *Public health research methods for partnerships and practice*

17. Goodman RM, Speers MA, Mcleroy K et al. Identifying and defining the dimensions of community capacity to provide a basis for measurement. *Health Educ.* 1998;25(June):258–278.
18. Hancock T, Minkler M. Community health assessment or healthy community assessment: Whose community? Whose health? Whose assessment. In: Minkler M, ed. *Community Organizing and Community Building for Health.* Brunswick, NJ: Rutgers University Press; 1997:148.
19. Costa S, Serrano-García I. Needs assessment and community development: An ideological perspective. *Prev Hum Serv.* 1983;2(4):75–88. http://www.ncbi.nlm .nih.gov/pubmed/10262480%5Cnhttp://www.tandfonline.com/doi/abs/10.1300 /J293v02n04_05.
20. Beaulieu LJ. Mapping the assets of your community: A key component for building local capacity. *South Rural Dev Center, Mississippi State, MS.* 2002;(SRDC-227):1–14.
21. Kretzman JP, McKnight JL. Asset-based community development: Mobilizing an entire community. In: Kretzman JP, McKnight JL, eds. *Building Communities from the Inside Out: A Path Toward Finding and Mobilizing a Community's Assets.* Evanston, IL: Northwestern University; 1993:345–354.
22. Norton BL, McLeroy KR, Burdine JN, Felix MRJ, Dorsey AM. Community capacity: Concept, theory, and methods. In: DiClemente R, Crosby A, Kegler MC, eds. *Toward a Comprehensive Understanding of Community Coalitions: Moving from Practice to Theory.* San Francisco, CA: Jossey-Bass; 2002:194–227.
23. Moore S, Shiell A, Hawe P, Haines VA. The privileging of communitarian ideas: Citation practices and the translation of social capital into public health research. *Am J Public Health.* 2005;95(8):1330–1337. doi:10.2105/AJPH.2004.046094.
24. Moore S, Haines V, Hawe P, Shiell A. Lost in translation: A genealogy of the "social capital" concept in public health. *J Epidemiol Community Health.* 2006;60(8):729–734. doi:10.1136/jech.2005.041848.
25. Coleman JS. Social capital in the creation of human capital. *Am J Sociol.* 1988;94(1988):S95. doi:10.1086/228943.
26. Gilbert KL, Quinn SC, Goodman RM, Butler J, Wallace J. A meta-analysis of social capital and health: A case for needed research. *J Health Psychol.* 2013;18(11):1385–1399. doi:10.1177/1359105311435983.
27. Kawachi I, Kennedy BP, Glass R. Social capital and self-rated health: A contextual analysis. *Am J Public Health.* 1998;89(8):1187–1193.
28. Helliwell JF, Putnam RD. The social context of well-being. *Society.* 2004; (August):1435–1446. doi:10.1098/rstb.2004.1522.
29. Putnam RD. *Bowling Alone: The Collapse and Revival of American Community.* New York, NY: Touchstone Books; 2001.
30. Putnam RD. Bowling alone: Americas's declining social capital. *J Democr.* 1995;6:65–78. doi:10.1353/jod.1995.0002.
31. Harpham T, Grant E, Thomas E. Measuring social capital within health surveys: Key issues. *Health Policy Plan.* 2002;17(1):106–111. doi:10.1093/heapol/17.1.106.
32. Szreter S, Woolcock M. Health by association? Social capital, social theory, and the political economy of public health. *Int J Epidemiol.* 2004;33(4):650–667. doi:10.1093/ije/dyh013.
33. World Health Organization. Ottawa Charter for Health Promotion First International Conference on Health Promotion. *Heal Promot.* 1986;1(4):WHO /HPR/HEP/95.1. doi:10.1017/CBO9781107415324.004.
34. Nicholas SW, Jean-Louis B, Ortiz B et al. Addressing the childhood asthma crisis in Harlem: The Harlem Children's Zone Asthma Initiative. *Am J Public Health.* 2005;95(2):245–249. doi:10.2105/AJPH.2004.042705.

Changing health outcomes through community-driven processes 313

35. Baum FE, Ziersch AM. Social capital. *J Epidemiol Community Health.* 2003;57(5):320–323. doi:10.1136/jech.57.5.320.
36. Ziersch AM, Baum FE, Macdougall C, Putland C. Neighbourhood life and social capital: The implications for health. *Soc Sci Med.* 2005;60:71–86. doi:10.1016/j.socscimed.2004.04.027.
37. Baum F, Ziersch AM, Zhang G et al. *People and Places—Urban Location, Social Capital and Health.* Adelaide, Australia: Flinders University; 2007. http://dspace.flinders.edu.au/xmlui/handle/2328/25237.
38. Wakefield SEL, Poland B. Family, friend or foe? Critical reflections on the relevance and role of social capital in health promotion and community development. *Soc Sci Med.* 2005;60:2819–2832. doi:10.1016/j.socscimed.2004.11.012.
39. Lomas J. Social capital and health: Implications for public health and epidemiology. *Soc Sci Med.* 1998;47(9):1181–1188. doi:10.1016/S0277-9536(98)00190-7.
40. Subramanian SV, Kim DJ, Kawachi I. Social trust and self-rated health in US communities: A multilevel analysis. *J Urban Health.* 2002;79(4 Suppl 1):S21–S34. doi:10.1093/jurban/79.suppl_1.S21.
41. Hodson R. Organizational trustworthiness: Findings from the population of organizational ethnographies. *Organ Sci.* 2004;15(4):432–445. doi:10.1287/orsc.1040.0077.
42. Singh JV., Lumsden CJ. Theory and research in organizational ecology. *Annu Rev Sociol.* 1990;16(1):161–195. doi:10.1146/annurev.so.16.080190.001113.
43. Crisp BR, Swerissen H, Duckett SJ. Four approaches to capacity building in health: Consequences for measurement and accountability. *Health Promot Int.* 2000;15(2):99–107. doi:10.1093/heapro/15.2.99.
44. Green L, Daniel M, Novick L. Partnerships and coalitions for community-based research. *Public Health Rep.* 2001;116(Suppl 1):20–31. doi:10.1093/phr/116.S1.20.
45. Goodman RM. A Construct for building the capacity of community-based initiatives in racial and ethnic communities: A qualitative cross-case analysis. *J Public Heal Manag Pract.* 2009;47405:1–8.
46. Foster-Fishman PG, Berkowitz SL, Lounsbury DW, Jacobson S, Allen NA. Building collaborative capacity in community coalitions: A review and integrative framework. *Am J Community Psychol.* 2001;29(2):241–261. doi:10.1023/A:1010378613583.
47. Gray B, Wood D. Collaborative alliances: Moving from practice to theory. *J Appl Behav Sci.* 1991;27(1):3–22. doi:10.1177/0021886391272001.
48. Kegler MC, Steckler A, Malek SH, McLeroy K. A multiple case study of implementation in 10 local project ASSIST coalitions in North Carolina. *Health Educ Res.* 1998;13(2):225–238. doi:10.1093/her/13.2.225.
49. Wandersman A, Goodman RM, Butterfoss FD. Understanding coalitions and how they operate: An open systems framework. In: Minkler M, ed. *Community Organizing and Community Building for Health.* 2nd ed. New Brunswick, NJ: Rutgers University Press; 1997:292–313.

Group discussion activity

Working with a community group or agency interested in refining its approach, building some evidence to demonstrate its effectiveness, and strengthening its capacity, develop a list of questions to learn more about the agency's mission, goals, daily activities, programs, resources, challenges, and membership. These questions can include items that might allow the group to summarize the issues the agency works on and how their activities help to meet their mission, achieve their goals, and address the key issues they are working on.

314 *Public health research methods for partnerships and practice*

Next, the group should identify leaders and members within the group and those who benefit from their services. In addition, discuss the stakeholders—identify groups the agency has worked with and groups that they might like to work with. This information can be used to better understand the internal mechanisms of the organization or group, to understand their impact, and to plan for future activities or to strengthen their interorganizational networks.

SELF-ASSESSMENT—WHAT DID YOU LEARN?

1. Which of the following statements is FALSE about good negotiators?
   a. They understand how to build key relationships.
   b. They identify what people need.
   c. They give people what they need and know how to get what they want in return.
   d. They find an approach that works for them and apply it to all situations.

2. Which of the following is a critical requirement for a strong coalition?
   a. An agreed-upon decision-making process
   b. Effective communication
   c. Respect
   d. All of the above

3. _____ is self-perceived personal power.
   a. Self-esteem
   b. Empowerment
   c. Spirit
   d. Health

4. A good leader _____.
   a. Tries to keep all of the power for himself or herself.
   b. Shuns the media.
   c. Is able to work with many different people.
   d. Focuses only on the actions of his or her organization.

5. A goal of community organizing is to _____.
   a. Change outdated and ineffective policies.
   b. Build a personal power base.
   c. Provide an opportunity for privileged people to build their power.
   d. Challenge people to act on behalf of their interests only.

Changing health outcomes through community-driven processes 315

6. Community organizing is _____.
   a. A process by which people come together to talk about matters connected to their health.
   b. A group of people who seek to amend errors in their community.
   c. A process to develop a sense of well-being in others.
   d. A process by which people organize themselves to take charge of their situation and to develop a sense of community together.

7. What is the recommended order for developing your action plan?
   a. Create a timeline of events, identify your issue, approach stakeholders, and delegate responsibilities.
   b. Delegate responsibilities, approach stakeholders, create a timeline of events, and identify your issue.
   c. Identify your issue, approach stakeholders, delegate responsibilities, and create a timeline of events.
   d. Approach stakeholders, identify your issue, create a timeline of events, and delegate responsibilities.

8. What is the primary purpose of a community advisory committee?
   a. Provide input and feedback on projects.
   b. Oversee the budget.
   c. Establish new partnerships for the organization.
   d. Draft the organization's strategic plan.

9. Which is NOT a top reason why people fail to volunteer to solve community problems?
   a. They are not being paid a wage.
   b. There is a lack of ownership of the problem.
   c. They feel that they lack the relevant skills.
   d. They feel that they lack the relevant knowledge.

10. The four approaches to building capacity include a top-down organizational approach, a bottom-up organizational approach, a partnerships approach, and an advocacy approach.
    a. True
    b. False

Conclusion
CRFT program implementation and evaluation

Melody S. Goodman and Vetta Sanders Thompson

Community-based participatory research (CBPR) is based on equitable community-academic partnerships with combined resources, knowledge, and skills. CBPR has been effective in engaging diverse, sometimes forgotten communities in the research enterprise by fostering collaborations among community health stakeholders and by enhancing community capacity for research and evaluation.[1,2] Inherent in the principles of CBPR is a commitment to community training and co-learning.[3] Training community members has the potential to increase capacity for full engagement and power-sharing in CBPR partnerships.[4–6] CRFT is an evidence-based model for increasing community capacity and enhancing the infrastructure for CBPR.

This book is designed to aid CRFT program adaptation, implementation, and evaluation in communities, populations, or settings other than the sites of the initial CRFT initiatives. The purpose of the CRFT program is to train community health stakeholders (e.g., community health educators, community health workers, patient navigators, health department staff, nurses, social workers, community members) to collaborate on community-engaged research to address health disparities. The program goal is to increase the role of minority and medically underserved populations in the research enterprise by enhancing capacity for community-engaged research. The objectives of the program are to:

- Increase research capacity among community health stakeholders.
- Promote partnerships between community members and researchers.
- Enhance community members' understanding of how to use research to improve health outcomes in their communities.
- Train community members to be critical consumers of research.[5]

Program implementation

We encourage purposeful selection of a diverse group of community health stakeholders for each cohort of the training program. Diversity among participants has been noted by program participants as a key attribute. For each of the review criteria (e.g., interest, research experience, and community

Conclusion 317

involvement), applicants are rated using a categorical scale (limited, meets, exceeds). We are not looking for applicants who exceed in every category; if they have already demonstrated excellence in all the categories, training is not needed. We are looking for applicants who exceed in some areas but are limited in others. This allows them to give to the program and to gain from it.

During the week before the first training session, we host an orientation session for the applicants who were selected. At the orientation session, fellows are given the course syllabus and materials needed to participate in the program. We discuss the purpose of the program and what is expected of the fellows. The orientation session concludes with a CRFT alumni panel. Panel members discuss their experience in the CRFT program and how they have used the program information subsequent to their participation. At the end of the orientation, if interested in participation, fellows sign the CRFT participant agreement. The agreement asks fellows to show passion, dedication, and commitment to learning; to make every effort to attend all sessions with no more than two absences; and to complete all homework assignments. It also asks fellows to make a commitment to the program evaluation by completing all assessments and evaluations.

Faculty are essential to the successful implementation of the program. Faculty are hand selected by the program director based on their topical expertise and experience with community-engaged research. Credentials are not what matters here. More important is the ability to explain complex topics to a lay audience and create a friendly and welcoming learning environment. Fellows are encouraged to ask questions during lectures, and it is often necessary for faculty to provide additional examples to clarify a topic. Faculty must be flexible in teaching styles and open to bidirectional learning. Program faculty include traditional faculty who span academic ranks (lecturers, assistant professor, associate professor, and professor) in addition to librarians, leaders of community-based organizations, and community health workers. We developed eight best practices for CRFT program implementation:[5,7]

1. Establish and use a community advisory board (CAB) for program adaptation and implementation. CAB members help to recruit participants, review applications for the program, and review pilot project proposals.
2. Tailor recruitment efforts for the population of interest. CRFT focuses on addressing racial health disparities and recruits minority and medically underserved populations most impacted.
3. Remove barriers to application and participation. We create résumé and reference letter templates, provide technical assistance during the application process, host information sessions for potential applicants, provide meals for evening sessions, provide parking validation or public transportation passes, and provide all the supplies necessary for participation.
4. Recruit a diverse, multidisciplinary faculty with demographics similar to the participants. Faculty are selected because of their expertise and experience with community-engaged research.

318 *Conclusion*

5. Provide training in multiple formats (e.g., large lectures, discussion, small group activities) to cater to the diverse learning styles of the participants.
6. Incorporate community-based homework assignments to enhance learning, allowing fellows to take what they learn in the classroom and apply it in their community.
7. Celebrate the accomplishment of fellows completing the program through a certificate ceremony and reception. This allows fellows to share this accomplishment with family, coworkers, and friends. It also introduces fellows to the community as key resources. Fellows demonstrate some of what they learn in the course by presenting their photovoice homework (or an activity/product suggested by the CAB) at the reception.
8. Conduct follow-up evaluation interviews shortly after the certificate ceremony to gain the best insights on the program and areas for improvement, thereby minimizing the amount of participant recall time between program completion and the interview.

On the website, we provide several documents and forms to assist with program implementation and evaluation. These include the CRFT application, application review template with criteria and scoring, participant agreement, ground rules, sample agenda, sign-in sheet, sample request for proposals, proposal review template, sample certificate of completion, evaluation documents (baseline assessment, final assessment, session evaluation template, mid-training evaluation, exit interview questions and consent form, faculty evaluation), and homework assignments. These documents serve as templates and should be reviewed by CABs and modified as needed.

Homework assignments supplement the interactive didactic training sessions and small breakout group experiential workshops that take place on site. Homework assignments are designed to help participants gain a more in-depth understanding of the topics in the curriculum and allow fellows to gain skills that can be used in completing community needs assessments. All homework assignments require fellows to go into their communities and collect data or to use existing resources; fellows have approximately 2 weeks to complete each assignment. We have developed, piloted, and refined four structured assignments (windshield survey, grocery store audit, community park audit, and photovoice) and created two new assignments (review of news article and reading a scientific article) that complement the 15-week training. Each assignment has a structured template that allows fellows to complete assignments easily in the field and to easily compare and analyze data collected. In essence, each homework assignment is a mini-research project that requires structured data collection (using an evidence-based tool) and synthesis of information to draw conclusions and increase understanding of community health.

The "Windshield Survey" assignment requires fellows to drive or walk slowly through a neighborhood and catalog types and conditions of residences, green spaces, residents, commercial areas, and community institutions.

This systematic, objective observation of the resources, infrastructure, and physical, social, and economic characteristics of a community is used to assess general community needs with respect to health, allowing the fellow to draw conclusions on the strengths, weaknesses, opportunities, and threats in a particular community.[2,8,9]

The "Grocery Store Audit" involves fellows recording the prices, quantity, and quality of goods and services at two grocery stores of their choice. If participants decide on a "big box" store, they are required to go to another store in the same chain but in a different community. Similarly, those who choose "mom and pop" stores visit a similar store in another community. This assignment allows fellows to compare grocery stores and to investigate potential disparities on the basis of the location or socioeconomic status of the stores' surrounding neighborhood.[10–12]

The "Community Park Audit" is similar to the grocery store audit but, instead, requires fellows to visit two parks in different areas and to record qualitative and quantitative details on park access, activity areas, quality, and safety.[13–16] The assignment allows fellows to compare recreational facilities and green space in two different neighborhoods. Completing this assignment after the grocery store audit drives home the fact that "place" is a major contributor to health, and disparities in the social determinants of health (e.g., access to healthy food options or safe spaces for physical activity) can lead to differences in health outcomes.

Photovoice, discussed at greater length in Chapter 11, is a group analysis method combining photography with grassroots social action and is commonly used in the fields of community development, public health, and education. Photovoice is often used with marginalized groups to provide insight into how they conceptualize their circumstances and their hopes for the future.[17–20] In the assignment involving photovoice, participants are asked to express their points of view by photographing scenes that highlight research themes. Common research themes may include community concerns, community assets, or health barriers and facilitators.[21]

In the "Photovoice" homework, fellows are asked to take a photo in their community that represents social capital (CRFT-STL Cohorts I and II) or the Black Lives Matter movement (CRFT-STL Cohort III) to demonstrate the potential community resources available to address health disparities. They reflect on their photo's subject and ways in which it might be used to bring about policy change.[22] These photographs are collaboratively interpreted in focus groups. Narratives around the images can be developed that explain how the photos highlight a particular research theme. These narratives are used to better understand the community and help to plan health or social programs that address community needs.[23]

The individual assignment culminates in a group discussion during the small breakout groups of the "Qualitative Methods" session. This is the one time that breakout group membership is not selected at random. Each group becomes a focus group composed of members whose photos are on a similar

320   *Conclusion*

topic (e.g., religion, health, and education), based on the review of CRFT program staff. Trained focus group facilitators (including some CRFT alumni) lead the group discussion. Each fellow is given the opportunity to present and discuss his or her photo in the focus group. After each photo is discussed, the group chooses a single photo to discuss in depth for the full cohort. These discussions also allow the fellows to experience participating in a focus group.

At the completion of the program, the "Photovoice" homework assignments are displayed for attendees of the certificate ceremony and reception to spark discussion about the training program and community issues identified by fellows. As a form of community health stakeholder consultation, photovoice is used to attempt to bring the perspectives of those real-world, lived experiences into the policy-making process.[24-26]

New Assignments. The two new assignments are designed to assist fellows in applying their new skills to understand research information. The areas of focus are the social determinants of health and quantitative data. The "Social Determinants of Health" assignment was included because of the strong health equity focus of CRFT. The "Social Determinants of Health" assignment asks fellows to read and reflect on a news article that addresses some aspect of health disparities or inequity. Fellows then identify one or more determinants of health mentioned in the article and then state the effects of these determinants and how they differ by race, gender, or income. Fellows are expected to be able to state the data methods, sources cited, and study limitations; they are also expected to be able to note the experts and stakeholders cited or quoted, as well as their roles in the research or issue. The final questions require fellows to discuss their reactions and position with respect to potential actions, policy recommendations, or both.

The "Quantitative Data" assignment focuses on reading and interpreting scientific findings in academic journals. Reviewing and interpreting the scientific literature that includes quantitative data are key components of evidence-based public health (EBPH). It was felt that this curriculum component should be represented among the homework assignments. Fellows read a journal article and answer items that ask about study design, including how and when data were collected, the outcome variable, and how the variable was measured. Fellows are asked to interpret a statistic from the results and to report findings from a study table. It is believed that the opportunity to engage with the scientific literature will boost the fellows' confidence during collaborations.

Program evaluation

We conducted a comprehensive (formative and summative), mixed-methods (qualitative and quantitative) evaluation of each cohort of the CRFT program. Methodological details and results of the evaluation are presented in detail elsewhere.[7,27] Over time, we have worked to reduce the participant's burden related to evaluation but maintain that a comprehensive evaluation is necessary for any

Conclusion 321

new implementation of the program. Participants take a baseline assessment before the first training session and a final assessment after the last training session. Initially, assessments consisted of 30 or more open-ended questions about program content. Questions were graded using a standardized rubric and scored as essentially correct (2 points), partially correct (1 point), or incorrect (0 points). We have replaced these questions with 10 multiple-choice questions, worth 1 point each, that assess research literacy. Each question requires knowledge of multiple topics taught during the training program and requires synthesis of information provided. We piloted these questions and conducted cognitive interviews with fellows to revise and refine the items. We also ask 20 multiple choice research knowledge items; each item covers a single topic.

In addition, participants complete a training evaluation halfway through the program, and evaluation questions are included on the final assessment. These evaluation questions ask fellows about their satisfaction with program logistics and how they are using the information learned in the program. Although these quantitative metrics provide key data, participants also complete follow-up evaluation interviews after the certificate ceremony. These semistructured one-on-one interviews provide important insight and context for quantitative results.[7]

In the follow-up evaluation interviews, fellows are asked about several topics related to program implementation: how they found out about the program; what they liked and did not like; their thoughts on the CRFT project team and faculty; the most useful information they learned in the training; how they use the training information and resources; whether they have shared the information with others; the barriers and facilitating factors for program completion; how to improve program logistics; their thoughts on the homework assignments, class size, and material covered; and whether they were interested in follow-up courses.

CRFT faculty members complete a short web-based evaluation survey after facilitating a CRFT session. Faculty are asked to rate the engagement of fellows in their session, the faculty's overall experience teaching the session, whether they would teach for the program in the future, whether they learned anything from fellows during the session, changes that need to be made to the program, and whether they would be willing to collaborate with fellows on a CBPR pilot project. One faculty member for CRFT-STL Cohort II stated, "The fellows had wonderful questions.... I hope the fellows are this engaged with other lectures. I received several extremely relevant questions following the lecture. It was clear they were transitioning the lessons of the lecture into their medical care." Another CRFT faculty member discussed learning from fellows: "The fellows suggested new ways that researchers benefit from working collaboratively with communities. The fellows have a more comprehensive view of issues that provides perspective on intervention strategies."

After each session, fellows complete a 10-question session evaluation that consists of six closed-ended questions with Likert response options and four open-ended questions. In the closed-ended questions, fellows are asked whether learning objectives are met, whether the information learned in the

322 *Conclusion*

session was helpful, whether concepts presented were understood, whether the facilitator was organized, whether the facilitator was knowledgeable about the subject, and the rating of the session overall. In the open-ended questions, fellows are asked for the three most important things learned during the session, what the fellows liked and did not like about the session, and additional comments and suggestions about the training session.

Evaluation metrics

We measure program commitment and engagement using attendance and homework completion rates. Based on data from the sign-in sheets, attendance rates are calculated as the percentage of cohort fellows present for each training session. We calculate homework completion rates as the percent of fellows completing an assignment. We measure increase in knowledge through change in baseline and final assessment scores for the program overall and for each session using pre- and posttest scores. We measure program satisfaction from the overall rating on the session evaluations. Outcomes of these evaluations are published and discussed in the literature.[4,5,7,27,28]

Overall, we have seen high levels of commitment and engagement in the CRFT program, statistically significant increases in research knowledge, and high levels of satisfaction reported by fellows in their evaluations. A CRFT-STL Cohort I fellow said, "I just liked the fact that it enhanced my knowledge, and it made me better equipped to do some of my own research and not be deathly afraid to pick up a journal article and read it." Another fellow stated,

> Actually, I liked every session of the training honestly, because every session was a lot of stuff I wasn't actually familiar with at all, as far as from a research perspective. I did data collection for research, but I never understood the foundation of how to collect the data, what type of data it was, so I learned a lot from just coming to every session.... I was just learning something new every day and [was] able to apply what I've learned in a more practical sense. Maybe, [I will] look at things from a more analytical perspective.

Pilot projects and other program outcomes

Development and implementation of CBPR pilot projects are key components of partnership development and extend the experiential learning of fellows to a research study. We developed an request for proposals (RFP) with broad categories (e.g., cancer disparities, social determinants of health, community heath, obesity, health of black women and girls) that allowed fellows to develop projects of interest to them. In its truest form, CBPR starts with an idea of importance to the community. As such, CBPR pilot projects must be an idea developed by fellows; once they have the topic, the CRFT project team assists fellows in identifying a faculty member with the necessary

Conclusion 323

content and/or methodological expertise. Fellows are responsible for building a research team consisting of a principal investigator, a co-principal investigator, co-investigators, a CRFT faculty collaborator, and community partners or a community-based organization with the skills and resources to conduct the proposed project.

The RFP outlines what is required in a 10-page proposal, including the abstract (500 words), specific aims (1 page), background/significance (2 pages), research plan (3 pages), evaluation plan (2 pages), and budget and budget narrative (2 pages). The background/significance section has to define the target population, community problem to be addressed, and service area need. It also has to place the proposal in the context of previous work done in the area and provide a rationale for why the proposed project is needed in the community or target population. The research plan states the problems and objectives, describes the research project scope and activities, and provides sample research materials (e.g., questionnaire, interview guide), a detailed description of community resources and collaborators (including letters of support), the timeline of activities, and conceptual maps. The evaluation plan has to include a logic model, a plan to measure the project results, the key impact of the project, and expected outcomes. The experience of writing a collaborative proposal and having it reviewed was new to some fellows and routine for others.

Two CBPR pilot projects were funded as part of the CARES program: the Truth Be Told project and the Brentwood Community Healthcare Assessment (BCHA).[29] Two CARES fellows from the BCHA team presented a poster on the study at the 2011 American Public Health Association Annual Meeting and Exposition.[30] In addition, several fellows were on the planning committee for the convening of the Think Tank for African American Progress–Long Island and became board members of the Long Island Think Tank for Black Progress, Inc., a community-based organization that was developed as a result of the convening.[31,32]

The CRFT CAB and CRFT faculty evaluate pilot project proposals. At least three people review each proposal, and funding decisions are based on scores for each of the following criteria:

- Potential for the project to address and improve health outcomes in the region (e.g., St. Louis Metropolitan Area).
- Demonstrated collaboration among CRFT Fellows.
- Demonstrated community-academic partnership (collaboration among CRFT Fellows and faculty).
- Quality of research approach, demonstrated use of research methods, and knowledge obtained in the CRFT program.
- Evidence of a strategic plan that engages community members, promotes academic-community collaboration, develops culturally appropriate approaches to meet the needs of diverse communities, and evaluates the project's impact on the specified population.
- A cost-effective, detailed budget and budget narrative.

324   *Conclusion*

- Demonstrated plans to expand and sustain funding sources beyond the anticipated CRFT seed grant and/or to promote broader community-based public health efforts.
- Significance of the problem addressed.
- Approach proposed to address specified problem.

The CRFT CAB selected two CBPR pilot projects from Cohort I to fund. The Healthy Body, Healthy Spirit project was a collaboration among four Cohort I fellows, a CRFT faculty member, and a church in North St. Louis, MO. The second project was The New Face of Homelessness, a study of the needs and concerns of homeless women 45 to 64 years of age. The New Face of Homelessness was a collaboration among four fellows, a CRFT faculty member, a shelter for homeless women in St. Louis that is now closed, and two residents of the shelter. This work received local media attention, including a cover story in the *St. Louis Post-Dispatch*, the regional daily, and two articles in the *St. Louis American*, a weekly newspaper focused on African American news with a local readership of over 200,000.

In addition, two other project teams submitted proposals, and, although not funded by the CRFT program, both projects subsequently found funding through other mechanisms (e.g., foundation, university).[5] There were no pilot projects for Cohort II because of limited funding. The GrassROOTS community foundation funded one project from Cohort III: Mental Health Literacy Among Unemployed African American Mothers, a collaboration among four Cohort III fellows, a CRFT faculty member, and a local community agency in St. Louis County, MO. Teams from The New Face of Homelessness and the Mental Health Literacy projects presented posters at the annual conference of the Institute for Public Health at Washington University in St. Louis.

On the basis of the discussion in the research ethics session, fellows who completed the Cohort I training decided to form a patient research advisory board (PRAB). The PRAB began meeting in July 2013 and elected to develop a planning committee consisting of 10 fellows to lead PRAB organizational development. The PRAB planning committee meets monthly, and the full PRAB meets quarterly. In its initial year, the PRAB planning committee worked to develop a mission, vision, goals, and objectives. They also developed a PRAB participant agreement, a process, and criteria to review patient-centered, community-engaged, and community-based projects and proposals. Eight Cohort II fellows joined the PRAB at its first general body meeting on September 30, 2014. The PRAB currently has 20 active members and started reviewing proposals in March 2015. The PRAB is involved in the development of several grant proposals with faculty at Washington University and serves as the CAB for programs affiliated with a local health department. CRFT faculty and staff serve as technical advisors to the PRAB. The PRAB is one example of how fellows translate increased knowledge and skills into action and research partnership development.

Conclusion 325

Several CRFT alumni serve on other CABs for programs and projects throughout Washington University (e.g., Occupational Therapy, Brown School of Social Work, CRFT CAB, Institute for Clinical and Translational Sciences, Institute for Public Health, Program to Eliminate Cancer Disparities), for national and state organizations (e.g., government, community-based organizations, foundations), and local St. Louis organizations (e.g., health department, community-based organizations, school-based health centers, advocacy and support groups, community health centers, hospitals, faith-based organizations, other universities). CRFT alumni have served as community representatives on grant review panels for Washington University (Institute for Public Health and Institute for Clinical and Translational Sciences) and a statewide health foundation.

Conclusions

CRFT provides a core curriculum and can be adapted to address particular health issues (e.g., cancer disparities or obesity) or issues relevant to certain populations (e.g., black women and girls) by adding additional sessions and by adapting examples, activities, and RFPs to focus on key issues or populations. The program has been implemented in urban (St. Louis, MO; Jackson, MS), suburban (Long Island, NY), and rural (Hattiesburg, MS) settings by academic institutions and a health department. Although this book is adapted from and designed for the CRFT program, other training programs focused on research literacy for lay audiences will find this a useful resource. We are committed to continued adaptation and evaluation of this curriculum for different ages and to health and social issues related to health. Thus, we ask others interested in or committed to CBPR to join us in this effort.

As scholars and researchers engaged in CBPR, we sought to share our efforts to facilitate CBPR as a component of the struggle for health equity. We encourage community-academic partnerships and collaborations to review this curriculum, to adapt it to the needs of their communities, and to use it to facilitate stronger partnerships. We believe that the more communities can embrace the knowledge that research provides and the more that they engage fully and productively in it, the more likely we are to attain health equity.

References

1. Israel BA, Coombe CM, Cheezum RR et al. Community-based participatory research: A capacity-building approach for policy advocacy aimed at eliminating health disparities. *Am J Public Health.* 2010;100(11):2094–2102.
2. Israel BA, Eng E, Schulz AJ, Parker EA, eds. *Methods in Community-Based Participatory Research for Health.* San Francisco, CA: Jossey-Bass; 2005.
3. Wallerstein NB, Duran B. Using community-based participatory research to address health disparities. *Health Promot Pract.* 2006;7(3):312–323.

326 Conclusion

4. Goodman MS, Dias JJ, Stafford JD. Increasing research literacy in minority communities: CARES fellows training program. *J Empir Res Hum Res Ethics.* 2010;5(4):33–41. doi:10.1525/jer.2010.5.4.33.

5. Coats J V., Stafford JD, Sanders Thompson V, Johnson Javois B, Goodman MS. Increasing research literacy: The Community Research Fellows Training program. *J Empir Res Hum Res Ethics.* 2015;10(1):3–12. doi:10.1177/1556264614561959.

6. Crosby LE, Parr W, Smith T, Mitchell MJ. The community leaders institute: An innovative program to train community leaders in health research. *Acad Med.* 2013;88(3):335–342. doi:10.1097/ACM.0b013e318280d8de.

7. Komaie G, Ekenga CC, Sanders Thompson VL, Goodman MS. Increasing community research capacity to address health disparities. *J Empir Res Hum Res Ethics.* 2017;12(1):55–66. doi:10.1177/1556264616687639.

8. Evenson KR, Sotres-Alvarez D, Herring AH, Messer L, Laraia BA, Rodríguez DA. Assessing urban and rural neighborhood characteristics using audit and GIS data: Derivation and reliability of constructs. *Int J Behav Nutr Phys Act.* 2009;6(44). doi:10.1186/1479-5868-6-44.

9. Callan LB. Adapting the windshield survey model to community health education. *HSMHA Health Rep.* 1971;86(3):202–203. http://www.ncbi.nlm.nih.gov/pubmed/23154435.

10. Baker EA, Schootman M, Barnidge E, Kelly C. The role of race and poverty in access to foods that enable individuals to adhere to dietary guidelines. *Prev Chronic Dis.* 2006;3(3):1–11.

11. Michigan Healthy Communities Collaborative. Nutrition Environment Assessment Tool (NEAT); 2011. http://www.mihealthtools.org/nea. Accessed February 22, 2017.

12. Vermont Departent of Health. Healthy Retailers Community Survey & Store Audit 2011–2012: a summary of results; 2012. http://han.vermont.gov/family/fit/documents/healthy_retailers_survey_audit_results_0912.pdf. Accessed February 24, 2017.

13. Kaczynski AT, Wilhelm Stanis SA, Besenyi GM. Development and testing of a community stakeholder park audit tool. *Am J Prev Med.* 2012;42(3):242–249. doi:10.1016/j.amepre.2011.10.018.

14. Floyd MF. Contributions of the community stakeholder park audit tool. *Am J Prev Med.* 2012;42(3):332–333. doi:10.1016/j.amepre.2011.12.002.

15. Floyd MF, Taylor WC, Whitt-Glover M. Measurement of park and recreation environments that support physical activity in low-income communities of color. Highlights of challenges and recommendations. *Am J Prev Med.* 2009;36 (4 suppl.):S156–S160. doi:10.1016/j.amepre.2009.01.009.

16. Taylor BT, Fernando P, Bauman AE, Williamson A, Craig JC, Redman S. Measuring the quality of public open space using Google Earth. *Am J Prev Med.* 2011;40(2):105–112. doi:10.1016/j.amepre.2010.10.024.

17. Ohmer ML, Owens J. Using photovoice to empower youth and adults to prevent crime. *J Community Pract.* 2013;21(4):410–433. doi:10.1080/10705422.2013.842196.

18. Morales-Campos DY, Parra-Medina D, Esparza LA. Picture this!: Using participatory photo mapping with Hispanic girls. *Fam Community Health.* 2015;38(1):44–54. doi:10.1097/FCH.0000000000000059.

19. Cabassa LJ, Parcesepe A, Nicasio A, Baxter E, Tsemberis S, Lewis-Fernandez R. Health and wellness photovoice project: Engaging consumers with serious mental illness in health care interventions. *Qual Heal Res.* 2013;23(5):618–630. doi:10.1177/1049732312470872.

20. Madrigal DS, Salvatore A, Casillas G et al. Health in my community: Conducting and evaluating photovoice as a tool to promote environmental health and leadership among Latino/a youth. *Prog Community Heal Partnerships Res Educ Action.* 2014;8(3):317–329. doi:10.1353/cpr.2014.0034.

Conclusion 327

21. Wang C, Burris MA. Photovoice: Concept, methodology, and use for participatory needs assessment. *Heal Educ Behav*. 1997;24(3):369–387. doi:0803973233.
22. Komaie G, Gilbert KL, Arroyo C, Goodman MS. Photovoice as a Pedagogical Tool to Increase Research Literacy Among Community Members. Pedagog Heal Promot. July 2017:2373379917715652. doi:10.1177/2373379917715652.
23. Catalani C, Minkler M. Photovoice: A review of the literature in health and public health. *Heal Educ Behav*. 2010;37(3):424–451. doi:10.1177/1090198109342084.
24. Castleden H, Garvin T, First Nation H. Modifying photovoice for community-based participatory Indigenous research. *Soc Sci Med*. 2008;66(6):1393–1405. doi:10.1016/j.socscimed.2007.11.030.
25. Mcknight JL, Kretzmann JP. *Mapping Community Capacity*. rev ed. Evanston, IL: Institute for Policy Research; 1996.
26. Kretzmann J, Mcknight J. Assets-based community development. *Natl Civ Rev*. 1996;85:23–29. doi:10.1002/ncr.4100850405.
27. D'Agostino McGowan L, Stafford JD, Thompson VL et al. Quantitative evaluation of the Community Research Fellows Training program. *Front Public Health*. 2015;3(July):179. doi:10.3389/fpubh.2015.00179.
28. Goodman MS, Si X, Stafford JD, Obasohan A, Mchunguzi C. Quantitative assessment of participant knowledge and evaluation of participant satisfaction in the CARES training program. *Prog Community Health Partnerships Res Educ Action*. 2012;6(3):359–366. doi:10.1353/cpr.2012.0051.
29. Goodman MS, Gonzalez M, Gil S et al. Brentwood Community Health Care Assessment. *Prog Community Heal Partnerships Res Educ Action*. 2014;8(1): 29–39. doi:10.1353/cpr.2014.0017.
30. Gonzalez MN, Pashoukos JL, Gil S, Ford E, Pashoukos DA. Assessing minority health care access in the Brentwood community. Poster presented at: American Public Health Association Annual Meeting and Exposition; October 29–November 2, 2011; Washington, DC.
31. Goodman M, Stafford J. Think Tank for African American Progress-Long Island. Paper presented at: American Public Health Association Annual Meeting and Exposition; November 2010; Denver, CO.
32. Mchunguzi C. Long Island Think Tank for Black Progress: Addressing the future of black girls on Long Island. Paper presented at American Public Health Association Annual Meeting and Exposition; 2011; Washington, DC.

Appendix: Self-assessment answer key

Chapter 1: Community-based participatory research

1. d
2. a
3. c
4. a
5. b
6. d
7. a
8. d
9. c
10. d

Chapter 2: Health disparities—Understanding how social determinants fuel racial/ethnic health disparities

1. b
2. a
3. d
4. a
5. a
6. d
7. b
8. c
9. d
10. a

Chapter 3: Community health and community-based prevention

1. b
2. b

Appendix   329

3. b
4. a
5. a
6. c
7. a
8. d
9. d
10. a

Chapter 4: Introduction to epidemiology

1. b
2. b
3. b
4. d
5. c
6. b
7. a
8. d
9. c
10. b
11. a

Chapter 5: Cultural competency

1. a
2. d
3. c
4. d
5. d
6. d
7. a
8. a
9. b
10. a
11. a
12. d

Chapter 6: Health literacy

1. d
2. d
3. b
4. d
5. c

330   *Appendix*

6. c
7. a
8. c
9. d
10. b

Chapter 7: Evidence-based public health

1. a
2. b
3. d
4. d
5. a
6. a
7. c
8. b
9. d

Chapter 8: Program planning and evaluation

1. b
2. a
3. b
4. a
5. c
6. b
7. c
8. a
9. a
10. d

Chapter 9: Research methods

1. d
2. d
3. a
4. d
5. a
6. a

Chapter 10: Quantitative research methods

1. d
2. c
3. a

Appendix 331

4. c
5. b
6. b
7. b
8. a
9. d
10. c

Chapter 11: Roles, functions, and examples of qualitative research and methods for social science research

1. b
2. d
3. c
4. a
5. a
6. d
7. d
8. b
9. a
10. b

Chapter 12: Research ethics

1. a
2. d
3. a
4. b
5. a
6. c
7. b
8. d
9. c
10. c

Chapter 13: Health services and health policy research

1. c
2. c
3. c
4. d
5. a
6. b

332   *Appendix*

Chapter 14: Developing a grant proposal

1. c
2. a
3. d
4. a
5. b
6. d
7. b
8. c
9. c
10. a

Chapter 15: Changing health outcomes through community-driven processes: Implications for practice and research

1. d
2. d
3. b
4. c
5. a
6. d
7. c
8. a
9. a
10. b

Index

A

Action research, 4
Adjusted odds ratios, 213
Affordable Care Act (ACA),
40, 261
Agency for Healthcare Research
and Quality (AHRQ), 267
Allocative health policies, 261
Alternative hypothesis, 208, 209
Ambiguous questions, 200
Analytic epidemiology, 77
Andersen Behavioral Model of
Health Services Use, 268
Association, definition of,
180–181

B

BCHA, see Brentwood
Community Healthcare
Assessment (BCHA)
Behavioral Risk Factor
Surveillance System
(BRFSS), 66, 138
Behavioral science theory,
138–139
Behavior questions, 224
Belmont Report (1979),
242–243
Bias
conscious and unconscious,
101
definition of, 176
measurement, 192, 198
nonresponse, 198
revelation, 226
sampling and coverage, 198
selection, 192

Bill & Melinda Gates
Foundation, 284
Bioethics, 240
Biological gradient, 83
Black Lives Matter movement,
302, 319
Breast and Cervical Cancer
Mortality Prevention Act
of 1990, 265
Breast and Cervical Cancer
Prevention and Treatment
Act of 2000, 267
Brentwood Community
Healthcare Assessment
(BCHA), 323
BRFSS, see Behavioral Risk
Factor Surveillance
System (BRFSS)

C

CAB, see Community advisory
board (CAB)
CARES program, 323
Case-control study design, 81
CBPR, see Community-based
participatory research
(CBPR)
Centers for Disease Control and
Prevention (CDC), 26
Chronic stress, 34
CLAS, see Culturally and
Linguistically Appropriate
Services in Health and
Health Care (CLAS)
Clinical epidemiology, definition
of, 132
Close-ended questions, 199

Cluster sample, 194
CNA, see Comprehensive needs
assessment (CNA)
Cohort study design, 80–81
"The Common Rule," 243
Community advisory board
(CAB), 65, 305, 317
Community Alliance for
Research Empowering
Social Change (CARES),
288
Community-based participatory
research (CBPR), 1–22
action research, 4
activity (group discussion),
17–18
activity (group problem
solving and planning),
18–19
agenda template, 20
basis of, 316
benefits, 6–7
community engagement, 2
cultural competency and, 96
definitions of community, 3–4
EBPH and, 139
example, 13–15
history, 4–5
implementation, 6–15
key principles, 6
learning objectives, 1
neighborhood, 3
outcomes, 12
partnership development, 7–9
process, 9–13
radical action research, 4
self-assessment, 1, 20–22
traditional action research, 4

334 *Index*

Community-driven processes, changing health outcomes through, 301–315
   Black Lives Matter movement, 302
   building capacity for community change, 305–306
   building community and organizational capacity, 308–309
   community advisory board, 305
   community coalitions, 303–304
   comprehensive needs assessment, 302
   grassroots organizing, 302
   group discussion activity, 313–314
   learning objectives, 301
   natural helper models, 304–305
   participation and membership in organizations, 306–308
   self-assessment, 301, 314–315
   structuring community engagement processes, 303–305
   tools and resources, 310
Community health and community-based prevention, 50–72
   activity (develop and evaluate a community health grant), 69–70
   analysis of existing datasets, 57, 63–64
   avoiding difficult areas, 67
   community analysis methods, 52–64
   community meetings, 55, 60–61
   community strengths, 66–67
   definition of community, 51
   engaging community members in the process, 65–66
   fortified dietary intervention, 65
   general public interviews, 52–59

group interviews, 54, 59
   identifying the health problems to target, 66
   identifying the history of a community, 66
   interpretation of records and transcripts, 55, 61
   key informant interviews, 52, 53
   learning objectives, 50
   observation, 54, 59–60
   PEST analysis, 56, 62
   photovoice, 57, 63
   public health matters, 50
   self-assessment, 50, 71–72
   survey, 58, 64
   SWOT analysis, 56, 61–62
   using community analysis data, 64–65
Community Networks Program (CNP), 13
Comprehensive needs assessment (CNA), 302
Concurrent validity, 201
Conference/Seminar grants, 285
Confounding variable, 198
Construct validity, 201
Convenience sampling, 194
CRFT program implementation and evaluation, 316–327
   Black Lives Matter movement, 319
   CARES program, 323
   community advisory board, 317
   evaluation metrics, 322
   faculty, 317
   "Grocery Store Audit," 319
   Likert response options, 321
   new assignments, 320
   patient research advisory board, 324
   "Photovoice" homework, 319
   pilot projects and other program outcomes, 322–325
   program evaluation, 320–322
   program implementation, 316–320
   request for proposals, 322, 323
   "Windshield Survey" assignment, 318
Criterion validity, 201
Critical race theory (CRT), 100

Cross-products ratio, *see* Odds ratio (OR)
Cross-sectional study design, 81–82
Cultural competency, 91–114
   action plan template, 108–113
   activity, 107–108
   CLAS standards, 101–104
   community resources, 111
   conscious and unconscious bias, 101
   consequences of culturally incompetent interventions, 101
   critical race theory, 100
   cultural competence, 94–96
   cultural humility, 104
   culture in broader context, 92–93
   definition of culture, 91
   diversity and culture, 93–94
   ever-changing culture, 93
   health disparities, 99
   learning objectives, 91
   need for culturally competent research and practice, 96–99
   planning table, 109
   practice standards related to cultural competence, 101–104
   race, ethnicity, and nationality, 92
   resources, 107
   self-assessment, 91, 113–114
   social determinants of health and critical race theory, 99–100
   who should practice cultural competency, 96
Culturally and Linguistically Appropriate Services in Health and Health Care (CLAS), 94, 101–104
Culture of Health Prize, 40

D

Daily life activity, using research in, 177
DASH trial, *see* Dietary Approaches to Stop Hypertension (DASH) trial

Index 335

Data
  acquisition, research ethics and, 248
  collection tools, 135–138
  definition of, 179
  health services research, 270–273
  matrix, 196
  primary, 182, 196
  qualitative, 165–166
  quantitative, 165–166, 196
  types, 184
Data collection methods (qualitative research), 222–233
  focus groups, 226–230
  interviews, 223–226
  photovoice, 230–233
Declaration of Helsinki (1964), 241–242
Department of Veterans Affairs (VA) medical centers, 263
Dependent variables, 179, 184
Descriptive epidemiology, 77
Devil's advocate questions, 225
Dietary Approaches to Stop Hypertension (DASH) trial, 79
Disparities Elimination Advisory Committee (DEAC), 13
Diversity, culture and, 93
Doctors' Trial, 241
Donabedian model, 268
Dose-response relationship, 83
Double-barreled questions, 201

E

EBPH, *see* Evidence-based public health (EBPH)
Emergency department (ED) visits, 262
Epidemiology, clinical, 132
Epidemiology, introduction to, 73–90
  activity, 88
  analytic epidemiology, 77
  basic epidemiologic measures, 83–86
  basic epidemiologic reasoning, 76–77
  biological gradient, 83
  biological plausibility, 83

case-control study design, 81
cohort study design, 80–81
consistency upon repeatability, 83
cross-sectional study design, 81–82
definition of epidemiology, 74–76
descriptive epidemiology, 77
determinants, 75–76
distribution, 75
dose-response relationship, 83
epidemiology triangle, 76
experimental study design, 78–79
federally qualified health center, 74
frequency, 74–75
incidence, 80
learning objectives, 73
loss to follow-up, 81
observational studies, determining causality in, 82–83
observational study design, 79–82
odds ratio, 85, 86
population, 74
quasi-experimental study design, 80
rates in epidemiology, 84–85
relative risk, 80, 85, 86
self-assessment, 73, 88–90
strength of association, 82
study design, 77–82
study validity, range of, 82
temporality, 82
Ethics, *see* Research ethics
Ethnic health disparities, *see* Health disparities
Evaluation, *see* Program planning and evaluation
Evidence-based public health (EBPH), 132–152
  activity, 149–150
  clinical epidemiology, definition of, 132–133
  common health theories and models, 140–141
  community engagement in assessment and decision-making, 139
  concerns, 144–145
  data collection tools, 135–138

decision-making using best available data, 134–138
definition, 132–133
disseminating of findings to key stakeholders, 143
evaluation types, 139
evidence-based medical practice and, 145–146
formative evaluation, 142
future of, 146
impact evaluation, 142
importance, 133
learning objectives, 132
levels of evidence, 143–144
logic model as planning tool, 139
outcome evaluation, 143
peer-reviewed studies, 134–135
process evaluation, 142
programmatic success, conducting evaluations to determine, 139–143
program-planning frameworks, application of, 138–139
qualitative methods, 138
quantitative methods, 138
resources, 145, 147
self-assessment, 132, 150–152
survey questions, types of, 136–137
using data and information systems systematically, 134
Expanded Food and Nutrition Education Program (EFNEP) curriculum, 65
Experience questions, 224
Experimental study, 78–79
External validity, 181, 201

F

Fabrication, 247
Falsification, 247
FDI, *see* Fortified dietary intervention (FDI)
Federal Housing Authority (FHA) loans, 32
Federally qualified health center (FQHC), 74
Federal Policy for the Protection of Human Subjects (1991), 243
Feeling questions, 224

336 *Index*

Focus groups, 226–230
  characteristics of, 227–228
  planning steps, 230
  questions, characteristics of,
    229–230
  questions, development of,
    228–229
Formative evaluation, 142
Fortified dietary intervention
  (FDI), 65
FQHC, *see* Federally qualified
  health center (FQHC)

G

General public interviews,
  52–59
Genetics, health literacy and,
  122–123
GI Bill, 32
Grant proposal, development of,
  280–300
  activities, 296–298
  budget narrative, 292
  co-principal investigator, 286
  description of grant proposal,
    280–281
  finding the appropriate grant,
    285–286
  foundations, 284
  funding sources, 283–284
  grant proposal components,
    288–295
  grant writing, 282–285
  learning objectives, 280
  letter of intent, 287–288
  logic model, example of, 293
  plan of action, outline of,
    286–288
  principal investigator, 286
  program staff, 287
  purpose of looking for a
    grant, 281–282
  research assistants, 286
  self-assessment, 280,
    298–300
  SMART goals, 288, 291
  specific aim, example of,
    289–290
  timeline development, 287
  types of grants, 284–285
Grassroots organizing, 302
"Grocery Store Audit," 319
Group interviews, 54, 59

H

Harlem Children's Zone
  Initiative, 307
Health disparities, 23–49
  activity (board game), 47
  chronic stress, 34
  cultural competency and, 99
  "culture of health," 40
  defining health disparities, 25
  health behaviors, social
    context, and social norms,
    34–37
  health equity, towards
    achieving, 37–41
  learning objectives, 23
  prioritizing health, 24–25
  race/ethnicity, socioeconomic
    status, and health
    disparities, 31–33
  racial/ethnic disparities
    in population health
    indicators, 25–29
  self-assessment, 23, 47–49
  social connectedness, 39
  social determinants of
    health (roots of health
    inequities), 29–30
  stress and coping, 33–34
Health equity, definition of, 37
Health literacy, 115–131
  activity, 128–129
  definition, 116
  effects, 116–119
  learning objectives, 115
  levels in the United States, 116
  measurement, 119–121
  modified Cloze procedure,
    120
  provider-patient
    communication, 118
  recommendations for
    materials development,
    121–122
  research example (health
    literacy and genetics),
    122–123
  self-assessment, 115, 130–131
Health services and health policy
  research, 258–279
  activity, 276
  allocative health policies, 261
  commonly cited health
    indicators, 262

conceptualizing health
    services utilization,
    268–269
  data, 270–273
  defining research questions,
    269–270
  emergency department visits,
    262
  example (opioid overdose
    deaths), 277–278
  feedback about existing
    programs, 265–267
  forms and categories of
    health policies, 261
  health services research,
    267–273
  learning objectives, 258
  metaphor, 264
  policy agenda, setting of,
    261–267
  public use and data sources,
    270–272
  regulatory health policies,
    261
  role of health policy in
    influencing health,
    260–267
  self-assessment, 258,
    278–279
  social determinants of health,
    259
Healthy People 2020, 40
Heckler Report, 99
HHS, *see* United States
  Department of Health and
  Human Services (HHS)
HHS Office of Minority Health,
  94
Human subjects research,
  247–248
Hypothesis, definition of, 178,
  191
Hypothesis testing, 208–211
  alternative hypothesis, 208
  definition of hypothesis test,
    208
  level of significance, 210
  null hypothesis, 208
  p-values and statistical
    significance, 210–211
  rules, 209
  statistical significance, 208
  steps, 209
Hypothetical questions, 225

Index   337

I

IBM Statistical Package for Social Sciences, 193
Ideal position questions, 225
"If-then" statements, 157
Impact evaluation, 142
Incidence, 80
Independent variables, 178, 184
Informed consent, human subjects research and, 247–248
Institute of Medicine (IOM), 95
  description of health literacy, 116
  recommendations, 95
Institutional review board (IRB), 96
  application status, 294
  roles and responsibilities of, 246–247
  system, 242
Integrated research, 221; *see also* Qualitative research and methods for social science research
Internal validity, 181, 201
Interpretive questions, 225
Interviews, 223–226
  categories, 223–234
  description, 223
  questions, 224–226
  questions to avoid, 226
IOM Roundtable on Health Literacy, 117
IRB, *see* Institutional review board (IRB)

K

Key informant interviews, 52, 53
Key questions, 229
Knowledge
  claims about, 221
  questions, 224

L

The Last Straw, 47
Leading questions, 200, 226
Letter of intent (LOI), 287–288
Level of significance, 210
Logic model
  example of, 159, 293
  as planning tool, 139
Loss to follow-up, 81

M

Measurement bias, 192, 198
Medicaid, 40, 260, 261
Medicare, 40
Memorandum of understanding (MOU), 10, 38, 287
Mentor–mentee relationships, 249
Mixed-methods research, 191, 221; *see also* Qualitative research and methods for social science research
Modified Cloze procedure, 120

N

National Breast and Cervical Cancer Early Detection Program (NBCCEDP), 265
National Center for Medical-Legal Partnership, 38
National Health Interview Survey (NHIS), 81, 138
National Health and Nutrition Examination Survey (NHANES), 75
National Institutes of Health (NIH)
  definition of health, 25
  -funded research, 247
  funding priorities of, 41
  grants, 285
  Office of Research Integrity, 247
National Research Act (1974), 242–243
Natural helper models, 304–305
New Deal era, 32
Newest Vital Sign (NVS), 120
The New Face of Homelessness study, 324
New York Foundation for the Arts (NYFA), 286
NHANES, 135
NHANES National Youth Fitness Survey (NNYFS), 203–206

NHIS, *see* National Health Interview Survey (NHIS)
NIH, *see* National Institutes of Health (NIH)
Nonresponse bias, 198
Null hypothesis, 208, 209
Nuremberg Code (1948), 241
NVS, *see* Newest Vital Sign (NVS)
NYFA, *see* New York Foundation for the Arts (NYFA)

O

Observation
  community analysis using, 54, 59–60
  unit, 196
Observational study, 79–82
Odds ratio (OR), 85, 123, 211–213
  adjusted, 213
  computation, 211–212
  example, 212
  interpretation, 212
OECD countries, *see* Organisation for Economic Co-operation and Development (OECD) countries
Office of Minority Health (OMH), 94
Open-ended questions, 199, 225
Opening question, 229
Opinion questions, 224
OR, *see* Odds ratio (OR)
Organisation for Economic Co-operation and Development (OECD) countries, 262
Ottawa Charter, 307
Outcome evaluation, 143
Outcome Model of Quality, 268
Outcome variable, 198

P

Parent-teacher association (PTA), 306
Patient-Centered Outcomes Research Institute (PCORI), 263

338   *Index*

Patient Protection and Affordable Care Act of 2010, 116
Patient research advisory board (PRAB), 324
Peer-reviewed studies, 134–135
PEST (political, economic, social, and technological) analysis, 56, 62
Photovoice, 57, 63, 230–233
  background and conceptual framework, 231
  methodology, 232–233
  rationale, 231–232
Plagiarism, 247
Planning grants, 285
PolicyLink, 39
PRAB, *see* Patient research advisory board (PRAB)
Predictive validity, 201
Predictor variable, 198
Pregnancy Risk Assessment Monitoring System (PRAMS), 193
Prevention, *see* Community health and community-based prevention
Primary data, 182, 196
Probability samples, 193
Process evaluation, 142
Program for the Elimination of Cancer Disparities (PECaD), 13
Program planning and evaluation, 153–173
  activity, 171–172
  engaging stakeholders, 154
  evaluation data, 167–168
  evaluation method, selection of, 164–166
  evaluation plan, development of, 162–164
  evaluation reports, writing of, 168–169
  expected resources, activities, and outcomes, 156
  identifying and prioritizing problems to address, 154–155
  "if-then" statements, 157
  interpretation of findings, 168
  learning objectives, 153
  logic model, example of, 159
  outcomes, 158
  outputs, 157–158

process and outcome evaluation, 164
program design and evaluation considerations, 166–167
program evaluation, 163
program planning processes, 154–158
quantitative and qualitative data, 165–166
research partners and consultants, 167
resources and inputs, 156–157
reviewing existing data, 155
self-assessment, 153, 172–173
SMART goal development, 158–162
visualizing your program, 155
Provider-patient communication, 118
PTA, *see* Parent-teacher association (PTA)
Purposive sample, 194

Q

Qualitative data, 165–166
Qualitative research and methods for social science research, 220–238
  comparing qualitative and quantitative research methods, 234
  data collection methods, 222–233
  definition of qualitative research, 221–222
  focus groups, 226–230
  interviews, 223–226
  knowledge, claims about, 221
  learning objectives, 220
  photovoice, 230–233
  reporting qualitative findings, 233
  self-assessment, 220, 236–238
  triangulation, 222
Quantitative data, 165–166, 196
Quantitative research methods, 188–219
  activity, 215–217
  alternative hypothesis, 208, 209
  analyzing survey data, 202
  census study, 192
  cluster sample, 194

convenience sampling, 194
data, 195–197
graphic methods, 202–208
hypotheses, definition of, 191
hypothesis testing, 208–211
learning objectives, 188
measurement bias, 192, 198
mixed-methods research, 191
nonresponse bias, 198
null hypothesis, 208, 209
observation unit, 196
odds ratio, 211–213
probability samples, 193
purposive sample, 194
questionnaire design, 198–202
quota sampling, 194
rare events, example of, 190
sampling and coverage bias, 198
sampling frame, 192
sampling methods, 192–195
selection bias, 192
self-assessment, 188, 217–219
simple random sample, 193
snowball sampling, 195
statistical significance, 208
statistics, definition of, 189
stratified sample, 193–194
survey methods, 197–198
systematic sample, 193
Quasi-experimental study design, 80
Questionnaire design, 198–202
  aims, 198–199
  ambiguous questions, 200
  close-ended questions, 199
  confounding variable, 198
  double-barreled questions, 201
  leading questions, 200
  open-ended questions, 199
  outcome variable, 198
  predictor variable, 198
  question style, 199
  survey instrument, 199–202
  validity, 201
Questions
  ambiguous, 200
  behavior, 224
  close-ended, 199
  devil's advocate, 225
  double-barreled, 201

Index   339

experience, 224
feeling, 224
hypothetical, 225
ideal position, 225
interpretive, 225
key, 229
knowledge, 224
leading, 200, 226
open-ended, 199, 225
opinion, 224
sensory 224
values, 224
Quota sampling, 194

R

Racial/ethnic health disparities,
  see Health disparities
Radical action research, 4
Randomized controlled trial
  (RCT), 78, 86
Rapid Estimate of Adult Literacy
  in Genetics (REAL-G),
  122
Rapid Estimate of Adult Literacy
  in Medicine (REALM),
  120
Rapid Estimate of Adult Literacy
  in Medicine-Revised
  (REALM-R), 120
Rare events, example of, 190
Regulatory health policies, 261
Relative risk (RR), 80, 85, 86
Request for Application (RFA),
  282
Request for proposal (RFP),
  282, 322
Research ethics, 239–257
  Belmont Report (1979),
    242–245
  beneficence, 244–245
  bioethics, 240
  case example, 240
  cases of research misconduct,
    250–252
  collaboration, 248–249
  conflict of interest, 248
  data acquisition,
    management, and
    presentation, 248
  Declaration of Helsinki
    (1964), 241–242
  description, 239
  Doctors' Trial, 241

Federal Policy for the
  Protection of Human
  Subjects (1991), 243
historical milestones, 240–243
human subjects research and
  informed consent, 247–248
institutional review board,
  roles and responsibilities
  of, 246–247
justice, 245
learning objectives, 239
mentor–mentee relationships,
  249
National Research Act (1974),
  242–243
Nuremberg Code (1948), 241
peer review processes, 249
protection of vulnerable
  populations, 246
publication and authorship,
  249
respect for persons, 243–244
responsible conduct of
  research and research
  misconduct, 247–250
safe laboratory and research
  practices, 248
self-assessment, 239, 255–257
small group discussion
  questions, 254–255
societal impact of research,
  249–250
Tuskegee syphilis study
  (1932–1972), 242
Research grants, 284
Research methods, 174–187
  activity, 185
  bias, definition of, 176
  clinical records, 182
  daily life activity, using
    research in, 177
  data collection methods,
    181–182
  data gathering, 181
  definition of association,
    180–181
  definition of research,
    175–177
  external validity, 181
  focus groups or interviews,
    182
  hypothesis, 178
  independent and dependent
    variables, 178–179, 184

internal validity, 181
learning objectives, 174
primary vs. secondary data,
  182–183
quantitative vs. qualitative,
  181
research settings, 179
scientific method, 176–177
self-assessment, 174, 187
source of research questions,
  178
study design, 183–184
surveys, 181–182
terminology, 186
RFA, *see* Request for Application
  (RFA)
RFP, *see* Request for proposal
  (RFP)
Robert Wood Johnson
  Foundation, 39, 284
RR, *see* Relative risk (RR)

S

Sampling and coverage bias,
  198
SCHIP, *see* State Child Health
  Insurance Program
  (SCHIP)
Scientific method, 176–177
Secondary data, 183, 196
Selection bias, 192
Self-assessment answer key,
  328–332
  community-based
    participatory research,
    328
  community-driven processes,
    changing health outcomes
    through, 332
  community health and
    community-based
    prevention, 328–329
  cultural competency, 329
  epidemiology, introduction
    to, 329
  evidence-based public health,
    330
  grant proposal, development
    of, 332
  health disparities, 328
  health literacy, 329–330
  health services and health
    policy research, 331

340 *Index*

program planning and evaluation, 330
qualitative research and methods for social science research, 331
quantitative research methods, 330–331
research ethics, 331
research methods, 330
Self-assessment questions
community-based participatory research, 20–22
community-driven processes, changing health outcomes through, 314–315
community health and community-based prevention, 71–72
cultural competency, 113–114
epidemiology, introduction to, 88–90
evidence-based public health, 150–152
grant proposal, development of, 298–300
health disparities, 47–49
health literacy, 130–131
health services and health policy research, 278–279
program planning and evaluation, 172–173
qualitative research and methods for social science research, 236–238
quantitative research methods, 217–219
research ethics, 255–257
research methods, 187
Sensory questions 224
Servicemen's Readjustment Act of 1944, 32
SES, *see* Socioeconomic status (SES)

Short Test of Functional Health Literacy in Adults (S-TOFHLA), 120
Simple random sample (SRS), 193
Single Item Literacy Screener (SILS) items, 120
SMART (specific, measurable, attainable, relevant/realistic, and time framed) goals, 158–162, 288, 291
Snowball sampling, 195
Social determinants of health, 30, 36
critical race theory and, 99–100
drivers of, 259
health disparities and, 99
Social science research, *see* Qualitative research and methods for social science research
Socioeconomic status (SES), 25
SRS, *see* Simple random sample (SRS)
SSI, *see* Supplemental Security Income (SSI)
State Child Health Insurance Program (SCHIP), 261
Statistical Package for Social Sciences (SPSS), 193
Statistical significance, 208
Statistics, definition of, 189
S-TOFHLA, *see* Short Test of Functional Health Literacy in Adults (S-TOFHLA)
Stratified sample, 193–194
Structural racism, 31
Supplemental Security Income (SSI), 261
SWOT (strengths, weaknesses, opportunities, and threats) analysis, 56, 61–62
Systematic sample, 193

T

Temporary Assistance for Needy Families (TANF), 261
Test of Functional Health Literacy in Adults (TOFHLA), 120
Think back questions, 229
Traditional action research, 4
Training grants, 285
Transition questions, 229
Tuskegee syphilis study (1932–1972), 97, 242

U

United States Department of Health and Human Services (HHS), 37
U.S. Census Bureau, 135

V

Values questions, 224
VA medical centers, *see* Department of Veterans Affairs (VA) medical centers

W

Washington University School of Medicine (WUSM), 13
"Windshield Survey" assignment, 318
W.K. Kellogg Foundation, 284
World Health Organization (WHO)
definition of health, 24, 259
Ottawa Charter for Health Promotion, 307

Y

Youth Risk Behavior Surveillance System (YRBSS), 194, 214